MARKETING BUDGETING
A Political and Organisational Model

MARKETING BUDGETING

NIGEL PIERCY

University of Wales Institute of
Science and Technology, Cardiff

CROOM HELM
London • Sydney • Dover, New Hampshire

658.154
P 618

© 1986 Nigel Piercy
Croom Helm Ltd, Provident House, Burrell Row,
Beckenham, Kent BR3 1AT

Croom Helm Australia Pty Ltd, Suite 4, 6th Floor,
64-76 Kippax Street, Surry Hills, NSW 2010, Australia

British Library Cataloguing in Publication Data

Piercy, Nigel
    Marketing budgeting: a political and
    organisational model.
    1. Marketing management – Finance
    I. Title
    658.1'55   HF5415.13

    ISBN 0-7099-2092-X

Croom Helm, 51 Washington Street,
Dover, New Hampshire 03820, USA

Library of Congress Cataloging in Publication Data

Piercy, Nigel.
    Marketing budgeting.
    Includes indexes.
    1. Marketing–finance. I. Title.
HF5415.122.P54   1986   658.1'54   85-28006
ISBN 0-7099-2092-X

Printed and bound in Great Britain
by Billing & Sons Limited, Worcester.

Contents

PART III AN EMPIRICAL STUDY OF THE POWER AND POLITICS OF MARKETING BUDGETING

PART IV CONCLUSIONS

Figures

Tables

Preface

Perhaps the commonest - and arguably the most critical - question asked by those concerned with planning and controlling marketing programmes is 'how much should we spend?'. Certainly, this question poses some of the most intractable problems for the marketing analyst and manager. Indeed, it may be that it is such intractability which explains the relatively scant attention given to this issue in the literature of marketing, or at the very least the type of treatment it receives. While that literature is replete with studies of marketing research techniques, consumer behaviour models, communication models, logistics systems, and so on, generally the analysis of the processual aspects of marketing, and particularly the processual aspects of resource allocation, are treated either simplistically or scarcely at all.

Given the very high and very visible levels of expenditure on such marketing activities as advertising and promotion, and the present context of an apparently hostile economic environment for many firms, then the lack of analysis of marketing budgeting and resource allocation processes is all the more surprising. It is this premise, therefore, which provides the starting point for what is attempted in this book.

It would be somewhat ambitious to propose to wholly remedy the identified shortcomings of the literature in a single book, but what is possible is to attempt some integration of the fragmented literature relevant to marketing budgeting, and to present some new empirical data in this area. This leads then to the synthesis of an organisational and political perspective on marketing budgeting, which is aimed at improving operational approaches to managing marketing resource allocation and at re-shaping perceptions of this topic in the business school curriculum, as well as at stimulating further research and analysis.

It should be noted that this present book does not stand alone in this context, but is part of a trilogy which has attempted to develop and apply this perspective on marketing management. First, in considering marketing information systems (Nigel Piercy and Martin Evans, Managing Marketing Information, Beckenham, Croom Helm, 1983), we took the view that the normative and techniques-oriented approaches to studying marketing information systems were severely limited and that there was advantage to be gained from a perspective that recognised the 'non-rational' and political uses made of marketing information, and that accepted the impact of political behaviour and organisational power on and in the design of marketing information systems.

Second, having examined the organisational aspects of information in marketing, attention was turned to the informational aspects of marketing organisation (Nigel Piercy, Marketing Organisation: An Analysis of Information Processing, Power and Politics, London, Allen and Unwin, 1985). In this analysis, three levels of marketing organisation were examined: the departmentation (and potential for disintegration) of the marketing department in the business unit; the centralisation or decentralisation of marketing responsibilities and functions in the complex organisation; and the internal structuring of a marketing department. This analysis rested on the interaction between: (a) information - taking the environment as the prime generator of uncertainty, which was conceived as an information processing burden, and taking marketing organisational structures as varying capacities for processing information; (b) organisational power - represented mainly by formal structures; and, (c) political behaviour - in terms of the control and shaping of information through structures and processes. An information-structure-power model was proposed as a vehicle for the operational study and design of the marketing organisation, and as a paradigm for conceptual analysis.

This third volume continues in the same vein by attempting an analysis of a major marketing decision area - resource allocation in marketing - using the conceptual framework provided by that information-structure-power model. The integration of these various pieces of work is to be found in a conceptual work: Nigel Piercy, Marketing Management: Structure and Process in Decision Making, London, Allen and Unwin, forthcoming 1987.

Turning to this present work, the starting point is to review and to attempt to integrate the two dominant approaches in the literature of budgeting for marketing.

The first of these approaches has been essentially prescriptive, involving the establishment of 'rational' decision rules to optimise the size and allocation of expenditure on marketing. The second approach has been to describe budgeting methods, and occasionally processes, leading some to develop from these studies normative models - either on the basis that 'what is should not be' because it is not rational or optimal, or that 'what is <u>should</u> be' since practices represent the 'pooled wisdom' of those in the field. These approaches are important, since, whatever practical or theoretical shortcomings they may have, together they represent the received theory of marketing budgeting.

However, the search for conceptual robustness and practical usefulness may be advanced in two further ways: the more general theories of budgeting found in other areas of study may be added to the available marketing concepts; and the organisational and informational aspects of budgeting (conceived here respectively as relating to organisational power and political behaviour) provide an additional source of analytical leverage not elsewhere applied to marketing budgeting. For present purposes, the central proposition here is that marketing budgets are best understood in the context of a corporate environment of organisational power differences, political struggles and bargaining.

The general aim is to arrive at a more comprehensive, and hopefully more realistic, understanding of how marketing budgets are determined, to serve a number of purposes. At one level there is value simply in developing a theoretical understanding of the dynamics of marketing budgeting processes, which goes beyond the received view in the literature. The extension of this, however, is in attempting to build a framework for analysing budgeting processes in practice, for those actually involved in those processes. By implication, at another level, those responsible for managing marketing budgets have a need for both predictive and control mechanisms.

The comments above imply the nature of the target audience for this book. First, there is the academic readership composed of those researching and studying marketing management, but also hopefully more generally those concerned with business policy, financial control and organisational behaviour. Second, it is to be hoped that there will also be a managerial readership composed of those participating in, and managing, the processes of marketing budgeting in the many different types of organisation to which this analysis is relevant. This said, it should be noted that this present book does not purport to be a guide to budgeting for the student or practitioner – that task is being attempted elsewhere (Nigel Piercy, <u>Budgeting for Marketing – Principles and Practices</u>, London, Allen and Unwin, forthcoming 1987).

It should be said that it may well be that the theses and conclusions advanced here are likely to be somewhat unwelcome to both marketing academics and practitioners, since they fly in the face of the ethos of 'rationality', and the advocacy of management science, which is implicit in a great deal of the prescriptive literature. The defence lies simply in the fact that the various empirical studies reported here are grounded in the reality of how organisations operate – for better or worse – and the focus is on how marketing budgets appear to be actually determined and may be predicted, and the implications of that actuality for management.

Gratitude is owed to the many individuals, both academics and managers, who offered advice and assistance in the course of this work, though particular thanks should be extended to Roger Mansfield for his guidance and methodological suggestions, to Jane Peregrine for her assistance in the research fieldwork, and to Stevie Burges for producing the original manuscript. Special thanks are reserved for Stevie's 'A' team of Sally Jarratt, Christine Long and Kath Hollister who descended at the speed of light to dissipate the usual last-minute panic and chaos, to get the work out at all costs – but particularly also for Stevie Burges for her encouragement to complete the project and her assistance in proofreading and indexing the volume.

This said, the inevitable residual shortcomings remain wholly the responsibility of the author. Apologies are offered to the reader for those flaws, though emphatically not for any controversy which the work may attract.

Nigel Piercy,
July, 1985
UWIST, Cardiff

1

Introduction - Aim and Purposes

The underlying goal of this work is to examine the process of marketing resource allocation - particularly, but not exclusively, in budgeting financial marketing expenditures - in terms of inputs to and outcomes of that process, and thus necessarily the approach taken is somewhat different to that found in the normal treatments of marketing budgeting. Specifically, the goal is to bring to bear certain of the findings and empirical tools established in other disciplines, to add a further dimension to the existing theory of marketing resource allocation or budgeting, through the development of a new conceptual frame of reference, which is supported by the presentation of new empirical data.

It may be noted that, in fact, this work does not stand alone, but is related to two earlier works (Piercy and Evans, 1983; Piercy, 1985b), and these antecedents are explicated in this chapter. It will be seen, thus, that the key concepts running through this analysis are: organisational structure in marketing, information processing and control, and the implications of these last factors for organisational power and political behaviour.

While this approach does not purport to provide a complete explanation of resource allocation behaviour in marketing, when it is taken in conjunction with the received prescriptive and descriptive theories, it provides a significant additional analytical lever of interest both to practitioners and to researchers or students of marketing.

The groundwork necessary before proceeding to the main body of the work is contained in this introductory chapter and consists of: a statement of the concept of marketing which is adopted for this study; the relationship between this work and theory development in marketing; the nature of the information-structure-power model; a clarification of the rationale of the general approach to be taken here; and an initial explication and justification of the resource allocation process in marketing as the topic for study.

MARKETING MANAGEMENT AND THEORY

The Definition of Marketing

An initial problem faced is that the term 'marketing' used above is itself somewhat problematic to isolate.   It will be seen that two difficulties arise – the marketing function in business organisations is subject to much criticism and attack at present (see pp. *102–110* below), and in Chapter 4 it will be seen that marketing both as a corporate function and an academic discipline is in a stage of transition in various ways, although both those discussions do, at least, imply some shared understanding of what marketing is – even if indicating dissension regarding what it should be. However, two further difficulties in pinning down the meaning of 'marketing' are that: different formal definitions abound in the literature;   and there are many elaborations of the 'philosophy' of marketing.

It should be stated quite explicitly at the outset that the view taken of marketing in this present study is biased and selective in that it concentrates on: <u>business</u> decision making, in a <u>corporate</u> setting, and is concerned therefore with a <u>managerial</u> focus.   This selectivity may be contrasted with the views of others.

There is, in fact, a demonstrably large array of formal definitions of marketing, and these have been reviewed by others at various times in the past two decades (e.g. Baker <u>et al</u>, 1967;   Crosier, 1975) without any clear conclusion being reached.   No such exhaustive review is attempted here, rather it is adequate for present purposes to compare one or two of the prominent views in US and UK literature.

In the UK, definitions by academic writers during the past twenty years have included the following:

> (a) Marketing is the primary management function which organises and directs the aggregate of business activities in converting consumer purchasing power into effective demand for a specific product or service and in moving the product or service to the final consumer or user so as to achieve company set profit or other objectives.   (Rodger, 1965)

> (b) Marketing is the way in which any organisation or individual <u>matches</u> its own capabilities to the wants of its customers.   (Christopher <u>et al</u>, 1980)

On the other hand, the main professional institute in the UK offers the view that:

> (c) Marketing is the management process responsible for

identifying, anticipating and satisfying customer requirements profitably. (Institute of Marketing)

In the US, the most prominent writer suggests that:

(d) Marketing is the social process by which individuals and groups obtain what they need and want through creating and exchanging products and value with others. (Kotler, 1984)

However, this last writer also defines marketing management as:

(e) the analysis, planning, implementation, and control of programs designed to create, build, and maintain beneficial exchanges and relationships with target markets for the purpose of achieving organizational objectives. (Kotler, 1984)

Perhaps the major contrast is between conceptualising marketing as a process of social or economic exchange, in (d), and marketing as a management function in (a), (c) and (e).

In fact there have been many who suggest that the search for a definition of marketing is likely to be fruitless (e.g. Matthews et al, 1964; Foxall, 1981), which is explained by such writers as arising from the 'amorphousness' of the field and the difficulty in combining consiseness and comprehensiveness. Certainly, pragmatically the meaning of marketing in the relatively concrete terms of organisational arrangements varies greatly (Hayhurst and Wills, 1972).

The classic study of the historical development of marketing (Bartels, 1962) offers some insight to this problem. Bartels argued that the history of marketing may be interpreted both in an absolute and relative manner. The former perspective, of an absolute viewpoint, suggests that marketing thought begins with simple enquiry and findings, progresses to the status of a discipline, finally to emerge as a science. The relative viewpoint appraises the stage of thought in relation to the circumstances bringing it forth, implying that completeness is defined as adequacy, which is to say that the body of thought is appraised not as an independent variable evolving of itself, but as one dependent on such factors as market problems and practices to determine its emergence, form and character.

The relevance to this present discussion is that the absolute perspective suggests the lack of definition or agreement on the marketing paradigm may be explained partly in terms of the evolution of the discipline, since the area itself may be an entity not stable enough to allow permanent definition, as it progresses to its assumed final state.

On the other hand, apparently divergent views may be explained from the relative viewpoint by arguing that the body of implicit and explicit theory constituting the field is a function of the circumstances surrounding it, where those circumstances may well both change over time and be substantially different for different organisations, suggesting the legitimacy and possibly inevitability of continued divergence in definition, and indeed understanding of the phenomenon.

It follows from our present emphasis on contingency theories (see pp. *121-130* below) that the latter argument is preferred.

On the other hand, it is possible to argue that the real divergence in views of marketing is actually rather limited, and reflects no more than differences in breadth of perspective (Bell, 1972), which allows for a continuum of views ranging from the marketing systems model of exchange patterns within an economy, to more limited views of the management of advertising and selling in organisations. In this present study, the bias is towards the latter area rather than the former, since the interest is in what has been defined above as marketing management.

One way of organising the various views of managerial marketing, developed elsewhere (Piercy, 1982), is to categorise concepts of marketing as relating variously to strategy, programmes and information. In the first area of marketing strategy, concern is with broad product-market direction, the form of competition to be pursued, 'marketing orientation', and so on. With the growth in corporate and strategic planning, what is less clear is how this area relates to the marketing sub-unit, if there is one. Such issues might be regarded as the task area of general rather than functional marketing management.

The second area - the marketing programme - is concerned with the management of the 'marketing mix' - product policy, pricing, distribution and marketing communications. The task activities concerned may be demonstrated by considering the responsibility patterns of chief marketing executives, as shown in Table 1.1. This area is apparently more easily identified with a marketing sub-unit as an area of functional management, although in fact, it would seem that there are many jurisdiction disputes and variations in practice (Piercy, 1985a), and it has been suggested that the real control of the marketing mix by marketing departments is commonly exaggerated by the literature (Hayhurst and Wills, 1972).

The third area - marketing information - may be associated with either of the first two: a general management service function, possibly associated with corporate planning, for scanning the environment and providing control data, or a marketing department function for the analysis, planning and control, of markets, marketing performance and the marketing environment (Piercy and Evans, 1983).

Table 1.1: Chief Marketing Executive Responsibilities

	% of CMEs directly controlling		% of CMEs directly controlling
Marketing research	67	Corporate planning	37
Marketing planning	65	Distribution relations	36
Corporate advertising	63	Product planning	33
Sales promotion	56	Product pricing	28
Sales training	54	Sales management	23
Product advertising	47	Product service	22
Sales research	44	Customer service	21
Merchandising	44	Export Sales	19
Public relations	44	Physical distribution	17
National accounts	42	Foreign marketing	13
New product planning	40	Mergers and new ventures	9

Source: Hopkins and Bailey (1971)

Interest in the present study is primarily in the second two areas: the marketing programme and marketing information, while our orientation is towards the management of these functions. Interest in marketing strategy formulation is reserved until a later date, when the power and politics of strategic choice in marketing are to be examined.

To summarise the sources of selectivity and bias in our present analysis of marketing: concern is not with the societal processes of marketing, the development of complex economy-wide or international exchange systems, nor with broad strategic formulation; concern is, however, with marketing, in the business organisation, and specifically with the management of the marketing programme and the use of marketing information.

Philosophies of Marketing

The abundancy of definitions of marketing, is equalled, if not surpassed, by prescriptive writings on marketing orientation, marketing 'myopia', the 'marketing concept', and similar philosophical notions.

For example, Kotler offers the view that the marketing concept is:

> The management orientation that holds that the key task of the organization is to determine the needs and wants of target markets and to adapt the organization to delivering the desired satisfactions more effectively and efficiently than its competitors. (Kotler, 1980)

It is argued that the implementation of such a concept requires the maintenance of a particular philosophy or managerial 'orientation'. In particular, Kotler saw three major implications of the marketing concept: customer orientation as a corporate focus; the need for integration of all 'customer-impinging' resources and activities in the company: and the pursuit of this path as a route to attaining corporate goals.

In attempting to operationalise marketing orientation, Hooley et al (1984) used the following definitions: marketing orientation - placing major emphasis on prior analysis of market needs, adapting products to meet them if necessary; selling orientation - placing major emphasis on advertising and selling to ensure sales; and production orientation - making what the firm can and selling to whoever will buy it.

In fact, the prescriptive views of marketing orientation and the marketing concept were advanced as the best way of avoiding such menaces as: the dangers of 'marketing myopia' - i.e. a shortsighted focus on technology and products rather than market needs; the less advanced selling concept, where 'selling is preoccupied with the seller's need to convert his product into cash; marketing with the idea of satisfying the needs of the customer' (Levitt, 1960); or the earlier stages in corporate development of 'production-orientation' (Levitt, 1977) or 'navel-gazing in the factory' (Adler, 1967). However, this view has attracted controversy on various grounds, although, the marketing concept still attracts support. For example, Cannon (1980) suggests that the real power of the marketing concept lies in the fact that 'firms or organizations will achieve their targets most effectively if they recognise that their prosperity is built up by meeting customer needs', while it would certainly seem that a lack of marketing orientation does lie at the heart of some of the commercial new product failures associated with the marketing of new technology (Piercy, 1984). In fact, recently, it has been suggested that harsh economic conditions have generated 'improvements' in marketing orientation (Hooley et al, 1984).

On the other hand, one recent attack on the marketing

concept (Austen, 1983) centres on overemphasis on the customer role, which it is believed results from marketing acting dogmatically as an 'article of faith', and providing an inappropriate perspective which confuses corporate and societal goals. This leads to the suggestion that a more appropriate view of the causality of success is one which depends on analysing complex, structural relationships rather than seeking a single 'key' to improved performance, be it the marketing concept or any other panacea.

Indeed, others have found difficulty in substantiating the hypothesised relationship between the implementation of the marketing concept and improved performance, either generally in major consumer goods firms (Davidson, 1975), or in improved new product development performance (Lawton and Parasuraman, 1980). In fairness though, other empirical workers have found a positive relationship between 'success' and the adoption of marketing concepts and organisation (Carson, 1968). It has been found, for example, that relationships between the marketing department and other sub-units, together with the level of marketing development, are reflected in results in terms of product development and customer relations (Tookey 1973; 1974); and that there is a link between success and the reflection of the market environment in organisation structure (Corey and Star, 1971).

Most recently, Hooley et al, (1984), in surveying UK firms, have suggested that there is some evidence that firms displaying 'genuine' marketing orientation are the most successful in profitability terms. Setting aside the issue of whether such results may be best explained by differences in the implementation of the marketing concept, or the appropriateness in different circumstances of the concept itself, what emerges quite clearly from the debate noted above is that the marketing concept has a variety of explicit organisational implications.

While accepting that structure is not the sole representation of the marketing concept - as emphasised by Ames (1970) in distinguishing 'trappings versus substance' in comparing token organisational change to real changes in the managerial attitude and frame of reference in decision making - it is possible to identify an organisational dimension of the marketing concept in the elevation and integration of the marketing sub-unit (Koch, 1962; Hise, 1965; Carson, 1968). One view of this kind is that:

> the marketing concept is perceived as the integration just below top management of those activities oriented primarily to customers ... In particular organizational terms this means that the chief marketing officer (regardless of his title) has authority over selling, advertising and marketing research. (Carson, 1968)

For this reason it is not possible to wholly isolate such 'philosophical' views from the issues with which we are presently concerned and two points are of note.

First, as noted by many writers, the 'philosophy' of marketing has implications for the departmentation of marketing, the existence of a chief marketing executive, the responsibilities of the marketing function, and indeed the status of marketing in a business. These are essentially structural attributes which it will be seen are relevant to assessing the organisational power of marketing.

Second, it was noted earlier that one source of power lies in the paradigm development of an area, or perhaps the ideology associated with it (Pfeffer, 1981a). Thus, one might be led to argue that the marketing sub-unit in a 'marketing oriented' firm is likely to be more powerful and politically influential, than a marketing sub-unit of similar appearance in another firm. In this sense, 'marketing orientation' may be taken as a proxy for paradigm development in assessing organisational power.

Thus, our concern is not with the study of marketing orientation or the marketing concept as such, but these issues as situational or contingent factors which may be related to the power of the marketing sub-unit and its political strength.

One further issue, from the points above is concerned with the development of marketing theory, and there is some value in attempting to position or locate the present work in relation to other theoretical contributions in marketing.

The Development of Marketing Theory

The Nature of Theory in Marketing. The question of the nature and meaning of theory and its development in marketing has received sporadic attention during the last twenty years. At one end of that period Halbert (1964) argued that 'Marketing ... has no recognised theoretical basis such as exists for many other disciplines, notably the physical sciences and, in some cases, the behavioral sciences'. At the other extreme of that period there is still what remains largely as speculation about 'what would be the characteristics of a general theory of marketing if we had one?' (Hunt, 1983), and it has been noted that:

> In recent years we have witnessed a considerable degree of dissatisfaction and controversy with the way research has been done in the discipline ... This author believes that at least part of the problem is due to a failure to mold together the theoretical domain with the empirical. (Bagozzi, 1984)

In fact, our present concern is not with the issues of

metatheory and the philosophy of science raised by such writers as those cited above, but with the nature of the received theory of the discipline in terms of the way in which this present study is related to that body of knowledge - accepting the more general shortcomings in the theoretical status of the discipline.   In particular, it is relevant to consider the sources of marketing theories, and the emergence of a marketing theory of the firm.

In considering the relationship of this present work to marketing theory development, it is argued that in many ways our present point of departure may be put in the context of the problems of implementing a 'marketing concept' of the type discussed above.   One analyst identifies the problems in implementing the marketing concept as: confusion about the meaning of the concept and its implications in the company;   unawareness among top management of marketing 'principles';   recruitment problems;   a lack of appropriate organisational structures, systems and procedures;   and resistance to change (McNamara, 1981), although most notably the underlying reasons for the existence of such barriers are not attacked.   In terms more congruent with our present thesis another writer categorises these problems as structural and human (Bonoma, 1983), and it has been suggested recently that 'marketing management research has emphasized only structural components.   Management issues have been neglected and, as a result, little is known about the process of marketing decision-making' (Dunn et al, 1985).

Accepting the practical significance of Dunn et al's (1985) injunction that we should be concerned with the behavioural mechanisms within firms that relate to success in implementing the marketing concept and marketing strategies (which does indeed indicate the direction in which we proceed here), it is also necessary to locate our efforts in the broader framework of marketing theory.

Sources of Marketing Theory.   If we stop short of holistic claims such as those of Alderson's (1957) functionalism, Hunt's (1983) 'general theories and the fundamental explananda of marketing', and Bagozzi's (1984) 'holistic construal', and accept the importance of more limited contributions to the understanding of specific issues in the marketing process, then two points may be made about the nature of the body of marketing theory, which are of direct relevance to our present focus.

Firstly, what passes for theory in marketing is to a large degree 'borrowed' from other disciplines (Cox, 1964), particularly the other social sciences.   Indeed, it is still arguable in the 1980s that relatively few contributions to marketing knowledge can claim to involve either concepts or methodologies developed within the discipline rather than borrowed from outwith – the most likely exception being the development of theories of consumer behaviour. For instance, Halbert (1964) suggested that, as shown in Table 1.2, the major conceptual contributions to marketing theory come from the behavioural and methodological sciences.

Table 1.2: Sources of Marketing Theory

	Contributions to Marketing Theory		
	Content (i.e. observations, measurements, and description of phenomena	Technique (i.e. methods of generating content)	Concept (i.e. abstractions, theories, generalised ideas)
Sources			
Marketing	Major	Minor	
Business disciplines (including law and economics)	Major	Minor	
Behavioural sciences	Minor	Major	Minor
Methodological sciences		Minor	Major

Source: Adapted by the Author from Halbert (1964)

The most important implication drawn from this is that the present study is an extension of that tradition of applying theories developed in other disciplines to the marketing process, since in this study we attempt to apply both techniques and concepts from other disciplines to resource allocation in marketing.

Further, however we should question the content of the existing theory of marketing in another respect. If it is accepted that marketing may be conceived and modelled as an exchange process (e.g. Hunt, 1983), then it follows that while there may be many parties involved in that process, two of them may be identified as the buyer (in some form) and the seller (of some kind). The point of this apparently obvious statement is that most theory construction in marketing has been concerned with buying and distribution and the acts of selling, rather than the actual operation or processual analysis of the seller organisation. This gap has been noted, for example, by Lutz in the following terms:

It has been extremely unfortunate that the vast bulk of theory-based behavioral research in marketing has been on consumer behavior ... if we truly believe that exchange is the fundamental building block of marketing, then, we have virtually ignored (in a scientific sense) the behavior of the party selling to the consumer. (Lutz, 1979)

To begin with, to pick up Lutz's qualification to his statement, we must accept that managers are quite likely to have implicit theories relating to this aspect of the marketing process, and it might be argued that much of what is attempted here is to develop an explicit theory of what is already understood implicitly. This is defensible on the grounds that while the manager 'is concerned with gaining a practical understanding of how his system works, this concern is manifested in finding rules of thumb and immediate guides to action ... It is this kind of theory development that supports the notion that experience is the best teacher. Yet to learn from experience one must have a framework of concepts within which to interpret past events; otherwise experience cannot be relevant and nothing can be learned from it' (Halbert, 1964).

The implication of the argument above, in terms of theory content, has been summarised by Hunt (1983) as the search for 'fundamental explananda in marketing', of the type summarised in Table 1.3. In these terms, our present interest lies in making a contribution to the second of the 'fundamental explananda', in investigating one aspect of 'the processes involved and organizational frameworks developed by sellers when engaging in exchange relationships' (Hunt, 1983).

This present work may thus be compared to other developments in marketing theory concerned with the development of a 'marketing theory of the firm'.

A Marketing Theory of the Firm. The major contribution to this area is Anderson's (1982) paper 'Marketing, Strategic Planning and the Theory of the Firm', in which he argued that 'marketing models implicitly assume a theory of the firm', and these implicit theories include the economic - neoclassical, market value and agency costs - and the behavioural - including the Cyert and March (1963) model and the Pfeffer and Salancik (1978) resource-dependence model. Of these models he concludes that:

theories of the firm developed in economics and financial economics emerged from a very different research tradition than the behaviorally oriented theories developed in management. This fact becomes particularly significant in considering their adequacy

---

Table 1.3: Fundamental Explananda in Marketing Theory

Basic Subject Matter	Fundamental Explananda	Research Questions
Exchange relation-ships	1. Behaviour of buyers directed at consummating exchanges.	1. Why do which buyers purchase what they do, where they do, when they do, and how they do?
	2. Behaviour of sellers directed at consummating exchanges.	2. Why do which sellers produce, price, promote, and distribute what they do, where they do, when they do, and how they do?
	3. The institutional framework directed at consummating and/or facilitating exchanges.	3. Why do which kinds of institution develop to engage in what kinds of functions or activities to consummate and/or facilitate exchanges?
	4. The consequences for society.	4. Impacts on society.

Source: Adapted by the Author from Hunt (1983)

---

as a framework for marketing theory development.   For example, the discipline of marketing appears to be committed to a research tradition   dominated by the methodology of inductive realism, yet it frequently employs the profit maximization paradigm of neoclassical economic theory ... In effect, marketing has rejected much of the philosophical methodology of economics while retaining a significant portion of its ontology. (Anderson, 1982)

Anderson's finding is that the need is for a theory of the firm which is consistent with the research tradition in marketing, which 'should deal explicitly with the role of marketing in the firm and should attempt to explicate its relationships with the other functional areas... and specify its contribution to the formulation of corporate "goal structures"' (Anderson, 1982).

Anderson's offering in this direction is a 'constituency-based theory of the firm', which recognises the coalition of interests, interfunctional dependence and rivalry and resource dependence concepts of behavioural theories of the firm.

In fact, Anderson's work has been criticised by Howard (1983) in his own proposal for a 'Marketing Theory of the Firm', where he claims that 'Anderson (1982) has carefully designed a descriptive theory ... but in this author's judgement it focusses upon the symptoms instead of the disease' (Howard, 1983). This judgement leads to a model of a demand and supply cycle describing customer and supplier behaviour, product hierarchies, and a customer decision system, but which returns ultimately to a somewhat naive reliance on notions of rational goals directing management choices and formal organisational structures for control.

This present work is more closely allied to Anderson's search for a model of managerial behaviour in marketing, although adopting a somewhat different perspective and not claiming to provide a full 'marketing theory of the firm'. We share Anderson's concern with the shortcomings of the economic theory of the firm, but we go somewhat further in adopting a behavioural analysis of managerial behaviour in marketing.

To summarise, we accept that the theoretical status of marketing remains limited, but do not here offer any holistic remedy to that shortfall. We proceed from that basis to study one aspect of the marketing process, which has received relatively little attention - the managerial decision making process in the selling organisation. Our efforts follow the tradition of constructing marketing theory by 'borrowing' conceptual frameworks from other disciplines. In terms of the location, in the general body of marketing knowledge, of what is attempted here, we may refer to the framework provided by Hunt's (1983) 'fundamental explananda' and what has been called a 'marketing theory of the firm'.

AN INFORMATION-STRUCTURE-POWER MODEL

Having attempted to position the present work in relation to the development of theory in marketing, the approach here may be further explicated. What we propose here is a model of the influences on decisional outcomes in marketing which reflect structure (power), and processual, and informational (political) sources. The development of the information-structure-power model was initiated in Piercy and Evans (1983) and synthesised in Piercy (1985b) and the theoretical development of the construct is detailed in Chapter 8.

The underlying hypothesis upon which the model is built is that decisional outcomes in marketing should be seen, at least in part, as the outcome of organisational variables, and as a starting point this hypothesis is summarised in Figure 1.1.

APPLYING THE MODEL TO MARKETING BUDGETING

As already stated, the area for investigation in this study is that of decision making on marketing expenditure in companies and its allocation to different segments. In some ways, this would appear to be a relatively unremarkable focus of attention, since it will be seen that there have been many studies of marketing budgeting - both descriptive and normative - and in this sense this work would appear to follow a well-trodden path. However, while the subject is apparently much-researched, the contention here is that the received theory is unsatisfactory in a number of respects, from the viewpoints of both managers and researchers. In particular, the explanatory power of the descriptive models of marketing budgeting is somewhat limited, while the relationship between prescriptive theories and actual management practices would seem tenuous in the extreme.

Why Power and Politics?

As noted above, the perspective adopted here relies on an information-structure-power model of marketing management, and we may expand briefly on the philosophy implicit in that model - although reserving detailed discussion until Chapter 8.

The notion of analysing the marketing budget as a political outcome - while contrasting dramatically with the 'rational', legitimate models commonly found in the marketing literature - has its justification in various sources.

On the broad front, in assessing the changing nature of strategic management, one analyst has concluded that:

> From a focus on efficient mass production, the internal concerns are shifting ... to managing the firm as a political (rather than consensual) environment. (Ansoff, 1979)

**Figure 1.1:   An Initial Information-Structure-Power Model of
Information Processing, Power, Politics and the
Marketing Organisation**

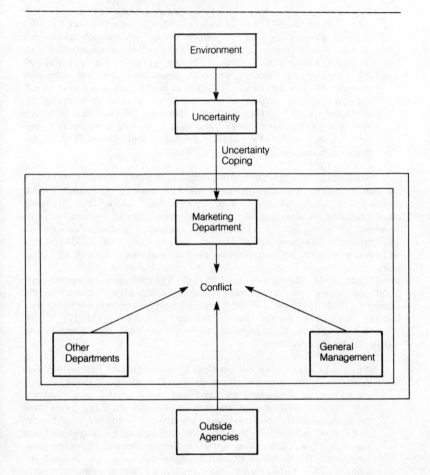

Similarly, it is suggested that the goals of the firm result
from the play of power between various internal and external
interests (Mintzberg, 1979), and the pervasiveness of power
and politics may be summarised thus:

> The subject of power is of interest primarily because of
> its importance for understanding what occurs in
> organizations ... It is not much of an exaggeration to
> claim that power and its effects are omnipresent in
> organizational decisions.   Power affects the allocation
> of resources both across departments and across
> personnel categories.   Power affects the succession of
> executives in organizations as well as the promotion of
> persons at all organizational levels. Power has effects
> on the structure that emerges in the organization,
> including its information system, and is affected by
> that structure.   (Pfeffer, 1981b)

In fact, the present interest is rather more limited –
to the resource allocation process for marketing – but it is
noteworthy that others have found the budgetary process
particularly susceptible to analysis using a political
framework as, for instance, in public sector budgeting
(Wildavsky, 1964).   As will be seen later, in addition to
Wildavsky's work in the public sector and more recent related
work by others (e.g.   Madsen and Polesie, 1981), the
political mode of analysis of budgeting has been adopted for
such purposes as studying capital budgeting in industry
(Bower, 1970; Pondy, 1970), and in analysing university and
social services budgeting (Pfeffer, 1977;   1978).   The
underlying proposition pursued by such workers was summarised
early on by Wildavsky:

> We shall conceive of budgets as attempts to allocate
> financial resources through political processes.   If
> politics is regarded as conflict over whose preferences
> are to prevail in the determination of policy, then the
> budget records the outcome of this struggle.   If one
> asks who gets what the (public or private) organization
> has to give, then the answers for a moment in time are
> recorded in the budget.   If organizations are viewed as
> political coalitions, budgets are mechanisms through
> which subunits bargain over conflicting goals, make
> side-payments, and try to motivate one another to
> accomplish their objectives. (Wildavsky, 1964)

To date, however, there has somewhat suprisingly been
little attempt to apply this form of analysis to marketing
budgeting, which provides the underlying motivation for what
is attempted here.   Indeed, it is tempting to note that
those who have specialised in the study of 'irrationality' in

consumer and buyer behaviour appear particularly resistant to studying their own managerial behaviour in similar terms, which returns us to the ontological problem discussed by Anderson (1982) of importing into marketing theory the assumptions and premises of disciplines like economics, which have quite different research traditions.

It is likely that this perspective will be ill-received by those seeking to analyse marketing expenditure decisions in the 'rational', legitimate terms of management science and bureaucratic decision making. Indeed, it has been noted by Pfeffer (1981b), in the more general field of management theory, that political analysis has been neglected for the very reason that it <u>does</u> provide an uncomfortable concept for managers and management theorists, since it conflicts directly with the managerial ideology of corporate goal-seeking rationality and the use of optimisation techniques in decision making.

As far as the use here of power and politics as explanatory variables is concerned, the view is quite simply that advocated by Pfeffer in the following terms:

> Power and politics are basic processes which occur in many organizations much of the time, and are empirically researchable and analyzable using a set of conceptual tools which are already largely in place. (Pfeffer, 1981b)

Indeed, this present writer's exploratory interviews with managers and others concerned with marketing analysis, carried out over a substantial period of time, suggested that such a view was far from being inconsistent with observations of the reality of marketing decision making – whether in terms of 'who has the Chief Executive's ear' or who controls the information on marketing effectiveness or who 'champions' or attacks marketing causes* – and that, at least at the anecdotal level, support exists for the approach taken.

However, even if it is accepted, at least as a working proposition, that the analysis of organisational behaviour

---

* That 'attacks' take place is no exaggeration. For example, in the chemicals division of a major oil multinational corporation visited, a senior member of the board of directors was on written record as stating: 'This word (marketing) was deleted from the (company) vocabulary some years ago and has no current meaning'. In this company there was no marketing department, little marketing information, and little marketing input to corporate strategy.

---

using the concepts of power and politics enjoys some validity in a general sense, this leaves open the question of why such an analysis should be considered applicable to the area of marketing and its resourcing.

Why Marketing?

If this present analysis is seen as an attempt to apply concepts developed in such literatures as those of organisation theory and organisational behaviour, to a particular area of context, then this opens the more general issue of organisational phenomena in marketing decision making processes, which was pursued in the earlier works of this trilogy (Piercy and Evans, 1983; Piercy, 1985b).

The case argued in detail in Chapter 4 is that there exists a need for a more rigorous approach to the structural and processual aspects of marketing. On this point there has been agreement for some time, although until recently progress in this direction has been hindered by the lack of suitable analytical tools.

In justice, there are some signs of progress towards a deeper processual analysis of marketing organisation, from various perspectives. While this present writer has been concerned with power and politics in marketing (e.g. Piercy, 1985b), others have advanced related, indeed interdependent, notions, for instance Scandinavian researchers (Hakansson and Ostberg, 1975; Hakansson, et al, 1979) have been concerned with social exchange and dependency between the marketing organisation and the environment, leading to a model relating marketing structures (and hence by implication power) to the type and level of environmental uncertainty.

Similarly, Nonaka and Nicosia (1979) identified the same gap in the theory:

> The marketing literature has essentially ignored the study of group behavior, especially the underlying organizational interactions. Yet the necessity and importance of filling the gap is self-evident. (Nonaka and Nicosia, 1979)

These last researchers were concerned with the impact of environmental uncertainty and instability on information processing and marketing structures, though extending their analysis to consider uncertainty reduction producing a locus of power in the marketing sub-unit.

Otherwise power in marketing has generally been concerned as an aspect of interorganisational relationships - typically in the channel of distribution - regarding which a large literature has been established (see pp. 194 - 197 below).

As far as political behaviour is concerned, it will be

shown that there are fragments of evidence that such phenomena occur in marketing decision making, and that these relate most particularly to information control by managers.

However, perhaps the most important argument is that if one accepts that under certain conditions or contingencies decisions are political outcomes, then the degree to which those conditions occur in, or even characterise, marketing decision making, provides a case for the political analysis of those marketing decision making processes.

The working hypothesis therefore is that marketing offers an untried, but potentially fruitful, area for political analysis.

Why Marketing Budgeting?

In fact, it may be argued that there are many decision areas in marketing which share the contingencies mentioned above – new product choices, product abandonment decisions, pricing choices, market selection, and so on. Indeed, it is intended that this line of marketing analysis should proceed in those very directions.

However, at the moment, for a number of reasons, attention focuses on the allocation of resources to marketing: (a) the relative ease of measurability of outcomes in terms of financial resources, manpower, facilities, and so on, compared to other possible areas of attack; (b) the lack of analysis of this area, discussed earlier; and (c) simply the importance of resource allocation to general and marketing management, as well as to others outwith companies. Indeed, there are those who suggest such expenditures are too high (e.g. Aaker and Carman, 1982). Consider, for instance, the data in Table 1.4, which demonstrate an outlay approaching £8,000 Millions on advertising in the UK, amounting to almost 3% of the Gross National Product. In addition, our view of marketing expenditure should be broadened to include personal selling and market research expenditure – the Census suggested that in 1981 some 123,500 people were employed in selling activities. If one takes the estimated average cost of £19,000 (Financial Times, 1982) to keep a sales person 'on the road', then expenditure here may amount to a further £2,350 Millions. Similarly it has been suggested that in the early 1980s, commissioned market research accounts for a further £130 Millions of expenditure. One may then make the crude calculation for 1983, as follows:

	£M
Media expenditure	3,580
Sales promotion	4,000
Sales personnel	2,350
Market research	130
	10,060

Table 1.4: UK Advertising and Sales Promotion Expenditure 1979-1983

		1979 £M	1980 £M	1981 £M	1982 £M	1983 £M
Total advertising media expenditure	(1)	2129	2562	2818	3126	3579
Total sales promotion expenditure	(2)	–	–	3000	3500	4000
				5818	6626	7579
% of UK Gross National Product				2.7%	2.8%	N/A

Sources: (1) Marketing Yearbook, 1983
         (2) Special Report, The Times, 4 June 1984, p.14

This suggests that overall marketing expenditure in the UK accounts for some of of the nation's Gross National Product. Indeed, advertising alone accounts for some 1.4% of GNP and 2% of consumers' expenditure, both which statistics have increased in the period 1970 to 1983 (Waterson, 1984). Even then one must recognise that there are other hidden costs - the cost of marketing personnel in non-selling jobs (of the order of 25,000 in the 1981 Census), the cost of in-house market research, administration, computing systems and so on.

Alternatively consider the significance of such outlays not to the national economy but to the individual company - consider the data in Table 1.5, showing the level of expenditure on media advertising alone by the fifteen largest advertisers in the UK. While valid comparisons are difficult, one finds firms like Cadbury Schweppes, Mars and

BL spending on advertising alone to the extent of 4-5% of sales revenue, a figure which rises as high as 10% for Proctor and Gamble, and runs at 1-2% for organisations like the Imperial Group and Beechams.

Table 1.5: The Major UK Advertisers, 1981

	Total Advertising Expenditure M
Unilever Plc	56.1
Cadbury Schweppes	34.6
Mars	35.9
Imperial Group	33.7
HM Government	30.3
Proctor and Gamble	24.9
Allied Breweries	24.3
Beecham Group	24.1
Rowntree Mackintosh	19.4
Nestle	18.2
Electricity Council and Boards	17.8
British Gas Corporation	17.1
Thorn EMI	16.0
Reed International	15.9
BL	15.8

Source: The Times 1000 1982-3

On these grounds alone marketing budgeting is of significance as an area for renewed study.

Even if one sets aside the sheer size of the resource commitment to marketing activities, the subject remains one of inherent fascination.   Indeed, the intrinsic interest of the topic of budgeting was encapsulated by one analyst in the in the following terms:

One is likely to think of budgeting as an arid subject, the province of stodgy clerks and dull statisticians. Nothing could be more mistaken ... Human nature is never more evident than when men are struggling to gain a larger share of funds or to apportion what they have among myriad claimants ... Budgeting deals with the purposes of men.   How can they be moved to cooperate? How can conflicts be resolved?   (Wildavsky, 1964)

There are several reasons for this breadth of definition. Perhaps the most important point is that if one is to examine the power and politics of corporate marketing, then increments in scarce resources like staffing and space may be as revealing, or possibly more revealing, than simply expenditure levels on advertising and the like, or even increments in those expenditures.

<u>Second</u>, it must be recognised that the 'marketing budget' as an identifying term suffers from some lack of precision simply because it is defined differently by different organisations.

Strictly speaking, a comprehensive marketing budget (e.g. Sevin, 1965; Gillingham, 1985) would include all the direct and indirect costs of the marketing organisation including: staff costs; office and equipment expenses; and the cost of each element of the marketing mix – product policy (e.g. packaging, new product launches, modification launches, etc.), pricing (e.g. discounts given, price lists, etc.), communications (e.g. advertising media and production costs, sales promotions, public relations, sales force office and field costs, etc.), distribution (e.g. transport of finished goods, storage, and warehousing, special deals with distributors, etc.).

In fact, there is little evidence to suggest that this is the normal practice in companies (Rayburn, 1981), and there are a number of reasons for this. To begin with, there has been some reluctance to identify marketing as a cost centre, in the full sense, in many organisations. It is easier, given the problems of cause and effect analysis, to regard marketing as no more than an overhead, or a charge against profits, rather than a creator of revenue and profit (Piercy, 1985a).

For present purposes, given the considerable lack of standardisation between companies in what are the components, if any, of the marketing budget, this is itself taken as a political outcome – at least at its extremes. In this sense, the working hypothesis is that the lack of a formally identified marketing budget suggests a low level of marketing department power. Similarly, a formal budget which is large and growing is linked to higher marketing department power, again as a working hypothesis. However these working hypotheses survive the empirical testing presented later, certainly the 'comprehensive' budget implies by its construction, a particular form of marketing structuring and a particular type and degree of marketing management responsibility. What limited evidence there is (e.g. Hayhurst and Wills, 1972) suggests that it is all too easy to exaggerate the real responsibilities of the marketing manager. From the prescriptive viewpoint it would be argued that if the marketing department has, for example, no responsibility for physical distribution, then it has no real place in the budget. Indeed, this returns us to the larger question of what marketing is, and therefore what is or is not a 'marketing cost'. Realistically, for present purposes, it is necessary to accept that the components of the marketing budget vary between firms.

In other words, the definition of the marketing budget is taken as a subjective outcome, which may be partly political in its own right, and we proceed on that basis.

Third, and closely related to the last point, there are clearly differences between organisations in the type of cost included in the marketing budget.

To begin with, the listing given above falls into the temptation of combining controllable and uncontrollable costs, which, at the very least, invalidates the use of the budget as a planning and control mechanism. This is not, however, to say that such practices do not occur. For example, in one company studied by the author, the largest component of the marketing budget was distributor commission, that is the difference between sales valued at list prices and revenues received from distributors, but, in fact, since commission rates were set by the finance department and top management, this was largely an uncontrollable factor for the marketing department and sales managers.

A related, and well-documented, technical problem is the danger of confusing overheads with direct or incremental costs. At its simplest, for example, the product manager may plan sales promotions and construct a budget for them, but is unlikely to be involved in determining the costs of administering the sales office and order processing system.

Lastly, it must be noted that there is even relatively little consensus about what specific items to include within the components of the marketing budget, even once they are accepted as part of that budget. For instance, while advertising would appear to be a clearly identifiable marketing activity, a recent survey by Patti and Blasko (1981) found considerable disagreement among large advertising spenders as to which specific items should be charged to the advertising budget.

Again, it may be that as well as technical, accounting differences, one should look for explanations of such practices in the power and politics of corporate resource allocation systems as they affect marketing. In fact, one management accountant was led recently to the conclusion that:

> Unfortunately, it may well be that many controllers have resigned themselves to assuming that marketing cost is an impossible area to control and analyze. (Rayburn, 1981)

However, Rayburn's survey (1981) did find that three-quarters of a sample of large industrial companies in the USA budgeted around (a) 'order-filling activities' - mainly physical distribution costs like transport, warehousing, order handling, credit and stocking; and (b) 'order-getting activities' - mainly advertising, sales promotion, and merchandising, which suggests that at least a workable frame of reference exists.

One accepts therefore that there are differences between companies in their definition of marketing budgets, with possible political implications, but may suggest that this is a variation around an established framework, rather a random process.

These points suggest that a number of qualifications should be expressed. While the term 'marketing budgeting' is used throughout, it is likely that the specific content of the marketing budget will vary substantially between companies. In many instances, the marketing budget is, in effect, no more than the budget for advertising and sales promotion. Indeed, this point is not unconnected with the analysis of the power and politics of budgeting. The substantive control of an important budget may in organisational terms be both a source of power and a sign of that power to others. On the other hand, illusory or symbolic control of an important budget item may be a sign of the power of others - it has recently been suggested, for example, that in companies with a large TV advertising spend, real control has passed from the marketing department to general managers and others (Wills and Kennedy, 1982). The term 'marketing budget' is therefore used both broadly - as including resources other than simply financial - and relatively loosely to reflect situational company differences in operational definition.

OBJECTIVES AND STRUCTURE

Given the introductory comments made above, the objectives of the study may be stated in the following terms.

First, the work seeks to identify, and to measure, political and power-based influences on the process of allocating resources to marketing, and hence on marketing expenditure.

Second, the work has the goal of applying the earlier developed information-structure-power model of marketing decision making to marketing budgeting. This implies that we take power as a structural/information processing variable, and political behaviour as an informational variable, both of which act through two sets of contingencies - strategic and political contingencies relating to the company's internal and external environments and the relationship between them. Budgeting methods and processes are thus taken as political in nature, relating to outcomes in budget increments, manpower and other resources.

Third, the study has the aim of adding to the under-standing of the corporate context or environment in which marketing decisions are made, in a way which may then be extended to areas of other than marketing budgeting.

Fourth, the study aims in this way to provide an additional theory of marketing resource allocation useful to those in the practical setting, and as a stimulant to further research and analysis.

These goals are pursued through the structure of the book in the following way.

Part I examines existing theories of budgeting in marketing - the normative or prescriptive, and the descriptive - and attempts to do so in a multidisciplinary context, but questions their adequacy in an organisational context.

Part II then turns from the received theory to the development of an organisational view of the marketing decision making processes, and from this, to the power and politics of marketing budgeting.

Part III introduces new empirical data from a survey of UK firms' marketing organisation and budgeting.

This leads then to the synthesis of an organisational/ political model of marketing budgeting in Part IV, and the identification of a range of implications of such a model for the practical management of marketing actions and resources, and the researching of that activity.

REFERENCES

Aaker, D.A. and Carman, J.M. (1982) 'Are You Over-advertising?', Journal of Advertising Research, 22 (4), 57-70

Adler, L. (ed.) (1967) Plotting Marketing Strategy, Simon and Schuster, New York

Alderson, W. (1957) Marketing Behavior and Executive Action, Irwin, Homewood, Ill.

Anderson, P.F. (1982) 'Marketing, Strategic Planning and the Theory of the Firm', Journal of Marketing, 46, Spring, 15-26

Austen, A. (1983) 'The Marketing Concept - Is It Obsolete?', Quarterly Review of Marketing, 9 (1), 6-8

Bagozzi, R.P. (1984) 'A Prospectus for Theory Construction in Marketing', Journal of Marketing, 48, Winter, 11-29

Baker, M., Braam, T and Kemp, A. (1967) Permeation of the Marketing Concept in Yorkshire Manufacturing Industry, University Press, Bradford

Bartels, R. (1962) The Development of Marketing Thought, Irwin, Homewood, Ill.

Bell, M.L. (1972) Marketing: Concepts and Strategy, 3rd ed., Houghton Mifflin, Boston, Mass.

Bonoma, T.V. (1984) 'Making Your Marketing Strategy Work', Harvard Business Review, 62 (2), 69-76

Bower, J. (1970) Managing the Resource Allocation Process, Harvard University, Boston, Mass.

Cannon, T. (1980) Basic Marketing, Holt Rinehart and Winston, London

Carson, T. (1968) 'Marketing Organization in British Manufacturing Firms', Journal of Marketing, 32 (2), 34-39

Cavanagh, G.F., Moberg, D.J. and Velasquez, M. (1981) 'The Ethics of Organizational Politics', Academic of Management Review, 6 (3), 363-74

Child, J. (1974) 'Management and Organizational Factors Associated with Company Performance', Journal of Management Studies, 11 (3), 175-189

Christopher, M., McDonald, M. and Wills, G. (1980) Introducing Marketing, Pan, London

Corey, E.R. and Star, S.H. (1971) Organization Strategy: A Marketing Approach, Harvard University, Boston, Mass.

Crosier, K. (1975) 'What Exactly is Marketing?', Quarterly Review of Marketing, 1 (2), 21-5

Cox, R. (1964) 'Introduction', in R. Cox, W. Alderson and S.J. Shapiro (eds.) Theory in Marketing, Irwin, Homewood, Ill.

Cyert, R.M. and March, J.G. (1963) A Behavioral Theory of the Firm, Prentice-Hall, New York

Davidson, J.H. (1975) Offensive Marketing, Penguin, Harmondsworth

Dunn, M.G., Norburn, D. and Birley, S. (1985) 'Corporate Culture - A Positive Correlate with Marketing Effectiveness', International Journal of Advertising, 4, 65-73

Financial Times (1982) 'The Falling Cost of a Salesman', Financial Times, 29 October 1982, 20

Foxall, G. (1981) Strategic Marketing Management, Croom Helm, Beckenham

Hakansson, H. and Ostberg, C. (1975) 'Industrial Marketing: An Organizational Problem', Industrial Marketing Management, 4, 113-23

Hakansson, H., Wootz, B., Andersson, O. and Hangard, P. (1979) 'Industrial Marketing as an Organizational Problem', European Journal of Marketing, 13 (3), 81-93

Halbert, M.H. (1964) 'The Requirements for Theory in Marketing', in R. Cox, W. Alderson and S.J. Shapiro (eds.) Theory in Marketing, Irwin, Homewood, Ill.

27

Hayhurst, R. and Wills, G. (1972) Organizational Design for Marketing Futures, Allen and Unwin, London

Hise, R.T. (1965) 'Have Manufacturing Firms Adopted the Marketing Concept?', Journal of Marketing, 29 (3), 9–12

Hooley, G.J., West, C.J. and Lynch, J.E. (1984) Marketing in the UK – A Survey of Current Practice and Performance, Institute of Marketing, Cookham, Berks.

Hopkins, D.S. and Bailey, E.L. (1971) The Chief Marketing Executive, Conference Board, New York

Howard, J. (1965) Marketing Theory, Allyn and Bacon, Boston, Mass.

Howard, J.A. (1983) 'Marketing Theory of the Firm', Journal of Marketing, 47, Fall, 90–100

Hunt, S.D. (1983) 'General Theories and the Fundamental Explananda of Marketing', Journal of Marketing, 47, Fall, 9–17

Koch, E.G. (1962) 'New Organization Patterns for Marketing', Management Review, February, 4–12

Kotler, P. (1980) Marketing Management: Analysis, Planning and Control, 4th ed., Prentice-Hall, London

Kotler, P. (1984) Marketing Management: Analysis, Planning and Control, 5th ed., Prentice-Hall, London

Lawton, L. and Parasuraman, K. (1980) 'The Impact of the Marketing Concept on New Product Planning', Journal of Marketing, 44 (1), 19–25

Levitt, T. (1960) 'Marketing Myopia', Harvard Business Review, July/August, 45–56

Lutz, R.J. (1979) 'Opening Statement', in O.C. Ferrell, S.W. Brown and C.W. Lamb (eds.) Conceptual and Theoretical Developments in Marketing, American Marketing Association, Chicago

McNamara, C.P. (1981) 'Time Is Running Out for Executives Still Flirting with the Marketing Concept', Sales and Marketing Management, 16 March, 103–4

Madsen, V. and Polesie, T. (1981) Human Factors in Budgeting: Judgement and Evaluation, Pitman, London

Matthews, J.B., Buzzell, R.D., Levitt, T. and Frank, R.E. (1964) Marketing, McGraw-Hill, New York

Nonaka, I. and Nicosia, F.M. (1979) 'Marketing Management, Its Environment and Information Processing', Journal of Business Research, 7 (4), 277-301

Patti, C.H. and Blasko, V. 'Budgeting Practices of Big Advertisers' Journal of Advertising Research, 21 (6), 23-9

Pfeffer, J. (1978) 'The Micropolitics of Organizations', in M.W. Meyer (ed.) Environments and Organizations, Jossey-Bass, San Francisco

Pfeffer, J. (1981a) 'Management As Symbolic Action: The Creation and Maintenance of Organizational Paradigms', in L.L. Cummings and B.M. Staw (eds.) Research in Organizational Behavior, Jai, Greenwich, Connecticut

Pfeffer, J. (1981b) Power in Organizations, Pitman, Marshfield, Mass.

Pfeffer, J. and Salancik, G.R. (1978) The External Control of Organizations, Harper and Row, New York

Piercy, N. (1982) Export Strategy: Markets and Competition, Allen and Unwin, London

Piercy, N. (1984) 'Marketing Systems and New Information Technology', in N. Piercy (ed.) The Management Implications of New Information Technology, Croom Helm, Beckenham

Piercy, N. (ed.) (1985a) Marketing Asset Accounting - Exploring the Marketing/Accounting Interface, EUROSAM, Bradford

Piercy, N. (1985b) Marketing Organisation: An Analysis of Information Processing, Power and Politics, Allen and Unwin, London

Piercy, N. (1986) 'The Marketing Budget: Rationality, Politics and Organisation', European Journal of Marketing, forthcoming.

Piercy, N. and Evans, M. (1983) Managing Marketing Information, Croom Helm, Beckenham

Pondy, L.R. (1970) 'Toward a Theory of Internal Resource-Allocation', in M.N. Zald (ed.) Power in Organizations, Vanderbilt University Press, Nashville, Tenn.

Rayburn, L.G. (1981) 'Marketing Costs - Accountants to the Rescue', Management Accounting, 62 (7), 32-41

Rodger, L.W. (1965) Marketing In a Competitive Economy, Associated Business Programmes, London

Sevin, C.H. (1965) Marketing Productivity Analysis, McGraw-Hill, St. Louis

Tookey, D.A. (1973) The Marketing Function in its Organizational Context, unpublished M.Sc. dissertation, University of Lancaster

Tookey, D.A. (1974) 'The Marketing Function in its Organizational Context', in R. Lawrence (ed.) Marketing as a Non-American Activity, Proceedings: Marketing Education Group Conference, University of Lancaster

Velasquez, M., Moberg, D.J. and Cavanagh, G.F. (1983) 'Organizational Statesmanship and Dirty Politics', Organizational Dynamics, 12 (2), 65-80

Waterson, M.J. (1984) 'Advertising Expenditure in the UK: 1983 Survey', International Journal of Advertising, 3, 249-68

Wildavsky, A. (1964) The Politics of the Budgetary Process, Little Brown, Boston

Wills, G. and Kennedy, S. (1982) 'How to Budget Marketing', Management Today, February, 58-61

PART 1

Marketing Budgeting in Theory and Practice

2

Normative Theories of Marketing Budgeting

INTRODUCTION

This part of the book has the goal of describing and contrasting the two dominant elements of the received theory of marketing budgeting: the <u>normative</u> – which seeks to prescribe to practitioners, on various implicit criteria, the budgeting methods which they should apply; and the <u>descriptive</u> – studies of the methods and processes which appear actually to be used in organisations.

It should be noted that the goal here is not to provide a guide to budgeting technique in marketing (a task attempted elsewhere (Piercy, forthcoming 1987), but to review very briefly the existing state of knowledge in this field.

The point should also be made that while the separation of prescription and description is convenient for present purposes, neither the precision nor the appropriateness of this distinction should be exaggerated. For instance, the basis of much of the normative work is the inadequacy of existing practices, which presumes some knowledge and understanding of the latter. More fundamentally, there is a central area between the prescriptive and descriptive, where the two merge – some normative work, for example, is based quite explicitly on the notion that management practices applied by successful organisations should provide a model to be applied by others.

It also emerges that the marketing literature makes relatively little distinction between <u>method</u>, or technique, and <u>process</u> in budgeting – a point which emerges most clearly in Chapter 3, and which is central to the approach developed in this present study.

For the moment, however, normative theories of marketing budgeting may be approached in the following way. First, the basis of prescription is examined, and then we proceed to describe briefly the type of tools and techniques offered by economic analysis, management science, and the marketing management literature, applied generally to the total marketing budget and to expenditure on the individual marketing mix elements of advertising, promotion, selling, and marketing research (though most commonly the former rather than the latter items).

THE BASIS OF PRESCRIPTION

The foundation of prescriptive or normative theories varies greatly, but they share the characteristic of stating what should be. This implies very clearly the existence of criteria and goals by which to judge what is or is not desirable.

To some extent it is the criteria of prescription which distinguish the various approaches taken, but as will be seen shortly they also demonstrate their limitations in the organisational context.

Firstly, there are the criteria of optimisation in using resources to maximise certain explicit functions – profit, sales, market share, efficiency, and so on – as in the case particularly of economic analysis, and management science models of budgeting and resource allocation. While the assumptions typically are great – that goals are explicit and quantifiable, and often that they are single; that managers thus seek the maximisation or optimisation of some known function; that information is freely available in one form or another; and that all major variables in a problem through a relevant time period are susceptible to quantification – on the face of things this would appear not to be unreasonable.

Secondly, there are criteria of 'rationality'. Certain budgeting approaches are expressed in terms of rational goal-seeking behaviour, and the systematic or logical approaches usable in implementing that behaviour. The 'objective and task' approach to advertising budgeting is of this type – objectives are set, implied tasks defined, and the costs of those tasks calculated. It may be that also included in this category should be the contributions of accountancy to the establishment and use of budgets in marketing (e.g. Bleil, 1983; Gillingham, 1985), although recognising that the goals of accountancy in this area reflect the multiplicity of uses made of budgets in organisations.

Thirdly, closely related to the notion of rationality in a general sense, are criteria of what may be called 'corporate rationality' or bureaucracy where, for example, budgeting systems are built around corporate missions and goals, as in output budgeting, and budgets are built from a zero-base rather than established by precedent, as in programme budgeting.

Lastly, though perhaps reflecting some notion of rationality, are deductive or judgementally normative approaches to budgeting based on the observation of <u>practice</u>, and judgement as to how methodology should be improved.

In this way, we may distinguish between normative theories based on: economic analysis, management science, and managerial models - ranging from the 'rational' or bureaucratic to the observation of 'best' or ideal practice, or the apparently unscientific derivation of principles on the basis of judgement.

THE BASIS OF ANALYSING BUDGETING

Following the type of distinction made in the accounting literature (e.g. Barrett and Fraser, 1977), it should be noted here that the main focus of attention is on the <u>operational</u> budget - i.e. basically the level of effort and hence expenditure on marketing and selling activities - rather than capital or financial budgeting.

It is also the case, as noted above, that budgets typically serve a variety of purposes in organisations - to plan expenditures, to motivate managers and operatives, to coordinate subunits, to link short-term actions to the long-term corporate plan, to control managers' performance, and so on (Piercy and Thomas, 1984). In our present analysis concern is essentially only with the first of these - the setting of the level of resources to be devoted to those activities designated as 'marketing' functions.

This said, one view of resource allocation emphasises that even in such a simple view of budgets they should be perceived as far more than simple accounts:

> Serving diverse purposes, a budget can be many things: a political act, a plan of work, a prediction, a source of enlightenment, a means of obfuscation, a mechanism of control, an escape from restrictions, a means of action, a brake on progress, even a prayer. (Wildavsky, 1964)

While this may seem fanciful, Wildavsky's view does emphasise the danger inherent in adopting a purely mechanical approach to budgeting - that of ignoring the managerial and organisational context in which that budgeting takes place.

This said, one substantial problem faced in attempting to escape from the paradigm provided by the received view of resource allocation and budgeting in marketing is still the lack of supporting material in the general literature. Rather than concluding that this evidences the validity of the received paradigm, it is perhaps indicative of the problems involved in the empirical study of this area - a point discussed in detail in Chapter 10. In fact, we are not alone in perceiving this problem.

One analyst on a more general note suggested some time

ago that:

> Only recently have the social sciences begun to direct substantial attention toward understanding the process of resource-allocation <u>within</u> the constituent institutions of society. (Pondy, 1970)

Indeed, later empiricists, concerned more specifically with sub-unit budgeting, concurred that 'there have been few empirical examinations of resource allocation within organizations' (Pfeffer and Salancik 1974). Perhaps the key point is that made by Bower in his qualitative study of capital budgeting:

> For purposes of management and research, adequate models of the allocation process are not available. I believe that this lack stems from the fact that prescriptive theories of economic choice have not yet been set in the context of the large organization's political process. (Bower, 1970)

Clearly, the thesis pursued in this present study is that this last point applies to marketing budgeting, and perhaps particularly so, compared to other areas of resource allocation.

None the less, our starting point is to examine in outline the normative approaches applied to resource allocation in marketing.

PRESCRIPTIVE THEORIES OF BUDGETING

Statements of the need for rigorous, integrated budgeting are to be found in both the general literature and that of marketing. For instance, in the former area one writer suggests:

> Budgeting, employed as a tool of both planning and performance measurement offers top management one of its best means for putting an organization on a single course and keeping it there. (Koltun, 1965)

Faith in such statements may be somewhat diminished by that writer's parallel assumption that 'Most of the company's expenses are known in advance and can be estimated (planned) with some degree of certainty' (Koltun, 1965). However, the centrality of budgeting remains uncontroversially an axiom of the normative theory (e.g. Barrett and Fraser, 1977; Lin, 1979; Piercy and Thomas, 1984).

Essentially the same point emerges in the literature of

marketing. For example, Turnbull's (1974) view of the need for an integrated approach to budgeting for marketing communications, echoes writers in the general literature, while the importance of taking a 'rational' approach to budgeting marketing expenses is predictably stressed by many analysts (e.g. Hurwood and Brown, 1970; Wills et al, 1972; Rayburn, 1981; Kotler, 1984).

The general literature has identified traditional approaches to budgeting as incremental, and imperfect in various respects (a view to which we return shortly), and a variety of approaches seek to replace and improve upon such practices in the marketing area.

Economic Analysis for Marketing Resource Allocation

Economic analysis has been applied conceptually to the total level of marketing effort (i.e. the total budget and resource allocation) (e.g. Kotler, 1984) and to particular individual elements of the marketing mix, most notably advertising expenditure (e.g. Corlett, 1984), promotional expenditure (e.g. Carlson and McDevitt, 1985) and sales force size (e.g. Dalrymple and Thorelli, 1984), and the key concept underlying such analyses is the marginality principle drawn from elementary economic theory.

In the general context, the economist's marginal utility principle suggests that profit will be maximised by increasing expenditure on marketing up to that point where the incremental pound (£) spent no longer yields more than an extra pound (£) of profit, i.e. net profits are maximised at the point where the marginal cost of marketing effort just equals the gross profit derived from the marginal sales increase generated, as suggested by the hypothesised relationships in Figure 2.1.

The principle of marginality is self-evidently linked to the notion of diminishing returns - the marginal effect of a given resource tends to decline as more is applied - through the non-linearity of the sales response function.

Interestingly, Kennedy and Corkindale (1976) made the observation that the marginal utility principle is synonymous with the principle of 'advertising as a fixed percentage of sales' - which purportedly is one of the commonest approaches to budget setting in advertising - a point discussed further below (pp. 78 - 80). Certainly, 'naive', univariate, time series analysis has been found to produce remarkably good predictions of aggregate advertising expenditure, as opposed to more complex models of consumption or other economic activity (Sturgess and Wilson, 1983).

One of the best-known and widely-cited applications of economic analysis to marketing resource allocation was presented by Palda (1969), which attempts to derive and explain normative prescriptions of the theory of the firm,

Figure 2.1: Marginal Analysis of Marketing Efforts

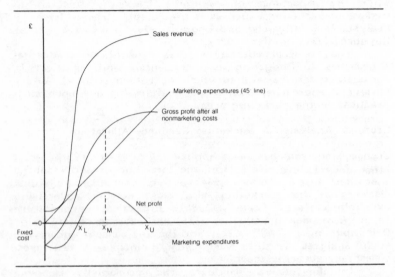

Source: Adapted by the Author from Kotler (1984)

designed to lead to the optimal input mix within the firm, relying heavily on the Dorfman-Steiner theorem (1954). This theorem sought to determine optimal advertising policy, taking into account the effects of price, quality and promotion, arriving at the conclusion, re-stated by Kennedy and Corkindale (1976), that for the monopolist, the optimal position is where:

$$\frac{Advertising\ (£)}{Sales\ (£)} = \frac{A\ T}{P\ Q} = \frac{E(Advertising)}{E\ (Price)}$$

where: A = number of advertisements
T = costs per advertisement
Q = production or sales volume
P = price per unit sold
E = (Advertising) = advertising elasticity of demand
E = (Price) = price elasticity of demand

It is this view which suggests that the optimal policy is a constant advertising/sales ratio - if E (Advertising) and E (Price) are in a constant ratio.

This type of approach has been criticised: for assuming that the isolated effect of advertising or other marketing effects on sales or profits is known or can easily be measured (Kennedy and Corkindale, 1976; Corkindale, 1983); for ignoring the complexities of the time effects of advertising and communications (Bass et al, 1961; King, 1984); and for not incorporating the changing costs over time of delivering an advertisement to a target audience (Schmalensee, 1972); to which may be added the broader implicit assumption that managers conceive the problems they face in these terms or, indeed, that they should do so.

None the less, what is still found in the marketing literature is the prescription of marginal analysis to analyse the known or hypothesised relationship between promotional expenditure and sales (e.g. Hurwood and Brown, 1970: Corlett, 1978; Doyle and Corstjens, 1982). Certainly such approaches may be defended to some extent in terms of providing an initial analytical framework, rather than actually determining budgets:

> There are grounds for doubting the economic significance of the whole business of writing down profit functions (or drawing curves) and finding points of zero partial derivatives (theoretical maxima or minima). Such devices are merely aids to thinking about practical problems and it may be an uneconomical expenditure of effort to devote too much ingenuity to developing them. Yet such devices are aids ... and if sufficiently flexible, they help us to find implications, interrelationships, and sometimes contradictions which might escape notice without them. (Dorfman and Steiner, 1954)

Indeed, empirical testing has suggested certain areas of validity in the economists' approach, reporting variously that: the marketing effort/sales ratio implies diminishing returns to scale, and that this model may be used to measure marketing effectiveness to optimise expenditure (Weinberg, 1956; 1960); that advertising/sales ratios vary across industries, which is attributable to price, sales levels, and type of product, and other factors (Doyle, 1968; Farris and Buzzell, 1979· Farris and Albion, 1981); that budget/sales ratios vary internationally suggesting the impact of cultural differences (Zif et al, 1984), that advertising/sales ratios, while varying across industries, are very close the 'optimum' defined by the Dorfman-Steiner theorem (Cowling, 1972), or conversely that firms may be substantially 'overadvertising' as a result of the difficulties of modelling responses (Aaker and Carman, 1982); and that advertising may vary within broad product categories for reasons such as price elasticity, the competitive situation, the rate of new product innovation, and the potential for market expansion (Telser, 1961).

That such studies are of value in developing economic theory there seems little doubt. What seems less evident, however, is the contribution of such work to advancing the analysis of marketing decision making within companies and the actual making of those decisions.

Management Science Models for Marketing Budget Determination

It follows from the econometric approaches discussed above that a major element of the prescriptive theory is provided by management science in the specification of models to describe, predict, and solve problems (e.g. Montgomery and Urban, 1969).

For example, specifically in the marketing resource allocation area, recent contributions have included: a hierarchical linking of marketing resource allocations to market areas and product groups (Gijsbrechts and Naert, 1984); an interactive computer model to allocate promotional spending across brands (Basu and Batia, 1984); and a variety of other sophisticated models which attempt to determine and allocate marketing expenditures.

In fact, there have been a large number of more general treatments of the application of management science to marketing (e.g. Buzzell, 1964; Montgomery and Urban, 1969: Simon and Freimer, 1970; Kotler, 1971· Leeflang, 1974; Kotler and Lilien, 1984), with the shared approach, suggested by Montgomery and Urban, of providing a quantitative framework of technique for: (a) problem formulation, (b) hypothesis generation, (c) measurement of the relevant phenomena, (d) derivation of a solution or better understanding of the problem, (e) testing of results, (f) revisions and (g) the emergence of valid results.

A taxonomy of marketing models is not attempted here (e.g. see Aaker and Carman, 1982· Basu and Batia, 1984), although it is noted that strictly speaking some of the techniques here, such as experimentation and market testing, are more properly classified as marketing research than management science (as in, for example, Piercy and Evans (1983); Corkindale (1984): and Sunoo and Lin (1979)). The common element in these approaches is described by Kennedy and Corkindale (1976) as involving either (a) the derivation of equations which model the behaviour of a product in a market, to allow to a greater or lesser extent the evaluation of the effect of changes in marketing efforts/expenditures on sales or profit, and hence provide criteria for resource allocation; or (b) the attempt to systematise the management decision process, to deduce the most logical outcome from the available information, and thus to arrive at a suitable budget size.

While these approaches are, above all else, logical and

'rational', and certainly such forces as the increased availability of new information technology makes advanced methodology potentially far more widely accessible (e.g. Corkindale, 1984; Lancaster and Stern, 1983), modelling approaches to budget determination in marketing have been criticised for: (a) underestimating the problems in quantifying the values of the critical parameters and the completeness of models (Gilligan and Crowther, 1976) (perhaps most particularly in terms of carry-over effects and the cross-elasticity of marketing inputs (Bultez and Naert, 1984)); (b) ignoring the lack of management understanding of models; and (c) the implicit optimisation goals of such models. One early and much-quoted contention by a leading management scientist was that 'the big problem with management science models is that managers practically never use them' (Little, 1966), to which may be added the argument that the use of models may even be a largely symbolic action in pursuit of the appearance of rationality, rather than substantively determining budgets (Pfeffer, 1981).

Certainly, it will be seen the evidence of the use of management science in setting marketing budgets is that their application is severely limited in practice (pp. *78-80*).

Rational/Corporate Management Models of Marketing Budgeting

Related to the philosophy of management science are a variety of models of management budget-setting, which aim to make that process more 'rational' through improved systems of budgeting. The emphasis here is implicitly on applying technique to process.

Programme Budgeting. The general literature offers such techniques as Zero-Base Budgeting (ZBB) and Programme Evaluation and Review Technique (PERT), and other quantitative management techniques, as methods of overcoming the essentially incremental and fragmented nature of traditional budgeting (as described in Chapter 3).

ZBB involves each year reducing the budget to zero and justifying all expenditures, ideally in combination with a participative management style (Lin, 1979) – for example as contrasted with traditional budgeting by Wetherbe (1976).

While this would appear unremarkable as a rational approach to budget setting – in marketing as elsewhere – in practice ZBB has been associated with problems in its application: managers feel threatened, more information is demanded, the process becomes excessively time-consuming, people become demoralised, and one conclusion is that:

Games are played – pet projects are funded anyway, important projects are ranked low, so that those ranked higher will be funded.   (Joiner and Chapman, 1981)

It is also suggested that it is only in very limited circumstances that participation in the budgetary process can be effective (Brownell, 1980).

Indeed, at the extreme it has been suggested that the rationality of programme budgeting as a contribution to more effective management is, in reality, illusory.   It has been suggested that:

> The incremental, fragmented, non-programmatic, and sequential procedures of the present budgetary process aid in securing agreement and reducing the burden of calculation.   It is much easier to agree on an addition or reduction of a few thousand or a million than to agree on whether a program is good in the abstract ... agreement comes much more readily when the items in dispute can be treated as differences in dollars instead of basic differences in policy.   (Wildavsky, 1964)

This last analyst's thesis suggests that with programme approaches to budgeting, the policy implications of programmes cannot be avoided – indeed this is the whole point – so in effect conflict is heightened and 'the appropriate response is to be for or against rather than bargaining for a little more or a little less' (Wildavsky, 1964).

It would seem therefore that corporate, 'rational' models of budgeting processes, involve us inevitably in the additional complexity of how managers behave in organisations and the implications of this behaviour – a central point to which we return in Chapter 4.

Turning to the marketing area, various reflections of these models are found.

'Task' Approaches to Marketing Budgeting.   In the advertising and promotion field a great deal of mention is made of the 'objective and task' approach to budget-setting (e.g. Barnes et al, 1982;   King, 1984), though similar approaches have been proposed elsewhere, for instance, for market research budgeting (Batham, 1980) and sales force budgeting (Dalrymple and Thorelli, 1984).   The essence of this approach is that objectives are defined, the tasks thus identified as necessary to achieve those goals are costed, and the sum of those costs is the budget for the product or market, and in this way the total marketing budget accumulates by compiling the budgets for individual products and markets (e.g. Ule, 1957).

In general terms this approach to advertising budgeting may be summarised as defining a role in which the manager: (a) defines the role advertising is expected to perform in the marketing plan and what its specific objectives are;   (b) states how he believes these objectives can be met and what must be performed to put this into practice; and (c) estimates the costs of performing these tasks (Kennedy and Corkindale, 1976). In advertising this involves balancing media exposures and audience sizes through conversion rates, in personal selling comparing sales calls to customer numbers, and so on.

Explicitly central to such models is the statement of marketing goals, and in terms of establishing such objectives, managers are offered various models of market change, to provide a framework for operational goals, given the intractable difficulties in linking marketing inputs to sales and profits (a point to which we return shortly).

Perhaps the best known of such models are the Colley (1961) DAGMAR model (Defining Advertising Goals for Measured Advertising Results), which suggests that market forces of all kinds move individuals through various states – unawareness, awareness, comprehension, conviction, and actions – in the face of countervailing forces, such as competition, memory lapse, sales resistance, market attrition, and so on. The rationale of this model is that objectives and control measurements may be set in terms of quantitative changes within and between states. Similar approaches have been proposed by Strong (1925) – AIDA or Attention, Interest, Desire and Action, by Lavidge and Steiner (1961) – the 'hierarchy of effects' of awareness, knowledge, liking, preference, conviction, and purchase, by Rogers (1962) – in modelling the diffusion of innovation in terms of awareness, interest, evaluation, trial and adoption and by Kotler (1984) – in modelling communications as involving exposure, reception, cognitive response, attitude, intention and behaviour.

However, while providing at least the appearance of rationality and logic in budget setting, there are various flaws in the 'objective and task' approach to budgeting.

First, there is an implicit assumption of 'bottom-up' budgeting, rather than 'top-down', where a budget ceiling is imposed by senior management, which assumption may be compatible with concepts of participative management, but is far less so with an ethos of centralised management control.

Second, although frameworks exist for considering marketing objectives in quantitative terms, as discussed above, it is clear that practical difficulties exist in setting objectives without prior understanding of how the advertising/marketing process works (Corkindale and Kennedy, 1976) – an understanding which may prove elusive in the field. In its simplest form the approach also lacks any mechanism for placing priorities on objectives, or for comparing the cost of achieving a given objective with profit requirements.

Third, and perhaps most fundamental, is that the model implicitly assumes a knowledge of the sales response function - i.e. what specific tasks (and what amount of each activity) are necessary to achieve the sales volume objectives selected (e.g. Hanmer-Lloyd and Kennedy, 1981; Wills and Kennedy, 1982), and it has been noted that:

> The practical difficulties of isolating advertising's impact on sales, plus recognition that advertising's function is to communicate, have motivated adoption of the task method and accompanying measures of intermediate response ... The great stumbling block in using this approach as a planning tool, however, is that it requires knowledge about how levels of expenditures and various communication response measures are related, and how the latter are linked to the purchase behavior that is relevant to the attainment of marketing goals. (Lilien, et al, 1976)

In short, it is suggested that task models rely for their validity on a market stability and availablility of information which may be infrequently found, and 'In reality, many companies have been forced back from any attempt at task-related budgeting' (Wills and Kennedy, 1982).

Output Budgeting in Marketing. Related to the task approach to budgeting, though adopting a wider organisational perspective, are output budgeting methods reflecting the ZBB model discussed earlier (Wills et al, 1972; 1974).

The prescription here is a framework for planning and budgeting around a matrix of corporate missions and functional resources, of the type suggested in Figure 2.2. The thesis is that the 'true' objectives are corporate missions (expressed in terms of market segments and need satisfaction), where budgeting requires the determination of the necessary level of input from each area to achieve mission goals, so that:

> functions are not allocated a budget which is historically or arbitrarily defined and then exhorted to perform as effectively as they can within that budget. Rather the functional budget is the result of a careful statement of mission goals and an analysis of the requirements placed on functions in order that such goals might be fulfilled. (Wills et al, 1974)

While broader than the 'objective and task' approaches, this methodology would seem likely to suffer from the same flaws. Similarly, as a reflection of the ZBB model, the output budgeting method would seem likely to share the shortcomings of that model.

Figure 2.2: Output Budgeting in Marketing

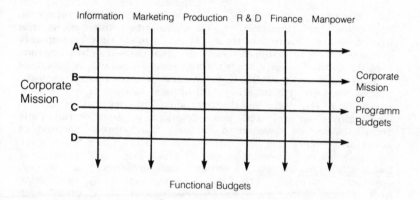

Functional Resources

Source: Adapted by the Author from Wills et al, (1974)

Judgemental Approaches to Marketing Budgeting

Finally, a variety of approaches to budget-setting rely either (a) on the application of heuristics or 'rules of thumb', or (b) qualitative, sequential appraisal of budget needs, normally derived from 'expert opinion'.

Heuristics. Commonly the literature of marketing has identified the 'rules of thumb' which may be used to establish budgets – such as, a given percentage of sales, the criteria of 'affordability', competitive parity, and so on. In view of their frequency in the descriptive literature – i.e. writings on what managers appear or claim to do – the characteristics of these approaches are summarised in Chapter 3, where it will be argued that such guidelines may be more closely related to control of budgets (against standards defined by top management) or the justification of budgets (against total performance) so that they may define parameters, rather than actually providing criteria for budget size determination in the first place.

For the same reason, the 'pooled wisdom' thesis is also examined at that point - i.e. the argument associated mainly with the PIMS and ADVISOR studies (pp. 80 - 86) that a rigorous analysis of industry practice will reveal the policies 'best' adopted, and the scope for what amounts to a form of imitation, although the interaction between firms makes imitation slightly more complex that it might at first seem.

For the present it is enough to note that such heuristics or decision rules dominate the managerial literature, in spite of their many logical flaws, arguably because of their apparent ease of application. Indeed, one recent writer, in contrasting the similar degree of reluctance of both British and American management to make use of marketing budgeting techniques, other than the most easily applied, concluded that much theoretical effort in developing sophisticated methodologies is misdirected, and should rather be devoted to refining the 'popular' techniques (Gilligan, 1977).

Sequential Appraisal. Other manifestations of 'expert opinion' represent attempts at systematising marketing budgeting on the basis of observation of 'best' practice in similar situations.

For instance, Broadbent (1970), in discussing advertising appropriations, proposed that the answers to four questions should determine the budget: (a) what can the product 'afford'; (b) what is the advertising task; (c) what are other competitors spending; and (d) what have we learned from previous years?

In a similar mould, the literature offers a 'business approach' to determining the budget for public relations activities consisting of: (a) identification of needs and objectives; (b) development of strategies and tactics; (c) identification of necessary activities; (d) establishing a timetable; (e) estimating the extent of the resources needed for each activity; and (f) estimating the cost and availablility of those resources (Tucker, 1981).

While such approaches are superficially appealing they tend to leave unanswered the same basic questions as the 'rational' corporate models discussed earlier.

CONCLUSIONS

This brief survey suggested that the normative literature of marketing budgeting allows distinctions to be made between (a) quantitative analysis including: economic analysis which applies the principle of marginality, but moves increasingly towards econometric measurement of marketing inputs and their effectiveness, to determine the expenditure level required to optimise one function or another; and the application of management science models and marketing experimentation methods to optimise expenditure, based on the measurement and modelling of effectiveness; and (b) qualitative models, including: rational, corporate approaches, such as the 'objective and task' methodology and its variants, programme and zero-base output budgeting; and judgemental approaches, relying on the prescription of norms like 'percentage of sales', and so on, as well as more subjective, sequential appraisal.

There are, in fact, many variants both on technique and in application to particular areas of marketing, which are not discussed here (see Piercy, forthcoming 1987).

The purpose of this survey was to uncover the general nature of the prescriptive theory, and to allow some commentary on the relationship between these norms and what is known of managerial practice. This contrast emerges most clearly at the end of the next chapter, but already certain limitations in the usefulness of the normative theory have become apparent.

Initially, in examining the criteria and goals implicit in the models reviewed here, it was noted that both the existence of relatively simple, often single, goals was assumed, as well as their nature - cost minimisation, sales or profit maximisation, and so on. There is also an implied assumption of 'rationality' - at least in the sense that goals will involve the optimisation of some legitimate function - and more generally in the sense of the corporate entity being goal-seeking and rational in the economic sense.

In fact, it is possible to take exception to the normative literature on two broad grounds: firstly, those underlying assumptions about managerial behaviour and organisational decision making, which are implicit in the models discussed; and secondly, the technical limitations of the models in coping with the complexity of marketing and market variables.

Organisational Objections

The point will be made shortly that the assumptions in the normative theory regarding goal-seeking and rational behaviour represent a somewhat limited view of managerial behaviour, since any attempt at analysing that behaviour would seem to require the incorporation of other concepts of organisational decision making, and the recognition of the existence of 'non-rational' behaviour. In essence the normative theory of marketing budgeting imports the assumptions of economics and management science, rather than

47

those of a behavioural theory of the firm (Anderson, 1982), a contrast reviewed in more detail shortly (pp. *114-118*).

In fact, the prescriptive attacks on marketing budgeting share one characteristic above all other similarities – the pursuit of economic rationality. This point is considered by one analyst in the following terms:

> everyone knows how decisions are made – by using rational criteria such as maximizing profit, or effectiveness or efficiency, or, in a more elaborate fashion, by maximizing subjective expected utility. (Pfeffer, 1977)

Such a view, it is argued, is widely accepted – and is implicit in many areas of prescriptive management theory – because 'rational choice is a valued social ideal' and because 'rationality is so desirable according to social values, the possibility of nonrational decision making is resisted' (Pfeffer, 1977), but in fact may be invalid and unreliable both descriptively and prescriptively on the grounds that:

> The problem is not that organizations do not seek to use rational bureaucratic criteria, but that it is impossible to do so because of dissensus concerning preferences, criteria, and definitions on what organizations should be doing. Unless such goals and criteria are shared among all participants in the organization, the use of power and influence is inevitable in organizational decision making. (Pfeffer, 1977)

Support for this assertion comes from the fragmented but growing literature recognising the role of power and social influence in determining decision outcomes in organisations. For example, Stewart (1979) pointed to instances where management arguments are couched in rational terms, but where the weighting and choice of what to put forward are politically determined by managers, and there have been a variety of examples of political influences in different management decision areas: in management information systems design and development (Keen, 1979; Markus, 1980); in the operation of matrix structures and product management (Corey and Star, 1972; Cunningham and Clarke, 1975); in relationships in the channel of distribution (Guirdham, 1979; Sibley and Michie, 1981); in organizational design (Tushman, 1975; Cobb and Margulies, 1981; Child, 1984; Piercy, 1985); and in financial management (Schiff and Lewin, 1970, Bower, 1970).

Similarly, Mintzberg <u>et al</u> (1976) analysed corporate strategy decisions in terms which revealed that multiple influences - many of which were judged to be 'political' in nature - had a variety of effects on the decision process: slowing it down, stopping it, sidetracking it, or recycling it back to an earlier phase, in a manner found to be protracted, bewildering and circuitous.

Indeed, one widely-cited view of organisational decision making is of a 'strategy of disjointed incrementalism' (Braybrooke and Lindblom, 1963), where decision makers redefine problems and adjust ends to the means available, of which it has been noted:

> of course, we know why decision making must be a disjointed process - it is always susceptible to intrusions from politically motivated persons. (Hickson et al, 1981)

It is in this way that one may take some exception to the rationality assumption and simplification in the prescriptive literature of marketing decision making generally and marketing budgeting in particular. It may be that the response from the advocate of rational budgeting methods is that if decision making is truly surrounded by these sources of nonrational behaviour, then steps should be taken to prevent this happening. While this may be a reasonable value-judgement, it has to be accepted too that such steps may be ineffective, and simply force 'nonrational' managerial behaviour to become unobtrusive (Pfeffer, 1981). Equally the value-judgement may be ideologically attractive but ill-founded in reality - it has yet to be shown that rational models of decision making are associated with superior decision outcomes to other modes of choices.

For example, analysis of the Polaris programme in the USA found that rational decision support techniques like PERT and CPA were no more than 'window dressing':

> Though the program innovativeness in management methods was, as I have tried to show, as effective technically as rain-dancing, it was, nevertheless, quite effective politically. The Special Projects Office quickly learned that a reputation for managerial efficiency made it difficult for anyone to challenge the ... development plan. (Sapolsky, 1972)

Similarly, Child (1974) suggested that the relationship between informal, overlapping channels of communication, and success, is clearer than that between sophisticated, formal management information systems and success, and others have postulated the existence of elements of ritual and myth in the use of techniques like ZBB and MIS (Jablonsky and Dirsmith, 1978; Jonsson and Lundin, 1977).

It was suggested at the outset that while the

assumptions of the normative literature may enjoy some validity, they represent only a single dimension of resource allocation, on the grounds that at one level budgets serve many diverse purposes, but also because at another level budgets have both a symbolic meaning and a substantive impact in organisations going beyond the simple accounting statement of resources allocated.

It is this perspective of analysis which is pursued in what follows here - the development of an organisational view of marketing budgeting, leading to the construction of a political model of that process in Part II; the introduction of empirical data in Part III, and a synthesis and interpretation in Part IV.

Technical Objections

Rather more simply dealt with is the existence of technical limitations in the methods, techniques and models which are provided by the normative literature, which provide the context for the organisational objections already discussed.

Since the concern here is not with methodology, one need do no more than point to such shortcomings as have emerged in the review above, with little further comment.

Economic analysis and management science models rely on: the availability of various data, and simplifying assumptions of several kinds to allow quantification and computation. Rational corporate models and judgemental approaches similarly assume the availability of data - notably regarding the sales response function - which would appear frequently invalid.

Without pursuing these points in detail, the working hypothesis is that the practical impact of normative models is limited - if that impact is conceived as the use of such methods by organisations to determine budgets. It may be that the theorist's contribution should be to continue to seek ways of overcoming the technical deficiencies of the models available, but the approach in this present study is to seek to provide an alternative perspective which is grounded in the organisational behaviour surrounding marketing resource allocation decisions.

However, before developing that case, we should examine the justification for the working hypothesis above to be found in the literature which describes marketing budgeting - a task carried out in the next chapter.

REFERENCES

Aaker, D.A. and Carman, J.M. (1982) 'Are You Overadvertising?', Journal of Advertising Research, 22 (4), 57-70

Anderholm, F., Gaertner, J. and Milani, K. (1981) 'The Utilization of PERT in the Preparation of Marketing Budgets', Managerial Planning, 30 (1), 18-23

Anderson, P.F (1982) 'Marketing, Strategic Planning and the Theory of the Firm', Journal of Marketing, 46, Spring, 15-26

Barnes, J.D., Moscore, B.J. and Rassouli, J. (1982) 'An Objective and Task Media Selection Decision Model and Advertising Cost Formulae to Determine International Advertising Budgets', Journal of Advertising, 11 (4), 68-75

Barrett, M.E., and Fraser, L.B. (1977) 'Conflicting Roles in Budgeting for Operations', Harvard Business Review, May/June, 137-46

Bass, F.M. et al (1961) Mathematical Models of Methods in Marketing, Irwin, Homewood, Ill.

Basu, A.K. and Batia, R. (1984) ADSPLIT: An Advertising Budget Allocation Model, Faculty Working Paper, University of Illinois at Urbana-Champaign

Batham, W.G. (1980) 'Planning Market Research Objectives and Strategies', ADMAP, October, 516-21

Bleil, G.B. (1983) 'Capital Budgeting in Marketing', Bank Marketing, January, 9-11

Bower, J. (1970) Managing the Resource Allocation Process, Harvard University, Boston, Mass.

Braybrooke, D. and Lindblom, C.E. (1963) A Strategy of Decision, Free Press, New York

Broadbent, S. (1970) Spending Advertising Money, Business Books, London

Brownell, P. (1980) Participation in the Budgeting Process: When It Works and When It Doesn't, Working Paper 172-80, Massachusetts Insitute of Technology, Boston, Mass.

Bultez, A. and Naert, P. (1984) Control of Advertising Expenditures: Based on Aggregate Models of Carryover Effects, Working Paper, European Institute for Advanced Studies in Management, Brussells

Carlson, D.C. and McDevitt, P. (1985) 'Budgeting Promotional Expenditures: Theory and Practice', Managerial Finance, 11 (1), 1-4

Child, J. (1974) 'Management and Organisational Factors Associated with Company Success', Journal of Management Studies, 11 (3), 175-89

Child, J. (1984) Organization: A Guide to Problems and Practice, 2nd ed., Harper and Row, London

Cobb, A.T. and Margulies, N. (1981) 'Organization Development: A Political Perspective', Academy of Management Review, 6 (1), 49-59

Colley, R.H. (1961) Defining Advertising Goals for Measured Advertising Results, Association of National Advertisers, New York

Corkindale, D. (1983) 'A Manager's Guide to Measuring the Effects of Advertising', Marketing Intelligence and Planning, 1 (2), 3-30

Corkindale, D.R. (1984) 'Measuring the Sales Effectiveness of Advertising', Journal of the Market Research Society, 26 (1), 29-49

Corkindale, D.C. and Kennedy, S.H. (1976) Measuring the Effects of Advertising, Saxon House, Farnborough

Corlett, T. (1978) 'Anyone for Econometrics?', ADMAP, August, 465-70

Corey, E.R. and Star, S. (1972) Organizational Strategy: A Marketing Approach, Harvard University Press, Boston, Mass.

Cowling, K. (1972) 'Optimality in Firms' Advertising Policies: An Empirical Analysis' in K. Cowling (ed.) Market Structure and Corporate Behaviour, Gray-Mills, London

Cunningham, M.T. and Clarke, C.J. (1975) 'The Product Management Function in Marketing', European Journal of Marketing, 9 (2), 129-49

Dorfman, R. and Steiner, P.O. (1954) 'Optimal Advertising and Optimal Quality', American Economic Review, 4 (5), 826-36

Dalrymple, D.J. and Thorelli, H.B. (1984) 'Sales Force Budgeting', Business Horizons, 27 (4), 31-6

Doyle, P. and Corstjens, M. (1982) 'Budget Determination for Highly Advertised Brands', Journal of Advertising, 1 (1), 39-48

Farris, P.W. and Buzzell, R.D. (1979) 'Why Advertising and Promotional Costs Vary: Some Cross-Sectional Analyses', Journal of Marketing, 43, Fall, 112-22

Farris, P. and Albion, M.S. (1981) 'Determinants of the Advertising-to-Sales Ratio', Journal of Advertising Research, 21 (1), 19-28

Gijsbrechts, E. and Naert, P. (1984) 'Towards Hierarchical Linking of Marketing Resource Allocation to Market Areas and Product Groups', International Journal of Advertising, 1, 97-116

Gilligan, C. (1977) 'How British Advertisers Set Budgets', Journal of Advertising Research, 17 (1), 47-9

Gilligan, C. and Crowther, G. (1976) Advertising Management, Philip Allan, Oxford

Gillingham, D.W. (1985) 'Marketing Expenditures: Investments or Expenses', Managerial Finance, 11 (1), 16-22

Guirdham, M. (1979) 'Boundary-Spanning and Inter-Organizational Relations: Theory and Marketing Implications', Proceedings: Marketing Education Group Conference

Hanmer-Lloyd, S. and Kennedy, S. (1981) Setting and Allocating the Marketing Communications Budget: A Review of Current Practice, MIRC Report 25, Cranfield School of Management Marketing Communications Research Centre, Cranfield, Beds.

Hickson, D.J., Astley, W.G., Butler, R.J. and Wilson, D.C. (1981) 'Organization as Power', in L.L. Cummings and B.M. Staw (eds.) Research in Organizational Behavior, Jai, Greenwich, Connecticut

Hurwood, D.L. and Brown, J.K. (1970) Some Guidelines for Advertising Budgeting, Conference Board, New York

Jablonsky, S. and Dirsmith, M. (1978) 'The Pattern of PBB Rejection: Something About Organizations, Something About PBB', Accounting, Organizations and Society, 3 (1), 13-32

Joiner, C. and Chapman, J.B. (1981) 'Budgeting Strategy: A Meaningful Mean', SAM Advanced Management Journal, 46 (3), 4-11

Jonsson, S.$^{\Delta}$. and Lundin, R. (1977) 'Myths and Wishful Thinking as Management Tools', in P.C. Nystrom and W. Starbuck (eds.) Prescriptive Models of Organization, North Holland, Amsterdam

Keen, P.F.W. (1979) Information Systems and Organizational Change, Working Paper 1087-79, Massachusetts Institute of Technology, Boston, Mass.

Kennedy, S.H. and Corkindale, D.R. (1976) Managing the Advertising Process, Saxon House/Lexington, Farnborough

King, S. (1984) 'Setting Advertising Budgets for Lasting Effects', ADMAP, July/August, 335-339

Koltun, A.B. (1965) 'The Profit Approach to Budgeting', Management Services, September/October, 47-52

Kotler, P. (1971) Marketing Decision Making: A Model Building Approach, Holt Rinehart and Winston, New York

Kotler, P. (1984) Marketing Management: Analysis Planning and Control, 5th ed., Prentice-Hall International, London

Kotler, P. and Lilien, G.L. (1984) Marketing Decision Making: A Model Building Approach, 2nd ed., Holt Rinehart and Winston, New York

Lancaster, K.M. and Stern, J.A. (1983) 'Computer-Based Advertising Practices of Leading U.S. Consumer Advertisers', Journal of Advertising, 12 (4), 4-9

Lavidge, R.J. and Steiner, G.A. (1961) 'A Model for Predictive Measurements of Advertising Effectiveness', Journal of Marketing, 25 (4), 59-62

Lilien, G.L., Silk, A.V., Choffray, J-M. and Rao, M. (1976) 'Industrial Advertising Effects and Budgeting Practices', Journal of Marketing, 40 (1), 16-24

Lin, W.T. (1979) 'Corporate Planning and Budgeting: An Integrated Approach', Managerial Planning, 27 (3), 29-33

Little, J.D.C. (1966) 'A Model of Adaptive Control of Promotional Spending', Operations Research, November, 25-32

Markus, M.L. (1980), Power, Politics and MIS Implementation, Working Paper 1155-80, Massachusetts Institute of Technology, Boston, Mass.

McCosh, A.M., and Maluste, R.D. (1981) 'Simulating the Forces Impinging upon the Research Budgets and Organisation of a Major Firm', R & D Management, 11 (1), 9-18

Montgomery, D.B. and Urban, G.L. (1969) Management Science in Marketing, Prentice-Hall, Englewood Cliffs, N.J.

Mintzberg, H., Raisinghani, D. and Theoret, A. (1976) 'The Structure of "Unstructured" Decision Processes', Administrative Science Quarterly, 21 (2), 246-75

Palda, K.S. (1969) Economic Analysis for Marketing Decisions, Prentice-Hall, Englewood Cliffs, N.J.

Pfeffer, J. (1977) 'Power and Resource Allocation in Organizations', in B.M. Staw and G.R. Salancik (eds.) New Directions in Organizational Behavior, St Clair, Chicago

Pfeffer, J. (1981) Power in Organizations, Pitman, Marshfield, Mass.

Pfeffer, J. and Salancik, G. (1974) 'Organizational Decision Making as a Political Process', Administrative Science Quarterly, 19, 135-51

Piercy, N. (1985) Marketing Organisation: An Analysis of Information Processing, Power and Politics, Allen and Unwin, London

Piercy, N. (1987) Budgeting for Marketing - Principles and Practices, Allen and Unwin, London

Piercy, N. and Evans, M. (1983) Managing Marketing Information, Croom Helm, Beckenham

Piercy, N. and Thomas, M. (1984) 'Corporate Planning: Budgeting and Integration', Journal of General Management, 10, (2), 51-66

Pondy, L.R. (1970) 'Toward A Theory of Internal Resource-Allocation' in M.N. Zald (ed.) Power in Organizations, Vanderbilt University Press, Nashville, Tenn.

Rayburn, L.G. (1981) 'Marketing Costs - Accountants to the Rescue', Management Accounting, 62 (7), 32-41

Rogers, E.M. (1962) Diffusion of Innovations, Free Press, New York

Sapolsky, H.M. (1972) The Polaris System Development, Harvard University Press, Cambridge, Mass.

Schiff, M. and Lewin, A.Y. (1970) 'The Impact of People on Budgets', Accounting Review, 45 (2), 259-68

Schmalensee, R. (1962) The Economics of Advertising, North Holland, Amsterdam

Sibley, S.D. and Michie, D.A. (1981) 'Distribution Performance and Power Sources', Industrial Marketing Management, 10, 59-65

Stewart, R. (1979) The Reality of Organizations, Pan, London

Strong, E.K. (1925) The Psychology of Selling, McGraw-Hill, New York

Sturgess, B.T. and Wilson, N. (1983) 'Forecasting Advertising Expenditure', International Journal of Advertising, 2, 301-16

Sunoo, D.H. and Lin, L.Y.S. (1979) 'A Search for the Optimal Advertising Spending Level', Journal of Advertising, 8 (3), 25-9

Telser, L.G. (1961) 'How Much Does It Pay Whom to Advertise?', American Economic Review, 51 (2), 194-205

Tucker, J. (1981) 'Budgeting and Cost Control', Public Relations Journal, March, 14-17

Turnbull, P.W. (1974) 'The Allocation of Resources to Marketing Communications in Industrial Markets', Industrial Marketing Management, 3, 297-310

Tushman, M.L. (1975) 'A Political Approach to Organizations: A Review and Rationale', Academy of Management Review, 2 (2), 206-16

Ule, G.M. (1957) 'A Media Plan for "Sputnik" Cigarettes', in How to Plan Media Strategy, American Association of Advertising Agencies, New York

Weinberg, R.S. (1956) 'Multiple Factor Break Even Analysis: The Application of O.R. Techniques to a Basic Problem of Management Planning and Control', Operations Research, 4, 152-86

Weinberg, R.S. (1960) An Analytical Approach to Advertising Expenditure Strategy, Association of National Advertisers, New York

Wetherbe, J.C. (1976) A General Purpose Strategic Planning Methodology for the Computing Effort in Higher Education, Unpublished Ph.D Dissertation, Texas University

Wildavsky, A. (1964) The Politics of the Budgetary Process, Little Brown, Boston

Wills, G., Christopher, M. and Walters, D. (1972) Output Budgeting in Marketing, MCB, Bradford

Wills, G., Christopher M. and Walters, D. (1974) 'Output Budgeting in Marketing', in G. Wills (ed.) Strategic Issues in Marketing, International Textbook, London

Wills, G. and Kennedy, S. (1982) 'How to Budget Marketing', Management Today, February, 58-61

Zif, J., Young, R.F. and Fenwick, I. (1984) 'A Transnational Study of Advertising-to-Sales Ratios', Journal of Advertising Research, 24 (3), 58-62

3

Descriptive Studies of Budgeting Practice

It was seen earlier that, for our present purposes of analysis, the literature of marketing budgeting falls into two broad categories: the <u>prescriptive</u> or normative, emphasising goal-seeking rationality and the corresponding techniques available to pursue this rationality; and the <u>descriptive</u>, which purports to assess actual managerial practice. It was also noted, however, that these categories are inevitably linked - for example in the sense that the prescriptive assumes knowledge of actual practice, while the descriptive frequently presumes a conceptual framework which is ultimately derived from the normative theory. Indeed, the relationship is frequently closer since the description of managerial practice has been used to provide the platform both for prescribing what organisations should <u>do</u> (taking advantage of the 'pooled wisdom' or experience learned by others) or what they should <u>not do</u> (because behaviour is judged to be non-rational and outcomes sub-optimal).

The procedure in this chapter is to consider the general attacks made on 'traditional' methods of budgeting, and then to expand on what is known descriptively of that traditional budgeting in the marketing context. This general discussion will be seen to imply a need to introduce a further distinction: that between <u>decision rules</u> or guidelines of various kinds in budget determination, and the <u>process</u> of budgeting, into which the decision rules should be fitted (in one sense or another, since the criteria may be less rules than tools of justification and legitimation).

THE CRITICISM OF 'TRADITIONAL' BUDGETING METHODS

The general literature has identified 'traditional' approaches to budgeting in organisations as incremental and highly imperfect in a number of respects. For instance, it has been noted that:

> Much current day budgeting is incremental in nature and

involves adding a given percentage increase to the preceding year's budget, to arrive at a new budget ... The approach is at best cosmetic and does little more than postpone the critical reallocation decisions. (Joiner and Chapman, 1981)

It was seen in Chapter 2 that many attacks have been mounted on this incrementalism and fragmentation, in terms of ZBB and programme budgeting and management science optimisation models of various types - these attacks being reflected in turn in the literature of marketing.

In fact, it was noted earlier that the techniques proposed to improve budgetary processes are themselves far from perfect, and one recent analyst suggested that:

I postulate that, for the most part, budgetary models have not described the rules being used by decision makers, but rather the structure of the problem they are solving. (Bromiley, 1981)

We return, shortly, to Bromiley's commentary on the barriers to budgetary reform.

First, however, it should be noted that the pressure for reform in marketing budgeting has tended to emphasise technique or method, rather than process and system in decision making. In fact, Bromiley (1981) suggests that in general budgeting research has followed one of two paradigms: (a) the routine, rule-applying, or 'aid to computation' approach; and (b) the bargaining, 'politicking' or game-playing approach. While it is not suggested that the latter approach is likely to provide a complete explanation of marketing budgeting, the omission of any significant attention to the analysis of behavioural aspects of marketing budgeting would seem a notable factor limiting understanding and, by implication, management control of that process.

For this reason, this present chapter examines first the processual aspects of marketing budgeting - as far as this is possible in the current state of knowledge - both in the sense of the formal systems adopted and their behavioural implications, and then secondly, the decision rules commonly described in the marketing literature and recent research into how they operate in practice.

THE TASK ENVIRONMENT FOR BUDGETING

Returning to the analysis of budgetary decision making provided by Bromiley (1981), he suggested that the analysis of budgeting behaviour should proceed from the distinction between task environment, information processing, and problem space.

In this model, the task environment (i.e. the

organisation and the budgetary process) structures the problem faced by the budgetary decision maker in the following ways: (a) by defining the major difficulty faced (e.g. the allocation compared to total funds available); (b) by defining what are acceptable solutions to the problem; (c) by defining the starting point for search, since 'Almost all decision sessions in the budget process start off with at least one reference point (last year's budget, the initial request, the department request, the last working figures developed)' (Bromiley, 1981), with the implication that 'the starting point will influence the outcome either because budgeters are looking for one solution (not enumerating all feasible solutions before choosing one) or because they make less than optimal adjustments based on the inclusion of new information': (d) by defining what information is available, which is important since, 'Budgeters have a large store of background information. The budget process defines what information they will have ready at hand and relevant to the decisions being made – that which is demanded in the budget requests. Information the budgeters do not have cannot influence their decisions' (Bromiley, 1981); (e) by providing certain heuristics and priorities to guide search, for example the chief executive's directive to make a certain allocation; and (f) by constraining the decision process, for example with deadlines. In this way it is argued that the first two facets of the task environment define the feasible region within which decision outcomes must lie, while the other four facets influence the problem solving which takes place within that feasible region.

Bromiley's prime concern was with budgetary reform in the public sector, but his conclusion is of some appositeness for our present purposes here. The major implication of Bromiley's analysis is that if budgetary innovation – through technique, process revision, or more sophisticated information systems – amounts to no more than changing the search made within a given task environment, then it will be substantially circumscribed in the effect it can have: 'If the basic task environment remains the same, adding new information can at best only alter the choice within that task environment' (Bromiley, 1981).

For present purposes this view is of some interest for a number of reasons. It suggests firstly, that the underlying limitation of the prescriptive literature may be that it does not even attempt to operate on the task environment for marketing budgeting, so whether our goal is to improve the management of marketing budgeting, or more conservatively simply to understand better what happens, then one area of focus should be on the task environment, rather than on budgeting techniques. Secondly, Bromiley's view makes explicit the role of information – as defined in various ways by the task environment – in influencing budget decisions, which becomes increasingly significant as our present analysis proceeds. **Thirdly,** this model suggests that our approach should be to study processual aspects of budgeting – administrative systems, organisational structure, and information systems – to provide the context into which can be placed the heuristics and other techniques popular in the literature. We are provided, thus, both with a platform upon which to build an analysis of the descriptive theory of marketing budgeting, but also with an orientation which leads to modelling of the power and politics of marketing budgeting, since it will be argued there that organisational structure and information are both related dimensions of organisational power and politics.

With this justification, we turn to examine the descriptive evidence relating to processes of marketing budgeting, and then turn to the decision rules uncovered empirically.

BUDGETING PROCESSES

A General Model of Budgetary Behaviour

In the general literature perhaps the classic, qualititative study is Wildavsky's <u>The Politics of the Budgetary Process</u> (1964; 1979), which provides a useful – indeed, central – frame of reference for what follows here. The Wildavsky work, through detailed observation of public sector budgeting in the US, established a number of descriptive parameters which provide a framework for the discussion below.

First, Wildavsky emphasised that budgets – which in his sociological analysis were the outcome of political struggles – establish <u>precedent</u>:

> Once enacted, a budget becomes a precedent: the fact that something has been done will vastly increase the chances that it will be done again. Since only substantial departures from the previous year's budget are given intense scrutiny, an item that remains unchanged will probably be carried along the following year as a matter of course. (Wildavsky, 1964)

Clearly the ZBB and programme budgeting techniques, discussed earlier, are explicitly designed to counteract the effect of precedent, though as noted they may have mixed effects (pp. *41-42*).

Second, Wildavsky considered the <u>calculations</u> used by decision makers in budgeting and the resulting tendency to <u>incrementalism</u>. His starting point was the hypothesis that the complexity of projects is such that decision makers have only a limited understanding of them. Since different methods of calculating budgets lead to different budget sizes, decision makers face considerable difficulty. These difficulties lead to the adoption of a variety of coping mechanisms or aids, which, though imperfect, allow decisions to be made. The effect of these decision aids is that budgeting becomes: (a) experiential - i.e. rough guesses are made, and subsequently modified; (b) simplified - for example, 'calculations may be simplified by lowering one's sights'; and (c) incremental - 'The largest determining factor of the size and content of the year's budget is last year's budget. Most of the budget is the product of previous decisions' (Wildavsky, 1964).

The studies suggested that budget users have to calculate how much to ask for, as well as how much to spend of what they already have, while on the other hand decision makers have to calculate how much to give - in both cases these calculations depending in large part on predictions of the reactions of others. The conclusion reached after studying the tactics of budget calculation was that:

> Budgeting turns out to be an incremental process, proceeding from an historical base, guided by notions of fair shares, in which decisions are fragmented, made in sequence by specialized bodies, and coordinated through multiple feedback mechanisms. The role of participants and their perceptions of each others' power and desires, fit together to provide a reasonably stable set of criteria on which to base calculations. (Wildavsky, 1964)

Indeed, it is of some note that the Cyert and March work, A Behavioral Theory of the Firm (1963), which was formulated at much the same time as the original Wildavsky research, also produced a number of hypotheses relating to sub-unit budgeting and resource allocation. Cyert and March suggested that there was a tendency, as part of the 'quasi-resolution of conflict', in the coalition of interests within an organisation, for allocations to be based on arbitrary rules which maintained the position of organis-ational members, involving, for example, the use of standard industry or organisational budgeting rules, to avoid uncertainty and to gain the appearance of rationality. In this way, they hypothesised that budgeting tended to be incremental rather than comprehensive, since bargaining over historical precedents was potentially disruptive. The effect is that the historical budget may be taken as a given factor and the area of conflict limited to bargaining over incremental resources. In this way stable relationships are maintained among coalition members.

Third, Wildavsky identified the use of budgetary strategies, that is, deliberate political behaviour by participants to maintain or increase their budgets.

Continuing with the general notion of political behaviour, this suggests both the possibility of unsanctioned goals being sought and unsanctioned methods being used by budgeters – in terms, for example, of information distortion, game-playing, and bargaining outwith the legitimised framework. This aspect of budgetary behaviour is explored further in contrasting rational and organisational perspectives of marketing budgeting later in this chapter, which leads to the analysis of the power and politics of marketing budgets in Part II of the book.

The next question is the degree to which the dimensions of budgeting in this general model of precedent, calculation, incrementalism and budgetary strategies, which provides a general paradigm dating back some twenty years, may be found in the empirical studies of marketing budgeting processes.

Marketing Budgeting Behaviour

In fact, budgeting for marketing has not been studied empirically, or analysed explicitly in the terms introduced above, though there is scope here for integrating the fragments of evidence and comment which do exist.

Precedent in Marketing Budgeting. The proposition from the general literature was that the prime determinant of one year's budget was that gained in the previous year.

In the entirely 'rational' sense, the precedent of previous allocations is largely irrelevant – hence the zero-base of ZBB and programme budgeting. None the less, the descriptive study of marketing budgeting shows some recognition of the importance of precedent in providing the base from which budgets are established.

At the conceptual level, Kotler (1972) suggested that marketing budget determination, in practice, tended to ignore market potential and differences in the effectiveness of different marketing actions at different times, and to amount thus to no more than 'budgeting by precedent'. Similarly, Cravens et al offered the proposition that:

> In practice, top management's frame of reference for total expenditures is frequently what has been done in the past and the market program is often determined by increasing or decreasing the last period's resource allocation. (Cravens et al, 1980)

At the empirical level, in a rare study of its type, Briscoe (1972) studied the marketing and marketing information systems developed at the British Steel Corporation. In this study, the formal budgeting system required each department to draw up plans for expenditure on marketing variables, which were then to be consolidated and coordinated centrally by the Divisional Accountant. In practice, Briscoe found that – apparently because of the lack of market information – budget allocations for marketing variables were determined by the much simpler approach of modifying the previous year's budget, in the light of sales managers' proposals and the constraint of divisional liquidity. The effect found by Briscoe was that in times of low profitability and liquidity, the budgets for marketing variables (mainly advertising and promotion) tended to be reduced, because the executives involved could not generate the information necessary to establish the value of marketing to the Division.

Thus, it would seem that there are some grounds for accepting the proposition that marketing budgets are, at least in part, determined by precedent within the organisation.

However, the implications of the theoretical commentary and empirical work like Briscoe's are somewhat greater.

One point of interest is the suggestion that the effect of precedent is more widely significant, on the grounds that it is implicit and institutionalised in the budgeting norms and concepts of affordability (see pp. *78–80* below), which are commonly cited in the literature.

While only testable empirically, one working hypothesis is that the point of reference which defines 'affordability', or the 'acceptable' expense/sales ratio, may be determined by past experience (i.e. precedent) as well as economic factors like liquidity. It has been noted by one analyst that:

> the marketing budget is not determined on independent grounds, but rather as a residual coming out of a budget-planning process. The marketing budget is established, in effect, as the amount the company can 'afford'. (Kotler, 1972)

The implications to be pursued are: that a circularity in logic may exist – taking marketing as an overhead charged against profit, rather than an influence on sales and profit; that the budgeting process is thus worthy of greater attention; and that 'affordability' and, indeed, competitive parity, may well be related to precedent. The same analyst later commented:

> Given the uncertainty, marketing management tends to set the marketing budget on the basis of a conventional percentage to sales, recent or expected. This percentage is based on what competition may be spending or what the company thinks it can afford. (Kotler, 1976)

It seems, therefore, reasonable to suggest that the

determination of norms or conventions relating to marketing budget size depends, at least partly, on precedent. It will be argued in due course that the use of precedent in this way is, in effect, a political process, in the sense that the norms and guidelines which become institutionalised are a reflection of organisational power differences (see pp. 255-69 below).

Indeed, recent qualititative research in the UK provides some support for the contention that precedent and company norms are significant in budget determination. Wills and Kennedy (1982) reported that in their small sample of large UK firms, under modern conditions there was an increased tendency for the marketing director to negotiate for his budget with the board of directors, and that in such negotiations:

> he will know the constraints within which he is expected to work and will not be prepared to present the board with an 'excessive' budget, which he suspects will be unacceptable. This process of dialogue and negotiation leads to the perpetuation of historical behaviour: the knowledge of what the next level of management anticipates can only encourage the presentation of cases which give no surprises. (Wills and Kennedy, 1982)

On the more specialised allocation issue of dividing marketing expenditure above- and below-the-line, the same study noted that:

> some companies have their own conventions regardless of external influences. They may even have formally stated policies, such as '60% of expenditure above the line'. In discussing the budget split, few ... argue the case without incorporating norms of this kind. (Wills and Kennedy, 1982)

This work is also suggestive of Wildavsky's notion that it was the prediction of what was acceptable to others that was at the centre of successfully obtaining a budget - a point to which we return below.

It would seem, therefore, that there is some evidence that precedent is significant in marketing budget determination, and, indeed, may be implicit in certain of the decision rules which have been described (see pp. 78 - 80 below).

Further, 'budgeting by precedent' implies the incrementalism also described by Wildavsky (1964), which is considered in the next section below.

Methods of Calculation in Marketing Budgeting. Again following Wildavsky's general model, we may consider the calculation methods associated with marketing budgeting, in coping with the complexity faced by decision makers.

In fact, the marketing literature is replete with decision aids and guidelines, although it might well be suggested that there is less guidance as to their applicability to different cases or situations.

For example, the Marketing Society (1967) grouped calculation devices into 'supply methods' – involving the allocation of a fixed amount to advertising through some heuristic calculation – and 'demand methods' – which rely on the measurement or assumption of market responses and the tasks required to achieve goals, as in the 'objective and task' approach discussed earlier.

A more exhaustive taxonomy was attempted by Mitchell (1979), whose classification of common approaches to calculating advertising budgets included: (a) percentage methods – distinguishing between the expense/sales ratio as a way of determining the budget, and as a way of describing a budget actually determined in some other way; (b) 'affordable' methods – based on cash flow and financial position; (c) 'all available funds' methods – for example, for new product launches; (d) competitive parity method; (e) task and objective methods; (f) marketing programme methods; (g) adaptive methods – updating the budget from feedback; and (h) mail order methods – for that specialised channel of distribution.

Similarly, empirical workers in the USA (Lilien et al, 1976) suggested that the budgeting methods commonly used by companies fell into three categories: (a) guidelines or 'rules of thumb', like sales ratios, matching competitors, industry norms, and the like; (b) task methods, relying on the establishment of marketing objectives and communication goals to illustrate budget priorities and needs; and (c) explicit modelling and experimentation of the type discussed in Chapter 2, usually viewed as expensive and difficult to apply. These researchers concluded:

> In the light of the dearth of available empirical knowledge about market response to industrial advertising, management in the field must ordinarily depend on some blend of judgement, experience with analogous situations, and simple rules-of-thumb guidance in setting budgets. Heuristics like 'x per cent of expected sales' and the 'objective and task' method are the principal approaches to budgeting that industrial advertisers report using. (Lilien et al, 1976)

Attention turns later in this chapter to the decision rules which managers report using, but for the moment the recognised calculation methods may be contrasted with the corporate setting for decision making to produce the following propositions.

Following the Wildavsky style of analysis, it is suggested that marketing budgeting in practice tends to be: <u>experiential</u> - in the sense suggested earlier that rough guesses are made and subsequently modified; <u>incremental</u> - or largely determined by changes to the base represented by the existing budget; and <u>simplified</u> - as decision makers attempt to cope with complexity and diversity through uncertainty-avoiding mechanisms.

Experiential Budgeting in Marketing. It will be argued later (pp. *270 - 272*) that the uncertainty surrounding the effectiveness of marketing efforts is a central contingency associated with the emergence of political behaviour to influence budget size and allocation (Piercy, 1986), but for the moment we may consider what evidence there is of a lack of systematisation of marketing budgeting in practice.

It will be seen shortly that the budgeting methods described by managers are usually unsophisticated, and perhaps surprisingly there appears no clear relationship between the sophistication of budgeting methods and budget size (Gilligan, 1977; Jobber, 1980), although it is true that one study of small industrial company behaviour noted that:

> objectives were not set, and the establishment of budgets was not usual ... (few) companies had established budgets of any form related to marketing communications; all other companies allocated resources on an <u>ad hoc</u> and unplanned basis. (Turnbull, 1974)

Certainly, as will be demonstrated shortly, it is true that the literature identifies a variety of decision guidelines and rules for budgeting, although it has been noted that, even among large advertisers, in effect 'most firms are budgeting by ear' (San Augustine and Foley, 1975). Similarly, in the industrial marketing area, empirical workers have found that:

> Decisions about marketing budgets are usually made in a seat-of-the-pants fashion ... Few guidelines are available to aid product managers in determining the appropriate size and mix of their marketing efforts. (Lilien and Little, 1976)

In fact, the MIT workers on the ADVISOR studies (see pp. *80 - 85* below) found that their evidence supported the existence of economies of scale in marketing, as well as threshold effects and the interaction between advertising and selling, but concluded:

the study of the effects of industrial advertising has not yet provided guidance to industrial advertisers faced with specific expenditure decisions, and current budgeting practice reflects this lack of knowledge about response. (Lilien et al, 1976)

It would seem, thus, that to the earlier discussion of precedent as an influence on marketing budgeting, should be added the related experiential dimension (which will later be stressed as a response to unresolved uncertainty).

Simplification in Marketing Budgeting. As discussed in more detail shortly (pp. *78 - 80*), the available empirical data suggest that the budgeting of marketing expenses in practice relies on a variety of 'rules of thumb'. In the terms pursued here, such rules amount to attempts to avoid the complexity of measuring marketing effectiveness at different points on the sales-response function, in favour of simpler methods.

It was noted earlier that the determination of corporate norms or conventions, and perceptions of 'affordability' are arguably linked to precedent and the politics of the organisation.

Certainly, it is demonstrable that such methods of calculation suffer from an unavoidable circularity of logic, since marketing costs are taken as a dependent - an outcome of the budgetary process, frequently treated as an overhead - rather than as an independent variable which influences the amount and type of business done.

However, that such flawed approaches are applied would seem well-established in the empirical literature. For example, Marschner noted in his research that advertising expenses in companies were treated 'largely as a dependent variable on sales, rather than one of the independent variables affecting sales' (Marschner, 1967). Similarly, Taplin (1959) noted a tendency for advertising costs to be regarded as a deduction from profit, rather than a determinant of revenue. More recently, it has been suggested at the practical level that the management reaction in many companies to economic recession has been cost-cutting, leading to the paradox that:

if advertising has any effect in stimulating demand, it would seem sensible to strengthen it at this time. However, the conventional corporate response is to regard all marketing expense as a managed cost - that is, one that can be cut when funds are scarce. (Williamson, 1981)

Indeed, recent empirical work offers some confirmation of this form of management behaviour and its underlying assumptions: 'Today, boardrooms are setting marketing budgets by allocating the residual revenue after deducting operating costs and profit contribution' (Wills and Kennedy, 1982). Correspondingly, it was noted by the MIT empiricists that:

> The weaknesses of percent-of-sales decision rules are well-known, but the most fundamental objection is that they implicitly make advertising a consequence rather than a determinant of sales and profits and can easily give rise to dysfunctional policies. (Lilien et al, 1976)

While the logical flaw is apparently self-evident - if cutting marketing expenses does not further reduce sales, then presumably those expenses were not needed in the first place - for present purposes what is demonstrated is a tendency to use methods of simplification in budgeting for marketing.

Incrementalism in Marketing Budgeting. To some extent also implied by the notion of precedent as a determining force is the incrementalism phenomenon in budgeting - attention being given only to changes in the base and to fragments of the total - as argued for example, by Wildavsky (1964) and Cyert and March (1963).

It was noted earlier too that 'the market program is often determined by increasing or decreasing the last period's resource allocation' (Cravens et al, 1980), and this form of budget-setting was demonstrated in such studies as Briscoe (1972). Indeed, Taplin's much earlier study of advertising had highlighted one perception of the reality of incremental approaches to budgeting, in a respondent's comment that: 'The first half-million we have to spend anyway. All the fights are about the last twenty thousand' (Taplin, 1959). In this sense, the essence of traditional methods of budgeting for marketing is the 'line-item budgetary form', leading to sequential consideration of fragments of the total budget and to the analysis only of changes, not of total budgets.

Predicting Reactions. One implication of the points above is that, in the absence of sophisticated budgetary methods, the determination of the budget may be taken as a process of negotiation, and thus partly an outcome of the interaction between organisational participants, either as members of groups or as individuals. In Wildavsky's terms, success in obtaining budgetary resources is partly determined by the ability to predict what will be acceptable to others (allowing for a certain amount of change in that amount through persuasion and social influence).

As noted, Wills and Kennedy (1982) pointed to the significance in marketing budgeting of the presentation by the chief marketing executive of a budget request which he judges to be acceptable and expected. Others too have found empirically that in the process of marketing budgeting 'the interaction of the marketing director and the board is important' (Hammer-Lloyd and Kennedy, 1981).

This point is not developed further for the moment, other than in noting that if the role of bargaining, and social interaction and influence in determining the marketing budget is allowed, then this clears the way to the case to be made for analysing the marketing budget as a political outcome.

The Process of Marketing Budgeting

The last point above leads necessarily to the consideration of what is known of the budgetary process in marketing resource allocation.

A General Model. One example of the general models of marketing budgeting which have been proposed is summarised in Figure 3.1. Taking as context the difficulties of predicting the sales-response function, which relate to: (a) the indirect, nonlinear relationship between marketing actions and sales; (b) the impact of competitive and environmental factors; (c) the interaction between different elements of the marketing mix; (d) the cumulative and lagged time effects of marketing actions; and (e) consequent variations of efficiency in marketing actions, Guiltinan and Paul (1982) suggest a four stage budgeting process, which is described below.

First, a 'baseline budget' is established, such as the previous year's budget, although it is adjusted to account for such factors as: maintaining a 'percentage of sales' norm to expected sales; maintaining competitive parity; pursuing individual product objectives (e.g. based on portfolio analysis); product profitability considerations; and, judgements of productivity.

Second, based on marketing objectives, methods are chosen and costed, for example, design and media costs in advertising. **Third**, experiments and tests may be run to evaluate the proposed programme, and **fourth**, the budget (or the objectives) may be revised, on the basis of the costs anticipated, the results of tests, and the impact of other marketing programmes being operated by the company.

In fact, the Guiltinan and Paul model can claim validity only in the prescriptive sense, although it provides a starting point contrasting what is known of actual budgeting processes in marketing and the prescriptive theory.

Figure 3.1: A Normative Model of the Marketing Budgeting Process

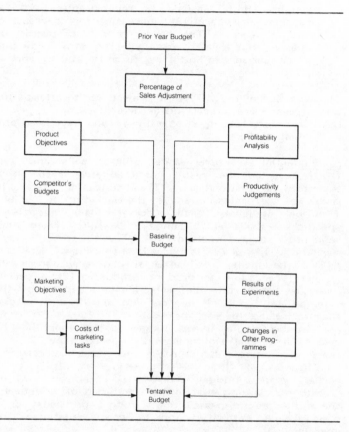

Source: Adapted by the Author from Guiltinan and Paul (1982)

The ADVISOR Project. Turning to the empirical evidence available, the MIT workers, cited earlier, in the ADVISOR study suggested that marketing budgeting (for industrial products) should be seen as a two-stage process: (a) the total marketing budget is set (where 'marketing' refers primarily to advertising and personal selling), which may be taken as a fraction of sales revenue; (b) a decision is made on what fraction of that marketing budget is to be allocated to advertising. The researchers uncovered a conceptual framework for that budgeting process:

the decision maker has a checklist of product-market factors that are relevant to the budget decision (e.g. stage in life cycle, plant capacity, and number of customers). The values for the factors are known roughly (High versus Low, for example), and each is considered separately, increasing or decreasing the budget score. The result is not a specific budget number, but a relative budget-size, e.g. a 'low budget', in comparison to industry norms. (Lilien and Little, 1976)

The objective of the ADVISOR project was to attempt to make this process more logical and accurate (see pp. *80 - 86* below). More recent, comparable results have been obtained by British workers.

A Sequential/Structural Model. First, Wills and Kennedy (1982) reported the results of qualitative research among seventeen large UK firms. They suggested that: 'In the model which operates nowadays, the marketing budget is set at a number of levels, each successive level becoming more specific' (Wills and Kennedy, 1982). Their model of sequential stages involved the following steps: (a) total marketing expenditure is agreed, with minimal detail on how it is to be spent; (b) after this general agreement, the budget is allocated to product groups; (c) a decision is made on the split between above- and below-the-line expenditure; and (d) then detailed consideration is given to the precise mix for each brand.

In their study it was suggested that there has been a recent 'structural tightening-up' in what they refer to as the 'negotiating structure', and they dismissed the significance of the task-budgeting concept, discussed earlier, where a budget accummulates from brand and product objectives, claiming that either the board of directors takes the initiative and passes down budget decisions, or (more commonly) 'a bottom-up and top-down negotiation process operates'.

Perhaps the most interesting implications of this study are those which in fact were made least explicit: (a) that in large companies the influence of the marketing department on budget size appears to be declining; (b) that organisational structure (e.g. primarily the brand manager structure) influences budget size; (c) that the starting point in putting total figures on the budget remains uncertain and obscure; and (d) that the budgeting process is prone to social influence attempts and information selectivity and distortion. Each of these points will be developed later.

MCRC Processual Models. Second, in the UK, Hanmer-Lloyd and

Kennedy (1981) reported in more detail on related qualitative research into marketing communications budgeting, carried out by the Marketing Communications Research Centre (MCRC) at Cranfield School of Management. Their general conclusions were that taking budgeting as an 'organisational process': (a) there is increasing emphasis on profitability and cost-effectiveness; (b) there is a trend to centralise corporate decisions; (c) participation in marketing budgeting decisions is broadening – 'the inputs of production management and accounting personnel appear to be playing an increasingly important role'; (d) trade marketing personnel deal directly with major retailers; and, (e) the current inflation of marketing communications costs is incurring greater scrutiny of those costs by management.

Hanmer-Lloyd and Kennedy suggested that there were three basic models of budgeting, as represented in Figure 3.2: (a) bottom-up budgeting – where the initiative lies with brand management; (b) bottom-up/top-down budgeting – with greater negotiation between senior management and marketing and product managers; and (c) top-down/bottom-up budgeting – where the initiative rests with senior management personnel and various types of committees.

In this scheme, **bottom-up budgeting**, placing initiative at the brand manager level, is taken as representative of the UK approaches of the 1960s and 1970s. While the MCRC researchers claimed that this model still operated in some companies, it was not found in their study, apparently because of the growing need for a corporate decision-making perspective, and the need for continuity in managing brands, while product managers continue to move on rapidly to new jobs.

Alternatively, **bottom-up/top-down** budgeting assumes far greater negotiation and a more limited role for the product manager. The tendency identified by the MCRC research was that of centralising decision making and involving other, non-marketing functions earlier in the process. The advantages of this model are: the greater impact of overall strategy on decisions; closer control of product manager 'optimism'; and easier allocation of funds to new products. The disadvantages are seen as: frustration at the product manager level as brands are 'undersupported' because of wider corporate goals; and a tendency for the marketing manager to stay within a known, expected level of expenditure irrespective of market opportunities or threats.

The **top-down/bottom-up** model is essentially similar to the last model, but with greater control over the budget at the top management level and a greater trend towards committee-based decisions. In this model, top management receives sales and profit forecasts and calculates a 'given' level of expenditure, with little room for negotiation especially when profits are under pressure. Thus, the

Figure 3.2: Processual Models of Marketing Budgeting

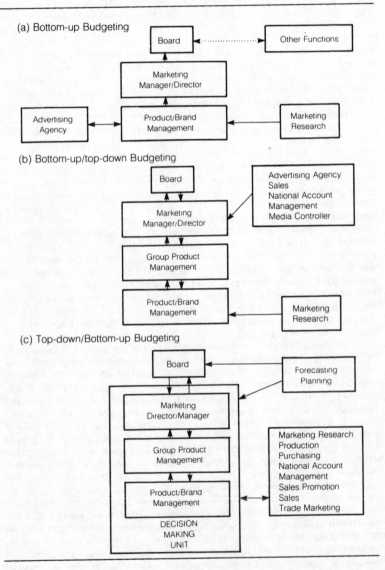

(a) Bottom-up Budgeting

(b) Bottom-up/top-down Budgeting

(c) Top-down/Bottom-up Budgeting

Source: Adapted by the Author from Hanmer-Lloyd and Kennedy (1981)

marketing spend is tied closely to sales revenue, liquidity and profit requirements – one implication being that when sales go down then the marketing spend goes down.

The researchers noted that in the top-down/bottom-up approach the tendency was for the marketing director to take action to obtain a budget and only then to decide how to use it – suggesting the exact reverse of the task-oriented budgeting model of the prescriptive literature:

> What it has meant is that budgets are seen initially as sums of money and not always in terms of what is needed to carry out certain tasks. Thus, the key step in the process becomes getting the budget numbers agreed.
> (Hanmer-Lloyd and Kennedy, 1981)

The MCRC researchers considered that this last model highlighted two of the basic trends emerging in their study: (a) the greater involvement of senior management personnel in initial planning, and (b) greater links between marketing and other functional departments in the early planning stages. The essence of this model was the role of interfunctional committees, to gain coordination and the dissemination of information, but at the potential cost of: (a) vested interests – 'the functional areas can be criticised for arguing more for their 'corner' than for the company as a whole'; (b) the dominance of production interests and profit data over marketing goals and information; and (c) the time taken to act.

In summary, the researchers suggested that their study illustrated four important trends in marketing budgeting practice at present: the increased role of senior marketing management in the construction of brand plans with a reduced role for the product/brand manager; the increased use of committees; the increased input of other functional areas into marketing plans; and structural changes which are being made to reflect these developments.

In the companies studied, the bottom-up model was the least representative of practice, and the researchers found that many companies were moving towards top-down/bottom-up, while most firms were located between bottom-up/top-down and top-down/bottom-up.

For the purposes of this present study the MCRC findings are of some note in several respects: first, it seems that the role of the marketing department in the process of determining the marketing budget may be limited in some major companies, and may be declining over time for a variety of reasons; second, it follows that influences on marketing budget size come from top management and their advisors and increasingly from non-marketing functional departments; third, in this approach, marketing budgeting is seen as a process of negotiation at a number of levels, suggesting a key role for advocacy and bargaining at each level; fourth, by implication, what is described is an internal competition for resources and for the control of resources, which may be identified with conflict; and finally, it emerged that the control and manipulation of information was central to such budget negotiations.

Implications of Budgeting Process Models. This section has demonstrated the existence of empirical evidence that marketing budgeting may be viewed as an organisational process characterised by social interaction and negotiation for resources, in a way suggestive of the conclusion that the use of decision rules and models may be more complex than is commonly suggested by the literature.

The key elements established by these models – such as sequential decision making, structural influences, departmental competition to control marketing budgets and resources, committee-based decision making, the centralisation of budget authority and involvement, and the significance of social interaction and negotiation – will be pursued in the next part of the book, specifically in the context of constructing a model of the power and politics of marketing budgeting.

However, following the general logic implied by the Wildavsky (1964) model, attention should be given to two last issues: conflict and budgetary strategies.

Conflictual Aspects of Marketing Budgeting

The existence of conflict over the size of the allocation of resources to and within marketing will be discussed in some detail later, as part of the argument that marketing budgeting may exhibit those conditions and contingencies associated with the emergence of political behaviour, but for the moment the central point may be made rather more simply.

The simpler prescriptive models of resource allocation make a number of critical assumptions that preclude the significant emergence of conflict about budgets: (a) that a known, quantified, fully operational, normally single, corporate/owners' goal provides the criterion of choice; (b) that all other interests are subordinate to that goal; and (c) that accurate information is freely available on the outcome of expenditures.

In fact, it may be demonstrated that these assumptions are largely invalid in practice: goals are multiple, hierarchical and frequently uncertain, implying multiple criteria of evaluation; personal individual and functional department interests enter into decision making; and there is frequently high level of uncertainty surrounding the effect of expenditures on the marketplace.

The implication is that the marketing budgeting process

may be conflictual and, indeed, some evidence suggests that this is so. For example, Wills and Kennedy (1982) noted some 'jostling for authority' over the marketing budget, with sales departments, the board, and committees all seeking some level of discretion over the marketing budget. Similarly, Hanmer-Lloyd and Kennedy (1981) noted of the phenomenon of emerging trade marketing departments that 'Some companies' sales departments see this as a way of moving funds out of the marketing budget into the sales budget'.

That such conflict is linked to political behaviour in distorting and manipulating information also emerges in some areas of the marketing literature, for example in studying product management (Cunningham and Clarke, 1975) or in retail managers' sales forecasting (Lowe and Shaw, 1968), and more recently it was found that 'some marketing personnel are plainly 'selective' in gathering information to help substantiate a particular viewpoint' (Wills and Kennedy, 1982). This information 'management' issue has been reviewed elsewhere (Piercy and Evans, 1983), and is pursued in later chapters.

For the moment a prima facie case exists for the proposition that marketing budgeting may operate as a conflictual process.

Budgetary Strategies in Marketing

It will be recalled from the general model of budgeting, that the conclusion reached was that:

> The budget represents an outcome of a bargaining process which occurs within organisations over the setting of priorities for action which become represented in the budget. (Cyert and March, 1963)

By implication, in that bargaining process those seeking particular goals may indulge in orchestrated behaviour to achieve what they want - or perhaps more simply 'politicking'.

The notion that the budgetary process includes such behaviour - the development and pursuit of 'budgetary strategies' - is central to developing a political model of budgeting, which is a task carried out in the next part of the book.

For the moment it is enough to note that sufficient case evidence (as cited above) exists of political behaviour in marketing budgeting to allow us to proceed.

Implications

This part of the book has reviewed marketing budgeting not as an isolated decision, but as an organisational process. This has been attempted by taking an early, and arguably seminal, empirical work from the general literature (Wildavsky, 1964), and testing its conceptual applicability to the fragmented evidence of budgetary behaviour in marketing.

It was established that there is a supportable case for the proposition that Wildavsky's model fits many practical cases of marketing budgeting.

It was found that both the conceptual and empirical literatures of marketing support the notion of <u>precedent</u> as an underlying determinant of marketing budget size and allocation.

Similarly, it emerged that the methods of budget <u>calculation</u>, which are commonly described in the literature, offer some confirmation that marketing budgeting may by analysed as experiential, incremental and simplified.

Thirdly, it was established that the available studies of marketing budgeting <u>processes</u> suggest that analysis should take account of a variety of organisational issues.

Finally, it was seen that there is some support for the working hypothesis that marketing budgeting may in some circumstances be taken as characterised by <u>conflict</u> and the pursuit of <u>budgetary strategies</u>, or political behaviour, by the parties <u>involved</u>.

This case produces the foundation for Part II of the book, which builds a model of the power and politics of marketing budgeting. Before moving to his stage, however, we review briefly the descriptive empirical evidence relating to decision rules in marketing budgeting, and finally make explicit the contrast between 'rational' and organisational models of marketing budgeting decision making.

DECISION RULES IN MARKETING BUDGETING

A descriptive treatment of the marketing budgeting literature, however brief, would be incomplete without examining the evidence relating to the decision rules which appear to be common in practice. More than pursuing completeness, however, this part of the literature is significant as the basis of the general conception of marketing (mainly advertising) budgeting, and to some extent as providing an insight into how managers perceive, or possible rationalise, the marketing budgeting decision.

Two areas merit attention: the decision rules managers claim to use make budget decisions, and the 'pooled experience' work by the PIMS and ADVISOR studies.

Common Decision Rules

A large number of descriptive empirical studies have approached this area by directly questioning managers as to how they set budgets, to arrive at the conclusion that simple heuristics like 'per cent of sales', 'affordability' and 'matching competitors' are commonly applied.

It should be borne in mind that the methodology (particularly the sampling) used varies considerably between these studies, and that in almost all cases the respondents were asked directly what budgeting methods they used (with all the attendant problems of respondent attribution, desire to appear 'rational', legitimation, simplification, and so on). However, a number of general points may be made.

First, the research literature suggests that there has been and apparently continues to be, a widespread reliance on 'rules of thumb' and simple formulae in setting budgets (e.g. San Augustine and Foley, 1975; Rabino, 1984). This picture of managerial behaviour is displayed in studies dating from the 1950s until the 1980s (e.g. Taplin, 1959; Rabino, 1984).

Second, the commonest budgeting methods, of the type discussed, are sales ratios (for example, advertising as a fixed proportion of present, past or expected sales), fixed sum approaches, or 'no method' in the formal sense, with the suggestion that there is 'a similar reluctance among both British and American management to make use of advertising budgeting techniques other than those easily applied' (Gilligan, 1977).

Third, it would seem that commonly the expense to sales ratio is a relatively constant value, and it was noted in one of the early studies of advertising that:

> Not only were conventional appropriation ratios normally observed, but more attention was paid to the maintenance of advertising expenditure as a percentage of turnover than to the absolute size of advertising expenditure. (Taplin, 1959)

It will be recalled that Kennedy and Corkindale (1976) drew the parallel between this phenomenon and the economist's marginal utility approach (pp. *37 - 40*).

Fourth, there are some indications that over time there has been (at least the appearance of) increasing use of 'objective and task' budgeting methods (e.g. Jobber 1980; Patti and Blasko, 1981; Blasko and Patti, 1984), although there is far from universal agreement on this point (e.g. San Augustine and Foley, 1975· Wills and Kennedy, 1982).

Fifth, similarly there have been some suggestions that more sophisticated measurement programmes and modelling techniques have made inroads into budgeting practice. This was found most particularly in the consumer goods field, and paradoxically more in Europe than the USA (Permut, 1977; Lancaster and Stern, 1983). In fact, however, the extent of such inroads would appear very limited in absolute terms (e.g. Lilien and Weinstein, 1981).

Finally, as noted earlier, there appears to be no clear relationship between the sophistication of budgeting methods used and the size of the budget concerned (Gilligan, 1977; Jobber, 1980). This said, at one limit – the very small industrial advertising budget – methods would appear unsophisticated (Turnbull, 1974), in the way that might reasonably be expected.

These studies may be taken as representative of the received understanding of budget calculation methods common in marketing. However, recent attention has been on the extent to which such guidelines may, in fact, reflect 'pooled experience'.

'Pooled Experience' – From Description to Prescription?

Two projects in this area merit some attention: the PIMS (Profit Impact of Marketing Strategy) study, and the ADVISOR work.

PIMS. This study was initiated at General Electric in 1960, and has since been associated with Harvard Business School, the Marketing Science Institute, and the Strategic Planning Institute (Schoeffler et al, 1974). The underlying approach of this work was to collect detailed empirical data from a large number of businesses, as input to computer models relating each factor studied to corporate performance in profitability and cash flow.

PIMS indicated that profitability was influenced by some thirty seven basic factors, which together explained more than eighty per cent of profitability variation in the businesses studied. Of these factors, the six most influential were: (a) market share; (b) product/service quality; (c) marketing expenditures – total costs of advertising, sales force, sales promotion, marketing research and marketing administration, but not physical distribution costs; (d) R & D expenditures; (e) investment intensity; and (f) corporate diversification.

The focus of PIMS was on the complete strategy for a business and the determinants of corporate success or failure, suggesting that some nine influences provide eighty per cent of the determination of that success or failure. In approximate order of importance these influences were found to be: (a) investment intensity; (b) productivity; (c) market position; (d) growth of the served market; (e) product/service quality; (f) innovation/differentiation – including new products, R & D, and marketing efforts; (g) vertical integration; (h) cost push; and (i) current strategic effort.

For present purposes interest is mainly in those PIMS findings relating to discretionary budget allocations, and the marketing expense/sales ratio in particular.

For instance, in studying the impact of the marketing expense/sales ratio on rate of return, findings (Buzzell et al, 1975; Abell and Hammond, 1979) included those summarised in Figure 3.3.

While such general findings offer some insight into the impact of marketing expenditure on profit and cash flows, and thus what might be the appropriate level of marketing/sales in a given situation, the descriptive models are then used to provide decision making guidelines for managers in specific businesses through the reports produced: (a) the PAR report - comparing a given business with others; (b) the Strategic Sensitivity report - predicting what would happen if certain strategic changes were to be implemented; and (c) the optimum strategy report - predicting the combination of strategic variables to produce the best profitability and cash flow.

It is in this sense that the description of variables is developed into prescriptive guidelines for decision makers, resting on the underlying proposition that the 'pooled experience' or 'collective wisdom' of a large number of firms provides guidance to optimum policies, on the grounds that it is reasonable to presume that of the other companies 'In a pragmatic way, on average, they have converged through experience on good decisions' (Lilien and Weinstein, 1981). Thus, it is argued to be possible to infer norms for such areas as marketing communications budgets (Buzzell and Farris, 1976; Farris and Buzzell, 1979).

ADVISOR. Based on the same 'pooled experience' concept of PIMS, but concerned specifically with marketing budgets, the ADVISOR project was initiated by Lilien and his co-workers at Massachusetts Institute of Technology in the 1970s (Lilien and Little, 1976; Lilien et al, 1976; Lilien 1978a, 1978b; Lilien and Weinstein, 1981).

As in the more general PIMS study, the ADVISOR project was based on the collection of data from firms to build a data-base from which to model decision making and to infer spending norms. ADVISOR I collected data from twelve companies covering 66 diversified industrial projects, and taking the two-step budget model discussed earlier (pp. *71-72*) found the norms to be:

	Median	Range for 50% of products
Advertising	$92,000	$16,000-$272,000
Advertising/Sales	0.6%	0.1%-1.8%
Marketing/Sales	6.9%	3%-14%

Figure 3.3: PIMS and Marketing Expenditure Norms

(a) High investment and intense marketing adversely affects profits:

	LOW	6%	11% HIGH
LOW	33	29	25
89%	24	19	10
130%	11	9	9
HIGH			

Investment/Value Added (vertical axis) — Marketing/Sales (horizontal axis)

(b) Intensive marketing in low market share businesses gives low profitability:

	LOW	6%	11% HIGH
LOW	20	13	7
26%	21	19	19
63%	34	31	34
HIGH			

Relative Market Share (vertical axis) — Marketing/Sales (horizontal axis)

(c) Intensive marketing and high R & D gives low profitability:

	LOW	6%	11% HIGH
LOW	21	21	21
1.3%	22	23	19
3.7%	19	22	10
HIGH			

R & D/Sales (vertical axis) — Marketing/Sales (horizontal axis)

(d) Intensive marketing plus low quality gives low profitability:

Quality	Marketing/Sales		
	LOW 6%	11%	HIGH
LOW			
	17	14	5
6%			
	22	19	18
36%			
	32	25	25
HIGH			

Marketing/Sales

(e) High market share produces positive cash flow, but only when marketing intensity is low:

Marketing/ Sales	Relative Market Share		
	HIGH 65%	31%	LOW
HIGH			
	7	4	−4
11%			
	6	4	0
6%			
	9	0	0
LOW			

Relative Market Share

(f) High investment and intensive marketing drains cash:

Investment/ Value Added	Marketing/Sales		
	LOW 6%	11%	HIGH
LOW			
	8	8	6
80%			
	6	2	0
120%			
	0	−3	−6
HIGH			

Marketing/Sales

The ADVISOR 2 study aimed at providing a quantitative framework to analyse budget decisions. As noted earlier, their model is of a decision maker with a checklist of factors, each known only approximately, which are considered separately and sequentially, each adding to, or subtracting from, a final budget score.

In this model the level of advertising and marketing expenditure was found to be determined by a few key factors (primarily sales levels and customer numbers), as summarised in Table 3.1.

Table 3.1: ADVISOR Study Influences on Budgets

Factors determining the size of the marketing budget	Factors determining the size of the advertising budget
Sales	Sales
Number of users	Number of users
Customer concentration	Customer concentration
Fraction of sales made to order	Fraction of sales made to order
Respect/customer attitude differences	
Proportion of direct sales	
Stage in life cycle	Stage in life cycle
Product plans*	Product plans*
Product complexity	Product complexity

---

* Discussions by the writer with one of the MIT researchers in 1981 suggested that the 'product plans' factor is the only area where organisational issues might be reflected in the model, in the sense that plans and priorities could be influenced by members of the organisation, but no explicit attention was given to such questions in the ADVISOR work.

The ADVISOR work also studied annual budget changes, relating marketing budget change to changes in market share, changes in product plans, and changes in the number of competitors, modified by the number of customers, their concentration, and the size of the advertising budget.

In response to claims by the PIMS workers that the ADVISOR work lacked generality (Farris and Buzzell, 1980), a replication was carried out in Europe (Lilien and Weinstein, 1981) suggesting that the same strategic variables had approximately the same explanatory power in Europe as in the USA. It was found, though, that there was some evidence of a different style of advertising use in Europe, where product-company factors (product plans and fraction of sales) have less effect, while the budget adjusts more radically to key market factors like the number of users.

The ADVISOR work may be taken as (a) specifying norms to provide points of competitive comparison;   (b) providing an insight into the key budget factors;   (c) generating certain general findings about budgeting, for instance –
- the marketing/sales ratio falls through the product life cycle,
- the higher the purchase frequency, the higher the advertising/marketing ratio,
- the higher product quality/uniqueness, the higher the advertising/marketing ratio,
- the higher the market share, the lower the marketing/sales ratio,
- the higher the sales concentration, the lower the marketing/sales ratio,
- the higher the customer growth rate, the higher the marketing/sales and advertising/marketing ratios;
(d) providing similar findings about the allocation of advertising budgets to different media;   and (e) in the ADVISOR 2 work, establishing optimisation models for setting advertising and marketing budgets.

As in the case of the PIMS work, the ADVISOR project may be seen as a way of systematising the experience of companies to establish norms and prescriptive models, or moving from the simple description of heuristics and 'rules of thumb' to understanding the source of such decision guides and applying them more scientifically.

Implications

The received theory in this area consists of descriptions of the decision rules managers recognise and claim to use, and attempts through the 'pooled experience' concept to arrive at some degree of optimisation through the insight provided by 'collective wisdom'.

In neither case is attention given to the issues of organisation and process, which were discussed in the last section. It is this gap to which attention now turns.

CONCLUSIONS: RATIONALITY VERSUS REALITY?

As the counterpart to Chapter 2, this chapter has attempted a review of the descriptive theory of budgeting and resource allocation in marketing.

The starting point was to recognise the attacks made on 'traditional budgeting' as incremental and fragmented and suboptimal, in the sense of not conforming with the criteria of 'rationality' discussed in Chapter 2. However, assuming that it is not acceptable or possible simply to follow the prescriptive directions and dictates outlined earlier, to overcome the deficiencies of managerial practice in budget-setting, our search is for greater insight into budgeting behaviour. One such insight is provided by the concept of the task environment as a point of focus, with the suggestion that much of the emphasis in the literature on technique - i.e. on how decision makers structure budgeting problems - provides only a limited understanding of how budgeting takes place.

Our review of the descriptive evidence of marketing budgeting practices followed this direction by adopting an organisational model and fitting to that model what is known of the budgeting process in marketing, with a fair degree of success. With this preparation and the prescriptive models put to one side for the moment, it is possible to move from the organisational model - of procedure, incrementalism, process and conflict - to the analysis of marketing budgeting as a political process.

Before making this progress, however, it was also necessary to recognise the 'decision rule' evidence which has accumulated, confirming that decision makers apply simple guidelines to budgeting decisions in marketing, together with the 'pooled experience' models which link description to prescription. This had two purposes: to illustrate the contrast which exists between prescriptive theories and how managers perceive their behaviour; and to provide further foundations for the notion that the fuller implications of uncertainty and complexity in setting marketing budgets have been largely neglected by the received literature.

It is this key distinction between 'rationality' and what may be discussed as organisational or behavioural reality at which we have now arrived.

Rational Versus Organisational Theories of Management Decision-Making

Given the largely normative nature of the bulk of marketing writing, this present study, and its perspective of political decision making, is likely to provoke substantial objections from the point of view of those advocating 'scientific' approaches to solving marketing problems. Indeed, such objections were characteristic of the early discussions in the exploratory stage of this study, with business theorists and managers in the UK and USA.

In fact, we are not alone in the implied rejection of rational management models as explanations of managerial behaviour. For instance, one attack on the rational ethos in management theory was provided by Cohen and March's (1974) comments on planning, which suggested that plans were often only symbols, with planning little more than a pretext to allow a number of activities which were valuable to powerful interests to take place.

There remains, therefore, a need to demonstrate the grounds on which this departure from, what may be seen as, the accepted theory of marketing decision making in particular, is proposed.

In fact, it is argued by one analyst that the use of power in resource allocation decisions is not merely common, but almost inevitable, and Pfeffer's controversial paper concluded:

> The problem is not that organisations do not seek to use rational bureaucratic criteria, but that it is impossible to do so because of dissensus concerning preferences, criteria and definitions on what organizations should be doing. Unless such goals and criteria are shared among all participants in the organization, the use of power and influence is inevitable in organizational decision making ... Since there is no way of rationalizing away the dissensus, political strength within the coalition comes to determine which criteria, whose preferences are to prevail. (Pfeffer, 1977)

Indeed, pursuing this style of argument leads to the conclusion not that the use of power to gain desired outcomes is unusual, but that its pervasiveness is hidden: in the way that problems are defined (Hedberg et al, 1975); and in the way organisational rules are made and the language used as symbolic legitimation of what happens as the result of power (Pfeffer, 1981a, 1981b). At his most extreme, Pfeffer (1981a) argues that planning and rationality constitute the 'religion' of the formal organisation, producing a feeling of legitimacy and orderliness for decision making, which is actually based on power.

The implication is that many of those involved will prefer not to be aware, not to notice, and not to report that decisions are made through political processes. Apart from the issue of social legitimacy, there is also the feeling that politically derived decisions are inferior to those based on rational models (which presumes that the outcomes are different).

Certainly, for present purposes, enough evidence exists to cast doubt on the notion, implicit in much marketing literature, that management science holds the key to analysing and controlling decision making. The conditions surrounding many decisions favour the use of power through political processes, and it will be argued shortly that this is particularly true of many marketing decisions. The argument that rational methods should be used at all costs, and that it is the problems of implementing such approaches that should preoccupy researchers, holds little attraction at this stage, on the grounds of the covertness and pervasiveness of power, and the lack of evidence that rational methods produce superior results. Thus, this source of objection to the basic thrust of the present study is dismissed for the time being.

Rationality in Budgeting

The vantage point usual in the marketing literature, following the identification of the contrast between prescriptive and descriptive or practitioner views on budgeting, is to criticise the latter. Exceptions are suggestions that the best course would be to devote attention to improving the heuristics used by managers rather than criticising them (Gilligan, 1977) or to work from the 'pooled experience' to greater systematisation (Lilien et al, 1976). However, for present purposes the interest here is somewhat different, since our goal is to establish the extent to which behavioural and organisational factors influence marketing budget decisions.

Early recognition of the difference between economic and organisational views of budgeting was provided by the Wildavsky model, which noted that the rational-economic, normative models of budgeting have value, but that:

> The crucial aspect of budgeting is whose preferences are to prevail in disputes about which activities are to be carried on and to what degree, in the light of limited resources ... one may purport to solve the problem of budgeting by proposing a normative theory (or a welfare function or a hierarchy of values) which specifies a method for maximizing returns from budgetary expenditures. In the absence of ability to impose a set of preferred policies on others, however, this solution breaks down. It amounts to no more than saying that if you can persuade others to agree with you, then you will have achieved agreement. (Wildavsky, 1964)

A similar argument is advanced by Pondy (1964) who noted that:

> The engineering economics literature and the accounting literature treat the budgeting and resource allocation problem solely as a problem in economics ... it proved helpful to interpret capital budgeting for resource allocation as a process of resolving intergroup conflict. (Pondy, 1964)

The thesis of the Pondy work on capital budgeting was that 'bargaining and compromise take precedence over analytical efforts' (Pondy, 1964), and as noted this led to the conclusion that budgeting can be viewed as a process of resolving conflicts within the organisation.

In a comparable argument in the accounting field it has been suggested that the prevailing emphasis is on technical rather than organisational issues, which is limited in perspective, and that:

> An organizational view of budgeting also highlights the social as well as economic and technical nature of budgetary outcomes ... 'The budget' is a reflection of the underlying political structure of the organization, as well as economic constraints and opportunities and the technical procedures out of which it arose. It has a social as well as an economic significance, reflecting the outcomes of debates over organizational power and influence, the social location of uncertainties and constraints within the organization and the allocation of organizational resources. (Hopwood, 1981)

Indeed, a recent analysis by Hopwood of the existence and use of political strategies in budgeting, which relied essentially though implicitly on Wildavsky's model being applied to a business context, concluded that:

> Such strategies are a response not only to the uncertainties and complexities which are inherent in the budgetary process, but also to the fact that budget demands reflect individual and group ambitions. Intertwining the logic of both economics and politics, the demands are strategies in an intensely serious game. The ability to estimate 'what will go' is a vital skill. Managers seek out facts and opinions, in order to arrive at an estimate of what they should ask for in the light of what they can expect to get and then, with due 'padding' to allow for anticipated cuts, they seek to market their budgetary demands. The support from others is actively canvassed and demands are packaged in the most attractive way. (Hopwood, 1981)

Comparison may be made with the Schiff and Lewin studies of budgeting, which emphasised the creation of organisational slack by budgetary decision makers. These researchers concluded that:

> the budget preparation process is a highly participative effort on the part of all managerial levels. This is because managers bargain about the performance criteria by which they will be judged throughout the year and for resource allocations. (Schiff and Lewin, 1968)

There would seem to be grounds therefore for the argument that some contrast exists between the rational economic models of the prescriptive literature and the insights offered by behavioural and organisational factors.

Rationality and Marketing Budgeting

Recognition of this contrast in the marketing literature was provided by Marschner (1967), in an empirical study of advertising budget allocations, where it was argued that:

> 'Theory' tends to ignore one of the essential elements in the behavioral structure of the large, modern, corporate organizations: the omnipresent element of compromise. Today's businessmen often may not insist upon - or even search for - the best solution to the problem. His organization is too large, too complex, and the facts he needs to obscure ... This means a solution he can justify (or rationalize) to his superiors, 'sell' to his peers, and pass on to his subordinates with the assurance that they will consider it logical and acceptable enough to act upon it in a predictable way. (Marschner, 1967)

Once this last point is given, then one implication of the behavioural rather than economic view of the firm is to highlight the creation of 'organizational slack'. As noted in the general budgeting area, it has been found that 'managers will create slack in budgets through a process of understating revenues and overstating costs' (Schiff and Lewin, 1970). More specifically related to the marketing area, it was found that:

> Marketing expenses result from many programs ... which are viewed by management as niceties. These programs appear on budgets, but the commitment of resources to them is contingent on progress made during the year. (Schiff and Lewin, 1968)

In other words, in this study there was not merely the

creation of slack in marketing budgets but <u>through</u> marketing budgets. One such example of the manipulation of the marketing budget for coalition goals was where 'management appears to have deliberately evened-out reported income by decisions to expend or defer advertising costs of new products' (Schiff and Lewin, 1968).

Less explicitly, a directly comparable phenomenon was identified in a NICB survey of advertising budget-setting:

> Whatever method may be favored, companies by and large are flexible in their approach to budget-setting ... it is apparent that companies generally provide themselves with room to manoeuvre and avoid being locked in by an unalterable budget. (Hurwood, 1968)

This 'flexibility' - which may be compared to organisational slack - was evidenced by budget meetings, committees, reviews and the establishment of contingency and reserve funds for marketing expenditures.

It is also characteristic of the behavioural theory of the firm that the <u>lack of information</u> and ability to handle information should lead to 'bounded rationality'. Various of the studies cited earlier in the general budgeting area make some play of the lack of understanding of projects by those making budget decisions, leading to the search for ways to simplify the decision. For example, it is noted:

> For the men concerned with budgeting, finding some method of calculation that will enable them to make decisions is no small task. So they take short cuts. They specialize. They use the past as a rough experiential guide to the present, and they use decisions made in increments to gather information on consequences. They make decisions repetitively and sequentially ... They fragment their areas of concern so that they are not dealing with too much at any one time, and they rely on feedback for information. (Wildavsky, 1964)

Lastly, given the existence of conflict and the need for compromise, the process of creating slack in budgets, and a lack of objective information, there is some need to consider the emergence of particularist criteria in resource allocation and 'nonobjective' decision guidelines. Pfeffer's study of resource allocation makes the point that 'criteria for allocating budgets can be developed to favour any one of a number of subunits in the organization' (Pfeffer, 1977).

In a similar way to Pfeffer's discussion of the selective use of objective criteria as a prime political strategy (Pfeffer, 1981b), Perrow earlier made the point that:

> organizational members are in a continual contest for control over organizational resources and that an inevitable consequence of this struggle is the use of particularist criteria in decision making - criteria that derive from the particular perspective or goals of the contending groups. (Perrow, 1972)

One illustration of this process is provided in the Corey and Star (1972) study of matrix management, which found that in the struggle for resource control between programme and resource managers 'Resource managers tend to influence strategy in such a way as to preserve and nurture resource strength' (Corey and Star, 1972). Similarly, Pondy argued that resource allocation is a constitutional question and that:

> To understand how an organization chooses a specific allocation pattern ... we need to examine more closely the internal dynamics of communication, persuasion, and the exercise of personal power. (Pondy, 1970)

Pfeffer summarises this issue in the following terms:

> In the allocation process, there are typically available a number of legitimate, objective criteria. Organizational members use power and influence to have those criteria selectively used that tend to favour their own relative positions. (Pfeffer, 1977)

If the points above are added to the Pfeffer (1981b) argument about the institutionalisation of organisational attributes, then it may be arguable that the heuristics of marketing budgeting are one such attribute, the institutionalisation of which may represent a statement of the distribution of power in the organisation.

If the comments made here regarding the contrast between the rational budgeting models and the emergence in empirical studies of behavioural and organisational insights are accepted for the moment, then there would appear to be grounds which offer some justification for the proposition that marketing budgets may be political outcomes.

This proposition is defensible on the grounds that the typical budget-setting methods are susceptible to political analysis, both in the sense of being themselves political outcomes which reflect relative power (since the powerful choose criteria which favour themselves), and also in the sense of representing superficially objective criteria for achieving or legitimising political ends. The underlying premise is that the use of heuristics, guidelines, and other rules of thumb is a way of influencing budget size, used by those who have power. Indeed, the desire to retain control of the outcome may provide one reason for the lack of use of the more sophisticated methods of budget setting. (It is not necessarily the case that more sophisticated methods would be non-political, since it may just be that they transfer power to others).

It is now possible to turn to Chapters 4 to 6 where we seek to reinforce this relatively speculative argument in two ways. First, the model of the contingencies for the use of power and politics may be used to test the marketing budgeting decision with regard to the characteristics which make it generally more or less subject to political influence. Second, a consideration of the informational and structural aspects of budgeting provides a basis for a more general proposition about the relationship between organisational power and the marketing budget.

REFERENCES

Blasko, V.J. and Patti, C.H. (1984) 'The Advertising Budgeting Practices of Industrial Marketers', Journal of Marketing, 48, Fall, 104-110

Briscoe, G. (1972) The Sources and Uses of Marketing Information in the British Steel Corporation (Special Steels Division), Centre for Industrial Economic and Business Research, University of Warwick

Bromiley, P. (1981) 'Task Environments and Budgetary Decision Making', Academy of Management Review, 6 (2), 277-88

Buzzell, R.D. and Farris, P.W. (1976) Industrial Marketing Costs, Marketing Science Institute, Working Paper, Boston, Mass.

Cohen, M. and March, J.G. (1974) Leadership and Authority, McGraw-Hill, New York

Cravens, D.W., Hills, G.E. and Woodruff, R.B. (1980) Marketing Decision Making, Irwin, Homewood, Ill.

Cunningham, M. and Clarke, C.J. (1975) 'The Product Management Function in Marketing', European Journal of Marketing, 9 (2), 129-49

Cyert, R.M. and March, J.G. (1963) A Behavioral Theory of the Firm, Prentice-Hall, Englewood Cliffs, N.J.

Farris, P.W. and Buzzell, R.D. (1979) 'Why Advertising and Promotional Costs Vary: Some Cross-Sectional Analyses', Journal of Marketing, 43 (4), 112-122

Farris, P.W. and Buzzell, R.D. (1980) 'A Comment on "Modelling the Marketing Mix for Industrial Products"', Management Science, 26 (1), 97-100

Gilligan, C. (1976) 'Budgeting for Advertising: Time for a New Approach', Advertising Quarterly, Winter, 32-5

Gilligan, C. (1977) 'How British Advertisers Set Budgets', Journal of Advertising Research, 17 (1), 47-9

Guiltinan, J.P. and Paul, G.W. (1982) Marketing Management: Strategies and Programs, McGraw-Hill International, Kogakusha

Hanmer-Lloyd, S. and Kennedy, S. (1981) Setting and Allocating the Communications Budget: A Review of Current Practice, Marketing Communications Research Centre, Cranfield School of Management, Beds

Hedberg, B., Edstroem, A., Mueller, W. and Wilpert, B. (1975) 'The Impact of Computer Technology on Organizational Power Structures', in E. Grochla and N. Szperski, (eds.) Information Systems and Organization Structure, de Gruyter, Berlin

Jobber, D. (1980) 'Advertising Budgeting: How Industrial Goods Companies Decide', Management Decision, 18 (5), 276-81

Joiner, C. and Chapman, J.B. 'Budgeting Strategy: A Meaningful View', S.A.M. Advanced Management Journal, 46 (3), 4-11

Kotler, P. (1972) Marketing Management: Analysis, Planning and Control, 2nd ed., Prentice-Hall International, London

Kotler, P. (1976) Marketing Management: Analysis, Planning and Control, 3rd ed., Prentice-Hall International, London

Lancaster, K.M. and Stern, J.A. (1983) 'Computer-Based Advertising Budgeting Practices of Leading U.S. Consumer Advertisers', Journal of Advertising, 12 (4), 4-9

Lilien, G.L. (1978a) ADVISOR 2: A Study of Industrial Marketing Budgeting, Part 1 - Background Data and Norm Models, Massachusetts Institute of Technology, Working Paper 991-78, Boston, Mass.

Lilien, G.L. (1978b) ADVISOR 2: A Study of Industrial Marketing Budgeting, Part 2, Massachusetts Institute of Technology, Working Paper, 992-78, Boston, Mass.

Lilien, G.L. and Little, J.D.C. (1976) 'The Advisor Project: A Study of Industrial Marketing Budgets', Sloan Management Review, 17, 17-33

Lilien, G.F., Silk, A.V., Choffrey, J-M. and Rao, M. (1976) 'Industrial Advertising Effects and Budgeting Practices', Journal of Marketing, January, 16-24

Lilien, G. and Weinstein, D. (1981) Do European Industrial Marketers Budget Differently? An International Comparison Via the ADVISOR Model, Massachusetts Institute of Technology, Working Paper, 1222-81, Boston, Mass.

Lowe, E.A. and Shaw, R.W. (1968) 'An Analysis of Managerial Biasing: Evidence from a Company's Budgeting Process', Journal of Management Studies, 5 (3), 304-315

Marschner, D.C. (1967) 'Theory Vs Practice in Allocating Advertising Money', Journal of Business, 40, 286-302

Marketing Society (1967) Setting Advertising Appropriations, Marketing Society, London

Mitchell, L.A. (1979) 'Common Approaches to Budgeting for Advertising', Management Decision, 17 (5), 359-67

Permut, S.E. (1977) 'How European Managers Set Advertising Budgets', Journal of Advertising Research, 17, 75-9

Pfeffer, J. (1977) 'Power and Resource Allocation in Organizations', in B.M. Staw and G.R. Salancik (eds.) New Directions in Organizational Behavior, St. Clair, Chicago

Pfeffer, J. (1981a) 'Management as Symbolic Action: The Creation and Maintenance of Organizational Paradigms', in L.L. Cummings and B.M. Staw, Research in Organizational Behavior, Jai, Greenwich, Conn.

Pfeffer, J. (1981b) Power in Organizations, Pitman, Marshfield, Mass.

Piercy, N. (1986) 'The Marketing Budget: Rationality, Politics and Organisation', Managerial Finance, forthcoming

Piercy, N. and Evans, M. (1983) Managing Marketing Information, Croom Helm, Beckenham

Rabino, S. (1984) 'Is Advertising Budget Planning Changing?', International Journal of Advertising, 3, 149-59

San Augustine, A.J. and Foley, W.F. (1975) 'How Large Advertisers Set Budgets', Journal of Advertising Research, 15 (5), 11-16

Schiff, M. and Lewin, A.Y. (1970) 'The Impact of People on Budgets', Accounting Review, 45 (2) 259-68

Schoeffler,, S., Buzzell, R.D. and Heany, D.F. (1974) 'The Impact of Strategic Planning on Profit Performance', Harvard Business Review, March/April

Taplin, W. (1959) 'Advertising Appropriation Policy', Economica, 26, 227-39

Turnbull, P.W. (1974) 'The Allocation of Resources to Marketing Communications in Industrial Markets', Industrial Marketing Management, 3, 297-310

Wildavsky, A. (1964) The Politics of the Budgetary Process, 1st ed., Little Brown, Boston, Mass.

Wildavsky, A. (1979) The Politics of the Budgetary Process, 3rd ed., Little Brown, Boston, Mass.

Williamson, B. (1981) 'Salesmen and the Slump', Marketing, 5 (7), 27-31

Wills, G. and Kennedy, S. (1982) 'How to Budget Marketing', Management Today, February, 58-61

PART TWO

An Organisational and Political Perspective for Marketing Budgeting

4

Developing an Organisational
Perspective on Marketing

INTRODUCTION

The discussion at the end of Chapter 3 highlighted the
distinction between 'rationality' in the sense that this term
is used in the literatures of economics, management, and
management science, and the concepts of decision making
established by those concerned with the behaviour of
individuals and groups in organisations. The role of Part II
is to explore further those latter concepts, in searching for
greater insight into marketing decision making processes, and
marketing budgeting in particular.

The Corporate Environment

It has been argued elsewhere by this writer (Piercy, 1984a)
that generally most studies of marketing have concentrated on
the description and analysis of the key areas of marketing
decision making - strategic paradigms and choices, and the
tactical management decisions relating to the marketing mix
elements. However, the suggestion in that article was that
such a framework for understanding and managing marketing
decision making is inadequate in at least one vital respect -
it ignores the fact that most major marketing decisions are
not made by owner-manager entrepreneurs who relate only to
the marketing environment of customers, competitors and
international economic forces, but by professional managers
who make decisions within an organisation (Piercy, 1984a).
The importance of giving explicit recognition to the
organisational setting of marketing decision making is to
suggest the existence of a range of pressures and
constraints, arising not directly out of the marketplace or
indeed directly from any other external source, but from
within the organisation itself. (This is not to deny the
argument, to which we return shortly, that organisational
characteristics reflect those of the environment).
      The central hypothesis advanced in that paper was that
the corporate setting may be considered in some situations to

be just as powerful a determinant of decisions made, as is the external competitive or marketing environment, with the objective of showing how this may occur - and to add to the marketing analyst's armoury a further element in the model of how marketing operates - the corporate environment.

In fact, others have linked corporate environment, in terms of such variables as culture and climate, generally to corporate success (e.g. Peters and Waterman, 1982; White, 1984), as well as more particularly to marketing effectiveness (Deshpande, 1982; Parasuraman and Deshpande, 1984; Dunn et al, 1985). Similarly, as noted earlier, Anderson's (1982) work makes explicit the impact of the coalition of interests in an organisation on marketing and strategic planning.

The dimensions of that corporate environment include such factors as: the organisation's structure; the development of norms of behaviour within an organisation; the impact of corporate ideology and culture; the effect of management style; the functioning of information networks; and all those other characteristics - some overt but many covert and implicit - of an organisation surrounding the decision maker.

In fact, the thrust of the argument in Part II is that the two of the most critical elements of the corporate environment for marketing decision making processes are organisational power and political behaviour, although it will be seen that these attributes are in reality intertwined with the other elements of the corporate environment.

There are, in fact, two broad reasons for adopting an analytical approach which is grounded in such organisational theories. The first, is simply that a gap exists in the received literature and understanding of marketing decision making, which may be productively analysed in this way. The second reason is that marketing as a business function is arguably in a continuing process of relatively turbulent transition in terms of such factors as organisational status, departmentation, structuring, and so on, in such a way that it may be argued that the organisational perspective is potentially even more illuminating that it might have been at an earlier stage in marketing's development. These questions are considered in turn below.

MARKETING IN TRANSITION

The historical evolution of marketing has been analysed elsewhere (Piercy, 1985) where the main implication drawn was that the corporate positioning of marketing - assessed in terms of such factors as departmentation, the existence and status of a chief marketing executive, the formal responsibilities of the marketing sub-unit, and the informal status and influence of that sub-unit - is neither homogeneous between organisations nor discernably stable over time. In particular, various factors suggested that the marketing influence may be diminishing in certain companies where the marketing sub-unit has matured, and attention may be drawn to the following points in support of that conclusion.

Attacks on the Marketing Concept. In recent years there has been a trend towards questioning the value of the 'marketing concept' (and thus its implications for the position of the marketing sub-unit). For example, one leading analyst in the UK has concluded of the received view of the marketing organisation, that:

> Marketing textbooks have not caught up to how the changing corporate superstructures have affected the organization of marketing. The new structures have diffused marketing decisions and curtailed the autonomy of marketing management... the new divisional and multilateral structures move integration outside the marketing function and given strategy to division and programme general management. (Doyle, 1979)

Indeed, other attacks are far more virulent than Doyle's. There has, for example, been some attention directed to the idea of abandoning the apparently 'bankrupt' marketing concept (Bell and Emory, 1971) and all that it implies for organising marketing activities, on the grounds that:

> In the early 1950s, the marketing concept emerged and became enthusiastically acclaimed as an article of faith ... Yet it has not worked. Nor can it ... the marketing concept should be either deliberately discarded or left to crumble under the weight of its own irrelevancies. (Sachs and Benson, 1980)

Similarly, in the US managers have been attacked both at the corporate level (Hayes and Abernathy, 1980) and at the marketing function level (Wind, 1981) for a lack of creativity and adaptability in relation to market environments.

The implications of such views have been highlighted by writers like Haller, who suggests that 'Marketing as we know it will disappear sometime in the 1980s. It has not kept pace with developments in other parts of the business world' (Haller, 1980b). Haller's conclusion is that strategic planning structures will replace the marketing department, since he claims that: 'The marketing concept is dead. Strategic management is the only hope' (Haller, 1980a).

In fact, there is some danger of taking too universal, or indeed too pessimistic, a view, since, for example, such disillusionment is not reflected in a recent survey of UK business school academics (Doyle and Saunders, 1980) and Buell (1982) has recently described strategic planning as actually 'setting the stage for marketing in large American companies'. It remains the case too that some argue that the role of the marketing concept is of growing rather than declining importance (McNamara, 1981; Parasuraman, 1981).

It is true, though, that the 1972 UK research into marketing organisation (Hayhurst and Wills, 1972) made much of the 'corporate planning backlash' reasserting the role of general management in the face of the growing diffusion of the marketing concept. Accepting that this diffusion is itself somewhat problematic as an issue for analysis, there remains, perhaps, the need for some scepticism about the validity of the wilder and more extreme prognoses in the popular literature of marketing.

This said, whatever conclusion is reached about the changing corporate role of marketing, and the consequent development of new structural forms, there would seem justification for claiming that some degree of change would appear to be taking place in the received view of that role. For instance, it is only very recently that marketing writers have begun to recognise the problems created by the existence of large numbers of mature and declining markets in corporate portfolios, and the consequent need for different marketing approaches - which in turn have their own structural implications (Buell, 1982; Hooley et al, 1984).

The Implications of New Information Technology. For more than a quarter of a century it has been recognised that the development of electronic information technology would have major impacts not simply on processes of production and administration, but on the shape of organisations themselves (for example, see the review provided in Piercy, 1984b). Indeed, the effects seem inevitably to extend to the relationships between organisations, in ways which affect the marketing sub-units in them.

The contributions to a recent review of the management implications of new information technology (Piercy, 1984b) suggested that the actual impact of the technology on organisations remained ambiguous, and indeed that it may be contingent upon a variety of factors, but particularly the choices made by management.

The organisational issues highlighted are various. **First,** traditional computerisation provided a pressure for centralisation of information and its processing, while new microelectronic technology may either reinforce this centralisation of control <u>or</u> offer the potential for decentralising control and authority. Decisions reached on the location of authority and the degree and type of control exercised, have clear implications for the responsibilites and role of the marketing department.

Second, there have been many suggestions that human inputs may increasingly be replaced by intelligent machines, both in operative tasks and also in management decision making. While the fact that this may be possible does not necessarily mean that it will happen, the implications for marketing include the replacement of routine human inputs by machines - as in, say, order processing, clerical market research work, advertising/promotion control, and perhaps much of what has fallen in the past to the product/brand manager - as well as the possible replacement of whole management levels in marketing - as, for instance, in the retail setting, where the automation of stock-holding and scanning to collate sales data may remove the need for the general area management structure.

One possibility, therefore, is a reduced marketing department in manpower terms. Added to this simple effect on departmental size, is the more general impact of the routinisation of work. It will be seen shortly that some suggest a division of the marketing department's activities into routinised activities (and by implication the relatively low level and non-strategic) and planning and development, in what amounts to the disintegration of the marketing department.

Third, at the level of the individual manager, the administrative concept of the limited span of control may have become misleading, in the sense that the new technology increases the manager's ability to process information and thus to supervise others. The outcome of such a prognosis is the 'flatter' organisation structure, where much of the middle management role is removed. This too may have substantial implications for the size and structuring of the marketing department.

Fourth, the enormously increased potential for electronic communications transcends organisational boundaries. At one level this may lead to the 'macro-marketing information system' (Piercy and Evans, 1983) based on the electronic sharing of information between manufacturers, distributors and even major end-users of products. However, more covertly there are signs that the 'cost' of obtaining such a level of networking or information sharing includes giving up marketing decision making discretion, either in submission to the reality that the controller of the information (hypothesised to be usually the distributor) has the balance of bargaining power, or in a more cooperative form of joint decision-making in the 'electronic channel of distribution'.

The latter situation amounts to what has been described as 'quasi-integration as a mechanism for controlling external dependencies' (Blois, 1980), where 'firms' marketing behaviour is developed to take account of the degree of concentration which exists in most markets' (Blois, 1978). In such situations too, one may anticipate the effective relocation of the responsibility and hence formal power of the manufacturer's marketing department, through the absorption by top management of the critical negotiations with other organisations, and the surrender of autonomy in new product policy, pricing and marketing communications to external organisations – the corollary being the development of a more powerful marketing department in the retailer or distributor organisation.

While much remains speculative in this area, it is important to note that the organisation of marketing in the future will inevitably reflect the impact of new information technology in some of the ways discussed above and that the dramatic effect of the technology serves to underline the significance of the concept of information processing to many of the assumptions we make about the organisation of marketing. Thus the potential impact of new information technology on marketing operations may be shown to include: greater decentralisation of management control; the replacement or automation of human information processors; the replacement of levels of supervisory or middle management; the organisational separation of routinised and non-routinised aspects of marketing; broader spans of control, leading to the 'flatter' organisation structure; and the increased potential for integrated communication-information systems that transcend the organisation's boundaries, possibly leading to the 'quasi-integration' of firms such as manufacturers and retailers.

In each case there are implications for the future organisation of marketing – its autonomy, its responsibilities, its task content, its management levels, its staffing, its external environmental relationships, and not least its control of information – since the integrated communication-information system implies information sharing, and access for other departments, managers, distributors, and so on – and thus its loss of control of critical contingencies such as sales forecasting and customer communications. By implication, one is also describing potential changes in the power of the marketing department through changes in sub-unit interdependencies.

In various ways – reduced control of critical contingencies, less ability to control information, loss of critical functions, reduced numbers – one possible impact of NIT on the marketing department is potentially to substantially reduce its power.

However, in each case above, we have stressed the potential of NIT, implying that potential to be realised only by managerial choice, (with what that implies in turn for the influences or politics acting on managerial choice processes).

The Disintegration of the Marketing Department. Finally, for the reasons suggested above and others laid out elsewhere (Piercy, 1985b), the concept of a life cycle of marketing development suggests that we may see, in some companies, the disintegration or even the disappearance of the marketing department.

The available evidence is variable, but there are some signs that the criticisms of marketing, noted above, are reflected in the realities of corporate marketing, in terms of such factors as: the abandonment of brand and product management by some companies – the organisational form which was widely associated with the implementation of the marketing concept; reduced formal responsibility and authority for the marketing department, even in such areas as advertising and sales promotion, as a result of increased top management intervention, formal corporate planning, and the greater involvement in marketing decisions of non-marketing functional managers; the development of business sector or segment management between the chief executive and the operations level, pushing marketing's influence down towards operations; a greater managerial emphasis on strategic management and corporate planning; and the growth in trade marketing departments out of key account sales operations dealing directly with major customers.

Expanding briefly on these arguments, one point emerging from a variety of sources is that the central focus or emphasis of corporate management shows signs of changing. At one level this is taken as an indication that marketing orientation was a fad or fashion, although more fundamentally it may be argued that the pressures on management have themselves evolved, thus changing priorities and urgencies. If one follows the general logic of the Cyert and March (1963) model of managers giving sequential attention to goals, it may simply be that in certain circumstances the mature corporation reaches a point where marketing goals become, at least temporarily, less urgent than others.

Indeed, such a suggestion is not new (e.g. see Hayhurst and Wills, 1972; Doyle, 1979; Morein, 1975; Haller, 1980a; 1980b; and Buell, 1982).

However, one implication would seem to be of a 'post-marketing orientation' future, where, if it exists, the marketing department operates as a functional area in parallel with other resource specialists, but that coordination, integration and strategic decisions may be made elsewhere. Indeed, it is possible to make more explicit the implications of these prognoses.

One possibility is that the integration of certain independent functions to create a marketing sub-unit may be followed by the disintegration of the functions of the marketing department. Such disintegration may involve the 'hiving-off' and separation of control of certain task activities, and the recognition that changing circumstances have 'diffused marketing decisions' (Doyle, 1979). As suggested above, it has been noted recently that large consumer goods companies are establishing trade marketing departments to deal with major retailers, as a reflection of their bargaining power (Wills and Kennedy, 1982). It has been suggested that trade marketing may represent simply a new task specialisation within marketing, reflecting the importance of key accounts, or may move outside the marketing department (Hanmer-Lloyd and Kennedy, 1981). To the extent that trade marketing is separated from the marketing department in companies facing highly concentrated buying power in the channel of distribution, the power of the marketing department relative to others is likely to be reduced.

Similarly, it has been found that the real control of marketing functions has actually been unified only to a limited extent in many companies – frequently areas like sales, physical distribution, pricing and so on, have been managed as separate entities to marketing (Hayhurst and Wills, 1972). Even then, formal responsibility may be greater than real authority, in that it has been suggested, for example, that senior management and interdepartmental intervention in advertising decisions increases as the size of expenditure becomes larger (Hanmer-Lloyd and Kennedy, 1981; Wills and Kennedy, 1982; Piercy, 1985).

In addition to certain task specialisations moving outside the marketing department, it has been proposed that there may be a split between marketing planning and the management of operations. Campbell and Kennedy (1971) argued that 'there is as much routine in marketing as in any other area of management (and) ... The routine in marketing must be accepted and provision made for it in the company structure', suggesting thus that routine tasks could be separated from the management role in marketing. This thesis was extended by Hayhurst and Wills (1972) in their proposition that the organisational problem for the future of marketing would 'include most notably the routinization of most operational marketing activities and their analytical separation from the marketing development task of the business; (and) the fusion of R & D planning activities with Marketing Development'.

In this approach, the operational marketing tasks would, by implication, be the residual responsibility of the marketing department, while a new location would be required for marketing development. Hayhurst and Wills (1972) argued for the joining of this element of marketing with technical research and development, their interests being linked by the key concept of technological forecasting, to choose long-term strategies for the future, although they also suggested that there was a need for the development of integration with financial departments in strategic analysis.

By implication the latter developments suggest the development of a formal corporate/strategic planning organisation incorporating marketing development, the planning of R & D, financial analysis and planning, and presumably also production and manpower planning.

Such a scenario would be compatible with Doyle's comments noted earlier, and a somewhat diminished role for the marketing department.

To this may be added the more recent suggestion that 'quasi-integration' between firms (Blois, 1979), enhanced by new information technology and networking (Piercy, 1984b), may lead to the sharing of marketing responsibilities between members of the channel of distribution, which in turn implies less autonomy for the traditional manufacturer's marketing department.

The most extreme prediction derived from the disintegration of the unified marketing department is its disappearance - literally, or at least effectively.

At one level, the adoption of the strategic management concept may imply organisational change of the type proposed by Haller (1980a), i.e. that the unified marketing department will cease to exist in favour of a structure based on implementing a strategic planning concept (see Piercy, 1985).

At a less extreme level, Wills (1980a) has used the dichotomy between planning and operations (discussed above) to explore the notion that marketing should not be represented on the board of directors as a line function. His logic points to a 'hiving-off' of marketing planning to a corporate planning unit and the 'renaissance of sales authority' covering operational marketing activities. His central point was the proposition that the marketing director should be replaced by a sales director and a distribution director. Later he extended this case and was able 'to contemplate the renaissance of the old role of Commercial Director, who took care of the company's external relationships' (Wills, 1980b).

Again in both such situations the marketing department would effectively disappear.

Finally, a somewhat less extreme reaction to the pressure of change on the marketing organisation is concerned not with the primary departmentation issue, but the internal structuring question. This is reflected, for instance, in the prediction that:

> The scope of much of marketing's conventional organizational points of reference will crumble, however. The points of contact with finance and research and development will lead to a wide variety of new organizational forms for marketing to attempt to

enhance effectiveness in rapidly changing circumstances such as product innovation. (Hayhurst and Wills, 1972)

For example, the matrix structure implies change both in departmentation and internal structuring for marketing (Corey and Star, 1971; Piercy, 1985), as do other proposals, which centre on the establishment of new venture departments, the development of intra-marketing teams (Doyle, 1979), and product-line management (Morein, 1975) with the introduction of business sector or category managers (Buell, 1982).

The implication of such points for our present purposes is to suggest that the corporate role of marketing is far from being unambiguous or stable either across organisations or within a particular company. This underlines the argument that the organisational and processual aspects of marketing are not just important per se, but actually increasingly and urgently so. The implicit hypothesis is, of course, that importance, in these terms relates to influencing organisational outcomes in some way.

It is to this last point that attention turns next. We examine first the relationship between marketing and organisation, and then expand on different concepts of organisational decision-making, before returning to the importance of structure and information in marketing.

MARKETING AND ORGANISATION THEORY

The Lacuna in the Marketing Literature

Justification of the approach taken in this study lies partly in the contemporary changes in the corporate position of marketing discussed above, but also in the argument that only very limited, genuinely analytical, attention has, in the past, been devoted to issues of structure and process in marketing. This gap in the literature has been noted by others, but little progress towards filling it has been apparent. For example, some twenty years ago, Howard noted that: 'Organization theory is an aid to understanding many marketing problems. Its general application is to the organizational influences on the marketing executive's decisions', (Howard, 1965). That last writer was led to conclude that:

The consequence of not having a satisfactory theory of marketing organization is shown by the two different ways the topic has been treated in the marketing literature, when marketing organization is dealt with at all ... the treatment is a description of the formal organization rather than how it works ... The alternative approach has been to ignore organization and treat the decision-maker implicitly as though he were uninfluenced by the human pressures around him. (Howard, 1965)

Discussions between Professor Howard and the writer in the exploratory stages of this work suggested that little progress had been made by marketing analysts to respond to that challenge.

Indeed, more recently researchers at Stanford made the similar point that:

The marketing literature has not addressed itself to the explicit study of organizational design of people/activities ... The marketing literature has essentially ignored the study of group behavior, especially the underlying organizational interactions. Yet the necessity and importance of filling this gap is self-evident. There cannot be optimal nor near-optimal marketing management decisions without near optimization of the underlying organizational designs. (Nonaka and Nicosia, 1979)

In fact, the earlier review of organisational studies in marketing (Piercy, 1985) suggested that: while most marketing writers offer some commentary on organisational issues, this is indeed normally restricted to the description of alternative structural devices; while there have been various empirical studies in the past twenty years, they have typically been very limited in scope; and little use has been made in the marketing literature of the received body of organisation theory.

We may expand briefly on each of these last points.

First, it will be recognised, without detailed citation evidence, that marketing textbooks normally at most do no more than to describe the internal structuring of the marketing sub-unit - by function, market, and so on - product and brand management systems, and new product organisational forms. In fairness, it was noted by two empirical workers in the UK:

It is probably because of the difficulty of delineating any really standardised marketing structure that one finds the dearth of literature on this subject, beyond the comparatively short sections which most authors give to the four generalised approaches ... We found some shortage of material on the problems of decentralisation in marketing, and the same deficiency occurs with information on delegation of authority in the marketing organisation beyond the usual platitudes. (Hayhurst and Wills, 1972)

It is suggested, however, that the criticisms made by Howard (1965) and Nonaka and Nicosia (1979) remain valid.

Second, there has been a reasonable number of empirical studies of marketing organisation in the past twenty years, both in the USA and the UK - again reviewed and cited more fully in Piercy (1985) - but these have also been concerned primarily with such questions as: the description of the internal structuring of marketing and only to a more limited extent the organisational positioning of the marketing department (e.g. BIM 1961; Hooley et al, 1984); the adoption or otherwise of the 'marketing concept' and the 'marketing orientation' displayed by firms (e.g. Weigand, 1961; Hayhurst and Wills, 1972; Hooley et al, 1984); or the study of the operational use of particular organisational forms such as product management, new venture departments, or matrix structures (see Piercy, 1985, Chapter 6, for a review of sources).

If one searches for recognition in the marketing literature of the 'inevitable duality of structure and process' (Weick, 1969), then that search is rewarded only in certain fragments of the literature. There has, for instance, been some note of the interpersonal influence modes used by product managers (e.g. Venkatesh and Wilemon, 1976) and of what amounts to political behaviour by product and brand managers (e.g. Cunningham and Clarke, 1975). More recently some attention has been given to the impact of environmental uncertainty on marketing organisation (Nonaka and Nicosia, 1979; Weitz and Anderson, 1981), and in a related way to the social exchange between an organisation and its environment as a determinant of the structural attributes of the marketing sub-unit (Hakansson and Ostberg, 1975; Hakansson et al, 1979).

In fact, it is from these fragments that what is attempted here is built, and more will be said of them later.

Third, this writer suggests that relatively little use has been made in the marketing literature of organisation theory, other than that associated with classical, administrative theorists. A review of organisation theory may reasonably distinguish the following: classical theories - based on the division of labour and balanced by unity of control, in the traditional concept of a pyramidal hierarchy; human relations approaches - challenging the underlying assumptions and effects of the classical school, and emphasising instead the social and emotional needs of individuals; sociotechnical models - taking the organisation as a system interacting with the environment and focusing on the interaction between human, technological, and social inputs; and contingency theories - which relate the organisation's structure to situational factors in the environment, the technology employed, and so on.

Examining the literature of marketing organisation suggests that the bulk of the material produced is grounded in classical theories, with attention focusing on such issues as: the base for dividing labour and decentralisation in the marketing department; the specific, formal responsibilities of the chief marketing executive and the delegation of responsibilities; the development of detailed, written role descriptions; or in areas like product management, the lack of correspondence between authority and responsibility; and more generally such questions as line/staff conflicts.

Interestingly, a recent paper (Ruekhart et al, 1985) similarly attacks traditional approaches to the study of the marketing organisation, but on the grounds that such approaches: through focusing on broad macro-organisational forms overlook variations required by different kinds of organisations; ignore the issue of whether any particular task should be performed within the firm or by an external agent; and do not explain linkages between the structure of marketing activities and subsequent performance.

There has admittedly been some attention, though it is limited, to human relations approaches in marketing, for instance in the suggestion that the emergence of participative, low-structure systems of management may be paralled with the adoption of the marketing concept (Douglas, 1967), or the proposal that 'management by objectives' be adopted in marketing (Migliore and Stevens, 1980) or participative group management methods in the sales force (Likert, 1962).

It is only comparatively recently that any recognition has been given to sociotechnical and contingency concepts in marketing organisation. Certain works, such as those mentioned above by Nonaka and Nicosia (1979), Hakansson et al, (1979) and Weitz and Anderson (1981) have attempted to relate marketing departmentation, decentralisation and internal structuring to such factors as environmental attributes, and social exchange. In related work Deshpande (1982) attempted to relate the use of marketing research information to structural attributes of the marketing organisation, and John and Martin (1984) link the 'credibility' of marketing plans to organisation structure.

It is from this last point that this present study departs, in taking a contingency view of marketing organisation (see pp. *119 - 129* below) and in focusing attention on the processual question of the interaction between structure and information. Indeed, it is noteworthy that even when a contingency analysis for marketing organisation has been proposed (Weitz and Anderson, 1981; Ruekhart et al, 1985), such works have emphasised only structure and not process, and thus not taken account of the interaction. A significant exception to this is found in Wensley (1985). This departure leads us, in Chapter 9, to a somewhat novel view of resource allocation and budgeting in marketing, which contrasts with the received marketing literature.

MODELS OF ORGANISATIONAL DECISION MAKING

Perhaps the most important implication of taking on board the notion that there are organisational dimensions of marketing - structure as information processing capacity, environments as creators of information processing burdens and critical contingencies, managerial choices subject to political pressures within and outwith the organisation, and so on (Piercy, 1985) - which are of far greater significance than simply the choice of decentralisation base (to divide marketing by function, product, market, and so on) is that structure and process influence decisional outcomes.

Put more simply, it is hypothesised that the way in which a company is run - in terms of its structure and internal systems - influences both the way or process in which decisions are made and the outcomes of those decisions or decision-making processes.

One way of summarising the essential point to be made about organisational decision making is to distinguish between alternative models of that process, in the way attempted by Pfeffer (1981). These distinctions are summarised in Table 4.1, and the main points of Pfeffer's paradigm are discussed below.

Rational Decision Making

Prominent in the literature - particularly the prescriptive literature - rational models presume: that consistent, congruous goals exist among members of an organisation; that search produces a set of alternatives from which choice must be made; that likely outcomes of alternatives are accurately assessed; and that the alternative selected is that maximising the likelihood of attaining goals.

In pursuing the question of what differences may distinguish rational decision making from political behaviour, it is suggested that:

> rational organizations can be distinguished from the more political organizations by investigating the extent to which the choices made consistently reflect the preferences of certain groups within the organizations ... The rational model presumes that information and value-maximization dictate choice; the political model presumes that parochial interests and preferences control choice. (Pfeffer, 1981)

Table 4.1: Models of Organisational Decision Making

Dimensions of the Models	RATIONAL	BUREAUCRATIC	DECISION PROCESS/ ORGANISED ANARCHY	POLITICAL POWER
GOALS	Consistent and shared	Reasonably consistent	Unclear ambiguous - they may be constructed after the event to rationalise actions	Consistent for individuals but pluralistic across the organisation
POWER/CONTROL	Centralised	Less centralised, more use of rules	Decentralised - anarchic	Shifting between coalitions and interest groups
DECISION PROBLEMS	Orderly and substantively rational	Rational in procedural sense - as in programmes and standard operations	Ad hoc	Disorderly - characterised by interests struggling and political behaviour
RULES AND NORMS	Optimisation	Precedent and tradition	Segmented, episodic, participative	Free play of internal forces - conflictual
INFORMATION PROCESSING REQUIREMENTS	Extensive and systematic	Reduced by use of rules and procedures	Random collection and use of information	Information used politically - distorted, selected, etc.
BELIEFS ABOUT CAUSE AND EFFECT OF DECISIONS	Probabilities or outcomes known	Consensual - shared acceptance of rules	Technology seen as unclear ambiguous	Disagreement about technology
DECISIONS	Made to maximise value	Made through programmes and routines	Not linked to intention - result from interaction of individuals, problems and solutions	Result from bargaining and interaction of interests
IDEOLOGY	Efficiency and effectiveness	Stability, fairness, predictability	Playful, loose coupling random	Struggle and conflict producing winners and losers

Source: Adapted by the Author from Pfeffer (1981)

Bureaucratic Decision Making

The essential characteristic of bureaucratic approaches to decision making is that choices are made according to 'procedural' rationality rather than 'substantive rationality' (Simon, 1979). Associated primarily with the work of March and Simon (1958) and Cyert and March (1963), bureaucratic decision processes involve: goals as systems of constraints which decisions must meet; 'bounded rationality' which suggests that search is limited and stops when a satisfactory alternative is found; uncertainty tends to be avoided; conflict is never fully resolved; and objectives are attended to sequentially.

The organisation thus learns rules of action or standard operating procedures as a guide to action and choice, as in the effect of historical precedent on decisions.

Pfeffer (1981) then distinguishes bureaucratic organisations from the more rational in their less extensive information search, and heavier reliance on rules, standard operating procedures and precedent, although the distinction between bureaucratic and political models is more problematic:

> In bureaucratic organizations, changes in resource allocation patterns should either follow a proportional basis, be based on some standard measure of operations and performance, or reflect an attempt to shift the resources to better achieve the goals and values of the organization. By contrast, political models of organizations would suggest that power would best predict changes and shifts in decisions and allocations. (Pfeffer, 1981)

Decision Process Models

The approaches characterised as decision process models assume less rationality and greater randomness than the bureaucratic theories – the assumption of pre-defined, known preferences is dropped. Such models suggest that: there are no overall organisational goals to be maximised by choice – or even that choices made may determine goals since the meaning of action is retrospective (Weick, 1969); and that there are no powerful interests with preferences and the resources to obtain them.

For example, the 'garbage can model' (Cohen et al, 1972) suggests that 'a decision is an outcome of an interpretation of several relatively independent "streams" within an organization' (Cohen et al, 1972) and it was concluded that:

> although the processes within the garbage can are understandable and in some ways predictable, events are

not dominated by intention. The processes and the outcomes are likely to appear to have no close relation with the explicit intention of actors. In situations in which load is heavy and the structure is relatively unsegmented, intention is lost in context dependent flows of problems, solutions, people, and choice opportunities. (Cohen et al, 1976)

Pfeffer (1981) suggests the key distinguishing characteristic of such models is the lack of intention – whether rational, bureaucratic or political in derivation.

Political Models of Decision Making

Finally, political concepts of organisational choice arise out of the pluralistic, coalitional view of organisations associated with March (1962) and Cyert and March (1963). Such approaches are characterised by: the lack of control devices that enforce a coherent and unified set of goals and definition of technology; conflict existing between interests, sub-units and sub-cultures in the organisation; action resulting from bargaining and compromise; and when preferences conflict the distribution of power determining the outcome of the decison process.

Pfeffer concludes of the distinguishing characteristics of political models that:

Power models can be distinguished from rational models if it can be demonstrated that either no overarching organizational goal exists or even if such a goal does exist, decisions are made which are inconsistent with maximizing the attainment of the goal. Power can be distinguished from chance or organized anarchy models by demonstrating that actors in organizations have preferences and intentions which are consistent across decision issues and which they attempt to have implemented. (Pfeffer, 1981)

We proceed to a fuller analysis of the nature of power and politics in the next chapters.

Implications for Understanding Organisational Decision Making

Pfeffer's interpretation of the paradigm discussed above is that it may not be necessary to choose between the analytical frameworks, but that one might attempt to apply any or all of the models to a given situation. In fact, others suggest that the different models may typify certain organisations, at least for given periods of time – e.g. in one study Butler et al (1977) distinguished between 'paralytic' and 'politicking' organisations.

Equally, the concept of contingencies associated with the use of power and politics (see pp. *199 - 214* below) suggests that if political models do not typify an entire organisation, they may be valid in certain areas of it, at certain times, and (of particular note here) they may be particularly valid for certain types of decision.

Implications for Understanding Marketing Budgeting

The intention here is to argue that (at least some) marketing resource allocation decisions are capable of valid analysis using the political model of decision making.

Accepting the caveat that power and politics do not by any means explain all that happens in organisations, then equally the same is true of the rational and bureaucratic theories - they do not alone provide a complete, let alone universal, explanation of behaviour in organisations.

For example, if the contents of Chapters 2 and 3 on marketing budgeting methods are compared with the models of organisational decision making discussed above, then various suggestions are possible. Most of the budgeting methods in Chapter 2 share the assumptions and pre-conditions of rational decision making models. This would seem true of economic analysis, management science models, marketing research and experimentation, and programme budgeting. Other forms of budgeting which are prescribed - sequential and objective and task methods - or which are described - common decision rules and process models - conform to the conditions of bureaucratic decision making models. It is only through re-working the available data, as in Chapter 3, that it becomes apparent that there are also observable political elements in marketing budgeting methods and processes, which have received little explicit recognition in the marketing literature.

The working hypothesis is that the insight into marketing budgeting offered by rational and bureaucratic models is limited and progress is possible by a political analysis, to which we turn in Chapter 9.

STRUCTURE AND INFORMATION IN MARKETING

The first use made of the conceptual framework described above - and the departure that it represents from the received marketing paradigm - was to reconsider the question of organisational design (OD) in marketing (Piercy, 1985).

The key theoretical sources of that latter approach to OD in marketing (Piercy, 1985) took as a starting point the March and Simon (1958) challenge to classical theories, leading to the Cyert and March (1963) behavioural theory of the firm and a focus on uncertainty coping as a behavioural phenomenon. The progression was then to consider information processing models of organisations (Galbraith, 1973; Tushman and Nadler, 1978) with their sources in the concept of uncertainty coping (Lawrence and Lorsch, 1967; Thompson, 1967; Duncan, 1972), and the identification of organisational information processing strategies (Galbraith, 1972; 1973) which involve both structural (information processing capacity) and information systems change. This leads to the measurement of information processing burdens from the environment and the information processing capacities of alternative structures as keys to OD.

The conclusion advanced in Piercy (1985) was that we could proceed from these theories, together with certain fragments of the marketing literature, to an analysis of the information/structure characteristics of the marketing organisation, firstly, in a contingency view of marketing organisation, but secondly, in viewing these organisational dimensions as determinants of decisional outcomes.

A Contingency View of Marketing Organisation

The Boundary Spanning Role. The marketing department has frequently been conceived as filling a critical boundary role, linking the firm to its channels of distribution and to its markets (e.g. Guirdham, 1979). The implications of filling such a role are various (e.g. Aldrich and Herker, 1977), but of particular importance here are the facts that: boundary-spanning activities are centred on coping with uncertainty, and interpreting for the inner parts of the organisation the pool of information which is the environment; thus, boundary-spanning emphasises information processing, but also information control (Pettigrew, 1973) and the absorption of critical uncertainties to allow the organisation's core to make decisions and plan under conditions of 'pseudo-certainty'; by implication, the boundary-spanning role is potentially a powerful one, if the information controlled and the uncertainties absorbed are critical to the organisation; and the boundary-spanning role provides a critical link between environmental characteristics and organisational structure (Aldrich and Herker, 1977).

In fact, Jemison (1984) has reviewed the limited literature on the boundary-spanning role in organisations, suggesting that this role gains influence in organisations through coping with dominant environmental contingencies to create dependencies for other parts of the organisation. The activities associated with this role were: (a) information acquisition and control; (b) domain determination and interface; and (c) physical input control, where the relative importance of those activities in gaining influence is determined by the technology of the organisation. Jemison's (1984) empirical work found that some 60% of the variance in influence in strategic decision was associated with boundary-spanning activity. He concluded that:

> Departments that are responsible for dealing with the environment are more influential in strategic decision making. Thus, the key to gaining and maintaining intraorganizational power seems to be in dealing with the environment. (Jemison, 1981)

In related work Dollinger (1984) has attempted to link the fulfilment of boundary-spanning roles, as information processing functions, with financial success. Boulton et al (1982) studied the strategic planner as a boundary spanner 'gatekeeping' between environmental uncertainty and internal decision making. In fact, little explicit attention has been given to this concept on the marketing literature, although Guirdham (1979) has attempted to use the paradigm to study sales activities and recently Lysonski (1985) has approached product management in this way.

On this basis we proceed as follows: to consider the development of a contingency view of marketing organisation, derived from concepts of environmental characteristics; and then to develop in the next chapter a more explicit consideration of the power of the marketing department.

Information Processing and Marketing Organisation. The general point is that the concept of information processing links marketing structures to the environment, and thus to marketing decision making. On the one hand, this suggests implicitly that the identification, definition, and allocation of 'marketing' tasks is central to structural choice - in the sense that the information processing burden in a limited-function marketing unit is necessarily smaller than that in a fully integrated marketing department, but that that choice of tasks may vary between organisations. It has been pointed out, for example, in the context of the potential information exchange with the environment:

> This potential is, however, never completely realised. The degree to which it is realised depends on the organizational design of the marketing function (notice, not the marketing department, which in many situations only performs a part of the marketing function). The organizational design is of central importance as it determines the structure of information and social exchange between the seller and its customer. (Hakansson et al, 1979)

This, in turn, may be expressed in terms of differences in

departmental power - to which we return in the next chapter.

However, to pursue the information processing/structure relationship, the starting point is with the suggestion that the problem in traditional approaches to studying the marketing organisation, which rely on charting formal positions and relationships, is that they ignore the real information processing functions and informal interactions between people.

For example, one unusual recognition of this structure/ information relationship in marketing theory, is Deshpande's (1982) study of the impact of the structure of the marketing organisation on the use of marketing research information.

More appositely, Nonaka and Nicosia (1979) have partially constructed an information processing view of the marketing organisation, which draws on the concepts discussed earlier, developed by organisational theorists like Lawrence and Lorsch (1967), Thompson (1967) and Duncan (1972). Their view is generated from the proposition that:

> the organization of a firm is designed for the purpose of processing environmental information ... Accordingly, we propose to look at the <u>environment as a generator</u> of information and at the <u>marketing department as a processor</u> of environmental information. (Nonaka and Nicosia, 1979)

They suggest that the environment (essentially markets) has two dimensions: certainty/uncertainty and homogeneity/heterogeneity. These dimensions may be conceived, and indeed measured, in informational terms, where: <u>certainty/ uncertainty</u> relates to the quality of information in terms of its reliability and time-span, and <u>homogeneity/heterogeneity</u> relates to the quantity of information indicated by the number of information sources and the amount of data generated by each source.

In these terms, high uncertainty exists where marketing information is low in reliability and short in time-span, and environmental heterogeneity exists where the quantity of information is high - there are many sources producing a high volume of information.

Nonaka and Nicosia (1979) concluded that the optimal design of the marketing organisation was that which matched the variety of the environment conceived in terms of uncertainty and heterogeneity.

It is evident from this argument that one major issue emerging is the nature of the links between environment - and particularly differentiation in environments - and marketing organisation structure.

A Contingency Model. Contingency theories in the field of organisational theory have some parallels in marketing analysis (Jerman and Anderson, 1978; Piercy, 1978). Indeed, the literature of marketing has implicitly recognised the contingency concept in various statements such as:

> Marketing organization structure is everywhere shaped by a host of unique factors, such as company objectives, management's philosophy of organization, management's view of marketing, the importance of different marketing tools, the types and numbers of products, and the character of competition. (Kotler, 1972)

In fact, a contingency concept of organisation is implicit in the Hakansson et al (1979) and Nonaka and Nicosia (1979) work discussed below, and is explicit in Weitz and Anderson (1981) and a recent conceptual paper by Ruekert et al (1985) (which was produced independently and concurrently with the author's own contingency analysis of the marketing organisation (Piercy, 1985)).

Building upon such views, we may discuss the main areas of contingency, or variability between the situations in which companies find themselves : firstly, as environmental and informational in character; secondly, as corporate and managerial differentiation; and, thirdly, as reflecting marketing strategy differences.

Environment and Marketing Organisation - At the general level, concern has been expressed recently about the impact of a hostile environment on the operation and organisation of marketing. At a slightly more analytical level, however, it has been noted that:

> Observation of the marketing activities of firms producing a wide range of products makes it clear that certain policies and organisational structures have been developed in response to the type of market structure. (Blois, 1978)

Similarly, Corey and Star (1971) suggested that it is the segmentation of markets which provides the primary source of internal differentiation:

> Organization design begins with the market. Businesses are structured to carry out strategies in the markets they serve. It follows that as market conditions evolve, as strategies are reshaped, and as customer groups change in character, organization structure must change accordingly. (Corey and Star, 1971)

In line with the 'strategy and structure' thesis, Corey and Star suggested that the central problem in structuring around the product-market is that of balancing, on the one hand, pressures to group markets together (to gain economies of scale in such activities as advertising, selling and logistics) to form an entity with market integrity, and on the other hand, the problems of market diversity, since if markets grouped together are diverse, the company is likely to be less responsive to customers and opportunities.

The prescriptive force of the Corey and Star work has been pursued elsewhere, in the context of the situational determinants of marketing structure (Piercy, 1985), but for the present we may focus on the question of how environmental variety is manifested.   In the Galbraithian terms outlined earlier (pp. *118 - 121*), if we are to view structures as information processing capacities (and to measure those capacities), then we must take the environment as an informational burden, and thus consider its informational characteristics.

Weitz and Anderson (1981) suggest that the environment may be analysed in terms of: its complexity, the interconnectedness of key elements, and its predictability, the following way.

Environmental complexity - refers to the number of elements in the environment which are relevant to the organisation, such as the number of product-markets served. Structural complexity may be related to environmental complexity:

> Organizations dealing with noncomplex environments have one advantage: there are fewer critically important information categories necessary for decision making. (Jurkovich, 1974)

Environmental interconnectedness - is concerned with the interdependence of key elements of the environment where an example of high interconnectedness is the commercial aircraft market in which there are few customers, each of whose purchase decisions affect each other (Weitz and Anderson, 1981).

Environmental predictability - relates to the degree to which variation in the environment is stable or unstable, thus increasing or decreasing uncertainty.   Again, predictability varies directly with the availability and quality of information.

Weitz and Anderson (1981) have proposed a model of marketing structuring which relates these dimensions of the environment directly to marketing organisation, with implications both for the internal structuring of the marketing function, its differentiation horizontally from other functions and the consequent needs for integration.

However, a more explicitly informational analysis of this issue is provided by the works of Hakansson and Ostberg (1975) and Nonaka and Nicosia (1979).

First, Hakannson and Ostberg (1975) used the Aston concepts to relate the organisation of marketing to different environments, where the environment was analysed in terms of uncertainty (arising from complexity, unpredictability, and so on) and also in terms of varying levels of social exchange required. The concept of social exchange refers to the level of buyer-seller interaction imposed by different market types. These writers hypothesised three situations: with a standardised product and low uncertainty, there would be no need for social exchange; with a more complicated product and higher uncertainty from the exchange process and market heterogeneity, there would be a higher need for social exchange; while with a complex product and high uncertainty, there would be a high need for social exchange.

Hakansson and Ostberg distinguish between uncertainty and social exchange, but these are interrelated and are linked by the concept of information processing:

> The need for information processing is ... related to the degree of uncertainty in the situation, that is the need for information processing is highly correlated with the need for social exchange. There are, subsequently good reasons to believe that an organization structure facilitating social exchange also will make information processing easier. (Hakansson and Ostberg, 1975)

In fact, it is possible to go somewhat further and to see the demand for social exchange as an aspect of uncertainty facing the marketing organisation - that aspect involving efforts to recognise demands and to create informational responses - and that in these terms social exchange and uncertainty are dual aspects of the environment defining the total information processing burden faced.

Hakansson and Ostberg propose three organisational forms of marketing, in the following way, distinguished by uncertainty and social exchange, and using Pugh's structural variables as summarised in Figure 4.1. **The communication-oriented marketing organisation** occurs with a complex product and thus a high need for social exchange and an extensive power-dependence relationship between buyer and seller, and marketing has to be organised to facilitate contacts in many dimensions - managers, technical specialists, selling, and so on - so the marketing function cannot be localised in a single department. Since uncertainty arises from dynamic changes in the environment, specialisation within marketing is difficult since generalists are more effective than specialists, and there is a need for active communication between all persons involved. Environmental change makes standardisation and formalisation difficult and promotes decentralisation. **The activity-**

oriented marketing organisation occurs with a complex product and a heterogeneous but static market, the seller supplements standard market offerings, making a specialised marketing department effective. This separate function operates to standard rules to cope with its limited interdependence with other departments. The marketing task may be divided and specialists used, and this clear-cut division of work makes standardisation and formalisation effective. Highly standardised internal communications and extensive control systems, together with specialised decision making provides a tendency to centralisation. **The non-existent marketing organisation** is associated with a low level of uncertainty, and limited market contacts (and thus little social exchange) - if the product is, for example, simply put 'on the market', there is no marketing organisation or structure. In these circumstances, standardisation is high in dealing with the market, as is centralisation of authority to general management, but there is, by definition, no marketing specialisation or

Figure 4.1: Uncertainty and the Structural Variables of the Marketing Organisations

	High Uncertainty	Limited Uncertainty	Low Uncertainty
Specialisation - the division of labour	Moderate	High	Low
Standardisation - the existance of procedures	Moderate	High	High
Formalisation - the writing down of rules, procedures, etc.	Moderate	High	Low
Centralisation - the locus of authority for decisions	Low	Moderate	High
Configuration —the 'shape' e.g. length of chain of command	High	Moderate	Low
	↓	↓	↓
	Communication oriented marketing organisation	Activity - oriented marketing organisation	Non existent marketing organisation

Source: Adapted by the Author from Hakansson and Ostberg (1975)

formalisation.

While much is arguably speculative in this thesis, examples of all three types of marketing departmentation are described in the research findings here (pp. *332-341*), and certainly the approach demonstrates the power of the information processing concept in linking environment type to the structuring of marketing, and indeed the form or existence (or otherwise) of a marketing department.

This perspective is of direct relevance to the case developed that marketing departments vary in their power and responsibility, for a variety of reasons. For instance, if the Hakansson and Ostberg (1975) model were pursued to its logical extreme, it might be argued that it is only in situations of limited uncertainty that marketing departments gain formal power - in high uncertainty, power and responsibility is distributed more generally, while in low uncertainty there may be little or no formal marketing power. This is not to say, however, that the communication-oriented marketing organisation may not be politically effective and potent in influencing decisions, but that this is not obviously achieved through formal authority.

Indeed, this point may be pursued in the sense that the power of the marketing department may be more explicitly linked to its success and effectiveness in processing information and thus absorbing uncertainty. It has been pointed out that market or environmental uncertainty may well be absorbed by other departments or outside agencies:

> So far all marketing activities concerned with processing market information have been assumed to be grouped within the so-called marketing department. But, in reality, the problem is to allocate, in some optimal fashion, groups of such marketing activities within and across firms. Thus, the optimization of the design of a marketing department depends on the optimal allocation throughout the firm - and even throughout the marketing channel - of all marketing activities concerned with processing market information. (Nonaka and Nicosia, 1979)

The challenge posed by inter-departmental 'competition to control' uncertainty absorption (Piercy, 1979), and the growing power of the marketing channel enhanced by new information technology (Piercy, 1984b) providing a critical area of 'environmental resource dependence' (Pfeffer and Salancik, 1978), are additional complications to the environmental information processing and structure relationship.

A somewhat different formulation, though comparable to Hakansson et al (1979), again based on a contingency analysis (Ruekhart et al, 1985), but grounded solely in the US rather than European literatures, suggests four 'archetypal' marketing structures – the bureaucratic, the organic, the transactional and the relationship – differing in the structural characteristics of centralisation, formalisation and specialisation, but also introducing the distinction between internally organised activities and those involving transactions with the environment (e.g. contract purchase of market research) and relations with the environment (e.g. a contract with an advertising agency).

A last point worthy of note on this present issue relates to the difference between the managerial or organisational perception of the environment, and the reality of that environment, as embodied in Weick's (1969) concept of enactment. Nonaka and Nicosia (1979) make the point that it is managers' perceptions of environmental characteristics which affect decisions, including those on structure, suggesting the complication that marketers may both create market heterogeneity and uncertainty through product differentiation and aggressive market segmentation, but also may act to reduce uncertainty through choices of marketing methods and structures.

Earlier, drawing on case study research, the main point to be made was summarised: 'a firm can only modify its organisation in relation to the marketing situation in so far as it knows and understands the situation' (Tookey and McDougall, 1969). This point underlines the importance of the information function in a prescriptive sense, and confirms the implicit significance of the information processing concept, but also leads us towards the addition of managerial and marketing factors to our contingency view of marketing organisation.

Management and Marketing Organisation. We have already discussed the thesis that strategy determines structure suggesting that, at least in adopting a prescriptive viewpoint, there is a degree of managerial discretion or choice in making structural decisions, even though that choice is itself based on environmental perceptions and thus the informational characteristics of existing structures, as well as such unknowns as managerial attitudes, philosophy, style, and so on. At its simplest, there may be little or no formal marketing organisation in a company simply because managers choose not to have one.

One way of making this discretion explicit has been provided by Baligh and Burton (1976; 1979) in advocating that organisations make a choice of the appropriate degree of implementation of the marketing concept, suggesting that there is no one 'best' level of marketing orientation for all organisations. Actually this view assumes that 'marketing orientation' does have structural implications, which is not necessarily the case, but if it is given that there may be such structural implications of the marketing concept, it is argued that its implementation is far from being costless, and further that using market-based criteria for all decisions is not appropriate to all firms. They conclude:

> An organization should strike a balance between the marketing concept and other organizational considerations, in particular its structure. The basic notion is quite simple – the implementation of the marketing concept is costly – both in fact and opportunity – and not all organizations require the same environmental awareness to survive and prosper. (Baligh and Burton, 1979)

In this sense, the existence of managerial differentiation should be seen as a further contingency shaping marketing organisational design to implement chosen strategies, and more situationally as representing managerial attitudes, philosophy and preferences.

Marketing Factors and Marketing Organisation. While still linked to the environment faced, and the managerial perception of it, we should also recognise that the marketing strategy and thus the marketing programme to be implemented, is directly a determinant of marketing organisation structure, in defining the tasks to be carried out and external relations to be managed. It has been noted that:

> In marketing, optimum size is a function of the size and geographic scope of the served market, the relative concentration of customers, their information and service needs, and the nature of the distribution systems (wholesale and retail) needed to reach them. (Corey and Star, 1971)

Indeed, the ignored significance of the impact of market structure has been recognised elsewhere:

> the literature on both consumer and industrial marketing fails to take account of the impact of observable features of the structure of modern markets on marketing activities. (Blois, 1978)

This would suggest that the choice of marketing methods (e.g. a reliance on personal selling compared to media advertising) and the level of marketing investment should be recognised as determinants of marketing organisational structure, as should the relationships developed with outside organisations.

At its simplest, the specific marketing tasks designated will determine the resources required both in type and amount, and thus the administrative arrangements required. In fact, this relationship is not necessarily obvious, since, for example, as marketing expenditures grow, their control may well pass outside the marketing department, leading to the paradox that marketing departments may have less authority and power as the marketing resource allocation increases (see pp. 23-24 above).

On the other hand, dependence on certain areas of the environment – for example, key retailers – may change the structural forms used, as in the emergence of trade marketing departments, and reduce the discretion and authority of the marketing department.

While closely related to the environment and to the exercise of managerial discretion, we should recognise marketing factors as part of our contingency view of marketing organisation.

The Implications of Structure, Information and Process for Marketing Resource Allocation

The diversity of structures used in practice suggests the lack of universal remedies to marketing organisational needs and problems, and the value of a contingency view of marketing organisation.

Such a contingency view rests initially on the relationship between the environment (here taken primarily as a creator of information processing burdens from market heterogeneity and uncertainty) and the implied need for information processing capacity in structure.

This form of analysis offers both some prediction of variations in the type of marketing department to be found and explanations of those variations, including the existence or not of a specialised marketing department of whatever type, and its structural form. Thus, analysis of the environment in terms of the information processing concept (and what it implies for uncertainty absorption and organisational power) would seem to be at the heart of the question of organisational analysis and design for marketing.

To the environmental contingency may be added two other general factors: the existence of managerial choice or discretion, and by implication the formal, explicit definition of the marketing task facing the organisation.

The argument above was originally constructed in pursuit of such a theory of organisational design for marketing (Piercy, 1985), but its implications for decision making in marketing are numerous.

The argument is that the key variable of the control of marketing resource allocation process (of the type described in the last chapter) will be determined, at least partly, by the structural arrangements for marketing and their implications for information processing and control. Secondly, it is suggested that the actual resource outcomes may also thus reflect structure and information processing capacity, at least under certain contingencies, through the impact of the latter on process. While it may be perceived as contentious, such a thesis is supportable from the material presented and developed in the following chapter, though clearly testable only empirically.

Perhaps the outstanding implication of this argument - both in its description of signs of marketing transition and in the comparison implied between the underlying assumptions of marketing theories and in the insights obtainable from other literatures - is that we should expect the power of the marketing sub-unit to differ between organisations, to reflect internal questions of the stage of the marketing life cycle reached and the political outcome of conflicts between different functional interests, as well as the external issues of channel and marketplace demands and pressures on the marketing interest in the company. If such differences exist they should be measurable and to some extent explainable in the terms discussed. Further though, if those differences are measurable, then so too should be their effects and consequences.

In particular, in seeking conceptual and secondary empirical support for this thesis two central concepts are pursued in the next two chapters. The structure of the marketing sub-unit - its departmentation, location, responsibilities, internal division, and so on - is pursued as an indication of the organisational power of that sub-unit derived from environmental dependencies of various kinds. At the same time that structure represents an information processing capacity, demonstrating the link to the second key concept of information. Information is pursued as a determinant of power of the non-formal type and as a major resource relevant to understanding political behaviour undertaken to influence decisions such as resource allocation. These variables are explored in detail in the next chapters, prior to being integrated in the information-structure-power model of marketing, and being brought to bear in the empirical work reported in Part III.

CONCLUSIONS

Following the statement of the direction and orientation of this present analysis outlined in Chapter 1, and the review of our area of research interest in Part II - marketing resource allocation and budgeting - this chapter sought to justify that direction and orientation by uncovering the implicit organisational dimensions of marketing.

First, the concept of the 'corporate environment' for marketing management was introduced as an influence on the outcomes of marketing decisions, which is demonstrably both significant and yet largely ignored by the marketing literature. Over and above the intrinsic importance of the corporate setting in which marketing decisions are made, the argument was underlined by showing that the role and status of corporate marketing remains somewhat ambiguous and nebulous, is variable between organisations, is the subject of contemporary criticism, and is in a process of reappraisal and change - in the light, for example, of new information technology, strategic planning methods, complex matrix organisation structures, and so on. The conclusion advanced is not merely that the organisational dimensions of marketing are worthy of study as decisional influences because of their omission from the literature, but that a focus on the structural and processual aspects of marketing is urgently needed and is potentially far more insightful at the present time than might have been the case in any earlier period.

Second, following this introduction the discussion explored further the relationship between marketing and organisational theories. It was demonstrated that although there have been some analysts who noted the gap in the marketing literature relating to organisational questions, the conceptual and empirical literature continues for the most part to offer little more than the superficial description of structural bases of decentralisation in marketing (although there are certain important exceptions to that conclusion). By and large the use of organisational theories by marketing analysts has been restricted to the application of the 'principles' of the classical, administrative school, with some limited recognition of humans relations concepts. Only very recently has any attention been given to the, now quite dated, contingency theories of organisation or to the potentially insightful information processing theories of structure. An explication and modelling of the organisational dimensions of marketing has been provided suggesting that the relationship between information processing, organisational structure, and the environment was a valid analytical framework for studying marketing (Piercy, 1985).

Third, the thrust of this argument was demonstrated further by examining a paradigm of contrasting models of organisational decision making - the rational, the bureaucratic, the decision process or organised anarchy, and the political. Having concluded that no single model offers universal explanation and that it was desirable to apply the different approaches to different situations, it was found that the analysis of the received theories of marketing budgeting reviewed in Chapters 2 and 3 demonstrated primarily the assumptions of rational and bureaucratic decision making, suggesting a further dimension to the lacuna in the established paradigm of marketing decision making and of marketing budgeting in particular.

Fourth, the exploration of the organisational dimensions of marketing was completed by a preliminary consideration of the structure/information relationship in marketing and reviewed a contingency theory of marketing organisation developed in Piercy (1985). The conclusion reached was that a structure (organisational power)/information (power and political behaviour) relationship lay at the heart of the certain decision making processes.

Our underlying hypothesis was then revealed: that, depending on certain contingencies to be made explicit, structure and information processing determine the control of resource allocation processes, and through the control of those processes the actual resource allocation outcomes.

With this preliminary justification completed, attention now turns to the conceptual core of this study: the nature of power and politics, the framework of an information-structure-power model of marketing, and then, in conclusion to this part of the study - a model of the power and politics of marketing budgeting.

REFERENCES

Aldrich, H. and Herker, D. (1977) 'Boundary Spanning Roles and Organization Structure', Academy of Management Review, 2, 217-30

Baligh, H.H. and Burton, R.M. (1979) 'Marketing in Moderation - The Marketing Concept and the Organization's Structure', Long Range Planning, 12 (2), 92-6

Bell, M.L. and Emory, C.W. (1971) 'The Faltering Marketing Concept', Journal of Marketing, 35, 37-42

BIM (1961) A Survey of the Functions of Marketing, Product and Brand Managers, British Institute of Management, London

Blois, K.J. (1978) 'Market Structure and Marketing Policies', European Journal of Marketing, 12 (6), 571-8

Blois, K. (1980) 'Quasi-Integration As A Mechanism for Controlling External Dependencies', Management Decision, (18) 1, 55-63

Boulton, W.R., Lindsay, W.M., Franklin, S.G. and Rue, L.W. (1982) 'Strategic Planning: Determining the Impact of Environmental Characteristics and Uncertainty', Academy of Management Journal, 25 (3), 500-509

Buell, V.P. (1982) Organizing for Marketing/Advertising Success, Association of National Advertisers, New York

Butler, R.J., Hickson, D.J., Wilson, D.C. and Axelson, R. (1977) Organizational Power, Politicking and Paralysis, Working Paper, Organizational Analysis Research Unit, University of Bradford

Cohen, M.D., March, J.G. and Olsen, J.P. (1972) 'A Garbage Can Model of Organizational Choice', Administrative Science Quarterly, 17, 1-25

Cohen, M.D., March, J.G. and Olsen, J.P., (1976) 'People, Problems, Solutions and the Ambiguity of Relevance', in J.G. March and J.P. Olsen (eds.), Ambiguity and Choice in Organizations, Universitetsforlaget, Bergen

Corey, E.R. and Star, S. (1971) Organization Strategy: A Marketing Approach, Harvard University Press, Boston, Mass.

Cunningham, M.T. and Clarke, C.J. (1976) 'The Product Management Function in Marketing', European Journal of Marketing, 9 (2), 129-49

Cyert, R.M. and March, J.G. (1963) A Behavioral Theory of the Firm, Prentice-Hall, Englewood Cliffs, N.J.

Deshpande, R. (1982) 'The Organizational Context of Market Research Use', Journal of Marketing, 46, Fall, 91-101

Dollinger, M.J. (1984) 'Environmental Boundary Spanning and Information Processing Effects on Organizational Performance', Academy of Management Journal, 27 (2) 351-68

Douglas, J. (1967) 'A Comparison of Management Theory Y with the Marketing Concept', in E.J. Kelley and W. Lazar (eds.) Managerial Marketing: Perspectives and Viewpoints, 3rd ed., Irwin, Homewood, Ill.

Doyle, P. (1979) 'Management Structures and Marketing Strategies in UK Industry', European Journal of Marketing, 13 (5), 319-31

Doyle, P. and Saunders, J. (1980) 'The Future of Marketing: Views from Two Ivory Towers', Management Decision, 18 (5), 254-69

Duncan, R. (1972) 'Characteristics of Organizational Environments', Administrative Science Quarterly, 17, 313-27

Galbraith, J.R. (1972) Designing Complex Organizations, Addison-Wesley, Reading, Mass.

Galbraith, J.R. (1973) 'Organization Design: An Information Processing View', in J.W. Lorsch and P.R. Lawrence (eds.) Organization Planning: Cases and Concepts, Irwin, Homewood, Ill.

Guirdham, M. (1979) 'Boundary Spanning and Inter-Organizational Relations: Theory and Marketing Implications', Proceedings: Marketing Education Group Conference

Hakansson, H. and Ostberg, C. (1975) 'Industrial Marketing: An Organizational Problem?', Industrial Marketing Management, 4, 113-23

Hakansson, H., Wootz, B., Andersson, O. and Hangard, P. (1979) 'Industrial Marketing as an Organizational Problem', European Journal of Marketing, 13 (3), 81-93

Haller, T. (1980a) 'An Organization Structure to Help You in the 80s', Marketing Times, 27 (3), 45-6

Haller, T. (1980b) 'Strategic Planning: Key to Corporate Power for Marketing', Marketing Times, 27 (6), 18-24

Hanmer-Lloyd, S. and Kennedy, S. (1981) Setting and Allocating the Marketing Communications Budget: A Review of Current Practice, MCRC Report 25, Cranfield School of Management, Marketing Communications Research Centre, Cranfield, Beds.

Hayes, R.H. and Abernathy, W.J. (1980) 'Managing Our Way to Economic Decline', Harvard Business Review, July/August, 67-77

Hayhurst, R. and Wills, G. (1972) Organizational Design for Marketing Futures, Allen and Unwin, London.

Hooley, G.J., West, C.J. and Lynch, J.E. (1984) Marketing in the UK - A Survey of Current Practice and Performance, Institute of Marketing, Maidenhead

Howard, J.A. (1965) Marketing Theory, Allyn and Bacon, Boston, Mass.

Jemison, D.B. (1981) 'Organizational Versus Environmental Sources of Influence in Strategic Decision Making', Strategic Management Journal, 2, 77-89

Jemison, D.B. (1984) 'The Influence of Boundary Spanning Roles in Strategic Decision Making', Journal of Management Studies, 21 (2), 131-152

Jerman, R.E. and Anderson, R.D. (1978) 'Marketing: A Contingency Approach', Quarterly Review of Marketing, 4 (1), 9-17

John, G. and Martin, J. (1984) 'Effects of Organizational Structure of Marketing Planning on Creditability and Utilization of Plan Output', Journal of Marketing Research, 21, May, 170-83

Kotler, P. (1972) Marketing Management: Analysis, Planning and Control, 2nd ed., Prentice-Hall, Englewood Cliffs, N.J.

Likert, R. (1962) 'New Patterns of Sales Management', in M.R. Warshaw (ed.) Changing Patterns in Marketing Management, University of Michigan, Ann Arbor, Mich.

Lysonski, S. (1985) 'A Boundary Theory Investigation of the Product Manager's Role', Journal of Marketing, 49, Winter, 26-40

McNamara, C.P. (1981) 'Time is Running Out for Executives Still Flirting with the Marketing Concept', Sales and Marketing Management, 16 March, 103-4

March, J.G. (1962) 'The Business Firm As A Political Coalition', Journal of Politics, 24, 662-78

March, J.G. and Simon, H.A. (1958) Organizations, Wiley, New York

Migliore, R.H. and Stevens, R.E. (1980) 'A Marketing View of Management by Objectives', Management Planning, 28 (5), 16-19

Morein, J.A. (19-75) 'Shift from Brand to Product Line Marketing',, Harvard Business Review, September/October, 55-63

Nonaka, I. and Nicosia, F.M. (1979), 'Marketing Management, Its Environment and Information Processing: A Problem of Organizational Design', Journal of Business Research, 7 (4), 277-301

Parasuraman, A. (1981) 'Hang On To The Marketing Concept!', Business Horizons, 224, 38-40

Parasuraman, A. and Deshpande, R. (1984) 'The Cultural Context of Marketing Management', in Proceedings of the American Marketing Association, American Marketing Association, Chicago

Peters, R. and Waterman, R. (1982) In Search of Excellence, Harper and Row, New York

Pettigrew, A. (1973) The Politics of Organizational Decision Making, Tavistock, London

Pfeffer, J. (1981) Power in Organizations, Pitman, Marshfield, Mass.

Pfeffer, J. and Salancik, G.R. (1978) The External Control of Organizations: A Resource Dependence Perspective, Harper and Row, New York

Piercy, N. (1978) Low Cost Marketing Analysis: An Alternative Technology, MCB, Bradford

Piercy, N. (1979) 'Behavioural Constraints on Marketing Information Systems', European Journal of Marketing, 13 (8), 261-70

Piercy, N. (1983) 'Information Processing - The Newest Mix Element' in M.J. Thomas (ed.) Marketing: Bridging the Gap Between Theory and Practice, Proceedings: Marketing Education Group Conference, University of Lancaster

Piercy, N. (1984a) 'The Corporate Environment for Marketing Management and Marketing Budgeting', International Marketing Review, 1 (3), 14-32

Piercy, N. (1984b) The Management Implications of New Information Technology, Croom Helm, Beckenham

Piercy, N. (1985) Marketing Organisation: An Analysis of Information Processing, Power and Politics, Allen and Unwin, London

Piercy, N. and Evans, M. (1983) Managing Marketing Information, Croom Helm, Beckenham

Ruekhart, R.W., Walker, O.C. and Roering, K.J. (1985) 'The Organisation of Marketing Activities: A Contingency Theory of Structure and Performance', Journal of Marketing, 49, Winter, 13-25

Sachs, W.S. and Benson, G. (1980) 'Let's Be Realistic and Junk the Venerable Marketing Concept', Marketing Times, 27 (3), 7-9

Simon, H.A. (1979) 'Rational Decision Making in Business Organizations', American Economic Review, 69, 493-513

Thompson, J.D. (1967) Organizations in Action, McGraw-Hill, New York

Tookey, D.A. and McDougall, C.M.H. (1969) Marketing Organization Structure, Ashridge Management College, Berkhamsted

Tushman, M.L. and Nadler, D.A. (1978) 'Information Processing as an Integrating Concept in Organizational Design', Academy of Management Review, 3 (3), 613-24

Venkatesh, A. and Wilemon, D.L. (1976) 'Interpersonal Influence in Product Management', Journal of Marketing, 40, 33-40

Webster, F.E. (1981) 'Top Management Concerns About Marketing: Issues for the 1980s', Journal of Marketing, 45, Summer, 9-16

Weick, K.R. (1969) The Social Psychology of Organizing, Addison Wesley, Reading, Mass.

Weigand, R.E. (1961) Changes in the Marketing Organization, in Selected Industries, 1950-1959, Unpublished Ph.D Thesis, University of Illinois

Weitz, B. and Anderson, E. (1981) 'Organizing the Marketing Function', in AMA Review of Marketing 1981, American Marketing Association, Chicago

Wensley, R. (1985) 'Strategy As Maintaining a Viable Organizational Entity in a Competitive Market', in H. Thomas and D. Gardner (eds.) Strategic Marketing and Management, Wiley, Chichester

White, J. (1984) 'Corporate Culture and Corporate Success', Management Decision, 22 (4), 14-19

5

Organisational Power

INTRODUCTION

While the existence and significance of organisational power and politics as determinants of decisional outcomes has emerged at a number of points throughout the first four chapters, it is now necessary to make more explicit the meaning and nature of these phenomena, leading to an analysis of their impact on resource allocation in the remaining chapters of Part II.

The main thrust of the argument so far may be summarised as follows. **First**, it was seen in Chapters 2 and 3 that existing studies of marketing budgeting either described in a relatively superficial way what managers claim to be their budgeting methods, or prescribe what should be done, in rational economic terms. Relatively little attention – conceptual or empirical – has been given to the processes of marketing budgeting, and that which has been so dedicated is supportive of the hypothesis that there may be organisational influences on the budgeting process and its outcome, which are frequently covert and implicit.

Second, it was seen in Chapter 3 that a modest reorganisation of the descriptive data of marketing budgeting allows a reasonable fit with the criteria of Wildavsky's (1964) model of the politics of budgetary decision making, while in Chapter 4 it was seen that it is possible to formulate a model of the corporate environment for marketing which makes explicit the nature of the influences on marketing decision makers which are of an organisational source.

Third, at the end of Chapter 3, it was seen that one thesis is that the emergence of the use of power and political behaviour may be inevitable in certain situations – or may simply be implicit in those situations – in the absence of any other way of making practical choices. In Chapter 4 it was seen that one paradigm suggests that theories of organisational decision making may be organised into different schools of thought producing different assumptions about and models of that process. It was seen that the majority of writings on marketing budgeting share the assumptions and conceptual framework of the classic, rational model or the bureaucratic model of decision making. It will be argued shortly that many of the conditions surrounding marketing budgeting – either through the very nature of the area of decision or through the contingencies which may occur – are those which are far more compatible with the political model of decision making than the bureaucratic or rational. It was seen at the end of Chapter 2 that the conceptual leverage provided by models of power and politics has proved useful in analysing other resource allocation processs, in a variety of contexts, and it is suggested that a similar approach may validly be applied to marketing budgeting (this argument is brought to its conclusion in Chapter 9).

While, by implication, the political perspective is only one among a number of distinctive ways of analysing managerial decision making behaviour, and therefore is unlikely to explain all marketing budgeting outcomes in all situations, the working hypothesis here is that it will offer insights into process and outcome not provided by other approaches

Fourth, it was seen that there is evidence that marketing as a formally recognised and organised corporate function would seem to be in a period of transition, and we have discussed elsewhere a life cycle of marketing development and the 'post-marketing concept' firm (Piercy, 1985), suggesting both ambiguity and instability in the corporate position of marketing. We added to this the following arguments: that organisational issues are potentially insightful but largely neglected in studying marketing; that it is possible to link marketing processes to the environment and the company as a boundary-spanning activity – though not necessarily formally organised – by specifying the 'organisational dimensions of marketing'; and that a contingency theory of marketing organisation relates the structural position and form of marketing to the environment, to management policies, and to strategic marketing choices. This provides then a partial justification for studying the power of the marketing sub-unit in an organisation (which power is conceived here primarily in structural terms), and the political activity which emerges (which is taken here as relating primarily to the control of information and of its processing), as a way of analysing marketing decision making.

The procedure in the following chapters is first to pursue a more rigorous definition of power and politics (Chapters 5 and 6), since these terms have been used only in a general sense in the earlier discussion; but also since power and politics are not taken as complete or universal determinants of behaviour, we then examine the contingent conditions surrounding the use of power and politics (Chapter 7). The following chapter provides a re-statement and re-working of the information-structure-power theorem developed in Piercy (1985), as an analytical framework for the study of marketing decision-making. It is then possible (Chapter 9) to turn attention to the available studies of resource allocation which have adopted a political perspective, and specifically to highlight the implications for marketing budgeting. This concludes Part II of the book and clears the way for the empirical approach and data presented in Part III.

THE RECOGNITION OF POWER

It was seen earlier that it is possible to model organisational decision making in alternative paradigms - one of which relies on the concepts of power and politics to explain and predict managerial decision-making behaviour. Indeed, there have been many who have advocated the value of adopting this model, in the right circumstances, for example: to understand the dynamics of sub-unit conflict (Tushman, 1977); to comprehend individual managerial success and to develop young managers' skills (Kotter, 1977); or simply on the grounds of the ubiquity of the phenomena since it may be argued that 'All life is a game of power ... in every organisation there exists a built-in or "house" power game, the rules and rewards of which are established by the management' (Korda, 1975); and it has been noted in a similar way by one analyst that:

> Power struggles, alliance formations, strategic manoeuvering and 'cut-throat' actions may be as endemic to organizational life as are planning, organizing, directing and controlling. (Schein, 1977)

In fact, the literature of organisational behaviour is replete with references to the significance of organisational power - if not to the accompanying facility for political action (Bacharach and Lawler, 1980). For instance, in 1952 one writer considered:

> The executive is a tactician and philosopher ... Power relationships are inherent in every administrative situation. The executive must be fully aware of their necessary implications, and prepared to struggle openly for power and for survival. (Dimoch, 1952)

Similarly, in 1964 Crozier saw power as the 'new central problem in the theory of organization', while another theorist advanced an 'information conception of power'

(Stincombe, 1968). Others have suggested, in the managerial literature, for example, that: 'The competition for power is characteristic of all political structures. And, whatever else they may be, business organizations are political structures' (Zaleznik, 1970), and that 'the effective performance of most managerial jobs requires one to be skilled at the acquisition and use of power' (Kotter, 1977).

On the other hand, it has been noted that such references to power and politics as the last two above are actually comparatively rare in the management literature (Allen et al, 1979; Pfeffer, 1981b). This absence may be explained in various ways: the concepts involved are problematic in definition and measurement – power has been described, for example, as a 'bottomless swamp' (Dahl, 1957) and 'the messiest problem of all' (Perrow, 1970), and some conclude that the concept of power remains 'elusive' (Golding and Jones, 1977); power may explain some outcomes but not all; and the notion is ideologically troublesome for the socialisation of managers, since in management development and even communications 'topics such as power and politics are basically incompatible with the values and ideals being developed' (Pfeffer, 1981b). Indeed, it may simply be managers are 'uncomfortable' in recognising the implications of power and its dynamics (Kotter, 1977), since after all, most would consider rationality to be the managerial ideal – an ideal which is apparently denied by the suggestion that significant decisions are the result of the use of power and political behaviour (although, as will be seen, that denial may not be as clear-cut as it might at first seem). Indeed, in considering the problem of the 'schizophrenia with which such concepts as power and politics have been treated' where these concepts are regarded 'either as pejorative terms or illegitimate as analytical concepts for use in understanding bureaucratic or rational systems of decision making' (Pfeffer, 1981b), it has been noted with somewhat heavy-handed irony that:

> At the time of the Nixon presidency, when rival coalitions within the federal government (for example, the FBI and the CIA) were frequently vying to outmanoeuver each other in a series of tactical initiatives designed to gain control over various domains of organizational power, sociologists were emphasising that the greater the size of the organization, the greater the propensity for the decentralization of authority. (Bacharach and Lawler, 1980)

Further, however, it is also demonstrable that the most effective use of power and politics in organisations is likely to be the most unobtrusive, either in the sense of surrounding processes with secrecy and 'confidentiality', or in the sense of legitimising power into the structure, so that it becomes recognised as, and indeed is, formal, legitimate authority (Pfeffer, 1977). In fact, in the sociological literature of community power it has been suggested that the frame of reference with which one approaches the organisation (and thus the choice of tools of analysis) will determine what power relationships one finds and the form they take (e.g. Bell and Newby, 1971); a point to which we return in Chapter 10 (pp. *289-94*).

Indeed, the following discussion demonstrates that it is just such issues which render complex the task of defining the meaning of power and politics.

Given such problems and barriers, the question as to why this approach should be pursued occurs. One answer to such a question is that:

> although there are many other, more tangible forces out there that affect what organizations do – such as the buying habits of clients, the invention of a new machine, an upturn in the economy – power is a major factor, one that cannot be ignored by anyone interested in understanding how organizations work and end up doing what they do. (Mintzberg, 1983)

In fact the definition and measurement of power remains problematic – demonstrated perhaps most aptly by the variety of contrasting and partly contradictory approaches taken by theorists and the general lack of empiricism (Ryan, 1984) – although it is worth noting that the problem is one troubling academics rather than managers, since the terms power and politics would seem to have some considerable degree of shared meaning in the practical decision making context (Salancik and Pfeffer, 1977; Mintzberg, 1983). The procedure here is to consider how power may be distinguished from influence and authority, and the various identified dimensions of power, before noting later what evidence there is available of the significance of power relationships in marketing decision-making.

DEFINING ORGANISATIONAL POWER

There are those who argue that the search for a definition of power is actually a fruitless exercise – since we should be more concerned with its operation and effect than its definition (Mintzberg, 1983); and because it may be no more than a 'sensitizing concept' (Bacharach and Lawler, 1980). This last argument would seem of some merit in the sense that the primitive concept of power should reveal complexity, integrate and lead to better defined or derived terms, and highlight the <u>forms</u> of the phenomenon (i.e. its basic pattern or configuration) and its <u>content</u> (i.e. aspects specific to a given situation). In particular, it would appear that in an enquiry of this present type the notion of the form of the phenomenon returns us to the question of definition and description, while the notion of content of the construct suggests the need to identify the sources of power in different situations and the characteristics of those situations.

Certainly some indirect support for the Bacharach and Lawler stance is provided by the paradox that while power is apparently readily understood and recognised as simply 'the ability of those who possess power to bring about the outcomes they desire' (Pfeffer and Salancik, 1977), it remains difficult to perceive a shared understanding of the phenomenon in the technical literature.

For example, on the one hand when Salancik and Pfeffer (1977) asked a group of managers directly to rate the 'influence' of their colleagues in their organisation, the majority accepted the concept and it was noted that 'Only one person bothered to ask, "What do you mean by influence?". When told "power", he responded, "Oh", and went on' (Salancik and Pfeffer, 1977) - the power ratings produced being reasonably consistent. Similarly, it has been suggested that 'everybody seems to know what it is except the experts' (Mintzberg, 1983).

On the other hand, there is considerable diversity in the views of power taken by theorists (e.g. Astley and Sachdev, 1984). One illustration of the diversity of theoretical views is provided by disagreement over whether power is context- or decision-specific. For instance, Pfeffer (1981b) claims that power is a characteristic of the relationship between social actors, so that it is context- or situation-specific, but:

> Although power is relationship or context specific, it is not necessarily specifically related to a limited set of decision issues. (Pfeffer, 1981b)

On this point Pfeffer's argument is internally inconsistent since he continues his thesis to suggest that certain contingencies surround the use of power (see pp. *199 - 214* below for a detailed discussion), which implies that if certain types of decision are characteristically associated with those contingencies, then the use of power may well be in that sense decision-specific. More fundamental contrasts emerge in the literature of community power where it is argued that power cannot be separated from the study of particular decisions and that participation in most community decisions is concentrated in the hands of a few, although different, small groups which make decisions on different community problems (Bell and Newby, 1971). Again the implication is that the use of power may characterise certain decisions.

The community power literature throws up another conflict in terms of frame of reference, since it is suggested there that the empirical methods used and particularly the basic questions asked are related to what is subsequently discovered, to the extent that 'in the study of community power the methods may even determine the findings' (Bell and Newby, 1971). The contrast made in supporting the pluralist rather than elitist frame of reference is between asking the question 'who runs this town?', thus implying that someone does, and 'does anyone run this town?'.

A further contrast emerges between those viewing power as a structural phenomenon (e.g. Astley and Sachdev, 1984) and those emphasising the social psychology of interaction. For instance, in the former area it has been asserted that:

> Although individual skills and strategies can certainly affect the amount of power and the effectiveness with which it is used, power is first and foremost a structural phenomenon, and should be understood as such. (Pfeffer, 1981b)

The supporting argument is that the structural nature of power arises from the division of labour and creation of departments in the organisation. (Since this perspective is favoured here, we return to it later (pp. 154-56)). On the other hand, the Bacharach and Lawler (1980) review emphasises power arising from social exchange and dependence between social actors, suggesting that structure is related to authority rather than influence (thus implicitly excluding formal authority as a source or outcome of power and politics). Given that power is embedded in the social relationship, they argue that it should not be treated as an attribute of the person, group or organisation, but that the relationship should be portrayed and understood in terms of dependence. A similar, though more qualified view is that:

> Individuals who control scarce resources and sources of uncertainty assume power over others, despite procedural safeguards intended to minimize such outcomes. This perspective on power is very much social psychological in that it identifies attributes of people - namely their positions and access to resources - but not organizational characteristics that stimulate or attenuate unplanned power relationships. (Meyer, 1978)

Even so, it might be argued that positions and resource-access are at least partly functions of structure, suggesting somewhat less disparity than might at first be perceived.

In fact, Hickson et al (1971) go somewhat further in reconciling the structure/social exchange debate by arguing that while power arises from the division of labour, the underlying reason for this is the imbalances created in interdependence, in the way argued by Thompson (1967).

In the section below an attempt is made to organise a selection of the available theoretical perspectives to highlight the central shared ground and also the conflicting concepts. It should be noted initially, however, that our interest is in power as a sub-unit phenomenon in organisations, rather than as a property of the individual, or as a philosophical construct (Cavanagh, 1984; Kenny and Wilson, 1984).

Concepts of Organisational Power

Taking first the conclusion of two recent reviewers, Bacharach and Lawler (1980) distinguish the forms of power as having relational, dependence, and sanctional aspects. Relational aspects of power - concerned with interactions between groups and individuals - have traditionally been those receiving greatest emphasis, and are found in a number of essentially sociological analyses (e.g. Weber, 1947; Parsons, 1956), taking interaction as the cornerstone and power as structural. Dependence aspects of power, on the other hand, are based on theories of social exchange (Blau, 1964; and others), where power derives in essence from having something upon which others rely, while sanctional aspects of power are concerned with the changes that the actors concerned can and do make in each other's outcomes.

In fact it is possible to pursue these sources further to identify a number of key attributes associated with power.

Influencing or Determining Behaviour. For example, one view is that:

> power is defined as the determination of the behavior of one social unit by another ... By power we mean the ability of a subunit to influence organizational decisions that produce outcomes favored by that subunit. (Hickson et al, 1971)

Within the broad area of behaviour determination, however, there are views which range from the philosophical (e.g. Siu, 1979) to the managerial or possibly manipulative (e.g. Goldhaber et al, 1979). In fact, one dissenting voice is provided by Mintzberg who defines power as 'the capacity to effect (or affect) organizational outcomes', and suggests that behaviour determination is a narrow conception of power, since:

> power as changing someone's behavior is a subset of power as effecting outcomes. Behavior needn't always be changed to get things done, nor must behavior necessarily be changed to have 'power'. (Mintzberg, 1983)

For present purposes, however, the view is taken that in the practical business organizational context with which we are here concerned, the changing of behaviour is effectively synonymous with the influencing of outcomes, since outcomes are viewed implicitly deterministically as the result of managerial action or inaction rather than as naturally occurring phenomena.

Overcoming Resistance or Coercion. It may be argued that implicit in determining behaviour and outcomes is the overcoming of resistance from those preferring other outcomes. Notionally, power could be exercised in the absence of resistance and thus without the need for any form of coercion. For example, Wrong (1968) adopts the classification of potential power, actual power and the potential for power, which supports the view that power may exist separately from its being used. Similarly, the Mintzberg definition above is concerned with a 'capacity' to influence rather than the use of power.

However, the pragmatic view is that if we take power only as a potential - even though we might measure the perception of that potential - rather than something that is used, then we are left with no obvious way of determining what has influenced an outcome. If behaviour takes place which matches the preferences of the powerful actor, without political actions being taken, then the outcome might as easily be determined by chance or coincidence as represent compliance with the wishes of the powerful actor. It might be argued that the empiricist's problem of detecting the capacity for influence, as compared to actual influence, is just that, and does not alter the fact of the existence of that capacity. Indeed, it may be that the existence of the capacity to influence itself amounts in some instances to determining outcomes through power - the status or reputation for being powerful may alone induce the less powerful to behave in ways they believe conform with the wishes of the powerful.

It should be noted that in the Pfeffer (1981b) model of contingencies for the use of power, in the absence of opposition there is no need for the use of power. Similarly, Hedberg et al (1975) adopt the stance that power can only be studied in situations of actual conflict.

Indeed, there is some support for this view of power as

overcoming resistance in many conceptual works. For example, it is implicit in the classic definition: 'A has power over B to the extent that he can get B to do something he would not otherwise do' (Dahl, 1957). Certainly, coercion features with varying degrees of explicitness in the definitions of power provided by others. Perhaps most prominent is Weber:

> Power is the probability that one actor in a social relationship will be in a position to carry out his will, despite resistance, and regardless of the basis on which this probability exists. (Weber, 1947)

Similarly, Bierstedt (1950) saw the incidence of power taking place only in the case of social opposition, a view echoed by Emerson (1962) and Blau (1964). These views, particularly latter, suggest that overcoming resistance is linked to dependence and resource control.

Resource Dependence. It is argued that the ability to influence outcomes and to control resources is linked to the dependence of the influenced on the influencer (Emerson, 1962; Blau, 1964; Thibaut and Kelley, 1975). For example, one view is that:

> power structures rest primarily not on social consensus ... but on the distribution of resources by means of which compliance with demands can be enforced. (Pettigrew, 1973)

The Pettigrew argument is that dependency results from an imbalance in exchange, to the advantage in power of one side and the disadvantage of the other. Implicit in the notion that resources confer power is the ability to control or monopolise the allocation of a resource, as well as the need or demand for the resource among those over whom power is presumed to be held. In this sense it is necessary to conceive of resources in a broad fashion – including, for instance, money, promotion, status, legitimacy, and so on.

However, of particular importance here is the inclusion of information as a key resource. Perhaps the clearest demonstration of this theme is provided by Pettigrew's (1973) study of an innovation decision process, where a 'technical gatekeeper' effectively shaped a major corporate computer purchase decision and directed it towards his preferred supplier by blocking 'unfavourable' information and feeding 'favourable' information to decision makers. Of central importance was the fact that the structural position of the gatekeeper was one of the factors allowing this use of information as a power resource.

An earlier writer, though taking a different view to

Pettigrew on social consensus, concluded of the lower participants in organisations that 'Within organizations one makes others dependent on him by controlling access to information, persons and instrumentalities' (Mechanic, 1962), while others take the similar view power should be conceived as 'influence associated with the capability of an individual's or a group's comparative advantage for providing information, materials, or other services to support other individuals' or groups' tasks' (Bariff and Galbraith, 1978).

This is, however, straying from the question of what power is, to that of how it is gained – a point we consider later (pp. *153-67*).

In this way, a review of some of the prominent authorities' views on defining power suggests that definition is problematic, but that we should recognise elements of: determination of the behaviour of others and outcomes of various kinds; coercion or overcoming resistance; and the exploitation of dependence and resource control. This leaves untouched what difference there may be between the commonly used terms of authority and influence, and power.

POWER, AUTHORITY AND INFLUENCE

Power and Influence

Turning first to the distinction between power and influence, on the one hand there are those who see relatively little difference between the two terms, and effectively equate power with influence over the behaviour of others (e.g. Dahl, 1957; Bacharach and Lawler, 1980). Mintzberg (1983) argues, for instance that while power is frequently taken to mean potential while influence is actual enactment, this distinction is of relatively little use, and he takes the terms as synonymous. Support for this comes from Kanter (1977) and McCall (1979). Others make a distinction based on relative strength rather than type, in taking power as coercion while influence is persuasion (Bierstedt, 1950), or in defining influence as the ability to restructure an opponent's perceptions, compared to power which is the capacity to restructure a situation (Macmillan, 1978).

For our present purposes there would seem little to gain in pursuing this distinction, and the term 'influence' is avoided, as far as possible, as ambiguous.

Power and Authority

There is seemingly a clearer and more fruitful debate on the difference between power and authority. At the simplest level, authority may be taken to be sanctioned jurisdiction over certain issues or resources, which is formally dispersed through the organisation by decentralisation around various bases. In this sense, delegated authority is what has been recognised as the legitimate power in an organisation to make certain decisions or to control certain resources (French and Raven, 1968). Support is provided by Hickson et al (1971) who took the view that 'authority will here be regarded as that part of power which is legitimate or normatively expected by some selection of role definers. Authority may be either more or less than power'. Similarly, Mintzberg (1983) takes authority as a subset of power, being that subset which relates to 'formal power, the power vested in office, the capacity to get things done by virtue of the position held'.

A slightly more complex view is provided by Hickson et al (1981) who contrasted perspectives on power as relating either to technique (the means to coordinate and reach organisational ends) and domination (the means for individuals and groups to pursue their own ends), and concluded:

> bureaucratic organization required some degree of obediance as an end in itself; obediance is due to a superior, not only because of his rational knowledge, but also because of the office he occupies. Authority, as a form of power, therefore takes on political connotations over and above its technical raison d'etre ... In this way power as technique supports power as domination, with ideologies of efficiency buttressing, disguising or justifying organizational inequality. (Hickson et al, 1981)

This suggests that authority is a structural aspect or source of power denoting both the formal and informal, and both sanctioned and unsanctioned uses.

Two further points must also be made. **First**, it is clear at the simplest level that there are sources of power other than the legitimate authority delegated to individuals and departments. For example, the simple French and Raven (1968) paradigm cited above recognises in addition to legitimate power or authority: reward power - based on the perceived ability to dispense real or symbolic values to others; coercive power - based on the perceived ability to dispense punishments; expert power - based on being perceived to have special knowledge or expertise; and referent power - based on personal attraction, friendship, and so on. As implied by Hickson et al (1981), to some extent these bases of power, possibly excluding the last, overlap with the delegation of formal authority - in the ability to control rewards and sanctions or being the expert in a field - but may go further. For instance, consider the proposition that 'lower participants', such as secretaries, junior management and the like, exercise power far removed from their structural location (Mechanic, 1962). While it is suggested, perhaps rather optimistically, that such personnel may rarely resist their supervisors' instructions (Pfeffer, 1981b), even if they do not they would appear to be able to shape at least some outcomes in significant ways.

Second, it may be that the appropriate perspective is to see formal authority as itself an outcome of political struggles, in the sense that authority is power which has become legitimated and accepted, following the development of social understanding and consensus within the organisation. If so, then it may be noted:

> Rather than seeing the exercise of influence within organizations as contests of strength or force, power, once it is transformed through legitimation into authority, is not resisted. At that point it no longer depends on the resources or determinants that may have produced the power in the first place. (Pfeffer, 1981b)

In fact, authority may well be resisted and there is ample evidence that it is (indeed in Pfeffer's own earlier work, e.g. Pfeffer (1978), and in his later points in the 1981 volume cited above concerning the unobtrusiveness of power use - reflecting perhaps the contrast between power and politics to be uncovered below, and the continuing struggle for the legitimation of their power among organisational sub-units).

In pursuit of this authority/power distinction, Pettigrew (1973), while also seeing authority as legitimated power, makes the point that there are conceptual problems related to the formal structure of power and legitimacy, particularly from the point of view of determining: the point at which people question the legitimacy of authority; the process of attaining and sustaining legitimacy; and simply the difficulty of knowing what is legitimate. This perhaps leads us back to the Pfeffer point that legitimation is itself a political activity and outcome reflecting power differences, but this is a point which is of some significance to the empirical study reported here, and it is discussed further later (pp. 287-88).

A somewhat different view is provided by Bacharach and Lawler (1980) - bearing in mind their case, discussed above, that power in their schema is derived from social exchange not structure - who take the content of the primitive term power as having two aspects: authority and influence. Their thesis is that it is authority that has a structural source (and relies for effect on coercion, renumeration, symbols and knowledge), while influence is drawn from personality, expertise and opportunity (and relies mainly on manipulating symbols and knowledge). In fact, this view merges power and politics in their concept of influence. Other objections to their model include the fact that Bacharach and Lawler appear to ignore the existence of social or other controls over the use of influence, in just the same way that led Crozier to criticise Dalton (1959) for being:

> so haunted by the fear of being misled by the formal structure and formal definitions of roles that, in his analysis of the ways managers really behave, he reports only irregularities, back-door deals and subtle blackmail ... No organization could survive if it were run solely by individual and clique back-door deals. (Crozier, 1964)

Implicitly they ignore the interaction of formal and informal power highlighted above by Hickson et al (1981) or, indeed, the fact that the use of influence may be sanctioned by the organisation (e.g. as shown in Cunningham and Clarke (1975) and discussed in Pfeffer (1981b)). It is also the case that 'influence' may be of a structural source – since structure defines at least one type of relationship and thus opportunity for the development and use of influence.

However, the conclusion of the Bacharach and Lawler work is of some interest, since they suggest that it is the influence (i.e. non-formal power) network rather than the authority structure which provides the best methodological framework for analysis:

> the study of authority to make decisions in organizations may be based solely on positional criteria, such as those revealed in organization charts, eliminating the need to examine interaction processes. By contrast, influence is the more elusive aspect of organizational power. Influence relationships do not always coincide with the authority structure; one may be independent of the other ... To identify the sources of influence, the links among key coalitions or interest groups, become critical. (Bacharach and Lawler, 1980)

In their main conclusion therefore – that to understand organisational outcomes it is necessary to look beyond the formal organisational structure – Bacharach and Lawler's work wouldseem to conform with the general thrust of the thesis developing here.

Thus far that thesis is that the definition of power remains problematic and the theoretical contributions display some divergence. None the less it is possible to identify common ground in understanding power as involving the determination of others' behaviour and outcomes, with some possibility of the overcoming resistance of those others by coercion, based on resource-dependence of one kind or another. Some divergence exists too in distinguishing power from 'influence' and from 'authority'. In the latter case it would seem reasonable to take authority as formally delegated power as opposed to other aspects of power, though there are some dangers in interpreting this distinction too strictly.

With these concepts of what power 'is' uncovered, attention turns to the sources and bases of power.

SOURCES AND BASES OF ORGANISATIONAL POWER

Much of what can be said here is either implied or stated explicitly in the earlier discussion, thus permitting some greater succinctness. We consider first some of the general views on the bases and sources of power and then focus on the strategic contingencies' theory and informational power. This latter focus is justified in two ways: firstly, it will be argued that the theories selected for detailed attention subsume and integrate many of the other statements which are available; secondly, it is information-resource dependence concepts of power which are chosen in this study as the most relevant to the study of marketing – the reasons for this choice will be explicated shortly.

Perhaps the classic statement of the bases of power is provided by the French and Raven (1959) model, cited earlier, which distinguishes coercive, reward, expertise, legitimate and referent power, to which was later added information power (Raven, 1974), and which may be compared to Etzioni's (1961) view of three forms of power: coercive, remunerative and normative (controlling symbolic rewards). However, the analytical limitation of these models is that they are concerned with the question of <u>how</u> power is enacted or used. While this question is important (see pp. *194 - 199* below for its relevance to marketing), it is not the question now addressed, which is where power comes from, and how it is sustained. It is this latter question, in particular, which is important if we are to analyse how the marketing sub-unit achieves a given level of power, how it sustains it, and how it may influence decisional outcomes through power. In fact, there are a number of ways of dealing with this question, which are now outlined. The major areas of note are: structural aspects of power; the role of uncertainty coping and dependency; resource (particularly informational resource) factors; and the environment. While these areas are separated for discussion it is inevitably true that they are highly interrelated so that separation is arbitrary, requiring therefore some effort at integration. This is provided in two areas: the strategic contingencies' theory as a general statement at this present stage, and the information-structure-power model of marketing organisation considered later (pp. *230-236*).

Organisational Structure As A Source of Power

As noted earlier, Bacharach and Lawler (1980) hold that organisational structure is the source of formal authority rather than influence or power, although it may be that this is simply to consider two aspects of power rather than anything more contentious. Certainly, it has long been accepted that formal status may not equate with real power. For example, it was noted earlier that 'it is not unusual for lower participants in complex organizations to assume and wield considerable power and influence not associated with their formally defined positions within these organisations' (Mechanic, 1962).

However equally, even though it is accepted that structure defines delegated authority or formal power, it would seem invalid not to accept too that structure may play a part in creating other types of power (Astley and Sachdev, 1984). The Hickson et al (1981) argument, cited earlier (pp. *150-51*), suggests that power as technique (coordination to achieve organisational goals), and thus structure, supports power as domination (or influence exerted for group/individual goals) or influence beyond that formally designated. Indeed, it has been suggested that formal structures may even be inconsistent with the technical demands of the work activities that they appear to enhance (Meyer and Rowan, 1977) and that:

> Though these structures are often rationalized as serving technical purposes they are also in some degree myths representing social purposes and interests which have gained an institutionalized status. (Hickson et al, 1981)

A simpler statement of this position is that:

> organizational structures create formal power and authority by designating certain persons to do certain tasks and make certain decisions and create informal power through the effect on information and communication structures within the organization. (Pfeffer, 1978)

In fact, it is widely recognised that power (at least formal, sanctioned power) arises from functional or task specialisation and the creation of interdependent sub-units. The supporting argument is that the division of labour creates technical economies and works to overcome the restrictions of bounded rationality and limited information processing capacity, but at the same time creates power differences which reflect the differing importance of the specialised tasks undertaken. Pfeffer (1981b) considers power is thus essentially a structural phenomenon, but he concludes :

> power is at once structurally determined but also is more than structurally determined; power is affected by the capacity of organizational participants to enhance their bases of power and to convince others in the organization of their necessity and value. (Pfeffer, 1981b)

The implication of such analyses is that structures are not simply a given, rationally-determined factor which determines formal power, since not only does structure appear to determine other elements of power, but also structure itself may be a political outcome, representing the struggle for power by members of the organization and the perpetuation of power through institutionalisation. On the last point it has been claimed, for example, that :

> Shifts in the control over information systems, shifts in control over resources, and the gaining and losing of discretion may be observed structural consequences of changes in the distribution of influence within organizations ... For it is the case that structure is at once both an outcome of the influence distribution and a determinant of power within the organization. (Pfeffer, 1978)

The implication of Pfeffer's view, which is pursued here, is that 'The explanation and analysis of organization structure will be enhanced if we consider not only the efficiency, performance and managerial aspects of structure, but the politics of organizational structures as well' (Pfeffer, 1978).

In fact, there seems some justice in the claim (e.g. Meyer, 1978; Pfeffer, 1978) that relatively little is known empirically of the interaction between power and structure. Certainly it has been shown that structural position is fundamental to mobilising power, with the 'gatekeeper' gaining strategic advantage from his structural location (Pettigrew, 1973), and other pieces of work suggest the potential insight which may be gained from studying this relationship. For instance, the matrix structure has been associated with changing power relationships (Corey and Star, 1971; Galbraith, 1973), with a 'pathology' of power struggles (Davis and Lawrence, 1978), and has been argued to be consistent with the political model of organisational decision making (Pfeffer, 1981b). Another relevant strand of theory is concerned with the power implications of the boundary role in the organisation which provides 'boundary impedance' (Allen, 1966) and strategic advantage to a 'gatekeeper' (Pettigrew, 1973) with the opportunity to act as a 'influence agent' (Spekman, 1979), and which links environmental characteristics to structure (Aldrich and Herker, 1977).

More generally the empirical work here attempts to explore the structure-power relationship in marketing, as a starting point in evaluating the influence on outcomes of that sub-unit.

Uncertainty Coping and Organisational Power

Perhaps the widest recent recognition has been to the claim that power in organisations is derived from the process of coping with uncertainty. (In fact, it will be seen that this process may be related in several ways to the structural issues discussed above - structural location provides the opportunity to cope with particular sources of uncertainty; structure represents information processing capacities and limitations; and so on). This perspective may be traced to the Carnegie work (particularly Cyert and March (1963)) and has been modified by others like Crozier (1964) who saw the distribution of power in organisations as being related to the absorption of critical uncertainties, and Thompson who advanced the proposition:

> The more sources of uncertainty for the organization, the larger the number of political positions in the organization, and the more dynamic the technology and the task environment, the more rapid the political processes. (Thompson, 1967)

More recently, Hickson et al (1971) and Hinings et al (1974) formulated and tested the well-known strategic contingencies' theory of intraorganisational power, which provides the main focus in this section.

The 'strategic contingencies theory of intra-organizational power' (Hickson et al, 1971; Hinings et al, 1974) proposed that the power of an organisational sub-unit would depend on its ability to cope with uncertainty - in the light of the ability of others to cope equally with that uncertainty, and the importance of that uncertainty to the organisation. The initial premise was that uncertainty lay at the centre of organisational power, but that:

> Uncertainty itself does not give power: coping gives power ... coping may be by prevention, for example a subunit prevents sales fluctuations by securing firm orders; or by information, for example, a subunit forecasts sales fluctuations; or by absorption, for example, a drop in sales is swiftly countered by novel

> selling methods ... By coping a subunit provides pseudo
> certainty for the other subunits by controlling what are
> otherwise contingencies for other activities. This
> coping confers power through the dependencies created.
> (Hickson <u>et al</u>, 1971)

Thus, uncertainty coping or absorption is quite explicitly a
form of interdependence creation, but at the same time one
which is potentially limited by the surrounding factors of
competition to cope with particular contingencies, and how
critical particular areas of uncertainty are to the
organisation:

> intraorganizational dependency can be associated with
> two contingency variables: (1) the degree to which a
> subunit copes with uncertainty for other subunits, and
> (2) the extent to which a subunit's coping activities
> are substitutable ... a third variable, centrality,
> refers to the varying degree to which the activities of
> a subunit are linked with those of other subunits.
> (Hickson <u>et al</u>, 1971)

The strategic contingencies' model is summarised in Figure
5.1, which demonstrates the argument that power through
uncertainty absorption is directly related to the uncertainty
of the inputs and the sub-unit's effectiveness in coping,
leading to the control of contingencies which are 'strategic'
because they are central to the organisation's work. Power
through this uncertainty coping is less to the extent that:
routinisation is high - coping involves no special expertise,
and substitutability is high - i.e. others can cope just as
well. This leads to a definition of the sub-unit's power,
in Kaplan's (1964) terms of: weight - the degree to which B
affects the probability of A behaving in a certain way;
domain - the number of people whose behaviour is so
determined; and scope - the range of behaviours of such
people which are so determined.
    We should expand briefly on a number of the points in
this theorem. First, Pfeffer (1977) notes a number of
processes involved in gaining power through uncertainty
absorption, which recognise the competitive element mentioned
earlier. These processes are: (a) being irreplaceable in
coping with a source of uncertainty, in the sense that:

> If uncertainty coping brings power only to the extent
> that such coping cannot be easily replaced, then to
> acquire power subunits will want to attempt to insure
> that their expertise cannot readily be acquired outside
> their boundaries. This may be done by destroying
> sources of information relevant to how the job is done
> ... developing specialized language and terminology

which inhibits the understanding of the job by outsiders, and by restricting the distribution of knowledge concerning how the task is accomplished (Pfeffer, 1977);

Figure 5.1: The Strategic Contingencies' Theory of Intraorganisational Power

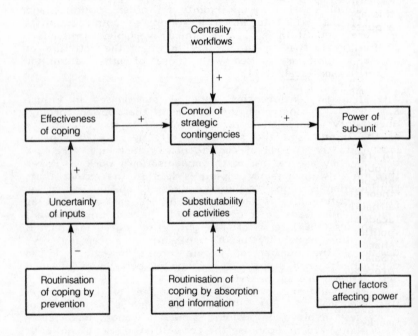

Source: Adapted by the Author from Hickson <u>et al</u> (1971)

158

(b) the subunit failing in its tasks, at least periodically, since 'one strategy to increase power is occasionally to cause problems which the subunit can then handle' (Pfeffer, 1977); (c) defining existing or new organisational problems as being within the subunit's particular expertise; (d) forming coalitions with those responsible for creating external contingencies, e.g. between industrial relations managers and union officials, or perhaps between sales managers and large buyers; and (e) controlling important resources and forming alliances to aid in coping with uncertainty.

This list is of some interest in suggesting that the ability to gain power through uncertainty absorption is itself a political process, with the location of uncertainty absorption a political outcome, representing the result of a struggle for jursidiction. For example, Pfeffer argues that what is most critical to an organisation is a dependent variable which is open to social contest within the organisations:

> the critical organizational uncertainties are defined by the organization. Indeed, it is the ability to institutionalize power and define critical resources and contingencies that leads to the fact that influence structures are typically more stable than the environments in which the organizations exist. (Pfeffer, 1978)

In the same way it is suggestive of the Pfeffer and Salancik (1978) agreement that the environment, through defining critical contingencies, acts to influence the distribution of intraorganisational power – an effect limited, though, by internal social contests and organisational actions to intervene in the environment. Finally, to the degree to which structure defines resource control, and areas of responsibility and jurisdiction, then it defines one dimension of the distribution of uncertainty absorption, and thus of power:

> Out of exchanges and the interdependencies created by them, emerge differences in power among organizational participants; its structure is thus to be interpreted in terms of domination rather than in terms of technical prescription. (Hickson, et al, 1981)

In this sense the strategic contingencies' theory is compatible with, and to some extent integrates, other theories of power.

Indeed, the structural and political interactional aspects of the theory were made partially explicit by Hinings et al (1974) who suggested that gaining power involved either the fortuitous allocation to a sub-unit of activities with high importance, or the sub-unit's own initiative in entering areas of high uncertainty. This last work tested the strategic contingencies' theory and reached the important, though qualified, conclusion that:

> Coping with uncertainty is the variable most critical to power, and it is the best single predictor of it, but it is far from being the only factor contributing to power. (Hinings et al, 1974)

The strategic contingencies' theorem is pursued later as the most relevant analytical framework in the empirical work, and its methodological aspects are discussed in Chapter 10.

Power-Dependence Theories

The concept of dependence is recognised in both the structural and strategic contingencies' perspectives. In the former, structure creates interdependencies of various types (Thompson, 1967). In the latter case the concept of centrality refers to the degree to which a sub-unit is an interdependent component of an organisational system, the elements of centrality being isolated by Hinings et al (1974) as: first, workflow pervasiveness – the degree to which the workflows of a sub-unit connect with the workflows of other sub-units; and second, workflow immediacy – the speed and severity with which the workflows of a sub-unit affect the final outputs of the organisation. These theorists noted in their original formulation that:

> The concept of work organizations as interdepartmental systems leads to a strategic contingencies theory explaining differential subunit power by dependence on contingencies ensuing from varying combinations of coping with uncertainty, substitutability and centrality. (Hickson, et al, 1971)

In fact, dependence is central to most concepts of power, simply because 'Power derives from having something that someone else wants or needs, and being in control of the performance or resource so that there are few alternative sources' (Pfeffer, 1981b).

Such dependency may involve: expertise and information (e.g. Crozier, 1964; Pettigrew, 1973); financial resources (e.g. Pfeffer, 1981b); sanctions (e.g. Bacharach and Lawler, 1980); or the absorption through some resource of uncertainty, where 'power resides implicitly in the others' dependence' (Emerson, 1962). It is claimed by Bacharach and Lawler that dependence theory provides the optimal framework for analysing power, based on their proposition that power is a function of dependence, where that dependence is based on the availability of alternative outcome sources and the value placed on the outcomes at stake, and conclude that: 'A power struggle is activated by attempts to alter the dependence relationship' (Bacharach and Lawler, 1980).

Accepting the reservation that dependence (or perhaps more strictly measurable dependence) may not alone be enough to predict power levels (Pfeffer and Salancik, 1978), the general proposition that dependency is a source of power seems unassailable, and almost self-evidently true. However, in attempting to operationalise dependency, interest has tended to centre more on specific, more easily measured, variables. Pfeffer (1981b) notes that empirical studies of dependency fall into two categories: first, examinations of resource provision between units; and second, the ability of sub-units to cope with critical uncertainties. In other words it would seem that dependence is conceived either in terms of resources or of uncertainty, and that these may be variants of each other (Pondy, 1977).

Resource Perspectives on Power

The concept of resources as a power source has emerged in the earlier points, but two further general points should be made, since the issue of resources lie at the centre of this present study. First, it is necessary to consider power from providing resources, and second, power from having resources. The related issue of using power to obtain resources is explored further as an aspect of the use or application of power (pp. 241 - 255), although it is inevitable that this issue should overlap with the question of resources as a power source.

On the first question - gaining power from providing resources - it has been noted that in relation to the organisation's environment 'the ability to obtain resources appears to be an important determinant of subunit power within a social structure' (Pfeffer and Salancik, 1978). This is directly comparable with the strategic contingencies controlled in the earlier model. Pfeffer (1981b) restates the claim that the sub-units providing the most critical or difficult to obtain resources come to have power in the organisation, where those resources are taken to include: money, prestige, legitimacy, reward and sanctions, expertise, and the ability to cope with uncertainty.

The second question is concerned with power through holding or controlling resources. In studying resource allocation it has been suggested that 'the allocation decisions themselves have consequences for the relative influence in the organization of the various groups and subunits' (Pfeffer, 1977). This argument has two sides. On the one hand, resource allocation decisions have symbolic value and reinforce the prestige and position of those who do well in the allocation process:

> Social power, after all, is not a physical reality. Uncertainty may exist in the organization as to the exact influence positions of various subunits and participants. Allocation decisions provide a reality by which power can be assessed. (Pfeffer, 1977)

It should be recognised, at the same time however, that gaining resources may be a symbolic rather than substantive outcome - a distinction developed by Pfeffer (1981a) - in the sense that the resources controlled may be non-strategic or their apparent 'ownership' may be illusory, and in such circumstances resource gains do not directly reflect power.

On the other hand, holding or controlling important resources, itself confers more power to be used in later activities. More recently, Pfeffer has formalised this argument in a model of the self-perpetuation of organisational power, where extra budget resources, additional personnel, information, and so on, can be used to provide more power in the future. This model is summarised in Figure 5.2, and it was hypothesised that in the business firm:

> If power is accrued to those units that best cope with the organization's critical problems, then once in power, these units can use their influence to ensure that they will remain with this uncertainty coping capacity. (Pfeffer, 1981b)

Information as a Power Source

It follows directly from the points above that information may be an important power source (Kenny and Wilson, 1984) - in structural interdependencies, in coping with uncertainty, and particularly in thus acting as an organisational resource: 'Information is, of course, one kind of resource, so the two perspectives on power acquisition are complementary rather than in conflict' (Pfeffer, 1977). This is of particular importance since it is argued that marketing is above all an informational function (pp. *118-30*).

The antecedents of the notion that information may act as a power source have already been cited, including March and Simon (1958), Simon (1962), Cyert and March (1963 and also Stinchcombe's (1968) 'information conception of power', where a decision unit's power is taken as the amount of information added. Wilensky (1967) noted that 'information is a resource that symbolizes status, enhances authority and shapes careers', and broadly similar conclusions are advanced

Figure 5.2:   Resources and Power

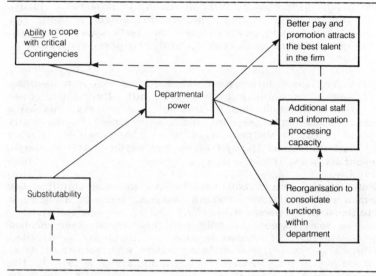

Source: Pfeffer (1981b)

by others (e.g. Hedberg et al 1979;   Bariff and Galbraith, 1978;   Pfeffer and Salancik, 1978;   Goldhaber et al, 1979; and Wildavsky, 1984).

Two aspects of information as a power source emerge: first, the simple possession and control of information;   and second, the manipulation or distortion of the information itself.

The power gained from holding and controlling access to information has been widely noted, for example in Mechanics' (1962) lower participants study.   Similarly, in the Crozier (1964)   study   maintenance   engineers   retained   power   by preventing others gaining knowledge about machine repair. Perhaps the now-classic example is the Pettigrew (1973) study of a complex purchase in a large organization, where the control of information by one manager was able to influence the decision in his favoured direction through the control of information - where that control was found to be a critical resource in mobilising power.   Pettigrew's 'gatekeeper' was in a position where:

> with control over information flow in the decision process, he was able to focus attention successfully on

>his demands, and at the same time, to hinder others from gathering support for theirs. (Pettigrew, 1973)

Comparable findings have been reported by others (e.g. Mintzberg, 1979; Piercy, 1979; Spekman, 1979; Markus, 1980).

This said, of course, information control alone is not adequate to explain power – the same tests apply as to the strategic contingencies' model – and Pettigrew concluded in his study that:

>Control over information was a critical resource used by Kenny for mobilizing power ... but this control over the information flow in the decision process, his more extensive role set, and his easier access to the locus of power in Michaels have to be considered in relation to how he was thought of by key members of the board. (Pettigrew, 1973)

Thus, information control was the key to understanding the politics of this decision making process, but operating in a broader social framework.

To some extent controlling information of itself implies the distortion of communication – through selectivity, withholding access, overwhelming others with volume of data, and so on – but further than manipulating access is the second aspect of informational power – manipulating the form and content of information.

Again, this is a well-documented phenomenon, and Wilensky 1967 observed that 'in reporting at every level, hierarchy is conducive to concealment and mis-representations', while Lynton (1969) considered that bargaining in organisations was likely to include: 'careful rationing of information and its deliberate distortion; rigid, formal, circumscribed relations; and suspicion, hostility and dissociation'. Similarly, Walton (1965) had noted the phenomena of minimum information disclosure, manipulation, defensiveness and distrust.

In the behavioural theory of the firm model, Cyert and March (1963) recognised the problem of information biasing, but expected it to be met effectively by counter-biasing. In fact, the conditions imposed by Cyert and March in their experiments place some doubt on the general validity of their expectation of effective counter-biasing, and others have quite different findings (e.g. Lowe and Shaw, 1968; Pettigrew, 1973; Cunningham and Clarke, 1975). Certainly, Allen et al, (1979) considered of the available political strategies and tactics that those of withholding or distorting information were the most dysfunctional.

For reasons which will be developed shortly (pp. *222 - 230*) the use of information as a power resource is taken as a prime vehicle for analysis, on the grounds that the marketing function is largely information-based.

Environmental Power Sources

Environmental influences should also be recognised, both in their own right and also as determinants of the allocation and location of intraorganisational power. It has been noted for instance that:

> The dynamics of the organization emerge primarily out of the flux and flow of internal politics and power struggles. But external influences have much more to do with who gains power and why. (Moore, 1965)

Similarly, it is suggested in Pfeffer and Salancik's resource-dependence perspective on the external control of organisations that:

> There is some evidence that the power of internal subunits varies with their relationship to critical environmental problems ... Since organizational decisions are based, at least partly, on subunit influence ... one might suggest that organizational environments come to affect organizational actions partly by affecting the distribution of power and influence inside the organization. (Pfeffer and Salancik, 1978)

However, in several ways this is no more than the counterpart to what has already been discussed - it may be that the critical uncertainties faced are (most likely) environmental in source; the formal structuring of interdependencies reflects the segmentation of the environment, and so on. One formal statement of this relationship is provided by Mintzberg (1983) who distinguishes between the internal coalition consisting of six sources of influence - the chief executive officer, operators, line managers, analysts of the technostructure, support staff, and the organisational ideology - and the external coalition, consisting of the owners; associates, such as suppliers and competitors; employee associations, like unions; and the organisation's publics, including general groups, special interest groups, and government. In the Mintzberg formulation, the particular configuration of power in an organisation depends on the relationship between the internal and external coalitions. In a similar way, Butler et al, (1977) worked from the premises that: a unit's potential for power is determined by its environmental setting, and by the 'rules of the game', to suggest empirically that externality of power produced a 'paralytical' organisation, while internality of power produced a 'politicking' organisation.

Other Sources of Power

While the discussion above has outlined the major groupings of theories about the sources of power in organisations, there are a number of less extensively developed points which should be regarded at least as caveats. These include situational or historical factors, personal or individual attributes, and symbols of power.

For instance, in their concluding remarks on the strategic contingencies' theory, Hickson et al (1971) recognised that factors other than uncertainty absorption influenced power, giving as examples such factors as: interdepartmental relationships of competition or collaboration; and the personal links of some individuals with top management. Another source observed that:

> A unit's influence has its roots partly in its strategic importance to the company and partly in nonfunctional circumstances such as tradition, or control over someone in top management, through, for example, family relationships. (Stymne, 1968)

Another view emphasises consensus as a source of power (Pfeffer, 1981b), particularly as it is represented by the level of paradigm development of different groups (Lodahl and Gordon, 1972). In other words the internal cohesion of a group - expressed in common perspective, values, and situational definition - provides a source of relative power over others. For instance, recently attention has focused on the role of language in this process (Moch and Huff, 1980).

Recognition must also be given to individual political skills which are associated with the successful use of power (Allen et al, 1979; Korda, 1975). For example, Pettigrew (1973) noted in his study that among other things the successful use of power depends upon tactical skills. Pfeffer (1981b) draws attention to the individual's position in a communication structure, and the power base provided by being in a 'strong' sub-unit, but also to personal characteristics in using power, in terms of appearance, verbal skills, articulateness, the ability to diagnose power situations, and understanding the 'rules of the game', although 'This knowledge is, to some extent cynical knowledge ... and, therefore, is not likely to be freely dispersed' (Pfeffer, 1981b).

Related to this is the assessed stature of the individual and the political access gained by the individual, as explanatory variables (Pettigrew, 1973).

Lastly, there is the issue of <u>symbols</u> of power - such as office 'territory', resources, privileges, and the like, as signs and thus as reinforcement of power (Korda, 1975).

IMPLICATIONS

To review what has been uncovered about organisational power, it will be recalled that the starting point was to make the contrasts between the ubiquity of power and its relative neglect in the management literature; and between the general shared meaning of the term but the problems in technical definition. While variations in perspective were found, there would seem some consensus that a definition of power should account for: one actor infulencing the behaviour of another and thus organisational outcomes of various kinds; the use of coercion or overcoming resistance to some degree; and resource-dependence as the key to determining the existence of power. Power was distinguished from authority - broadly conceived as the formally delegated, sanctioned aspect of power, though this distinction is far from clear-cut - and similarly the term 'influence' was to some extent distinguished, although in this latter case the distinction appeared less fruitful and was not pursued.

The review turned then from the question of what power is, to where it comes from, i.e. the bases and sources of power. The traditional paradigm of power bases describes types of power, but does not facilitate analysis of its sources. We turned therefore to consider separately the issues of: <u>organisational structure</u> as a source of power - both formal authority but also in terms of 'domination', status, information control, and so on - though recognising structure to be both a source and an outcome of power; <u>uncertainty coping</u> as a source of power, particularly as this was formulated in the 'strategic contingencies' theory of intraorganizational power'; <u>dependence</u> as a source of power, arising from differentiation and the structural division of labour, the location of uncertainty absorption, and other resource control; <u>resources</u> as a source of power, where those resources may be tangible or intangible; <u>information</u> as a power source, in the sense that information is one type of critical resource in organisations, which is subject to control and manipulation; the <u>environment</u> as a power source, or at least arbiter through creating uncertainties, influencing structure, and so on; and <u>situational</u> factors of various kinds. While these areas were assessed separately it emerged quite clearly that they were interrelated.

The major implications which are to be pursued in this study are: that structure lies at the centre of analysing power differences between sub-units; that the location of uncertainty absorption to cope with strategic contingencies will provide insight into the enactment and reinforcement of these power differences; and that among the resources important to creating such dependencies, information is one of the most significant. These implications will be pursued in the following chapters.

However, the immediate question to be studied is that of the nature of the related topic of organisational politics.

REFERENCES

Aldrich, H. and Herker, D. (1977) 'Boundary Spanning Roles and Organization Structure', Academy of Management Review, 2, 217-30

Allen, R.W., Madison, D.L., Porter, L.W., Renwick, P.A. and Mayes, B.T. (1979) 'Organizational Politics – Tactics and Characteristics of its Actors', California Management Review, 22 (1), 77-84

Astley, W.G. and Sachdev, P.S. (1984) 'Structural Sources of Intraorganizational Power: A Theoretical Synthesis', Academy of Management Review, 9 (1), 104-113

Bacharach, S.B. and Lawler, E.J. (1980) Power and Politics in Organizations, Jossey-Bass, San Francisco

Bariff, M.L. and Galbraith, J.R. (1978) 'Intraorganizational Power Considerations for Designing Information Systems', Accounting, Organizations and Society, 3, 15-27

Bell, C. and Newby, H. (1971) Community Studies, Allen and Unwin, London

Bierstedt, R. (1950) 'An Analysis of Social Power', American Sociological Review, 15, 730-8

Blau, P.M. (1964) Exchange and Power in Social Life, Wiley, New York

Butler, R.J., Hickson, D.J., Wilson, D.E. and Axelson, R. (1977) 'Organizational Power, Politicking and Paralysis', Organization and Administrative Sciences, Winter, 45-59

Cavanagh, M. (1984) 'Theories of Power', in A. Kakabadse and C. Parker (eds.) Power, Politics and Organization: A Behavioural Science View, Wiley, Chichester

Corey, E.R. and Star, S. (1971) Organization Strategy: A Marketing Approach, Harvard University, Boston, Mass.

Crozier, M. (1964) The Bureaucratic Phenomenon, Tavistock, London

Cunningham, M.T. and Clarke, C.J. (1975) 'The Product Management Function in Marketing', European Journal of Marketing, 9 (2), 129-49

Cyert, R.M. and March, J.G. (1963) A Behavioral Theory of The Firm, Prentice-Hall, Englewood Cliffs, N.J.

Cyert, R.M., Simon, H..A. and Trow, D.B. (1956) 'Observation of a Business Decision', Journal of Business, 29, 237-48

Dahl, R.A. (1957) 'The Concept of Power', Behavioral Scientist, 2, 201-15

Dalton, M. (1959) Men Who Manage, Wiley, New York

Davis, S. and Lawrence, P. (1978) 'Problems of Matrix Organizations', Harvard Business Review, May/June, 131-42

Dimock, (1952) 'Expanding Jurisdiction: A Case Study in Bureaucratic Conflict' in R.K. Merton et al (eds.) Reader in Bureaucracy, Free Press, Glencoe, Ill.

Emerson, R.M. (1962) 'Power-Dependence Relationships', American Sociological Review, 27, 31-41

Etzioni, A. (1961) A Comparative Analysis of Complex Organizations, Free Press, New York

French, J.R.P. and Raven, B.H. (1959) 'The Bases of Social Power', in D. Cartwright (ed.) Studies in Social Power, University of Michigan Press, Ann Arbor

French, J.R.P. and Raven, B.H. (1968) 'The Bases of Social Power', in D. Cartwright and A. Zander (eds.) Group Dynamics, (3rd ed.), Harper and Row, New York

Galbraith, J.R. (1973) Designing Complex Organizations, Addison-Wesley, Reading, Mass.

Golding, D. and Jones, D. (1977) Power and Control, MCB Management Bibliographies and Reviews, Bradford

Goldhaber, G.M., Dennis, H.S., Richetto, G.M. and Wiio, O.A. (1979) Information Strategies: New Pathways to Corporate Power, Prentice-Hall, Englewood Cliffs, N.J.

Hedberg, B., Edstroem, A., Mueller, W. and Wilpert, B. (1975) 'The Impact of Computer Technology on Organizational Power Structures', in E. Grochla and N. Szperski (eds.) Information Systems and Organizational Structure, de Gruyter, Berlin

Hickson, D.J., Hinings, C.R. Lee, C.A., Schneck, R.E. and Pennings, J.M. (1971) 'A Strategic Contingencies' Theory of Intraorganizational Power', Administrative Science Quarterly, 16, 216-29

Hickson, D.J., Astley, W.G., Butler, R.J. and Wilson, D.C. (1981) 'Organization As Power', in L.L. Cummings and B.M. Staw, Research in Organizational Behavior, Jai Press, Greenwich, Connecticut

Hinings, C.R., Hickson, D.J., Pennings, J.M. and Schneck, R.E. (1974) 'Structural Conditions of Intraorganizational Power', Administrative Science Quarterly, 19, 22-44

Kaplan, A. (1964) 'Power in Perspective', in R.L. Kahn and K.E. Boulding (eds.) Power and Conflict in Organizations, Tavistock, London

Kanter, R.M. (1977) Men and Women of the Corporation, Basic, New York

Kenny, G.K. and Wilson, D.C. (1984) 'The Interdepartmental Influence of Managers: Individual and Sub-Unit Perspectives', Journal of Management Studies, 21, 409-425

Korda, M. (1975) 'Power: How to Get It, How to Use It', Random House, New York

Kotter, J.P. (1977) 'Power, Dependence, and Effective Management', Harvard Business Review, May/June, 125-36

Lodahl, J. and Gordon, G. (1972) 'The Structure of Scientific Fields and the Functioning of University Graduate Departments', American Sociological Review, 37, 57-72

Lowe, E.A. and Shaw, R.A. (1968) 'An Analysis of Managerial Biasing: Evidence from a Company's Budgeting Process', Journal of Management Studies, 5 (3), 304-15.

Lynton, R.P. (1969) 'Linking an Innovative Subsystem into the System', Administrative Science Quarterly, 14 (3), 398-416

MacMillan, I.C. (1978) Strategy Formulation: Political Concepts, West, St. Paul

Markus, M.L. (1980) Power, Politics and MIS Implementation, Working Paper 1155-80, Massachusetts Institute of Technology, Cambridge, Mass.

McCall, M.W. (1979) 'Power, Authority and Influence', in S. Kerr (ed.) Organizational Behavior, Grid, Columbus, Ohio

Mechanic, D. (1962) 'Sources of Power of Lower Participants in Complex Organizations', Administrative Science Quarterly, 7, 349-64

Meyer, M.W. (1978) 'Recent Developments in Organization Research and Theory', in M.W. Meyer et al (eds.) Environment and Organizations, Jossey-Bass, San Francisco

Meyer, J.W. and Rowan, B. (1977) 'Institutionalized Organizations: Formal Structure as Myth and Ceremony', American Journal of Sociology, 83, 340-83

Mintzberg, H. (1979) 'Organizational Power and Goals: A Skeletal Theory', in D.E. Schendel and C.W. Hofer (eds.) Strategic Management: A New View of Business Policy, Little Brown, Boston, Mass.

Mintzberg, H. (1983) Power In and Around Organizations, Prentice-Hall, Englewood Cliffs, N.J.

Parsons, T. (1956) 'Suggestions for a Sociological Approach to the Theory of Organizations', Administrative Science Quarterly, 1, 63-85

Perrow, C. (1970) Departmental Power and Perspective in Industrial Firms', in M. Zald (ed.) Power in Organizations, Vanderbilt UP, Nashville, Tenn.

Pettigrew, A.M. (1973) The Politics of Organizational Decision Making, Tavistock, London

Pfeffer, J. (1977) 'Power and Resource Allocation in Organizations', in B.M. Staw and G.R. Salancik (eds.) New Directions in Organizational Behavior, St. Clair Press, Chicago

Pfeffer, J. (1978) 'The Micropolitics of Organizations', in M.W. Meyer et al (eds.) Environment and Organizations, Jossey-Bass, San Francisco

Pfeffer, J. (1981a) 'Management As Symbolic Action: the Creation and Maintenance of Organizational Paradigms', in L.L. Cummings and B.M. Staw (eds.) Research in Organizational Behavior, Jai Press, Greenwich, Conn.

Pfeffer, J. (1981b) Power in Organizations, Pitman, Marshfield, Mass.

Pfeffer, J. and Salancik, G.R. (1978) The External Control of Organizations: A Resource Dependence Perspective, Harper and Row, New York

Piercy, N. (1979) 'Behavioural Constraints on Marketing Information Systems', European Journal of Marketing, 13 (8), 261-70

Piercy, N. (1985) Marketing Organisation: An Analysis of Information Processing, Power and Politics, Allen and Unwin, London

Pondy, L.R. (1964) 'Budgeting and Intergroup Conflict in Organizations', Pittsburgh Business Review, 34, 1-3

Pondy, L.R. (1977) 'The Other Hand Clapping: An Information-Processing Approach to Organizational Power', in T.H. Hammer and S.B. Bacharach (eds.) Reward Systems and Power Distribution, Cornell University, New York

Ryan, M. (1984) 'Theories of Power', in A. Kakabadse and C. Parker (eds.) Power, Politics and Organization: A Behavioural Science View, Wiley, Chichester

Salancik, G.R. and Pfeffer, J. (1977) 'The Bases for Use of Power in Organizational Decision Making', Administrative Science Quarterly, 19, 453-73

Schein, V.E. (1977) 'Individual Power and Political Behavior in Organizations: An Inadequately Explored Reality', Academy of Management Review, 2 (1), 64-72

Simon, H.A. (1962) 'On the Concept of an Organizational Goal', Administrative Science Quarterly, 4, 1-22

Siu, R.G.H. (1979) The Craft of Power, Wiley, New York

Spekman, R.E. (1979) 'Influence and Information: An Exploratory Investigation of the Boundary Role Person's Basis of Power', Academy of Management Journal, 22 (1), 104-17

Stinchcombe, A.L. (1968) Constructing Social Theories, Harcourt Brace, New York

Thibaut, J.W. and Kelley, H.H. (1959) The Social Psychology of Groups, Wiley, New York

Thompson, J.D. (1967) Organizations in Action, McGraw-Hill, New York

Tushman, M.L. (1977) 'A Political Approach to Organizations: A Review and Rationale', Academy of Management Review, 2, 206-16

Walton, R.E. (1965) 'Theory of Conflict in Lateral Organizational Relationships', in P.R. Lawrence (ed.) Operational Research and the Social Sciences, Tavistock, London

Weber, M.L. (1947) Theory of Social and Economic Organization, Free Press, New York

Wildavsky, A. (1964) The Politics of Budgetary Decision Making, Little Brown, Boston

Wildavsky, A. (1984) 'Information as an Organizational Problem', Journal of Management Studies, 20 (1), 29-40

Wilensky, H.L. (1967) Organizational Intelligence, Basic, New York

Zaleznik, A. (1970) 'Power and Politics in Organizational Life', Harvard Business Review, May/June, 47-60

6

Organisational Politics

INTRODUCTION

There has been some tendency in the review above, in effect to equate the terms 'power' and 'politics' in their corporate setting. It may be arguable that this enjoys some validity in practical terms, although it may be demonstrated that there are certain differences in technical meaning which are apparent in the literature.

The recognition of politics in organisations may be traced essentially to the same sources as power – e.g. March (1962), March and Simon (1958), Cyert and March (1963) – and perhaps in a lesser way to analyses like that of Strauss (1962) who considered 'office politics' and 'bureaucratic gamesmanship'.

In fact, the Carnegie theorists have been subjected to some criticism, particularly for not going far enough with the analysis of political behaviour in organisations. For instance, Pettigrew (1973) claimed that March and Simon concentrated too much on the individual, to the neglect of the impact of organisational structure, and suggested that a political analysis:

> leads the argument away from woolly notions of satisficing towards the possibility of explaining choice among alternatives as a product of the strategic mobilisation of power resources. (Pettigrew, 1973)

While Pettigrew applauded the 'political realism' of Cyert and March, he criticised their neglect of such issues as: communications structures, external affiliations, organisational structure, and membership of sub-groups, with the effect that they 'dodge the issue of the potential role that powerful interests are likely to have in the search and choice processes' (Pettigrew, 1973).

Specifically, Pettigrew voices three objections to the 'behavioral theory of the firm': first, that the theory is untestable on an aggregated basis because it is presented in a universal and non-structural form; second, decisions are made not by individuals, but through processes affected by the organisation, thus 'Information failures that characterize "bounded rationality" are rooted in structural problems of hierarchy, specialization and centralization, and do not just reflect the malfunctioning of thought processes'; and third, the determinants of conflict are not explored.

The culmination of Pettigrew's argument, which is of some relevance to this study, is that in order to add to the existing theory it is necessary to explain the relationship between political strategies pursued and decisional outcomes, and that it is necessary to differentiate politics into power and authority.

The first of these points is pursued in the consideration of research problems in Chapter 10, while the second is relevant to the problem of defining organisational politics at this stage, and in fact some exception will be taken to Pettigrew's implied definition of power and politics.

Certainly, it would seem that many recent writers have claimed that politics are widespread and perhaps endemic to organisational decision making, in the sense for example that: 'Organizational actions result from political processes within organizations' (Pfeffer and Salancik, 1978), and that 'It is now accepted that organizational politics exist in every organization and are involved in almost every facet of organizational life' (Cobb and Margulies, 1981). On the other hand, as in the case of organisational power, it has been suggested that the use of political concepts in the management literature is relatively limited (e.g. Allen et al, 1979; Pfeffer, 1981). Some go even further, as far as politics are concerned, and Bacharach and Lawler (1980) suggest that while power has received some attention, it is in effect the underlying patterns of intraorganisational politics which have remained largely unexamined.

DEFINITION AND DESCRIPTION OF ORGANISATIONAL POLITICS

Similar problems in definition exist to those encountered earlier in considering power, and it is necessary again to review a variety of viewpoints. In particular, that review should consider: the relationship between power and politics; the issue of resources; conflict; and the nature of political actions or tactics.

Power and Politics Compared

One view of politics is that it is (at least partly) the process of gaining power:

Organizational politics involves those activities taken

within organizations to acquire, develop, and use power and other resources to obtain one's preferred outcomes in a situation in which there is uncertainty or dissensus about choices. (Pfeffer, 1981)

If one takes the partial premise that politics are aimed at gaining power, then the paradox is clear that the powerful have relatively little need to indulge in politics, because they have power already and by implication at least certain of the things they want are already sanctioned by the organisation.

On the other hand, to the extent that one regards politics as the use of power (thus presumably some power is held by the actor) then political behaviour is restricted to the powerful – those without power have no basis for political behaviour. In fact, this is probably to take too strict a view of the amount of power needed to exert influence on outcomes, and one might well either substitute the term 'influence' for power, or argue that all organisational participants enjoy some potential power and thus ability to indulge in political behaviour.

Actually, these points are rather more than a semantic debate – it is of some importance to consider whether power and politics are complements or substitutes, as will be seen in approaching the empirical study of the phenomena.

In fact, many writers do take politics as the use of power, as for example:

Organizational politics can be taken as the use of power to modify or protect an organization's exchange structure. An exchange structure is composed of an organization's resource distribution system and those who have the formal authority to decide to what purposes resources will be used. (Cobb and Margulies, 1981)

politics in organizations involve the tactical use of power to retain or obtain control of real or symbolic resources. (Bacharach and Lawler, 1980)

Clearly, this returns as to the original problem of deciding exactly what is meant by 'power' – it may be argued, for example, that power may be seen as either an object in its own right, as a conditioner (Johnston, 1978), or indeed both.

One view is that politics is a subset of power, being that subset which is 'informal power, illegitimate in nature' (Mintzberg, 1983), as compared to authority or formal power. Whether or not this view is fully accepted, it highlights the distinction between formal and informal, and by implication the sanctioned or legitimate and the unsanctioned and illegitimate. For instance, Mayes and Allen proposed the definition:

> Organizational politics is the management of influence
> to obtain ends not sanctioned by the organization or to
> obtain sanctioned ends through non-sanctioned influence
> means.   (Mayes and Allen, 1977)

While this view is perhaps even more explicit and revealing
of the practical nature of organisational politics, it should
be noted that there is some circularity of logic, since that
which is 'sanctioned' in the organisation is itself partly
the result of the use of power and political activity – as
noted above the powerful may not need to engage in politics
since what they want is organisationally sanctioned (Pfeffer,
1981).   Similarly, there is some problem in assuming that
that which is 'sanctioned' is necessarily 'right', since this
is to presume that the organisation knows in advance what is
best for it, so the management analyst should perhaps
recognise the 'acceptable' and 'unacceptable' faces of
politics – the former involving 'honest' disagreements over
the best way to achieve organisational goals, and the latter
the pursuit of vested interests which may differ from those
of the organisation.   Indeed, Pfeffer (1981) goes much
further in challenging views like that of Mayes and Allen,
and he takes exception to the implication of 'sinfulness' on
the grounds that what is sanctioned by the organisation is
itself an outcome of power and political activity.

Certainly, it has been suggested by Gandz and Murray
(1980) that in reviewing concepts of politics, we should
distinguish between the following: first, neutral
definitions, where politics is behaviour associated with the
use of power or influence, either in any conflict over scarce
resource allocation, or in any conflict over a policy
decision;   and second, self-serving definitions, where
politics is the pursuit of their own goals by individuals or
groups, which are either self-serving and contrary to
organisational effectiveness, or which involve self-interest
conflicting with the interests of any other member of the
organisation.   In this sense organisational politics involve
'intentional acts of influence to enhance or protect the
self-interest of individuals or groups' (Allen et al, 1979),
suggesting differences between organisational and individual
goals, the existence of some opposition and thus conflict,
and the condition of uncertainty which is denied by the
rational/bureaucratic   model   of   organisational   decision
making.

One related view has it that our concern in studying
politics should be primarily with upward influence attempts:

> while not all (or even most) upward influence involves
> political behaviour, most political behaviour (in

organizations) does involve upward influence. (Porter et al, 1981)

Porter et al contrast this view with the more common focus on downward influence (in leadership studies) and lateral influence (in studies of group dynamics). To some extent this perspective on politics by implication also underlines a distinction between power and politics, or at least between formal power and political influence. We return to the question of unsanctioned behaviour below.

For our present purposes, politics are taken as activities to gain, keep and to use power to influence outcomes, including in those activities, modes of behaviour, and goals which are not formally sanctioned by the organisation (and by implication in some cases not by the powerful).

Resources and Politics

Several of the definitions above pre-empt the argument that resources lie at the centre of analysing politics.

One of the older descriptions of politics is 'who gets what, when and how' (Lasswell, 1936), suggesting implicitly that politics is concerned with gaining resources of one kind or another. While it was seen earlier that some views take the position that politics may involve conflict over any policy decision, others like Harvey and Mills (1970) argue that it is essentially conflict over scarce resources which will be resolved by political proceses - i.e. coalition formation, bargaining and side-payments. In other words, it is claimed that:

> Typically individuals within ... subunits and hierarchical control positions will compete for scarce resources within an organisation. Successful resource acquisition will be highly dependent on political rather than rational-economic decison making. (Bariff and Galbraith, 1978)

Similarly, Pettigrew suggested that:

> Political behaviour is defined as behaviour by individuals or in collective terms of subunits, within an organization, that makes a claim against the resource sharing system of the organization. (Pettigrew, 1973)

Indeed, given scarce resources Pettigrew saw the emergence of politics as inevitable.

However, note that while the resource-claiming, resource-competition concepts of politics are apparently useful in supporting this present study's central thesis, there is some danger in taking too literal a view of 'resources' as they are conceived above. It has already been suggested that power itself is a resource to be competed for, and to this most certainly be added information (Pettigrew, 1973), if not more broadly 'information, persons, and instrumentalities' (Mechanic, 1962), as resources. The point is that resources can be widely defined in this context to include both tangible factors, such as money, facilities, and personnel, but also intangibles, such as information, status, legitimation, and the control of incidentals, for example office space, or indeed almost anything upon which value is placed by the people involved. However, the breadth of such a concept of resources somewhat reduces the value of the concept in isolating the meaning of politics other than as competition for things which people value.

This said, if one determining characteristic of politics is 'the ability of those who possess power to bring about the outcomes they desire' (Salancik and Pfeffer, 1977), and if it is accepted that there has to be something of value at stake, to make the efforts, costs, and risks of political action worthwhile, then resource control and competition may be taken as a significant element in a description of politics, though seemingly not a definitive one.

Conflicts of Preferences and Interests

Added to the notion of competiton for resources is the view that 'the inference is that politics involves how differing preferences are resolved' (Pfeffer, 1981). Indeed, it may be argued that if there were no difference in preferences or goals, there would be no need to use political behaviour to gain resources or any other outcome. Stating this more explicitly, one writer opines:

> Political action takes place when an actor, recognizing that achievement of a goal is influenced by the behavior of other actors in the situation, undertakes action against the others to ensure that its own goals are achieved. (Macmillan, 1978)

In fact, as will be seen later that the problem in demonstrating conflicts of preference and interest is that they are likely to be covert or hidden, because they are frequently not perceived as legitimate in organisational terms.

It was seen earlier that the pursuit of self-interest through political behaviour is central to some views although we made a distinction between what might be called the 'acceptable' and 'unacceptable' faces of politics, where the former might include advocacy of favoured projects or areas of expansion which are believed to facilitate achieving organisational goals, while the latter might include the same advocacy in pursuit of personal financial gain, promotion, and so on. Even so, there may be some coincidence between, for example, personal gain and what is 'good' for the organisation – indeed one might argue that the politically able and successful may be those best-suited to designing the organisation's future. Thus, to conflict with others in the organisation is not the same as to conflict with organisational goals (if the latter exist).

One broad view of politics which is of some interest at this point is:

> organizational political behavior is defined as:
> 1. Social influence attempts,
> 2. that are discretionary (i.e. that are outside the behavioral zone prescribed or prohibited by the formal organization),
> 3. that are intended (designed) to promote or protect the self-interests of individuals and groups (units),
> 4. and that threaten the self-interests of others (individuals, units). (Porter, et al, 1981)

These analysts emphasised both the resource-related and conflictual aspects of politics, and concluded that:

> This puts political behavior squarely in the camp of competitive as opposed to collaborative behaviour, and focusses on the zero-sum aspect of organizational resource allocation. It leads ... to the prediction that the scarcer the resources the higher the level of political activity. (Porter et al, 1981)

Accepting the competitive politics argument, there is, in fact, some room for debate as to the effect of resource scarcity on the propensity towards political behaviour and the perception of its likely success. It might well be, for example, that in times of extreme perceived resource scarcity in an organisation, the criticality of resource allocation causes tighter formal control and intervention, so allocations relate to the power distribution, rather than the influence attempts of political behaviour. We return shortly to this point.

For the moment it is enough to recognise that conflicting preferences and goals are central to the emergence of politics, and to consider this question further as a contingency for that emergence (pp. *200-214* below).

Political Tactics and Actions

While Chapter 7 turns to the process of power and politics in

Table 6.1: The Tactics of Organisational Politics

Tactics	Forms
Blaming or attacking others	Reactive – 'scapegoating' when the actor minimises association with an undesirable situation or result. Proactive – reducing the competition for scarce resources from rivals by making them 'look bad' in the eyes of the influential, e.g. blaming rivals for failures, denigrating their accomplishments as unimportant, poorly timed, self-serving, or lucky.
Use of information	Proactive, reactive or both. Lying/falsification – rare because of risk. Withholding information – where possibly detrimental to self-interest through: avoiding individuals/situations that might require explanations; distorting information to create an impression by selective disclosure, innuendo, or 'objective' speculation about individuals/events. Overkill – overwhelm the target with information to obscure details that could be harmful without the risk of withholding; providing volume of data to impress; giving an impression of logic with quantitative data.
Creating and maintaining a favourable image	Proactive. Image building – general appearance, dress, and hair style, sensitivity to organisational norms, drawing attention to successes, creating the appearance of being involved in important activities, developing a reputation for having attributes favoured by the organisation, taking credit for the accomplishments of others.
Developing a base of support	Proactive. Idea support building – getting others to 'understand' an idea before a decision is make; setting up a decision before it is 'made'; getting others to appear to contribute to an idea to assure their commitment.
Other tactics	Ingratiation/praising others. Forming coalitions and getting allies. Associating with the influential. Performing services or favours to create obligations.

Source: Adapted by the Author from Allen et al (1979)

use, part of the task of defining, or at least describing, politics involves exemplifying the type of behaviour concerned, i.e. the means and tactics employed.

For example, Johnston (1978) describes overt influence, manipulational influence, and influence-related gestures, while Allen et al's (1979) empirical study produced the classification of political tactics shown in Table 6.1, while Kipnis and Schmidt (1983) highlight the 'strategies of organizational influence' summarised in Table 6.2. Similarly Lewicki (1983) has provided a behavioural model of lying and deception in organisations.

Earlier, in considering 'office politics' Strauss (1962) distinguished the political techniques of: rule-oriented tactics - appealing to some common authority, referring to some rule, requiring written statements from others of the reasons for their demands, and requiring others to bear the cost of their demands; rule-evading tactics - going through the motions of complying with requests but with no no expectation of success, exceeding formal authority and ignoring others' requests; personal-political tactics - relying on friendships to modify others' requests, relying on favours, working through political allies in other departments; educational tactics - using direct or indirect persuasion; and organisational interactional tactics - seeking to change the interaction position, for instance through prior consultation, or seeking to take over other departments.

In another study, Izraeli (1975) examined the tactics of power expansion by the middle manager, identifying tactics of: neutralising potential opposition, through forming alliances with immediate subordinates; strategic personnel replacements, where the 'first lieutenants' are changed to give a new, politically circumscribed middle management; committing the uncommitted, through limiting the freedom of middle management to make free choices; and forming winning coalitions, by gaining direct backing from superiors' superiors.

At a somewhat lighter level, Korda (1975) has written about the personal characteristics and behaviour of political actors, and the political geography of offices and meetings, and such ploys as the 'information game', where it is noted of players.

> They not only obtain and control information, they know how to make it practically incomprehensible. The object is to render the information at their disposal as mysterious and inaccessible as possible, compiling it in such complex forms that only they can explain what (if anything) it means. (Korda, 1975)

Lastly, in considering the issue of upward influential

Table 6.2: Strategies of Organisational Influence

Strategy	Behaviour
Reason	The use of facts and data to support the development of a logical argument.
Coalition	The mobilisation of other people in the organisation. Sample tactic: 'I obtained the support of co-workers to back up my request'.
Ingratiation	The use of impression management, flattery, and the creation of goodwill. Sample tactic: 'I acted very humbly while making my request'.
Bargaining	The use of negotiation through the exchange of benefits or favours. Sample tactic: 'I offered an exchange (if you do this for me, I will do something for you)'.
Assertiveness	The use of a direct and forceful approach. Sample tactic: 'I demanded that he or she do what I requested'.
Higher Authority	Gaining the support of higher levels in the organisation to back-up requests. Sample tactic: 'I obtained the informal support of higher-ups'.
Sanctions	The use of organisationally derived rewards and punishments. Sample tactic: 'I threatened to give him or her an unsatisfactory performance evaluation'.

Source: Adapted by the Author from Kipnis and Schmidt (1983)

political behaviour Porter <u>et al</u> (1981), distinguish methods of influence as:

Methods		Predicted Relative Frequency of Use	Concealed: Means	Ends
I Sanctions	A Positive	Low		
	B Negative	Low		
II Inform- ational	A Persuasion	Low to Medium	Open	Open
	B Manipulative Persuasion	High	Open	Hidden
	C Manipulation	High	Hidden	Hidden

IMPLICATIONS

While organisational politics are widely recognised in the general context, as in the case of power this phenomenon is largely absent from the management literature.   Also in common with power, it was found that views as to the meaning of politics vary, although it seems reasonable to recognise as distinguishing characteristics: politics as the gaining and enactment of power, outside the formal authority system, in unsanctioned areas;   politics as resource-related in a general way; politics operating in a context of conflict; and politics as tactics or actions of influence.

For the purpose of this study the most significant implications are: that to study power alone would be somewhat limited in understanding outcomes;   that the interrelationship of power and politics is of some interest – be they complements or substitutes;   and that informational resources may lie at the centre of political behaviour – this last notion is pursued further shortly.

We have now examined the nature of power and politics in some detail, and the next chapters continue the argument by examining first the general process of using power and politics, and then the evidence of the significance of these phenomena in the marketing literature.

REFERENCES

Bacharach, S.B. and Lawler, E.J. (1980) Power and Politics in Organizations, Jossey-Bass, San Francisco

Bariff, M.L. and Galbraith, J.R. (1978) 'Intraorganizational Power Considerations for Designing Information Systems', Accounting, Organizations and Society, 3, 15-27

Cobb, A.T. and Margulies, N. (1981) 'Organizational Development: A Political Perspective', Academy of Management Review, 6 (1), 49-59

Cyert, R.M. and March, J.G. (1963), A Behavioral Theory of the Firm, Prentice-Hall, Englewood Cliffs, N.J.

Cyert, R.M., Simon, H.A. and Trow, D.B. (1956) 'Observation of a Business Decision', Journal of Business, 29, 237-48

Gandz, J. and Murray, V.V. (1980) 'The Experience of Work Place Politics', Academy of Management Journal, 23 (2), 237-51

Harvey, E. and Mills, R. (1970) 'Patterns of Organizational Adaptation: A Political Perspective', in M. Zald (ed.) Power in Organizations, Vanderbilt UP, Nashville, Tenn.

Izraeli, D.N. (1975) 'The Middle Manager and the Tactics of Power Expansion: A Case Study', Sloan Management Review, 16 (2), 57-70

Johnston, W.J. (1978) 'Marketing: The Social Psychology of Conflict, Power and Influence', American Behavioral Scientist, 21 (4), 515-34

Porter, L.W., Allen, R.W. and Angle, H.L. (1981) 'The Politics of Upward Influence in Organizations', in L.L. Cummings and B.M. Staw Research in Organizational Behavior, Jai Press, Greenwich, Conn.

Salancik, G.R. and Pfeffer, J. (1977) 'The Bases for Use of Power in Organizational Decision Making', Administrative Science Quarterly, 19, 453-73

Strauss, G. (1962) 'Tactics of Lateral Relationships: The Purchasing Agent', Administrative Science Quarterly, 7, 161-86

7

The use of power and Politics - a Contingency Model

INTRODUCTION

With the phenomena of power and politics defined, or at least described, attention may be turned to the ways in which organisational power and political behaviour are enacted and manifested in organisations, and how they determine outcomes. We then turn to examine the critical question of what evidence there is of such phenomena and behaviour in marketing - drawing on examples from both the marketing literature and broader studies. Finally, we examine the argument that power and politics emerge in decision making only under certain contingencies. The nature of those contingencies is discussed together with the available evidence of their existence or emergence in marketing decision making.

POWER AND POLITICS IN ACTION

While to some it might be thought to reflect on unhealthily Machiavellian frame of reference (e.g. Hunt and Chonko, 1984), the theoretical review of power and politics above comes to life only when power is seen to be used in organisations to achieve concrete outcomes of some kind. More conservatively as we move closer to the stage of operationalisation of the variables under study, it is necessary to consider how power is represented and how politics are enacted.

Games

At one level there are descriptions of 'games of power' (Korda, 1975), involving: games of weakness, i.e. avoiding victories over one's superiors and feigning a lack of power; the philosophy of 'nice guys finish first' - based on the observation that those who 'talk tough' seldom win; the strategy of expansionism - rather than waiting for promotion; the information game - of controlled access and interpretation; and games of manners and languages, together with the use of symbols and rituals of power (Korda, 1975).

More rigorous analysis at this level, of what are essentially the same phenomena is provided by Bardach (1977), who identified in the reactions to change in the US public sector 'counter-implementation' games of diverting resources, deflecting goals, and dissipating the energies of the change agents.   Similarly, in considering information systems change in organisations, Keen (1979) identified the political games played by resisters as: laying low; relying on social inertia; keeping a project complex, hard to coordinate and vaguely defined;   organisationally minimising the imple-menters' legitimacy and and influence;   and exploiting the implementers' lack of inside knowledge.

A Model of Political Enactment

A more structured analysis of political influence attempts was provided by Porter et al (1981), who identified a number of key considerations involved in the enactment of political behaviour;   first, the learning of political norms by actors within an organisation, through a process of attribution, although with the accompanying problem that:

> the signals by which an organizational member pieces together a picture of 'political reality' originate from the informal organization, and are apt to be sent in disguised format and against a noisy background. (Porter et al, 1981)

Second, situational factors are identified, in the sense that some organisational situations may be viewed as intrinsically political, in view of such factors as: uncertainty;   the importance of the issue to the larger organisation;   the salience of the issue to the individual; and resource scarcity.   Third, actor characteristics enter, including beliefs about action-outcome relationships, needs, the locus of control, the tendency to Machiavellianism, and the propensity towards risk-taking:

> To the extent that an organizational member is a risk seeker, it might be reasonable to expect that he/she would be tempted to engage in a political influence attempt (which can indeed be dangerous) that might be shunned by a risk averter. (Porter et al, 1981)

Fourth, there is the process of target selection, then fifth, the choice of methods of upward influence.

Their analysis, and emphasis on the individual, leads Porter et al to propose what they describe as an episodic model of upward influence, involving the cognitive elements of the recognition by the focal person of the opportunity to promote or protect self-interest, and recognition of an outcome: and decisional elements of the decision to attempt political influence, the decision to select a particular target, and the decision to use a particular influence method.

They propose that the recognition of opportunity is related to low structuring and high ambiguity (in a similar way to the argument presented by Thompson and Tuden (1959) and Pfeffer (1981), see pp. *201-204* below). The decision to engage in political behaviour is related to the actor's personal power, the salience of the issue to the actor, his personality traits, and his internalisation of norms condoning such behaviour. The selection of specific influence targets is related to perceptions of the target's power and the ability to approach targets successfully. The selection of an influence method is related to individual traits, risks and costs, the perceived normative climate, interpersonal attractions, and the perceived consequences.

A similar episodic model of power has been proposed by Cobb (1984) distinguishing between antecedent conditions and power episodes, in an attempt to integrate different empirical findings.

Alternatively, it is possible to examine not just models of the relatively overt games and political enactment behaviour of individuals, but the underlying process of political influence.

A Covert Process of Power and Politics

Turning to a view of politics as a process Pfeffer (1977) considered that 'Any discussion of the process of the use of power must consider the mechanisms through which power is exercised unobtrusively', which logic we follow here. Later, Pfeffer (1981) argued that while it seems that: power is most effectively implemented unobtrusively; the exercise of power and influence is facilitated by legitimation and rationalisation; and that strategies are adopted to gather support for the position taken; even so it is possible to identify a variety of underlying strategies or processes in the implementation of power and politics.

First, there is the selective use of objective criteria in decision making. As will be seen shortly (pp. *200-6*) it is characteristic of complex decisions that there are a multiplicity of interests, and thus criteria of choice, which might be applied. To the extent that the choice of criterion amounts to choice of outcome, it evidences the covert use of power:

In a decision situation, it is difficult and not very legitimate to argue for the validity and choice of a given course of action on the basis of the power of the social actors favoring that particular choice. Rather, choices must be legitimated and power is best exercised unobtrusively. One strategy, then, involves the selective stressing of certain criteria that favor the position advocated by the particular social actor in question. (Pfeffer, 1981)

A **second** and related point is the way in which information is used in decision making. It has long been recognised that information may serve a variety of 'non-objective functions' (e.g. see Piercy and Evans, 1983), for example to justify a decision already made (Cyert et al, 1956)). Inevitably, this issue returns us to Pettigrew's study of the control of information to influence outcomes, where he noted of the information gatekeeper that:

> Control over information was a critical resource used by Kenny for mobilising power. Because he sat at the junction of the communications channels between his subordinates, the manufacturers, and the board, Kenny was able to exert biases in favour of his own demands and at the same time feed the board negative information about the demands of his opponents. (Pettigrew, 1973)

However, central to Pettigrew's findings, as noted earlier, was that possessing information was not sufficient alone to mobilise power, but that tactical skills were required. The attributes of assessed stature, and access to the powerful or role set, revolve in Pettigrew's study around the expert, in the manifestation of political behaviour:

> The expert can maintain a power position over high-ranking persons in the organization as long as they are dependent on him for special skills and access to certain kinds of information. (Pettigrew, 1973)

In fact, Crozier (1964) argued that the expert's power is self-defeating and transitory. In Pettigrew's study one group of experts (the computer programmers) used their resources of technical knowledge and status to attempt (in fact, unsuccessfully) to maintain the dependency of others on them. When harassed they created barriers to protect their autonomy and developed high group cohesiveness. They protected their power base through a variety of tactics: developing norms which denied the competence of outsiders; developing protective myths; developing norms of secrecy, and protecting their knowledge base through control over training and recruitment. Eventually, though, the superior in question found other sources of expertise.

A **third** process element is the use of organisational secrecy as a covert means of influencing outcomes. By implication, in our pursuit of a political analysis of marketing organisation and budgeting, this last point is of some interest. For instance, Pfeffer's concern in studying resource allocation was with the political use of secrecy – as a particular form of information control – since in organisations:

> the limitation of access to information is used strategically by power holders to enclose and maintain their capability for action, in the organisation. Various aspects of an allocation decision may be kept secret. First, the information used to make the decision may be kept secret ... Second, the decision-making process itself may be secret ... And third, occasionally even the results of the decision making may be kept secret. (Pfeffer, 1977)

The argument is that withholding information prevents informed criticism, while obscuring the process makes attempts to influence it difficult for others, as does keeping the results of the process secret. At the same time, the secrecy surrounding the decision may be rationalised in terms of commercial confidentiality, the need to protect decision makers from influence, and so on. The contention is that:

> Secrecy almost invariably leads to decisions and a decision process that are different from what would otherwise have occurred. If this were not the case, there would be no point in secrecy and no necessity to develop and support the mythologies that support it. (Pfeffer, 1977)

A **fourth** point is concerned with the more general process of legitimation – the provision of rational or legitimate reasons and grounds to justify and explain outcomes that are favoured by the powerful or are politically determined. For instance, there is the use of such decision making procedures as committees to legitimise decisions already made, since:

> While the use of committees may provide legitimitation ... it is unlikely that it alters the final result. In most decision contexts, committees operate with the information provided to them, under the rules provided, and under time constraints. (Pfeffer, 1977)

Similarly, Pfeffer points to the effect of centralisation through majority rule – where the appearance of participative decision making is achieved, but in fact decisions are made centrally. Indeed, of a similar nature is the use of the 'outside expert' to provide an 'aura of rationality' and to render the use of power less obtrusive (Pfeffer, 1981).

Fifth, and yet more covert and unobtrusive is the process of controlling the agenda, since it is argued that: 'One of the best and least obtrusive ways of exercising power is to prevent the decision issue from surfacing in the first place' (Pfeffer, 1981). In this sense, keeping items 'off the agenda' for discussion and formal or open decision, and so on, amounts to the mobilisation of bias (Bell and Newby, 1971).

A **sixth**, and related, point is concerned with the process of what Pfeffer (1981) describes as 'affecting the decision process'.

It is suggested that political influence over decision making may be exerted unobtrusively through: control of the decision premises, that is influencing the criteria and assumptions made; controlling the considered alternatives, since 'it is clear that the final choice among alternatives will be heavily dependent on the alternatives which are considered at all, and which survive the initial winnowing process' (Pfeffer, 1981); and controlling the information about alternatives, which may be illustrated aptly from the Pettigrew (1973) study cited earlier.

Finally, attention is drawn to the process of coalition building, and the management of internal and external coalitions as a political strategy, possibly involving cooptation and committee manipulation (Pfeffer, 1981). Coalitional bargaining lies at the centre of the Bacharach and Lawler (1980) study of power and politics, where they classify tactics in terms of: improving the quality of the bargainer's alternatives, decreasing the quality of the opponent's alternatives, decreasing the value of the opponent to the bargainer, or increasing the value of the bargainer to the opponent.

Implications

In considering the use of power and politics to influence decision outcomes, it was seen that one may identify 'games' or tactical ploys, a political enactment model, and strategies in an underlying political process of influence. Together these concepts suggest that political influence is covert and unobtrusive while the use of power may be both implicit and unobtrusive. As will be seen, one implication is that the empirical study of such phenomena is problematic because they are hidden. However, we are also left with the conceptual difficulty of testing simply for the presence of political influence or the use of power, and deciding if an outcome is political – or whether it is rationally determined, the result of coincidence, or whatever. We also return to these questions in Chapter 10.

For the moment, however, we turn to the issue of whether power and politics in decision making, in the way that they have been explicated above, are detectable in the marketing literature.

POWER AND POLITICS IN MARKETING

Power and the Marketing Department

If the case to be presented later is to be acceptable, then it is desirable to make explicit the signs of power phenomena in the marketing function. In fact, the literature of marketing itself shows little sign of making great explicit recognition of power-dependence relationships in organisations, though fragments of evidence do exist, in various areas as demonstrated below.

For example, recently, in considering the relationship between marketing, strategic planning and the theory of the firm, Anderson (1982) made an attempt to introduce strategic contingencies' theory to the issue of the relationship between marketing and the other functions of the firm. The main point of Anderson's marketing constituency theory was that environmental coalitions place demands on organisations which result in a power struggle among internal groups or constituencies, and thus that group or function which adds most to successfully concluding negotiations with the dominant environmental coalition receives the greatest increase in status and influence. While such a model has clear antecedents in such works (discussed earlier) as Mintzberg (1979), Pfeffer and Salancik (1978) and Hickson et al (1971), it represents an unusually explicit recognition of power systems in marketing literature.

Certainly there has been some use made of the dependence/social exchange concept in examining the bases of power of product managers. For instance, Gemmill and Wilemon (1972) considered the sources of interpersonal influence used by product managers to gain support for their product lines, given their typical lack of formal authority over those controlling resources. Using the French and Raven (1968) paradigm, they found that two influence styles predominated: primary reliance on reward and coercive power; and primary reliance on expert and referent power, the latter being perceived as the more effective. They concluded that:

> This imbalance between authority and responsibility causes product managers either to succeed or to fail, depending upon their ability to use alternative forms of influence to gain support for their actions. (Gemmill and Wilemon, 1972)

Related work has examined the concept of social power in buyer-seller relations (Busch and Wilson, 1976) and in sales management (Ivancevich and Donnelly, 1970; Busch, 1980).

This amounts to some recognition of structural or positional power, as defined, for instance, by Hickson et al (1971), but perhaps even more of the significance of expert power and the informational advantages enjoyed and exploited by experts (Crozier, 1964; Pettigrew, 1973). While the reward/coercive power of the product manager was closely related to structural location, the amount of expertise attributed to them by others was found to be influenced by: their information; their previous performance; their work experience; and their ability to evaluate information from diverse sources. This suggests some confirmation of the notion that analysis of the marketing organisation should start with structure and then proceed to such informational aspects as control, criticality, monopoly and processing capacity.

Indeed, an earlier study of product management pointed out more explicitly that for the product manager 'The solving of some problems is usually a matter of bargaining and company politics' and that the product manager builds 'informal authority' through the 'case law' or precedents in earlier decisions (Evans, 1964).

Turning to the more general question of marketing structure as such, the empirical material discussed earlier suggests that one can distinguish dimensions of marketing power in the style of Kaplan's (1964) paradigm of weight, domain, scope. The evidence reviewed in Piercy (1985) suggested that marketing department influence was frequently restricted in all these dimensions – by virtue of such factors as: the 'sharing' of responsibility for marketing decision areas with increased top management intervention; the strength of other departments and the 'hiving-off' of parts of the unified marketing organisation; and the loss of control of certain task areas altogether.

For instance, ignoring for the moment the important differences between sales and marketing, Lawrence and Lorsch (1967) in studying two container organisations found that the sales department was perceived as the most influential, even though the market environment was seen as the least uncertain. Hickson et al (1971) commented that this was so because the sales department was high in workflow pervasiveness and immediacy, and

   although the market subenvironment was seen as the least uncertain, the sales unit was perceived as the most influential. Sales not only has the opportunity to cope with such uncertainty as may exist over customer requirements, it is highly central; for its activities connect it to both other departments – workflow

> pervasiveness - and if it ceased to work, production of containers would stop - workflow immediacy. The effects of centrality are probably bolstered by nonsubstitutability, since the sales department develops a necessary particularized knowledge of customer requirements. Production and research are, therefore, comparatively powerless in the face of the strategic contingencies controlled by the sales subunit.
> (Hickson et al, 1971)

It should, however, be noted that we argued above that the definition of what are the strategic contingencies for an organisation is to some extent itself a political outcome, and one which is capable of becoming institutionalised and thus reinforced.

The point is that both the actual criticality of the contingencies controlled and the institutionalisation of their importance, and thus their role as a source of power, may work either to the favour or the detriment of the marketing department:

> There is some evidence that the power of internal subunits varies with their relationship to critical environmental problems ... While marketing departments may have dominated many corporations during the 1950s and 1960s, there are indications that financial and legal departments may be increasing in importance.
> (Pfeffer and Salancik, 1978)

However, Perrow (1970), in studying the emergence of dominating groups in companies, found that in eleven out of twelve firms the sales department was the most powerful sub-unit, acting as the gatekeeper between the customer and the company.

On the other hand, the testing of the strategic contingencies' theory by Hinings et al (1974), found, in studying five brewing industry firms and two container organisations, that production was powerful right across the board - scoring highly on all the strategic contingencies measures, while marketing/sales was powerful in its own area, but not elsewhere. This suggested that simply coping with uncertainty alone was insufficient to allow domination, since it had to be accompanied by work flow pervasiveness and immediacy, and a low level of substitutability for the coping function. In the companies studied this consistently placed production in a more dominant position than marketing, although no claim was made that this group of firms was in any way a representative sample of industry more generally.

Lastly, one small empirical study in the marketing literature (Tookey and McDougall, 1969) unusually offers some explicit recognition of power differences between marketing departments in interdepartmental relationships, and the integration of marketing responsibilities, and the relationship of those differences with structure. Ultimately this work foundered on the problem of classifying environments and the intervening issue of the firm's understanding of those environments.

While the issue of organisational power and the marketing department has thus received relatively little attention, particularly in the marketing literature, it would seem that the fragmented evidence allows the following points: that interpersonal influence based on positional power, but also on expert status and informational advantage, has been found significant; that the power of the marketing department in different organisations varies in weight, domain and scope; and that the strategic contingencies' theorem of uncertainty absorption offers an apparently useful lever to make sense of power differences between marketing and other sub-units, in the light of findings relating to the organisational positioning, responsibilities and status, and integration of the marketing department compared to other 'constituencies' in the firm.

However, what remains to be considered, is the other face of influence in marketing in terms of organisational politics.

Politics and the Marketing Department

In fact there are some signs of the recognition of political behaviour in the literature of marketing management, though they are few and fragmented and normally do not make explicit use of a political frame of reference. We may, though, consider the following pieces of evidence from a variety of sources as indicators.

By way of introduction, Madison et al (1980) found in their survey that the departments in which organisational politics were perceived as most prevalent were marketing and sales, while accounting and finance were seen as lowest in political activity. It should be borne in mind, of course, that these data reflected organisational participants' attributions, so that it may be that they reflect the skills of the politically active in obscuring their behaviour rather than directly reflecting political activity.

None the less some other general recognition is provided by comments about the salesman's role in selectively passing on information to management (Albaum, 1964; Howard, 1965), and in the notion that change-oriented roles like market research are at best ambiguous (Kahn, 1964) and certainly bring researchers into conflict with the rest of the organisation (Krum, 1969; Schlackmann, 1979).

To pursue this last point, there has been some suggestion in the marketing research field that research is used as a tool to justify decisions already made and to encourage members of the marketing team to be 'properly optimistic' (Hardin, 1969). Similarly, others have suggested that the motivations for undertaking marketing research are frequently 'purely irrational or political' (Channon, 1968) although serving organisational needs for justification, reassurance, delaying decisions, conciliation, decisions, conciliation, ritual, and so on (Samuels, 1973; Ramond, 1974). Indeed, recent empirical work has made explicit a measurement of the 'political conceptability' of marketing research as an indicator of the use made of the research by managers (Deshpande and Zaltman, 1984).

In a related fashion, the area of <u>sales forecasting</u> would appear to show some signs of political behaviour. For example, a study of sales forecasting by retail shop managers (Lowe and Shaw, 1968) found that managers were prepared to bias sales forecasts to suit their own interests, where those interests included manipulating the reward system, gaining approval from superiors, and acquiring an increased share of scarce resources (see pp. *255-7* below).

Information biasing has also been discovered in the operation of the <u>product management</u> system in marketing. Cunningham and Clarke (1975) found that the reaction of product managers to high perceived risk was predominantly manifested in the adoption of organisational strategies (to reduce the amount at stake) or active information seeking (to increase subjective certainty). The reason for this behaviour was that product managers 'identified so strongly with their brands that they tried to increase their influence in decision-taking as risk increased, in order to counter the centralizing influence of company policy on important decisions' (Cunningham and Clarke, 1975). Linked to both these behaviours was biased information handling, to favour their organisational position and that of their products. Indeed, not merely did the majority of the product managers give numerous examples of deliberate information biasing – both 'legitimate' in situations like presentations to the sales force and 'illegitimate' in forecasting sales and making budget requests – but it emerged that this behaviour was acceptable and, indeed, expected by their superiors in the marketing organisation.

Further, the study found biased target setting to be almost a norm of product manager behaviour, of particular note as a way of obtaining resources for a product or brand:

> The most common behavioural strategy was to attempt to get low targets accepted in order to benefit from the rewards of over-achievement or to avoid the 'punishments' of failure to reach targets. (Cunningham and Clarke, 1975)

(Further detailed commentary on the resource allocation aspect of this study is given later, pp. *258-62*).

In a similar vein, another study of product management examined the interpersonal influence methods used by product managers to gain compliance from others, and found that: the most important interpersonal influence sources for product managers were human relation skills and technical expertise, followed by respect for organisational position; and for group product managers the most important sources of influence were perceived authority, respect for organisation position, and expertise (Venkatesh and Wilemon, 1976).

Similarly, another review of the product management system concluded of the product manager's role with staff and functional managers (over whom they typically had no formal authority):

> Through the integrative and linkages roles, product managers can apparently exercise influence on others by managing the product decision system rather than by making decisions themselves. (McDaniel and Gray, 1980)

It does appear, thus, that the product management system exhibits clear, empirically substantiated, signs of political behaviour, at least in the sense of manipulating information and exerting social influence over others.

Thus, while the amount of evidence is limited, the statement is advanced that marketing decision making does manifest political behaviour, as defined and described earlier, or at least that in certain circumstances it would appear to do so. Our attention turns, therefore, to the nature of those circumstances.

Perhaps the clearest point emerging is that power and politics in marketing are to some extent recognised, which provides some measure of support for the direction of this present study, but that there has been little or no systematic attempt to evaluate their impact and the management problems or opportunities created.

CONTINGENCIES FOR THE USE OF POWER AND POLITICS

In Mintzberg's (1979) analysis, a conflictual power configuration with a politicised internal coalition occurs only when there is an 'aberration' in any of the more legitimate power configurations. Another view is that decision making situations differ in terms of complexity and 'cleavage' of interests, suggesting that the type of decision making adopted will depend on the mix of these two properties (Astley et al, 1982). In fact, this provides a key to what little analysis there is of the conditions surrounding the use of power and politics - it occurs when there is no option.

A General Model of the Conditions for the Use of Power and Politics

The proposition advanced is that it is only under certain conditions that decisions are likely to be resolved through the use of power, or through political behaviour. What one seeks therefore is some mechanism for identifying, labelling, and operationally detecting those conditions. If this can be achieved, then one should be able to isolate those management decision making situations where 'rational' approaches are impractical and 'the use of power is virtually inevitable and furthermore it is the only way to arrive at a decision' (Pfeffer, 1981). It may be that one can argue that these conditions are common in marketing – indeed this thesis will be advanced shortly – but the point is that power and politics are unlikely to emerge in their absence and that some other model of decision making is likely to be more valid. The core of the argument is thus that in the conditions to be specified:

> There is no rational way to determine whose preferences are to prevail, or whose beliefs about technology should guide the decision. There may be norms, social customs, or traditions which dictate the choice, but these may all be efforts to legitimate the use of power to make its appearance less obtrusive. (Pfeffer, 1981)

One model of the contingencies surrounding the use of power and politics is provided by Pfeffer (1981) and is shown in Figure 7.1. Briefly these conditions may be described as follows.

Interdependence and Differentiation. From the discussion in Chapter 4, the term interdependence, in the sense of the links between differentiated sub-units in an organisation, is to some extent explicated. The basic structural argument is that differentiation makes interdepartmental dependencies and conflict inevitable (Lawrence and Lorsch, 1967), as well as external pressures causing internal units to accept compromise in their pursuit of goals (Thompson, 1967). This provides a precondition for the use of power and politics, on the grounds that there would otherwise be no basis for conflict or interaction. Hence, the more differentiated are the task roles of sub-units, the more disparate are the goals pursued and the beliefs about technology (see pp. 201 – 204 below). In the strategic contingencies' model this notion of interdependence was conceived as centrality, in terms of workflow immediacy and pervasiveness, and a lack of

Figure 7.1: Contingencies for Power and Politics in Decision Making

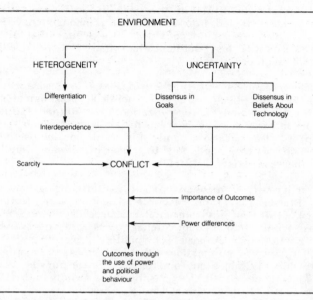

Source: Adapted by the Author from Pfeffer (1981)

substitutability.

Goal and Technology Dissensus. If there were no disagreement or uncertainty about goals, it is argued there would again be no basis for conflict, and similarly if there were no uncertainty about technology - in the sense of understanding and predicting the cause-and-effect relationships between actions and results - there would be no room for anything but computational or bureaucratic decision making. In turn, as noted above, goal and technology disagreements may be traced through departmental differentiation to conditions in the environment (Lawrence and Lorsch, 1967). The widely-cited Thompson and Tuden model (1959), shown in Figure 7.2, implies that it is only in conditions of consensus about both goals and technology (cause-and-effect relationships) that computational decision making is even possible. In all other situations, of varying types and levels of dissensus, then decision making is liable to processes of social influence. A similar point is made by Hedberg <u>et al</u> (1975) who argue that power is used in just this way, so that the point at which conflict arises, is when the decision making process changes from analysis to bargaining.

Interestingly, it is in the area of goal dissensus that Pfeffer (1981) is led into a surprising inconsistency in his analysis which we should consider. He argues that business organisations are less political than those in the non-profit or public sector:

> The reason is not that businessmen are more rational, more analytical, or less political administrators in these (business) organizations. Rather, business organizations have a reasonably agreed upon goal of profit maximization, and this goal consensus negates much of the need for the use of power that might otherwise exist. (Pfeffer, 1981)

This argument is inconsistent with Pfeffer's earlier work, e.g. Pfeffer (1977) on resource allocation and Pfeffer and Salancik (1978) on environmental resource-dependence, where it was found that organisational goals are themselves at least partly the outcome of political processes. More seriously, the suggestion that business organisations single-mindedly agree on, and take action to pursue, a single goal, let alone profit maximisation, is wildly adrift from the conceptual and empirical findings in this area.

We consider below certain of the empirical findings, which suggest that goal dissensus may be an important attribute of marketing decision making, but consider first the range of theoretical contributions from the general theory denying the validity of single goal or profit maximisation behaviour by business organisations.

While classic economic theory certainly did assume both single-goal and profit maximisation behaviour, it was noted recently that:

> the theory about the goals of the business has done a complete about-face in the last three decades or so, from a reliance on classical economic theory to an increasing attention to newer sociological themes, from the notion of given organizational goals to that of fluid power in and around the organization with no set goals, from an organization devoid of influencers to one in which virtually everyone is an influencer. (Mintzberg, 1983)

One can simply list the departures from classical theory to demonstrate the weight behind such an 'about-faced': (a) profit may not be the goal, e.g. Duncan (1945) and Baumol (1959) argued that firms pursue sales maximisation and others

---

Figure 7.2: Goals, Technology and Decision Making

GOALS

		Consensus	Dissensus
TECHNOLOGY (Relationship between actions and results)	Consensus	Computational/ bureaucratic decision making	Inspiration decision making
	Dissensus	Judgemental decision making	Compromise decision making

---

Source: Adapted by the Author from Thompson and
          Tuden (1959)

---

point to the pursuit of management preference functions and
societal goals (Williamson, 1963;   Sales, 1972);   (b)
maximisation may be neither possible nor sensible – it is
variously argued that firms 'satisfice' (e.g. Simon, 1962) or
set targets (e.g. Dean, 1951);   (c) goals are not single but
multiple – for example, Cyert and March (1963) pointed to
sequential attention to multiple goals, similar to
Papandreou's (1952) 'preference function' model, though
recognising a 'coalition of interests' rather than simply a
peak coordinator; and (d) organisations may, in practical
effect, have no goals, e.g. Mansfield (1985) argues that
there is effectively no such thing as an organisational goal,
in the sense of a motivating object leading directly to
action, and earlier Georgiou argued that rather than being
rational goal-seeking entitites, organisations are 'arbitrary
focusses of interests, market places whose structures and
processes are the outcomes of the complex accommodations made

by actors exchanging a variety of incentives and pursuing a diversity of goals' (Georgiou, 1973).

It would seem, therefore, that one may expect goal dissensus as much in the business organisation as in any other, and we proceed here on this basis.

Scarcity. Almost by definition if there were no conditions of scarcity, there would be little basis for conflict and thus no reason for power and politics to be involved (other than for their own sake, although that is a possibility which should not be dismissed out of hand (Cartwright, 1965)), though scarcity should be understood broadly – it may refer to status or image as well as to financial or other tangible resources.

Certainly it would seem that conflict may be associated with resource scarcity, and indeed may be intensified by resource scarcity (Cyert and March, 1963; Porter et al, 1981). Pfeffer concludes that: 'When the organization faces a constant, or worse yet, shrinking pool of resources, conflict and power struggles become more intense' (Pfeffer, 1981).

Conflict. The result of differentiation and inter-dependence, dissensus, and scarcity is conflict, either open or covert, when decisions are faced. Two further conditions, however, are necessary for political mechanisms to operate.

Importance of Outcome. Given that the use of power and political behaviour involve efforts, the use of resources and thus costs, and that there are risks involved – the blatent use of power may call forth reactions from others, and unsanctioned political behaviour may bring organisational disapproval and punishment – then the use of power and politics is not likely if only trivial outcomes are at stake. This said, of course, the judgement of the importance or triviality of outcomes is ultimately subjective, to the individual or group concerned.

Power Differences. It is suggested that: 'Political activity, bargaining and coalition formation occur primarily when power is dispersed. When power is highly centralized, authority makes decisions using its own rules and values' (Pfeffer, 1981).

The implication is that political contests take place in organisations only because there is some dispersion of power and authority.

In fact, there is some contentiousness implicit in this assertion. It is argued that:

> when power is highly concentrated, the other
> participants have little ability or motivation to engage
> in a contest for control which provokes the visible
> conflict and political activity observed when power is
> more equally distributed. (Pfeffer, 1981)

To some extent this is a logical extension of Pfeffer's
structural view of power, but it is one which may go too far.
It denies, for example, the power of the expert who may exert
upward influence, or indeed the exertion of any other kind of
power which is not directly related to structure. The view
also implicitly equates the use of power and political
activity - i.e. only the powerful use of politics - which
returns us to an earlier paradox (pp. *176-79* above). If one
regards political behaviour as lying essentially outside the
formal power structure, then power and politics are not
necessarily complementary - the non-powerful in the
structural sense may well exert an upward influence over
outcomes, in the way portrayed by Porter <u>et al</u> (1981) and
discussed earlier. It follows too from the earlier debate
that the formal concentration or centralisation of power - if
it is a political outcome, as argued - is related to the
skill exercised in making political behaviour unobtrusive,
rather than reducing political influences on decisions and
outcomes. Finally, the view is somewhat static, in ignoring
the possibly continuing struggle by the non-powerful to
redefine critical contingencies and resources to restructure
the power framework. For these reasons, Pfeffer's argument
on this point seems weak.

Outcomes Through Power and Politics. The existence of
these conditions is suggested to make the use of power almost
inevitable, not through choice of the participants but quite
simply through the lack of any other way to make a decision
and to resolve conflict, since 'There is no rational way to
determine whose preferences are to prevail, or whose beliefs
about technology should guide the decision' (Pfeffer, 1981).
While the use of power and politics may be hidden and
obscured - for instance, through 'rational' decision
guidelines (which are chosen selectively and thus may be seen
as a political mechanism) - this amounts to legitimation
rather than avoidance. Thus, the central proposition is
that:

> In situations of conflict, power is the mechanism, the
> currency by which the conflict gets resolved. Social
> power almost inevitably accompanies conditions of
> conflict, for power is the way by which such conflicts
> become resolved. (Pfeffer, 1981b)

This point proposed, the next question concerns the

extent to which such contingencies may arise in marketing situations.

Marketing Contingencies for the Use of Power and Politics

Following the model advanced above, we may examine the sources and existence of conflicts in marketing decisions and the potential for their political resolution.

Interdependence and Differentiation. From the discussion in Chapter 4, it follows that the existence of a differentiated marketing department is the subject of debate in terms of its control of specialised task activities and decisions and its success in filling a key boundary-spanning role (which in turn is related to the organisation's technology (Jemison, 1984)). This was, in an earlier work (Piercy, 1985), related to the organisation's environment, using the information processing concept to propose that the level and type of environmental uncertainty would imply different levels and types of marketing department specialisation. In political terms this suggests differences between which environmental contingencies are defined as most critical to an organisation, and the degree to which a boundary-spanning marketing organisation has a monopoly in coping with them.

The conclusion for present purposes would seem to be that differentiation and interdependence will vary between organisations depending on their environments, as will the ways in which those environments are perceived, enacted, and understood, and hence reflected in the marketing organisation. Thus, at one extreme we may have the integrated marketing department directly controlling the major marketing mix variables, which is highly differentiated from other departments, and controls critical factors like customer communications and sales forecasting, while at the other extreme there may be no formal marketing organisation or simply a limited staff function advising management, with no real control of decision areas or critical contingencies.

Goal and Technology Dissensus. On the general question of perceived levels of political activity, we noted earlier that Madison et al (1980) found that marketing/sales was perceived as high in political activity, compared for instance to accounting/finance. We expressed some reservation in that earlier comment about the validity of this type of measurement, but these researchers' finding was that:

> the 'politically active' functional areas are those in which uncertainty is most prevalent. Organizational members in such roles may need to rely on political skill to deal with the conflicting demands of intra- and

extra-organizational associates. Thus, norms that favour political influence as a means of conducting the day's business may arise, out of necessity in such sub-units. (Madison et al, 1980)

The source of that uncertainty may thus be environmental, but also perhaps reflect low paradigm development in marketing, and arise from the organisation or 'task environment' itself.

Turning first to **goal consensus**, in examining the general question of corporate goals and objectives, it was clear earlier that the prescriptive literature generally favours some concept of profit maximisation, albeit somewhat different in concept to the traditional or classical economist's view of that goal. Perhaps of greatest relevance is the emergence of a model of multiple goals, which are pursued sequentially (Cyert and March, 1963), suggesting immediately the potential for disagreement on what goals are in general, and specifically which of the multiplicity available should prevail at a particular time or in a particular decision. In fact, the multiplicity and non-maximisation characteristics of corporate objectives are generally confirmed by the empirical work in this area (e.g. Kaplan et al, 1958; Lanzillotti, 1958; Hague, 1971).

In the marketing area, one may distinguish firstly, actual differences in the goals of the marketing sub-unit, as compared to other parts of the organisation; and secondly, uncertainty as to what goals are, or which are the most relevant in different situations.

First, the problem of multiple, conflicting objectives has been recognised at a general level in diagnosing department conflict (Seiler, 1963; Lawrence and Lorsch, 1967) and in the analysis of company systems (Sengupta and Ackoff, 1965), as well as in investment appraisal when departments choose different criteria of evaluation reflecting their sub-unit goals - the finance department emphasising economic criteria, the legal department regulatory, the marketing department market share, and the production department operating efficiency (Pondy, 1964).

More specifically in the marketing area, Kotler (1965) noted that 'Marketing, in trying to mobilize the company's resources to develop customer satisfaction, often causes other departments to do a poorer job in their terms', which is to say that sub-unit goals differ, leading to conflict: with production (Perrow, 1970; Dutton and Walton, 1967; Shapiro, 1977); with R & D (Souder, 1981; Hooley et al, 1984); with accountancy and finance (Harrison, 1979); and even with purchasing (Sengupta and Ackoff, 1965), as well as actually within the marketing department itself (Evans, 1964).

Second, in addition to the existence of multiple,

conflicting objectives, there is also the evidence of dissensus over goals arising from uncertainty. For instance, in studying pricing decision making Hague (1971) distinguished between operational objectives - which set specific tasks with time limits and control measurements - and non-operational objectives which 'do not say, or even imply, exactly what action the firm should take to achieve them'. Apart from the fact that it was non-operational objectives rather than operational about which there was greatest consensus, in some firms operational objectives were effectively treated as non-operational, and a third type of objective laid down goals for the firm as a whole, but did not indicate how any particular department or product was expected to contribute. Given the surrounding confusion found in the study about what marketing's role and function in pricing should be, it seems fair to conclude that some uncertainty surrounded the objectives to be pursued in pricing decisions.

Similarly, in the Cunningham and Clarke (1975) study of product management cited earlier, product managers were questioned about brand objectives, and the researchers found some certainty about profit and sales volume objectives, but considerable uncertainty about objectives for brand share, growth, distribution, and brand development, and some uncertainty about objectives for brand image. Generally, it was suggested that there was uncertainty in all facets of company objectives, though less so about their nature or range than their relative importance, the company's view about acceptable attainment levels, and current brand achievement.

More recently, a study of advertising budgeting in major UK firms noted that in determining promotional expenditure companies tended to have 'norms' - sometimes even made explicit in terms like '60% of expenditure above the line' - rather than taking a more 'rational' approach, and that in comparing goals to budgets:

> The objectives quoted above tend to be very general, too open-ended to provide a very firm base against which achievement can be monitored. In part this generality is encouraged by a feeling that the achievement of promotional objectives can't be measured with any sort of accuracy; in part it stems from unwillingness of managers to commit themselves to very tight objectives. (Wills and Kennedy, 1982)

This is suggestive of both goal dissensus, but also a lack of understanding of 'cause and effect' or 'technology' relationships in marketing, to which we return shortly.

A recent study of marketing strategy choices, suggests that strategic marketing objectives are a function of managerial perceptions of the product-market environment and organisational reward systems, (Burke, 1984) and this may explain certain aspects of the dissensus discussed above.

Thus, as far as goal consensus is concerned in marketing, we may point to evidence both of conflicting goals in relations with other departments and between different parts of the marketing sub-unit, leading directly to conflicts, and also to goal uncertainty or ambiguity, contributing somewhat differently to goal dissensus in marketing.

Closely related to the last of these points is the question of **technology dissensus** in marketing. A lack of understanding, or at least demonstrable 'proof', of the cause-and-effect relationship between marketing efforts and results is in many ways a defining characteristic of marketing management. It has been noted:

> A real operational understanding of the effectiveness of marketing actions - the causal link, for example, between advertising and selling, and sales and profits - remains problematic in most companies. The elements of the marketing mix interact and there are time-lags and cumulative effects in assessing their impact on buyers and distributors, such that only sophisticated analysis can hope truly to measure marketing effectiveness. The use of complex survey methods, tests, and experimentation ... can make a contribution to such analysis, but such methods are technically sophisticated and expensive. (Piercy and Evans, 1983)

We may conceive of marketing inputs and outputs in the way suggested in Figure 7.3 where it is possible to measure inputs and outputs, but only to hypothesise the links between them.

While it is possible to measure intervening variables, such as awareness, attitude change, distribution penetration, and the like, and sometimes to demonstrate plausible relationships with the costs of product launches, advertising, selling and promotion and results in sales, cash and profits, certainly as to cause-and-effect remains typically problematic in dealing with marketing decisions. Indeed, it has been suggested that this uncertainty is compounded by 'research that tells lies' (O'Herlihy, 1981).

This central uncertainty has been uncovered particularly in advertising and promotion (Kennedy and Corkindale, 1976), but also in product management (e.g. Lysonski, 1985), personal selling (e.g. Semlow, 1959), pricing (e.g. Shapiro, 1968) and marketing research (Piercy and Evans, 1983).

It would seem, therefore, that in addition to goal dissensus, technology dissensus may typify the making of decisions on many marketing issues.

Figure 7.3: Marketing Inputs and Outputs - A Black Box Model

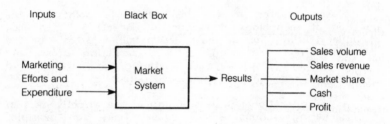

Source: Piercy and Evans (1983)

Scarcity. Accepting that scarcity is a prerequisite for political contests in decision making, it would seem likely that this condition is at least sometimes present in marketing decision making.

Certainly, there have been suggestions that economic recession has placed greater pressure on marketing budgets (Buell, 1982) and has imposed sometimes inappropriate pressures to 'cut-back' (Wilson, 1981), in ways generally suggestive of greater political involvement in resource allocation in times of decline rather than growth (Hannan and Freeman, 1978).

This said, resource scarcity is not likely to affect all organisations equally, nor all marketing departments.

Conflict. What would seem far more generally recognised is the existence of conflict between marketing and other sub-units, as well as between the elements making up a marketing department.

At the most general level, Kotler (1980) suggested the

type of common marketing department conflicts with other
departments summarised in Table 7.1.

By way of expanding this view, certainly in considering
relationships with the production department, studies have
suggested evidence of conflict (Dutton and Walton, 1966) and
that marketing and production are 'natural enemies' (Perrow,
1970). For example, Shapiro's (1977) empirical study was
concerned with production/marketing conflicts relating to
capacity planning, production scheduling, delivery and
physical distribution, quality assurance, breadth of product
line, cost control, new product launches, and adjunct
services, and Shapiro suggested that these conflicts were
directly explainable by: evaluation and reward system
differences; inherent complexity; differences in orientation and experience; and cultural differences, but were
further complicated by group decision making, technological
change, and increased company size. Others have suggested
that there is a far greater potential for conflict and
domination than cooperation between marketing/ sales and
production/engineering units (Weinrauch and Anderson, 1982;
Clare and Sanford, 1984).

Similarly, in interdepartmental relations with R & D
departments, Souder (1977; 1981) focused empirically on the
existence of 'disharmony' with marketing, finding both 'mild
disharmony', characterised by a lack of interaction and
communication, and 'severe disharmony', characterised by
deep-seated negative attitudes, lack of appreciation, and
distrust. Harmony was found only in a minority of cases,
characterised either by equality in political and decision
power, or by one party accepting the dominance or leadership
of the other.

In examining the relationship between marketing and the
finance/accounting department, Haller (1980) suggested that:

> Today's marketing executive fights a two-front war. The
> one front is the market, which is essentially the same
> as it has always been... The second front is in his own
> company. The 'enemy' is the financial guy who has the
> chief executive's ear. (Haller, 1980)

The loss of decision making power for accountants in the
marketing oriented company has aroused some criticism
(Bridges, 1971), while empirically, Harrison (1979) drew
attention to the ineffectiveness of links between accounting
and marketing departments, and the lack of enthusiasm among
accountants for the marketing approach, producing conflict
over budgets in marketing planning. More recently, Hooley et
al (1984) also found some evidence of friction between
marketing and the finance/accounting function in
marketing-oriented UK companies.

Commentary on other interface conflicts includes that

Table 7.1:   Conflicts Between Marketing and Other Departments

---

Department	Emphasis	Marketing's Emphasis
R & D	Basic research	Applied research
	Intrinsic quality	Perceived quality
	Functional features	Sales features
Engineering	Long design lead time	Short design lead time
	Few models	Many models
	Standard components	Custom components
Purchasing	Narrow product line	Broad product line
	Standard parts	Nonstandard parts
	Price of material	Quality of material
	Economical lot sizes	Large lot sizes to accord stockouts
	Large purchases	Immediate purchasing for customer needs
Production	Long production lead time	Short production lead time
	Long runs with few models	Short runs with many models
	No model changes	
	Standard orders	Customer orders
	Ease of manufacture	Product appearance
	Average quality control	Tight quality control
Finance	Strict rationales for spending	Intuitive arguments for spending
	Tight budgeting	Flexible budgeting
	Pricing to cover costs	Pricing for market development
Accounting	Standard transactions	Special terms/ discounts
	Few reports	Many reports
Credit	Full disclosure by customers	Minimum audit examination of customers
	Low credit risks	Medium credit risks
	Tough credit terms	Easy credit terms
	Tough collection procedures	Easy collection procedures

Source: Kotler (1980)

---

relating to sales and purchasing (Sengupta and Ackoff, 1965), and more generally the hostility towards change oriented functions like market research (Kahn, 1964; Deshpande and Zaltman, 1984), and the conflict between those who manage programmes (whether, for example, project or product centred) and those who control resources (such as the sales force, advertising, and so on) (Evans, 1964; Pondy, 1964; Argyris, 1967; Corey and Star, 1971; Eckles and Novotny, 1984). It would seem, therefore, that there is a reasonable amount of evidence of conflict associated with various aspects of marketing decision making within organisations.

Importance of Outcome. Any judgement of importance rests on knowing what and whose criteria are to be applied. Certainly there have been findings that as the size of marketing expenditure increases, then so does general management intervention, in marketing budgeting generally (Wills and Kennedy, 1982), and in controlling the detail of the allocation of advertising and promotional expenditures (Hanmer-Lloyd and Kennedy, 1981).

This said, the most that can be concluded is that the outcomes of marketing decisions may be highly important in organisations, but that this depends on other situational factors – for example, the relative size of the amount at stake, or how critical or strategic are the issues involved to the particular organisation.

Power differences. Again the argument must be that the power of the marketing department is highly variable (pp. *194-197*), so this too remains a situational variable, about which it would be wrong to draw too general a conclusion. In the terms introduced earlier the power of the marketing department relative to others will vary according to its uncertainty coping role – including its success in this role and the centrality of the contingencies concerned and the scope for routinisation and routinisation of this coping – whether this role is gained through the division of tasks bringing activities with high immediacy, or whether the opportunity is taken to enter areas of high uncertainty (Hinings et al, 1974). To this should be added the skill of the departments in mobilising support for their demands, whether through 'expert' status, structurally derived political access and role set, the successful control of key resources like information, or other factors (Pettigrew, 1973).

Outcomes Through Power and Politics. The hypothesis advanced, therefore, is that the contingencies encountered in marketing decision making are in some – and possibly many – cases frequently just those conditions described as leading to decisions being determined through power and politics, that is, particularly, goal and technology dissensus, and conflict arising through differentiation; in other cases the contingencies for power and politics are likely to occur in marketing, though may not necessarily be typical, that is, interdependence, scarcity, importance of outcome, and the existence of power differences.

It is on these grounds that it was considered earlier appropriate to introduce concepts of power and politics to the analysis of marketing organisation (Piercy, 1985) and now to a major strategic marketing decision making area, particularly to the extent that it is possible to identify particular, situational contingencies favouring power and politics in the marketing area. The occurrence of such contingencies is considered in the context of the power and politics of marketing budgeting at the end of this Part of the book.

REFERENCES

Albaum, G. (1964) 'Horizontal Information Flow: An Exploratory Study', Journal of the Academy of Management, March, 21-33

Argyris, C. (1967) 'Today's Problems with Tomorrow's Organizations', Journal of Management Studies, 4 (1), 32-55

Anderson, P.F. (1982) 'Marketing, Strategic Planning and the Theory of the Firm', Journal of Marketing, 46 (2), 15-26

Astley, W.G., Axelsson, R., Butler, R.J., Hickson, D.J. and Wilson, D.C. (1982) 'Complexity and Cleavage: Dual Explanations of Strategic Decision-Making', Journal of Management Studies, 19 (4), 357-75

Bacharach, S.B. and Lawler, E.J. (1980) Power and Politics in Organizations, Jossey-Bass, San Francisco

Bardach, E. (1977) The Implementation Game: What Happens After A Bill Becomes a Law, MIT Press, Cambridge, Mass.

Baumol, W.J. (1959) Business Behavior, Value and Growth, Macmillan, New York

Bell, C. and Newby, H. (1971) Community Studies, Allen and Unwin, London

Bridges, J.S. (1971) 'Implications of a Marketing Orientation for the Role of Accountants', Accountants' Journal, August 8-13

Buell, V.P. (1982) Organizing for Marketing/Advertising Success, Association of National Advertisers, New York

Burke, M.C. (1984) 'Strategic Choice and Marketing Managers: An Examination of Business Level Marketing Objectives', Journal of Marketing Research, 21, November, 345-59

Busch, P. and Wilson, D.T. (1976) 'An Experimental Analysis of a Salesman's Expert and Referent Bases of Social Power in the Buyer-Seller Dyad', Journal of Marketing Research, 13, February, 3-11

Busch, P. (1980) 'The Sales Manager's Bases of Social Power and Influence upon the Sales Force', Journal of Marketing, 44, Summer, 91-101

Cartwright, D. (1965) 'Influence, Leadership and Control', in J.G. March (ed.) Handbook of Organizations, Rand-McNally, Chicago

Channon, C. (1968) 'The Role of Advertising Research in Management Decision Making', Proceedings, Market Research Society Conference, Brighton

Clare, D.A. and Sanford, D.G. (1984) 'Cooperation and Conflict Between Industrial Sales and Production', Industrial Marketing Management, 11, 291-301

Cobb, A.T. (1984) 'An Episodic Model of Power', Academy of Management Review, 9 (3), 482-93

Corey, E.R. and Star, S. (1971) Organization Strategy: A Marketing Approach, Harvard University Boston, Mass.

Crozier, M. (1964) The Bureaucratic Phenomenon, Tavistock, London

Cunningham, M.T. and Clarke, C.J. (1975) 'The Product Management Function in Marketing', European Journal of Marketing, 9 (2), 129-49

Cyert, R.M. and March, J.G. (1963) A Behavioral Theory of the Firm, Prentice-Hall, Englewood Cliffs, N.J.

Cyert, R.M., Simon, H..A. and Trow, D.B. (1956) 'Observation of a Business Decision', Journal of Business, 29, 237-48

Dean, J. (1951) Managerial Economics, Prentice-Hall, Englewood Cliffs, N.J.

Deshpande, R. and Zaltman, G. (1984) 'A Comparison of Factors Affecting Researcher and Manager Perceptions of Market Research Use', Journal of Marketing Research, 21, February, 32-8

Dutton, J.M. and Walton, R.E. (1966) 'Interdepartmental Conflict and Cooperation: Two Contrasting Systems', Human Organization, 25 (3), 207-20

Eckles, R.W. and Novotny, T.J. (1984) 'Industrial Product Managers: Authority and Responsibility', Industrial Marketing Management, 13, 71-5

Evans, G.H. (1964) The Product Manager's Job, American Marketing Association, Chicago

French, J.R.P. and Raven, B. (1968) 'The Bases of Social Power', in D. Cartwright and A. Zander (eds.) Group Dynamics, (3rd ed.), Harper and Row, New York

Gemmill, G.R. and Wilemon, D.L. (1972) 'The Product Manager as Influence Agent', Journal of Marketing, 36, 26-30

Georgiou, P. (1973) 'The Goal Paradigm and Notes Towards a Counter Paradigm', Administrative Science Quarterly, 18, 291-310

Hague, D.C. (1971) Pricing in Business, Allen and Unwin, London

Haller, T. (1980) 'An Organization Structure to Help You in the 80s", Advertising Age, 51 (36), 45-6

Hanmer-Lloyd, S. and Kennedy, S. (1981) Setting and Allocating the Marketing Communications Budget: A Review of Current Practice, Cranfield School of Management, Cranfield, Beds.

Hardin, D.K. (1969) 'Marketing Research - Is It Used or Abused?', Journal of Marketing Research, 6, 239

Hannan, M.T. and Freeman, J.H. (1978) 'Internal Politics of Growth and Decline', in M.W. Meyer (ed.) Environment and Organizations, Jossey-Bass, San Francisco

Harrison, G.L. (1979) 'The Accounting/Marketing Interface', The Australian Accountant, August, 469-73

Hedberg, B., Edstroem, A., Mueller, W. and Wilpert, B. (1975) 'The Impact of Computer Technology on Organizational Power Structures', in E. Grochla and N. Szperski (eds.) Information Systems and Organizational Structure, de Gruyter, Berlin

Hickson, D.J., Hinings, C.R. Lee, C.A., Schneck, R.E. and Pennings, J.M. (1971) 'A Strategic Contingencies' Theory of Intraorganizational Power', Administrative Science Quarterly, 16, 216-29

Howard, J.A. (1965) Marketing Theory, Allyn and Bacon, Boston, Mass.

Hinings, C.R., Hickson, D.J., Pennings, J.M. and Schneck, R.E. (1974) 'Structural Conditions of Intraorganizational Power', Administrative Science Quarterly, 19, 22-44

Hooley, G.J., West, C.J. and Lynch, J.E. (1984) Marketing in the UK - A Survey of Current Practice and Performance, Institute of Marketing, Cookham, Berks.

Hunt, S.D. and Chonko, L.B. (1984) 'Marketing and Machiavellianism', Journal of Marketing, 48, Summer, 30-42

Ivancevich, J.M. and Donnelly, J.H. (1970) 'Leader Influence and Performance', Personnel Psychology, 23, Winter, 539-49

Jemison, D.B. (1984) 'The Importance of Boundary-Spanning Roles in Strategic Decision Making, Journal of Management Studies, 21 (2), 131-52

Kahn, R.L. (1964) Organizational Stress: Studies in Role Conflict and Ambiguity, Wiley, New York

Kaplan, A.D.J., Dirlam, J.B. and Lanzillotti, R.F. (1958) Pricing in Big Business, Brookings Institute, Washington, D.C.

Keen, P.G.W. (1979) Information Systems and Organizational Change, Working Paper 1118-80, Massachusetts Institute of Technology, Cambridge, Mass.

Korda, M. (1975) Power: How to Get It, How to Use It, Random House, New York

Kotler, P. (1965) 'Diagnosing the Marketing Takeover', Harvard Business Review, November/December, 70-71

Kotler, P. (1980) Marketing Management: Analysis, Planning and Control, 4th ed. Prentice-Hall International, London

Krum, J.R. (1969) 'Perceptions and Evaluations of the Role of the Corporate Marketing Research Departments', Journal of Marketing Research, 6, 459-64

Lanzillotti, R.F. (1958) 'Pricing Objectives in Large Companies', American Economic Review, 48, 921-40

Lawrence, P. and Lorsch, J. (1967) Organization and Environment, Harvard UP, Boston, Mass.

Lowe, E.A. and Shaw, R.A. (1968) 'An Analysis of Managerial Biasing: Evidence from a Company's Budgeting Process', Journal of Management Studies, 5 (3), 304-15.

Lysonski, S. (1985) 'A Boundary Theory Investigation of the Product Manager's Role', Journal of Marketing, 49, Winter, 26-40

Madison, D.L., Allen, R.W., Porter, L.W., Renwick, P.A. and Mayes, B.T. (1980) 'Organizational Politics: An Exploration of Managers' Perceptions', Human Relations, 33, 79-100

Mansfield, R. (1985) Company Strategy and Organizational Design, Croom Helm, Beckenham

McDaniel, C. and Gray, D.A. (1980) 'The Product Manager', California Management Review, 23 (1), 87-94

Mintzberg, H. (1979) 'Organizational Power and Goals: A Skeletal Theory', in D.E. Schendel and C.W. Hofer (eds.) Strategic Management: A New View of Business Policy, Little Brown, Boston, Mass.

Mintzberg, H. (1983) Power In and Around Organizations, Prentice-Hall, Englewood Cliffs, N.J.

Moch, M. and Huff, A.S. (1980) 'Chewing Ass Out': The Enactment of Power Relationships Through Language and Ritual, Working Paper 687, University of Illinois

O'Herlihy, C. (1981) 'Research That Tells Lies', Campaign, 9 October, 41-3

Papandreou, A.G. (1952) 'Some Basic Problems in the Theory of the Firm', in B.F. Hally (ed.) A Survey of Contemporary Economics, Irwin, Homewood, Ill.

Perrow, C. (1970) 'Departmental Power and Perspective in Industrial Firms', in M. Zald (ed.) Power in Organizations, Vanderbilt UP, Nashville, Tenn.

Pettigrew, A.M. (1973) The Politics of Organizational Decision Making, Tavistock, London

Pfeffer, J. (1977) 'Power and Resource Allocation in Organizations', in B.M. Staw and G.R. Salancik (eds.), Research in Organizational Behavior, St. Clair Press, Chicago

Pfeffer, J. (1981) Power in Organizations, Pitman, Marshfield, Mass.

Pfeffer, J. and Salancik, G.R. (1978) The External Control of Organizations: A Resource Dependence Perspective, Harper and Row, New York

Pfeffer, J. and Salancik, G.R. (1978) The External Control of Organizations: A Resource Dependence Perspective, Harper and Row, New York

Piercy, N. (1985) Marketing Organisation: An Analysis of Information Processing, Power and Politics, Allen and Unwin, London

Piercy, N. and Evans, M. (1983) Managing Marketing Information, Croom Helm, Beckenham

Pondy, L.R. (1964) 'Budgeting and Intergroup Conflict in Organizations', Pittsburgh Business Review, 34, 1-3

Porter, L.W., Allen, R.W. and Angle, H.L. (1981) 'The Politics of Upward Influence in Organizations', in L.L. Cummings and B.M. Staw Research in Organizational Behaviour, Jai Press, Greenwich, Conn.

Ramond, C. (1974) 'On Getting Research Used', Journal of Advertising Research, 14, 47-8

Sales, A. (1972) 'The Firm and the Control of its Environment', International Studies of Management and Organization, 3, 230-57

Samuels, J.A. (1973) 'Research to Help Plan the Future of a Sea-Side Resort', Proceedings: 12th Marketing Theory Seminar, University of Lancaster

Schlackmann, W. (1979) 'The Participation Concept As A Key Factor in Integrating Professional Services Within the Modern Corporation, Admap, 15 (6), 292-7

Seiler, J.A. (1963) 'Diagnosing Interdepartmental Conflict', Harvard Business Review, September/October, 104-14

Semlow, W.J. (1959) 'How Many Salesmen do you Need?' Harvard Business Review, May/June, 126-32

Sengupta, S.S. and Ackoff, R.L. (1965) 'System Theory From an Operational Research Point of View', IEE Transactions on Systems Science and Cybernetics, 1 (1) 9-13

Shapiro, B.P. (1968) 'The Psychology of Pricing', Harvard Business Review, November/December, 119-27

Shapiro, B.P. (1977), 'Can Marketing and Manufacturing Co-Exist?', Harvard Business Review, September/October, 104-14

Simon, H.A. (1962) 'On the Concept of an Organizational Goal', Administrative Science Quarterly, 7, 1-22

Souder, W.E. (1971) 'Effectiveness of Nominal and Integrating Group Decision Processes for Integrating R & D and Marketing', Management Science, February, 595-605

Souder, W.E. (1981) 'Disharmony Between R & D and Marketing', Industrial Marketing Management, 10, 67-73

Thompson, J.D. (1967) Organizations in Action, McGraw-Hill, New York

Thompson, J.D. and Tuden, A. (1959) 'Strategies, Structures and Processes of Organizational Design', in J.D. Thompson, P.B. Hammond, R.W. Hawkes, B.H. Junker and A. Tuden (eds.) Comparative Studies in Administration, Pittsburgh UP, Penn.

Tookey, D.A. and McDougall, C.M.H. (1969) Marketing Organisation Structure, Ashridge Management College, Berkhamstead

Weinrauch, J.D. and Anderson, R. (1982) 'Conflicts Between Engineering and Marketing Units', Industrial Marketing Management, 11, 291-301

Wills, G. and Kennedy, S. (1982) 'How to Budget Marketing', Management Today, February, 58-61

Wilson, C. (1981) 'When the Export Trade Gets Tough', Marketing, 3 June, 28-31

Venkatesh, A. and Wilemon, D.L. (1976) 'Interpersonal Influence in Product Management, Journal of Marketing, 40, 33-40

8

An Information-Structure-Power
Theory of Marketing

INTRODUCTION

The perspective developed from the earlier analysis of marketing information systems (Piercy and Evans, 1983) and marketing organisational structure (Piercy, 1985) – the main thrust of which has been elaborated in Chapters 5, 6 and 7 – is one which suggests that our approach to analysing marketing decision making behaviour should rest on the study of the interaction between information, structure and power in organisations.

The information-structure-power (ISP) model was introduced in Chapter 1 and this present chapter provides a more detailed reasoning for the model and concludes with a discussion of the analytical leverage it provides in approaching various aspects of marketing.

INFORMATION, STRUCTURE AND POWER IN MARKETING

Marketing Information

Marketing information is popularly regarded as centrally important in the marketing literature. Indeed, marketing is regarded by 'somewhat unique' in that information functions are commonly institutionalised within the marketing organisation (Deshpande, 1982). For example, one view is that:

> Good information is a facilitator of successful marketing action and indeed, seen in this light marketing management becomes first and foremost an information processing capacity. (Christopher et al, 1980)

To the extent that many of the major identifiable outputs of marketing are likely to be informational – marketing, sales and advertising plans and control reports; environmental intelligence reports; surveys, tests and market experiment results; sales forecasts; and so on – then such a proposition would appear reasonable. In fact, the significance of the information processing view of marketing is rather more fundamental than this, but let us pursue for the moment the conventional view.

The consequence of this view is that much attention in the marketing literature has been devoted to systematising and attempting to promote the use of techniques of marketing intelligence gathering, research and experimentation, and the development of formal marketing information systems (see Piercy and Evans, (1983) for a review of such sources). The implicit underlying assumptions of such approaches are typically that: better quality marketing information will produce better quality decisions; managers, if provided with such information, will use it in a 'rational' way; and that information is essentially neutral. In fact, the basis of such assumptions can be challenged.

The commentary below is organised into three parts: the organisational character of information, the relationship between information and structure, and the relationship between information and power.

Marketing Information and Organisation

If we return firstly to the general theory, there are some indications in the literature of management information systems (MIS) of a recognition of the danger in assuming a direct relationship between formal MIS development and effective decision making and organisational performance (Earl and Hopwood, 1979). For example, Grinyer and Norburn (1975) found no clear relationship between the formal MIS and financial performance, but rather that informal channels of communication and decision making were more associated with success in those terms. Similarly, Child (1974) found that financially successful companies tended to avoid sophisticated information and control systems in favour of informal practices. It was concluded by Earl and Hopwood that the link between MIS and decision making effectiveness has been presumed rather than successfully described or analysed and:

> Such presumptions are little more than abstractions from the complex reality of information planning in organizations. While they might simplify the information design process, their relationship to the realities of organizational life is questionable. (Earl and Hopwood, 1979)

There are some grounds, therefore, for attempting to proceed from the normative, 'rational' view of marketing information and marketing information systems (MkIS) to account for the 'realities' of organisational behaviour.

While the prescriptive literature proposes marketing information systems development as a logical response to information overload among marketing decision makers (Hulbert et al, 1972), it follows from the earlier commentary that information in a 'corporate environment' may be far from the neutral, rational decision making resource assumed.

Certainly, at one level there has been a persistent stream of descriptive studies suggestive of some considerable contrast between the prescriptive literature, and the practices commonly found in companies. For example, over a substantial period of time it has been found: that there is a low level of use of marketing research (BIM, 1962; Baker et al, 1967; BIM, 1970; Parsons and Foster, 1978); that there has been a very limited operational development of the MkIS in the UK (Jobber, 1977; Jobber and Rainbow, 1977; Fletcher, 1982); that the information techniques actually used by companies are unsophisticated (Permut, 1977) and lack integration (Westwood et al, 1975); that market research has low status in UK industry (Wills, 1971);   and that marketing managers have a high propensity for relying on short-term operating data (Aguilar, 1967).

However, rather than simply condemning such limitations in practice as are observed, it is possible to consider the reasons for such behaviour.

First, it is noted that the literature of marketing contains some contributions which cast doubt on the validity of the entirely economic-rational approach to generating and using marketing information, and some support is available elsewhere in the wider literature, while second, a deeper analysis shows some severe conceptual flaws in the rationalist assumptions as they apply to information systems, particularly regarding such factors as the possibility of objectivity in an organisation as it relates to its environment.

To begin with, consider what is known about the reasons for searching out marketing information.   It is widely recognised that 'search processes and information-gathering constitute significant parts of decision-making' (Cyert et al, 1956), and an entirely rational approach would suggest information seeking in marketing is undertaken in order to make choices and to reduce uncertainty, as formulated in the many prescriptive texts on marketing research and information systems.

However, it was noted earlier that information may be collected for 'nonobjective' functions of various kinds, but more fundamentally for reasons which are essentially political in nature.   For instance, thinking forward to the next stage of the argument it has been noted that:

Another critical determinant of the decision to collect information is the structure of the organisation. Information is never neutral. The more important a problem is, the more important it becomes to have information about the problem, and the more important are those who gather the information.
(Pfeffer and Salancik, 1978)

Certainly, information system studies suggest that the sub-units operating and controlling information systems tend to gain status and influence from this control (Hedberg et al, 1975; Bariff and Galbraith, 1978), and we should not neglect the argument in the MIS literature that change and increased sophistication are resisted not least because such processes redistribute the control of information, and thus by implication they redistribute power (Markus, 1980).

However, even this neglects the argument that the definition of which problems are the most critical is an organisational outcome which may result from political inputs. The recognition and definition of problems is not a 'given' but has to be generated in the organisation (Cyert et al, 1956), with the implication that:

subunits, which are themselves concerned with their own survival and power in the organization, would collect information which enhances their own value in organizational decision-making or which convinces others in the organization that they have information needed for organizational purposes ... attentional processes are determined by the organization's own structure of influence. (Pfeffer and Salancik, 1978)

The conclusion is that sub-units which are established to deal with some aspect of the environment will attempt to show that that aspect is the most important part of the environment, and that they are effectively dealing with it. A similar case, in yet more overtly political terms, is made by Earl and Hopwood, who postulate that:

far from creating a basis for dialogue and interchange, MIS tend to be used as 'ammunition machines' in decisions by compromise ... information systems serve to promote and articulate particular interested positions and values. Political processes in organizations give rise to the emergence and elaboration of information systems as one party or interested group seeks to influence others ... information systems may be used to perpetuate or modify decision-making processes and structures. By influencing the accepted language of negotiation, such systems can help to shape what is regarded as problematic, what can be deemed to be a credible solution and, most important of all, the criteria which are used in their selection. (Earl and Hopwood, 1979)

The **second**, though closely related, source of doubt regarding the validity of rationalist assumptions about marketing information systems, is at a somewhat more abstract level.

The Pfeffer and Salancik (1978) argument is that organisations are led to seek particular information about their environments as a result of various factors, including the ease of collection and the ease of processing and interpretation, as well as the supposed necessity for having the information. While this seems relatively unremarkable, its importance lies in describing the process of environmental enactment, as defined by Weick (1969): 'the human creates the environment to which the system then adapts. The human actor does not react to an environment, he enacts it'. The essence of Weick's argument is an objection to the predominant model of rational beings in an organisation who react to an external environment:

Rather than talking about adapting to an external environment, it may be more correct to argue that organizing consists of adapting to an enacted environment, an environment which is constituted by the actions of interdependent human actors ... This reasserts the argument that the environment is a phenomenon tied to the processes of attention, and, that unless something is attended to it doesn't exist. (Weick, 1969)

While there may be dangers in taking Weick's argument too literally or too far - firms are, after all, dependent on the environment for resources (Pfeffer and Salancik, 1978) and legitimacy (Mintzberg, 1983), and may be overtaken or traumatised by environmental changes in factors like market and societal demands - the case made is of some relevance to challenging the apparently self-evident rationality implied by the advocacy of upgrading information systems in marketing. The writers cited above conclude:

Theoretically, information systems are designed and created to provide the information the decision maker requires, but that is an impossible task because the decision maker does not know what he needs only what is available. The available information provides cues to what is considered organizationally important and provides the information which will tend to be used by decision makers. (Pfeffer and Salancik, 1978)

In other words, it may be argued that the environment is enacted through the information system, and the information system determines, in this way, to what part of the environment attention is given by those in the organisation. The extension of the argument is that this enactment has its source in the power distribution of an organisation and political behaviour by those seeking to improve or protect their position and to influence outcomes.

These points provide some justification for the proposition that the implicitly economic-rational approach to the generation and use of marketing information may rest on challengeable and untried assumptions. On the basis of this proposition, attention is turned to the overlapping structural and political aspects of marketing information.

Marketing Information and Structure

The comments above suggest that information may be approached as an organisational, and conceivably a political resource. Since structure is one aspect of the organisation, the importance of the information-structure relationship is implicit in what has already been discussed. It is enough therefore to summarise certain of the most important points to be made.

First, it follows from the last section that the decision to collect certain types of environmental information, or to 'enact' an environment is partly determined by the organisational forms used, in the sense that 'the attentional process is determined largely by the structure of the organization' (Pfeffer and Salancik, 1978). This factor been largely ignored by the marketing literature.

Certainly, the normative literature has given some limited recognition to the idea that 'The performance of the marketing information function is directly associated with the organisational structure of the department' (Slater, 1970), since structure represents formal and informal communication channels. Others claim that marketing information system developments have been impeded by the failure of companies to adopt new structures (Howard et al, 1975). Such issues are reviewed in Piercy and Evans (1983).

Perhaps more appositely, Blankenship and Doyle (1965) stressed the importance of the location of the market research department as a determinant of its use and influence, and Bellenger and Greenberg (1978) attempted a rare conceptual analysis of the impact of structure on marketing information needs and flows. Indeed, it is only recently that empirical work has focused on the fact that 'the structure of a marketing organization may impact on the use of research information by managers' (Deshpande, 1982), or the relationship between structure and effectiveness in the marketing planning process (John and Martin, 1984). It has been found, for example, that market research use is affected, among other factors, by organisational structure

(Deshpande and Zaltman, 1982; 1984).

Second, in terms of the information processing concept of organisation considered in Chapter 4 (pp. *118-27*), a structural form represents a given capacity for processing information. This concept has achieved some recognition. For instance, Nonaka and Nicosia (1979) proposed that a simple centralised marketing organisation was sufficient to process information from a homogeneous, certain environment, but that a complex, decentralised marketing organisation is needed to process heterogeneous, uncertain environmental information. This suggests that, given certain measurement problems are solved (Piercy, 1985), information processing burden and capacity provide a mechanism for organisational design in marketing, but, more importantly here, that structure and information are directly interrelated.

Third, from the earlier discussion, organisational structure – in the sense of hierarchy, specialisation and centralisation – provides a source of barriers to information flows and of information distortion. From the cases cited in product and sales management (pp. *194-99* above) it may be claimed that this point receives some limited support in the marketing literature.

If we take as granted the organisational attributes of information in marketing – 'nonrational' practices, uses and information functions; sub-unit political behaviour in collecting and controlling information; and environmental enactment – and in particular the structure-information interaction, where structure relates to the information attended to, the linking of information processing burdens and capacities, and barriers to information flows – then we have arrived at, and indeed partly pre-empted, the question of power.

Marketing Information and Organisational Power

From the points above, and the discussion in Chapters 5 and 6, information generally may be taken variously as a source of power, an outcome of power, and a political resource used in influence processes. There seems no reason why these arguments should be less valid in the management of marketing than they are elsewhere – indeed, it will be argued that quite the reverse is true.

First, at an abstract level it is possible to approach the link between information and power via the concept of 'environmental enactment' by reference to the creation of meaning in an organisation, emphasising the symbolic and ritualistic aspects of information generation:

> language, symbols, rituals, and ceremonies are used to manage the process by which actions and events are given meaning. The process is managed in such a way as to

provide legitimation and a supporting structure for the desired behaviors and actions which are to be carried out within the organization. (Pfeffer, 1981a)

One very practical implication of such a view is that information achieves its political status because it is used to justify actions, as noted earlier, and that it thus affects the distribution of power:

one critical form of political activity in organizations is the creation of meaning – meaning which justifies the positions of power of some participants, which justifies and rationalizes decisions and actions, and which discredits the motivation or information of opponents. (Pfeffer, 1981b)

Second, information may be controlled in the way discussed earlier, and one is led to accept that:

the information to cope effectively with uncertainty is distributed through organizations in a non-random way; some people/groups have more access to this than others and this gives them power. (Markus, 1980)

In fact, it is possible to point to some recognition of the particular applicability of this form of argument to marketing information and uncertainty coping. For instance, examples of the recognition of uncertainty coping in marketing were made explicit in the strategic contingencies work:

when a marketing department copes with a volatile market by forecasting and switching sales staff around to ensure stable orders, it acquires power. (Hickson et al, 1971)

A marketing department coped with market-share uncertainty by an explicit marketing policy, regular market-share forecasting and selective advertising. (Hinings et al, 1974)

Even closer to the heart of the matter is the Nonaka and Nicosia piece, which, while not providing extensive empirical support, argued that 'The relative power of a marketing department depends on its relative ability to contribute to uncertainty reduction in the environmental information'. They concluded:

firms face an increasing market variety, i.e. marketing information is becoming increasingly more heterogeneous and uncertain. Accordingly, the power of the marketing department within an organization would have to increase. (Nonaka and Nicosia, 1979)

In all such arguments, however, there remain the constraints of substitutability and centrality.

Third, the political use of information in terms of distortion and manipulation has already been documented (pp. *197-99*).

From these comments and the foundation established in the earlier chapters, it is possible to proceed to a statement of an information-structure-power theory of marketing.

A SYNTHESIS: THE INFORMATION-STRUCTURE-POWER THEORY

The Model

The model described below in a more refined form was first proposed in Piercy (1985) and is summarised in Figure 8.1.

The essence of the argument is contingent - the environment faced by an organisation creates a given number and level of uncertainties, which are taken to be the central problem faced by management (Crozier, 1964; Thompson, 1967; Galbraith, 1973). One part of this problem is market- and marketing-related uncertainty. (Market- and marketing-related uncertainties are defined as those which are identified by the organisation with, or as, marketing management task responsibilities, and those which the marketing area - sub-unit or otherwise - may seek to cope with, possibly in competition with others within or outwith the organisation).

This uncertainty may be conceived as varying in terms of a number of dimensions - complexity, predictability and interrelatedness (Weitz and Anderson, 1981), and those attributes may be reduced to measurement either as perceived uncertainty, or as instability (the quality of information) and heterogeneity (the quantity of information) (Nonaka and Nicosia, 1979).

In this way, environmental uncertainty may be thought of as the creation of a burden of information processing requirements (Galbraith, 1973), but also as a source of critical contingencies - i.e. factors which are, or at least which are perceived to be, central to organisational success (in whatever terms the organisation measures its performance) and to organisational survival.

It may be that the nature and level of uncertainty faced, and the contingencies or critical factors created, favour the creation of a boundary-spanning marketing department - to specialise in a defined area of the environment and by providing a structural capacity to cope with the information processing burdens and the critical

---

Figure 8.1:   A Model of Information Processing, Power, Politics and the Marketing Organisation

---

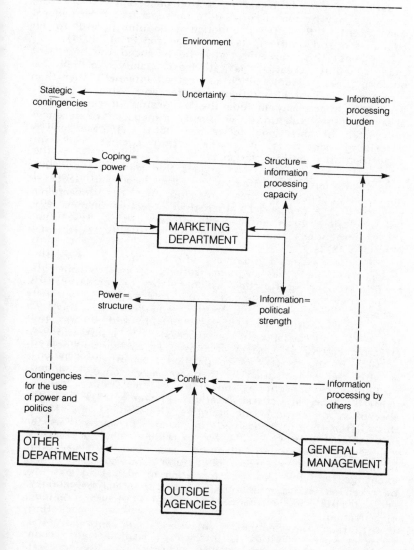

factors associated with that area.

It has been argued, however, that the nature of uncertainty may, in fact, not favour the creation of a marketing sub-unit - in situations of low uncertainty there may be no perceived need for a specialist marketing sub-unit, while in situations of very high market-related uncertainty, marketing and sales may be too significant to be separated from general management, R & D, production scheduling, and so on (Hakansson and Ostberg, 1975; Hakansson et al, 1979).

Against this, however, must be balanced the argument that sub-unit creation is at least partly, a political outcome (Leeds, 1967), which may reflect internal rather than direct environmental conditions (Pfeffer and Salancik, 1978). These conditions may include the 'ownership' of certain task areas by other sub-units, or simply managerial preferences for certain organisational forms - in both such cases one is describing conditions of power acting against marketing departmentation or integration.

In the same way, if one argues that marketing sub-unit departmentation is contingent on the form and level of uncertainty, one must bear in mind that the uncertainty concerned is a perceived rather than objective phenomenon, following the environmental enactment case (Weick, 1969), and these perceptions may in turn be politically determined (Pfeffer, 1978).

If we assume, however, first, that a marketing department exists in an organisation as an environmental boundary-spanning function which relates to certain critical contingencies - where criticality refers both to their perception as strategic and to the dependence of others on those who cope with them (Thompson, 1967) - and, second, that the marketing department is successful in maintaining an effective coping or control of those critical contingencies - possibly in the context of competition from others within or outwith the organisation - then we may conceive of the marketing department as powerful. This power derives primarily from structural location (Pfeffer, 1981) and the absorption of critical uncertainties (Hickson et al, 1971), this latter being conceived in turn, primarily, as an informational process - in, for example, sales forecasting, sales and advertising planning and control, marketing intelligence and research, distributor and customer social exchange, and the like. Information in marketing may also be taken as an important component of political behaviour - or attempts to influence decisional outcomes in the organisation.

In fact, the relationship between power and politics in terms of such activities as information manipulation remains ambiguous. One may either conceive of the powerful marketing department using marketing information as a resource to maintain or increase its power, or it may be that the powerful marketing department has no need for behaviour of this kind in relation to others (although this does not does not preclude the possibility of such behaviour within the marketing department itself). In the latter case, the absence of political behaviour would be explained by the argument that the formally powerful marketing department has little need for political behaviour, either because that formal power amounts already to the organisational institutionalisation of the goals of the marketing sub-unit and the marketing paradigm or ideology, or because formal power is more overt and susceptible to top management control, thus increasing the risks in political behaviour.

On the other hand, as noted, a marketing department may not exist at all, or may exist as little more than a symbol. We may argue that a marketing department is likely to be low in organisational power: where important boundary-spanning functions are carried out by others – whether by top management, another organisational sub-unit, or an outsider, such as a powerful distributor or an advertising agency; where those uncertainties organisationally defined as marketing-related are not critical or strategic to the organisation (itself an outcome which may be argued as above to be political in determination); or others cope more effectively with those uncertainties which are critical.

In such situations, one may conceive of the marketing department as low in organisational power, though depending on the reasons for a lack of formal structural power, the marketing sub-unit may be politically influential in the absence of formal power.

On the one hand, it is possible that the reasons for a marketing department having low formal power which are mentioned above may represent the status quo in a particular firm, or indeed the direction of a trend – for example: (a) in the concentration of power in the hands of a single distributor, or the 'Marks and Spencer syndrome', where marketing uncertainty is coped with outside the organisation; (b) or in the impact of new information technology on information access and sharing within the organisation, the channel of distribution, or the product-market, destroying marketing information 'monopolies' and automating certain information functions in marketing; (c) or the weakening of the marketing paradigm and the emergence of new corporate structures like the matrix, and new sub-units such as trade marketing, or strategic planning. In such circumstances, the outcome may not be just low power, but even the disintegration of the marketing sub-unit.

On the other hand, a marketing sub-unit which is low in formal or structural power may be politically influential, depending upon such questions as the resources available to support such influence – 'expert' status, information, access to the powerful inside and outside the organisation, and so on – and how 'politicised' is the organisation in question, as well as the more general contingencies surrounding the use of political activity to determine outcomes.

In fact, in either case, the use of power or the emergence of political forms of behaviour depends on the existence in relation to particular issues of political contingencies - particularly goal and technology dissensus, resource scarcity, and so on, leading to conflict. It has been suggested that these contingencies are likely to emerge in various areas of marketing decision making, and indeed may typify some such areas.

Ultimately, this model of the power and politics of the marketing organisation rests on the relationship between structure and information. The structural dimensions of departmentation, location with respect to others in and outwith the organisation, and the integration of functions within the sub-unit, define information processing capacity (a factor also influenced by the internal structuring of the sub-unit, organisational management style, and sub-unit interdependencies), and thus its ability to cope with uncertainty, both directly in planning and task performance but also indirectly through prevention or absorption. This is taken here as a definition of the organisational power of the marketing sub-unit.

However, what we are also describing is the definition of the potential for political influence, particularly through information control and manipulation. This may be conceived either as a support for formal power, or as an alternative way of determining outcomes in situations of uncertainty and conflict.

In this way it is possible to develop an information-structure-power theory of the marketing process in organisations. Certain aspects of this model are tested in the empirical work on marketing budgeting reported in Part III of the book. It is worth exploring, first some of the more general implications of this model.

Implications of the Model

Perhaps the first major implication of the ISP model of marketing is that our general **understanding** of the organisational functioning of marketing is likely to be improved by looking beyond the 'trappings' and examining the underlying processes of power and politics, and information processing as they affect corporate or managerial marketing behaviour. By examining the existing power structures and information processing behaviour, it is suggested that we may achieve more analytical leverage in understanding the decisions made, and in planning change, if that is the appropriate response.

Certainly, as will be seen in Part III, the empirical measurement of power remains problematic, though a variety of useful proposals exist for studying the indicators and symbols of power, in terms of such attributes as status, reputation, representation, and resources (Piercy, 1985), to allow an approach to be made to assessing power at a practical level.

In terms of **organisational design** for marketing, the model offers two insights which are absent from the extant literature of marketing organisation. The approach taken follows the suggestion that:

> It is likely that the relationship between structure and control is most productively examined in terms of information and the distribution of communication within social structures. Information is, after all, a prerequisite for control (Pfeffer, 1978)

The methodology involves the measurement of the characteristics of the information processing burden faced by marketing, and the evaluation of the information processing capacities of alternative marketing structures (Piercy, 1985).

The implications of the earlier discussion are: that the formal allocation of marketing task responsiblities creates power and the 'ownership' of certain activities; that organisational participants are likely to struggle over the allocation of discretion and resources; that structure lies at the heart of the ability to politically 'manage' information flows; and that marketing decision making is frequently characterised by high uncertainty, and is often shared.

The suggestion for an operational model of organisational design for marketing is that it should encompass the link between structure and the control of activities, the determinants of power and influence of departments, the attempt by participants to have their interests structurally institutionalised, and the varying capacities for structural alternatives to process information. This model was specified in Marketing Organisation: An Analysis of Information Processing, Power and Politics (Piercy, 1985).

In just the same way, the design of **marketing information systems** is proposed not simply as an exercise in matching information processing software and hardware with identifiable management information needs, but as involving organisational analysis of the political implications of marketing information and the structural requirements for meeting different objectives. This approach was detailed in Managing Marketing Information (Piercy and Evans, 1983).

Of greatest present moment, as the implications of the ISP model unfold, are those for **marketing decision making**. The ultimate importance of power and politics lies not in their intrinsic interest but in their impact on significant decisional outcomes. In this present study interest is focused on the allocation of resources to marketing, although it is intended that this approach should be extended to other decision areas, particularly in the choice of marketing strategy, new product selection, product deletion, and so on.

Various propositions may be worth exploring in this area. For example, it may be speculated that one of the, as yet undefined, characteristics of 'good' marketing management (whatever criterion is used) may turn out to be directly related to the use, management, and control of power sources and political influence. Certainly, as noted in Chapter 1, it is not possible simply to presume that power and politics necessarily have an adverse effect on organisational effectiveness. To the extent that such a view were supportable it would have considerable significance for such issues as the evaluation of marketing managers and for marketing education and training. We return to this argument in Part IV of the book.

More specifically, analytical leverage in understanding the dynamics of power and influence is central to predicting who will gain the resources they want and who achieves acceptance of their preferred courses of action. More deterministically, applying that same analytical leverage to the system of power and politics is a starting point in redesigning the system to alter its functioning, with the goal of managing outcomes or facilitating change in technology, strategic direction, external relationships, and so on.

Also, while the corporate power system is an attribute of one's own organisation, it follows that the same principles apply to understanding the behaviour of other organisations, in evaluating competitors and other outside bodies.

IMPLICATIONS

This chapter had the goal of applying the earlier theoretical analysis of organisation, power and politics to marketing, in the form of an information-structure-power model.

The first stage was to discuss the interrelationship between marketing information - viewed in its organisational setting - and structure, and then between information and structure and the key concept of power.

This led to a synthesis in the information-structure -power model or theory of marketing, followed by a discussion of the implications of this approach for the study and management of corporate marketing.

The ISP model provides the basis for the empirical investigation of marketing resource allocation described in Part III. The last task remaining in Part II is to pursue the logic of the ISP model by examining in Chapter 9 the power and politics of budgeting and resource allocation in marketing.

REFERENCES

Aguilar, F.J. (1967) Scanning the Business Environment, Macmillan, New York

Baker, M., Braam, T. and Kemp, A. (1967) Permeation of the Marketing Concept in Yorkshire Manufacturing Industry, University Press, Bradford

Bariff, M.L. and Galbraith, J.R. (1978) 'Intraorganizational Power Considerations for Designing Information Systems', Accounting, Organizations and Society, 3, 15-27

Bellenger, D.N. and Greenberg, B.A. (1978) Marketing Research - A Management Information Approach, Irwin, Homewood, Ill.

BIM (1961) A Survey of the Functions of Marketing, Product and Brand Managers, British Institute of Management, London

BIM (1970) Marketing Organization in British Industry, British Institute of Management, London

Child, J. (1974) 'Management and Organizational Factors Associated with Company Performance', Journal of Management Studies, 11 (3), 175-189

Christopher, M., McDonald, M. and Wills, G. (1980) Introducing Marketing, Pan, London

Corey, E.R. and Star, S. (1971) Organization Strategy: A Marketing Approach, Harvard University Press, Boston, Mass.

Crozier, K. (1964) The Bureaucratic Phenomenon, University of Chicago Press, Chicago

Cyert, R.M., Simon, H.A. and Trow, D.M. (1956) 'Observation of a Business Decision', Journal of Business, 29, 237-48

Deshpande, R. (1982) 'The Organizational Context of Market Research Use', Journal of Marketing, 46, Fall, 91-101

Deshpande, R. and Zaltman, G. (1982) 'Factors Affecting the Use of Market Research Information: A Path Analysis', Journal of Marketing Research, 19, February, 14-31

Deshpande, R. and Zaltman, G. (1984) 'A Comparison of Factors Affecting Researcher and Manager perceptions of Market Research Use', Journal of Marketing Research, 21, February, 31-8

Earl, M.J. and Hopwood, A.G. (1079) 'From Management Information to Information Management', in The Information Systems Environment, North-Holland

Fletcher, K.P. (1982) 'Marketing Information Systems: A Lost Opportunity', in Thomas, M.J. (ed.) Marketing: Bridging the Gap Between Theory and Practice, Proceedings: Marketing Education Group Conference, University of Lancaster

Galbraith, J.R. (1972) 'Organization Design: An Information Processing View', in J.W. Lorsch and P.R. Lawrence (eds.), Organization Planning: Cases and Concepts, Irwin, Homewood, III.

Galbraith, J.R. (1973) Designing Complex Organizations, Addison-Wesley, Reading, Mass.

Grinyer, P. and Norburn, D. (1975) 'Planning for Existing Markets: Perceptions of Executives and Financial Performance', Journal of the Royal Statistical Society, Series A, 70-97

Hakansson, H. and Ostberg, C. (1975) 'Industrial Marketing: An Organizational Problem?', Industrial Marketing Management, 4, 113-23

Hakansson, H., Wootz, B., Andersson, O. and Hangard, P. (1979) 'Industrial Marketing as an Organizational Problem', European Journal of Marketing, 13 (3), 81-93

Hedberg, B., Edstroem, A., Mueller, W. and Wilpert, B. (1975) 'The Impact of Computer Technology on Organizational Power Structures', in E. Grochla and N. Szperski (eds.) Information Systems and Organization Structure, de Gruyter, Berlin

Hickson, D.J., Hinings, C.R., Lee, C.A., Schneck, R.E. and Pennings, J.E. (1971) 'A Strategic Contingencies' Theory of Intraorganizational Power', Administrative Science Quarterly, 16, 216-29

Hinings, C.R., Hickson, D.J. Pennings, J.M. and Schneck, R.E. (1974) 'Structural Conditions of Intraorganizational Power', Administrative Science Quarterly, 19, 22-44

Hooley, G.J., West, C.J. and Lynch, J.E. (1984) Marketing in the UK - A Survey of Current Practice and Performance, Institute of Marketing, Cookham, Berks.

Howard, J.A., Hulbert J. and Farley, J.U. (1975) 'Organizational Analysis and Information Systems Design: A Decision Process Perspective', Journal of Business Research, 3 (2), 133-48

Hulbert, J., Farley, J.U., Howard, J.A. (1972) 'Information Processing and Decision Making in Marketing Organizations', Journal of Marketing Research, 9 (2), 75-7

Jobber, D. (1977) 'Management Information Systems in United States and British Industry', Management Decision, 15 (2), 297-304

Jobber, D. and Rainbow, C. (1977) 'A Study of the Development and Implementation of Marketing Information Systems in British Industry', Journal of the Market Research Society, 19 (2), 104-11

John, G. and Martin, J. (1984) 'Effects of Organizational Structure of Marketing Planning on Credibility and Utilization of Plan Output ', Journal of Marketing Research, 19, February, 14-31

Leeds, R. (1967) 'The Absorption of Protest: A Working Paper', in W.E. Cooper, H.J. Leavitt and M.W. Shelley (eds.) New Perspectives in Organization Research, Wiley, New York

Markus, M.L. (1980) Power, Politics and MIS Implementation, Working Paper 1155-80, Massachusetts Institute of Technology, Cambridge, Mass.

Mintzberg, H. (1983) Power In and Around Organizations, Prentice-Hall, Englewood Cliffs, N.J.

Nonaka, I. and Nicosia, F.M. (1979) 'Marketing Management, Its Environment and Information Processing', Journal of Business Research, 7 (4), 277-301

Parsons, M. and Foster, P. (1978) 'Notes on the Motivation and Methods of the Small Exporter', Industrial Marketing Digest, 3 (2), 130-5

Permut, S.E. (1977) 'The European View of Marketing Research', Columbia Journal of World Business, 12 (3), 94-104

Pfeffer, J. (1978) 'The Micropolitics of Organizations', in M.W. Meyer et al (eds.) Environment and Organizations, St. Clair Press, Chicago.

Pfeffer, J. (1981a) 'Management As Symbolic Action: The Creation and Maintenance of Organizational Paradigms', in L.L. Cummings and B.M. Staw (eds.), Research in Organizational Behavior, Jai Press, Greenwich, Conn.

Pfeffer, J. (1981b) Power in Organizations, Pitman, Marshfield, Mass.

Pfeffer, J. and Salancik, G.R. (1978) The External Control of Organizations, Harper and Row, New York

Piercy, N. (1985) Marketing Organisation: An Analysis of Information Processing, Power and Politics, Allen and Unwin, London

Piercy, N. and Evans, M. (1983) Managing Marketing Information, Croom Helm, Beckenham

Slater, A. (1970) The Organization Structure for Marketing Information, unpublished M.Sc. dissertation, University of Bradford

Thompson, J.D. (1967) Organizations in Action – Social Science Bases of Administrative Theory, McGraw-Hill, New York

Tushman, M.L. and Nadler, D.A. (1978) 'Information Processing as an Integrating Concept in Organizational Design', Academy of Management Review, 3 (3), 613-24

Weick, K.R. (1969) The Social Psychology of Organizing, Addison-Wesley, Reading, Mass.

Westwood, R.A., Palmer, J.B., Zeitlin, D.M., Levine, D.M., Thio, K. and Charney, R. (1975) 'Integrated Information Systems', Journal of the Market Research Society, 17 (3), 127-82

Wills, G. (1971) Marketing Research in British Industry, British Institute of Management, London

9

The Power and Politics of Marketing Budgeting

INTRODUCTION

Part II of the book concludes with a synthesis of what has been discussed in two areas: marketing budgeting (in Part I), and organisational power and politics and the marketing organisation (in the preceeding chapters of Part II). The goal is to apply the concepts summarised in the information-structure-power model of marketing to the area of resource allocation, leading in Part III to the introduction of new empirical evidence.

The pursuit of this goal involves first examining general models of the power and politics of resource allocation in organisations, and then turning to evidence of similar processes in marketing budgeting. In this latter area the available evidence amounts to no more than indications, since no existing study has adopted an explicitly political analysis of marketing decision making. In support of the last issue, we examine, thirdly, the case that may be made for claiming that the contingencies for the use of power and politics may be found in the particular area of marketing budgeting. Finally, we close Part II by drawing out the implications for the analysis of marketing budgeting, and construct a conceptual model of the power and politics of resource allocation in marketing.

THE POWER AND POLITICS OF BUDGETING

The purpose of this section is to review a number of studies of budgeting and resource allocation in the general literature, which take an explicitly political stance in their analysis. Reference has already been made to a number of such studies, and attention will be focused here on those which are most methodologically and conceptually revealing for our present purposes.

General Recognition of Budgeting Politics

One conceptual analyst of power in organisations describes

what he refers to 'the budgeting game' as:

> perhaps the best-known of the political games, and the
> one most extensively studied ... The tactics of the
> budgeting game are simple.   In the case of operating
> budgets, use every trick available to gain the largest
> possible allocation for the unit;   always ask for too
> much in the knowledge that a given percentage will be
> cut;   evoke all the 'rational' arguments that support a
> large budget and suppress those that do not, if need be
> distorting the truth about the real needs of the unit;
> and finally, when the budget is determined, make sure
> that every last penny is used up at year end, even if
> some of it is wasted, for whatever gets turned back will
> be subtracted from the next year's request.
> (Mintzberg, 1983)

Antecedents for such conclusions lie in the Cyert and
March (1963) study, where the general argument was that the
budget is an outcome of a political process of bargaining in
the organisational coalition of interests (see pp. *244 - 245*
below).   Of more immediate moment, however, are a variety of
empirical studies in the general literature concerned with
government budgeting, business organisation budgeting, and
that in public sector organisations like universities.

Budgeting in Govermental Organisations

The classic work here, to which considerable reference has
already been made (pp. *61-63*) is the Wildavsky (1964, 1968,
1979) work on the allocation of resources across government
agencies in the USA, which quite explicitly took 'budgets as
attempts to allocate financial resources through political
processes' (Wildavsky, 1968).   Indeed, more recently, it has
been noted that in order to obtain resources 'Even that
archtechnocrat, Robert McNamara, as Secretary of Defense
deliberately distorted the figures he gave to Congess on the
Vietnam War' (Mintzberg, 1983).

This, and indeed the later work to which we give
detailed attention shortly (pp. *250-254*), has focused on the
public sector, for reasons of data availability, ease of
access, and so on.   This highlights what may to some provide
a substantial objection.   It might be argued, for instance,
that while budgeting in the public sector is demonstrably a
political process, this behaviour is characteristic of the
public sector rather than of the budgeting process.   Thus,
the defender of the prescriptive theory of budgeting might be
led to argue that for a number of reasons business
organisations are 'rational' in their budgeting behaviour,
rather than political.

The important point is, however, that while political

processes may be more obscured in business organisations (and there are certainly problems of access and data availability in finding what budgets are, let alone how they were determined), there appears no conceptual reason why the same processes should not operate, in the appropriate circumstances or contingencies, as in public sector organisations.

Mintzberg (1983) suggests that budgeting is widely studied as a political process because 'it must be played more overtly and with more clearly defined rules... Managers must make their cases explicitly and formally, in accordance with set procedures at set times of the year'. In fact, this quotation contains something of a <u>non sequitur</u>, since apparently bureaucratic or rational systems may do little more than obscure the real use of power and politics. Although managers themselves would probably argue similarly that business budgeting is essentially rational because it is open and systematic, this is to risk obscuring real underlying process with superficial bureaucratic systems, and we reject the argument that public sector studies are irrelevant to business organisations for such reasons.

Similarly, as noted earlier, Pfeffer was led to argue somewhat strangely, and certainly inconsistently, that business organisations 'have a reasonably agreed upon goal of profit maximization, and the goal consensus negates much of the need for the use of power that might otherwise exist' and he suggested that 'The objective of profit maximization can serve as an archetype of what a consensually shared goal can accomplish, in terms of legitimating and organizing collective action' (Pfeffer, 1981). If taken to its extreme this argument would again be similar to that voiced by managers themselves – that budgeting is not political because profit maximisation provides both the objective and control mechanism. This would, however, be to take a somewhat simplistic view of organisational objectives (see pp. 201-204 above), and also to ignore the role of rationalisation and legitimation, given the uncertainty typically surrounding what is or is not profit maximising behaviour. This argument then is also rejected as a reason for concluding that business budgeting is necessarily less political than that in the public sector.

In fact, in unfolding his thesis Pfeffer finally conceded of Wildavsky's work that it is 'equally applicable to the analysis of resource allocation within other types of organization' and more generally that 'anecdotal evidence suggests that corporations are not as different as one might think, in terms of the influence of power and politics, from these public organizations' (Pfeffer, 1981). This leads us shortly to draw parallels between the Stanford public sector work and related studies, and business budgeting.

Budgeting in Business Organisations

In support of the last point, it is possible to cite a number of studies of budgeting in business firms, which display signs of the use of power and the emergence of political behaviour.

Cyert and March (1963). While the basis of A Behavioral Theory of the Firm was the computer simulation of a theoretical model of organisational decision making, rather than the direct study of organisational behaviour, its impact is such that the conclusions about budgeting merit attention.

Certainly, Cyert and March found case evidence of information distortion in budgeting to influence outcomes:

> The classic statment came from a staff member ... He told a group of men outside the company 'In the final analysis, if anybody brings up an item of cost that we haven't thought of, we can balance it by making another source of saving tangible'. (Cyert and March, 1963)

In their general model they postulated that budgeting was one of the areas where dependence was particularly conspicuous on 'information, estimates, and expectations that ordinarily differ appreciably from reality', and there was only limited consideration of alternatives, where 'The set of alternatives considered depends on some features of organizational structure and on the locus of search responsibility in the organization'.

The implications they drew were that budgeting could be related to the dimensions of their theory of the firm in the following ways: in the quasi resolution of organisationa! conflict – goals enter as independent constraints, but in resource rationing there was a tendency to use arbitrary allocation rules that maintained the relative position of coalition members, and a tendency to re-evaluate estimates which were difficult to defend as traditional organisational practice, by standard accounting procedure, or as giving an immediate return; in search behaviour – search was stimulated by a problem or failure, such as the need to cut costs, to improve profitability, or to increase sales, or to maintain the position of an organisational sub-group, where each type of search has a different organisational locus and consequences, and for an alternative investment to be introduced, a problem must be perceived by the organisation and the investment must be visible to that part of the organisation in which search is stimulated; in uncertainty avoidance – which involved extensive use of standard industry and firm rules, since widely shared criteria standardise dimensions within the environment and standardise decisions, leading to rule-directed behaviour, where the rules tend to be biased in the direction of producing data that lead to organisational acceptance of projects favoured by particular sub-units; and in <u>organisational learning</u> – adjustments over time in the aspirations of sub-units, in the criteria applied to projects, and in the search reactions to failure, in a behavioural model of resource allocation which is 'heavily history-dependent'.

They presented case evidence of the allocation of resources to projects in support of this approach, as well as in sub-unit resource allocations. They cited the results of studies by Seeber at Carnegie into the allocation of resources to R & D in one business which suggested that: most organisations were aware of, and probably used, simple rules like 'per cent of sales' to guide R & D allocations; there was pressure from sub-units to maintain absolute money allocations and, the logic of research, as well as difficulties in forecasting revenues, led to attempts to smooth allocations; target allocations were substantially influenced by estimates of 'per cent of sales' allocations made by other organisations; and organisational failure in profit or sales led to pressure to revise allocation rules. This suggested some confirmation of the general model, though the authors sought refinements to:

> provide specific understanding of the ways in which the demands of the various organizational subunits are mediated in the face of scarcity, the ways in which allocation rules change over time, and the ways in which causes are attributed to failures of various kinds. (Cyert and March, 1963)

Pondy (1964, 1969, 1970). At a similar time to the Cyert and March work, Pondy was studying capital budgeting, where his central focus was on sub-unit conflict, since he suggested:

> The engineering economics literature and the accounting literature usually treat the budgeting and resource allocation problem solely as a problem in economics ... it proved helpful to interpret capital budgeting for resource allocation as a process of resolving intergroup conflict. (Pondy, 1964)

His starting point was to take the organisation as a conflict system, where organisational participants had multiple group memberships and 'each subgroup engages in competition with every other subgroup for an adequate share of the available resources' (Pondy, 1964). Because of sub-group identity and goals which were only partly consistent, sub-group loyalty produced a situation where:

each functional department has a vested interest in each of its projects considered for the budget, and will find it hard to be objective in judging the entire set of projects or in genuinely accepting the budgeting decisions of an impartial budget committee. (Pondy, 1964)

Perhaps of greatest interest here was Pondy's recognition of the political consequences of sub-group conflict over budgets in organisations, since, he suggested:

Not only do subgroup loyalties distort the perceptions of investment projects they lead subgroups to adopt 'political strategies' for more nearly assuring approval of its projects. (Pondy, 1964)

While recognising that 'what strategies are adopted depends on the particular loopholes available in the budgeting system of the parent company', Pondy found that examples of such political strategies in budgeting included: where the company had long-range plans, putting a project in tentatively so that it gradually assumed a more certain status; when the budget committee asked divisions to rank proposed projects, the sub-unit put last those projects the budget committee was known to favour and was likely to approve anyway, and placed first those projects with least chance of approval otherwise; when the budget committee set a minimum rate of return requirement, then the sub-unit might 'doctor' the economic analysis of marginal projects, for example by judicial 'guessing' of uncertain figures.

Pondy examined the use of budget committees in resolving sub-unit conflict, suggesting that conflict among members appeared almost inevitable and that 'Though no direct evidence is available on how these conflicts of project preferences are settled, it is likely that bargaining and compromise take precedence over analytical efforts' (Pondy, 1964).

Pondy's theory, and empirical observations, suggested that project classification was one device used to resolve conflicts. Since sub-group loyalties are reflected in the criteria of project evaluation – the accounting/finance group stressed economic criteria, the legal group government regulations, and 'the marketing representative will insist that market share is really a more appropriate measure of the worth of a project than is rate of return' (Pondy, 1964) – in order to avoid resurrecting the criteria conflict for each project, the budget committee defined different investment categories, which thus legitimised the use of different criteria. For example, one classification found for projects was into: cost reduction; replacement; commercial; legal; and employee welfare categories - each category implying different criteria, and where that categorisation reflected the residue of past conflicts, and provided an institutional framework for resolving inter-functional conflict over the criteria for project evaluation. Two other devices - or 'defense mechanisms' - used by budget committees were: to divide budgets into parts to be authorised by the board in increments; and to put 'unsuccessful' projects into the long range plan, to handle the disappointment of 'losing' divisions.

However, even more covert was the difference between the projects chosen by an organisation and those actually implemented. For example, Pondy (in a private communication cited by Cyert and March, (1963)) found in one large manufacturing firm that the procedures for making 'technical' revisions to projects, in effect yielded somewhat different projects to those which had been originally approved - simply by modifying or elaborating approved projects with the partial substitution of non-approved projects. Indeed, Cyert and March found similar case evidence in their own work.

Pondy's research led to the general conclusion:

> two factors are sufficient for intergroup conflict to exist; subgroup loyalties and intergroup competition. Both these factors were shown to be present in the budgeting-resource allocation process in the modern, large corporation. Budgeting can therefore be viewed as a process of resolving intergroup conflicts. (Pondy, 1964)

Perhaps of even greater relevance, Pondy's subsequent work on the same process led to the suggestion that:

> To understand how an organization chooses a specific allocation pattern... we need to examine more closely the internal dynamics of communication, persuasion, and the exercise of personal power. (Pondy, 1970)

Bower (1970). Also of note in the capital budgeting area is Bower's detailed case study research, where his starting point was 'a growing awareness that the firm, in many respects, is a political organism' (Bower, 1970).

Bower's approach was to turn from the traditional theory of capital budgeting - emphasising financial analysis techniques - to approach the subject as a general management problem of: perception, analysis and choice; a social process of implementation; and a process of revising policy. One implication was that the submission of a project proposal should not be regarded as the starting point - where

247

financial analysis comes into play - but as one of the last stages of an 'unobserved process'. In particular, his findings suggested that the context of budgeting was a set of organisational forces that influenced the processes of project definition.

In his detailed conclusions, one significant element was the recognition of the politics of budgets, and the political manipulation of information. On the former point he found that:

> the process of bureaucratic politics is the explanation, or the content, of the process of impetus. Projects are counters in the games managers play to achieve organizational position. It may be clearer to think of the two interrelated systems involved in the organizational process of resource allocation in these terms: the process of distribution is technical-economic in content; impetus is political. (Bower, 1970)

On the latter point of information manipulation, Bower suggested, for example, that:

> A forecast, understood in context, must be regarded as a 'move' in a complicated game with economic, organisational, and interpersonal implications. (Bower, 1970)

Schiff and Lewin (1968, 1970). Turning to operating rather than capital budgets, Schiff and Lewin's studies demonstrated bargaining, and the creation of 'organizational slack', as well as the manipulation of budgeting systems, in ways which are suggestive of covert political behaviour, since they found that managers satisfied their personal aspirations through the creation of 'slack' in good years and the reconversion of 'slack' into reported profit in bad years.

In studying three large US corporate divisions, they concluded that:

> division management generally created slack in their budgets by underestimating gross revenue, inclusion of discretionary increases in personnel requirements, establishment of marketing and sales budgets with internal limits on funds to be spent, use of manufacturing costs which do not reflect process improvements operationally available at the plant, and the inclusion of discretionary 'special projects'. (Schiff and Lewin, 1970)

Since their analysis gave some explicit attention to marketing costs, Schiff and Lewin's work is cited again below (pp. *268-69*).   Their general findings, however, were that managers created slack in budgets through understating revenues and overstating costs, which is possible because:

> the budget preparation process is a highly participative effort on the part of all managerial levels.   This is because managers bargain about the performance criteria by which they will be judged throughout the year and for resource allocations.   The outcome is a bargained budget incorporating varying degrees of slack.   (Schiff and Lewin, 1968)

In their terms managers consciously and intentionally created, and bargained for, slack.   They concluded that:

> slack may account for as much as 20 to 25 per cent of divisional budgeted operating expenses ... Our results amply support the behavioral implications of the occurrence of slack as an unintended result of the budget and control system.   (Schiff and Lewin, 1968)

Moreover, however, we may interpret the use of simple decision rules to underestimate sales and overestimate costs, and the bargaining processes described by Schiff and Lewin as essentially political in nature.

Gandz and Murray (1980). In a study of the experience of workplace politics, Gandz and Murray measured the perceived politicisation of organisational processes among managers. They found that politicisation was widely recognised among managers, and that the issues seen as most highly political were promotions and transfers, recruitment, pay, and budget allocations.   They suggested that of the organisational processes considered:

> the ones that are seen as most politicized ... are those in which there are usually few established rules or standards and criteria tend to be "fuzzy" or open to great subjectivity.   Those seen as least political ... are those in which policies, some objective criteria, or precedents exist.   (Gandz and Murray, 1980)

It was also found that the perceptions of managers were that the climate was most political at higher managerial levels and less political at lower levels.

On one hand this confirms that budgeting is perceived as a political process, although the Gandz and Murray thesis is that politics is a 'subjectively experienced phenomenon' - i.e. political behaviour is taken as attributed by others rather than measured in any more objective way (see pp. *292 -94* below).

Collins et al, (1983). In an overt, and admittedly somewhat superficial, study of behaviour by managers in budgeting, Collins et al studied the influence acts summarised in Table 9.1, and factor analysed their responses to identify four 'gameplay factors' in budgeting: devious, economic, incremental and time factors. Of these factors the devious and incremental were explicitly political in nature.

Budgeting Studies in US Universities, Social Services, and Schools

The works cited to this point demonstrate general recognition of the power and politics of budgeting, the description of these phenomena in public sector budgeting, and their existence in business organisations. We turn now to a collection of studies originated or inspired by Pfeffer and his co-workers. While these studies were carried out in public sector organisations - universities, social services, and school districts - their relevance to this present study is considerable and will become clear as we proceed.

Pfeffer and Salancik (1974). The first of several studies of resource allocation in US universities was at the University of Illinois, and focused on twenty-nine academic departments, using budget data over a thirteen year period. The dependent variable was the average proportion of the 'general funds' budget (i.e. budgets not controlled by contract or bequest) received by each department. Explanatory variables included: the proportion of teaching done by each department, and committee representation. The finding was that both the power indicators measured (Committee and Research Board representation) and workload (hours taught) significantly affected budget allocations. This finding remained even when controlling for department size or national reputation of departments. It was also found that differences in teaching costs did not overturn the finding, and that powerful departments were able to increase their share of resources regardless of their share of students taught, while in less powerful departments resources were lost when student demand fell and only gained through demonstrating greatly increased student demand in the department.

Pfeffer and Moore (1980). The Illinois study was replicated at the University of California and extended to include the paradigm development of departments. The results were consistent with the Illinois study, suggesting power, as well as enrolments, affected the change in budget and faculty resources over time, as well as absolute resource

---

Table 9.1: Political Influence Acts in Budgeting

Influence Acts	Labels
Trying hard to keep what was in last year's budget	Horatio at the Bridge
Getting changes in one's budget by seeking incremental changes over prior budgets	Incremental Change
Soliciting help of persons other than one's boss to get desired budgetary amounts	Seeking other's help
Relying on friendship with one's boss to get a desired budget	Friendship with boss
Inviting boss to work area to assess budgetary needs	On site visit
Waiting for right time to ask for certain items in the budget	Waiting for right time
Telling the boss the operation must be shut down if budgetary request is not granted	All or nothing
Asking for small amount initially with the hope of getting larger amounts in succeeding budget periods	Camel's nose
Presenting the boss with the facts to get budget requests	Present facts
Getting budgetary amounts by showing that request will pay for themselves	It'll pay for itself
Getting budgetary requests by convincing boss a crisis exists	Crisis
Putting some likely-to-be-cut items in the budget request in order to protect other items	Sacrifical lamb
Attaching particularly desired items to already approved items to guard against a disapproval	Piggyback

---

Source: Adapted by Author from Collins et al, (1983)

---

allocations. There was also evidence that paradigm development had a positive effect on the level of resource allocation, and that the change in enrolments interacted with paradigm level to affect changes in resource allocations. The researchers' explanation was that departments with more consensus about educational and research issues (high paradigm development) and the ability to more predictably produce research results, were more successful in using enrolments and change in enrolments to gain extra shares of resources.

Hills and Mahoney (1978). A related, though methodologically different, study at the University of Minnesota, also found evidence that power affected resource allocations and that this was particularly the case in periods of greater resource scarcity.

Implications of the University Studies. In reviewing the university studies, Pfeffer (1981) suggested that: they confirm the notion of universities as political coalitions, where, among other factors, power relates to resource allocation outcomes; and they provide evidence of the unobtrusiveness of the use of power and the dominance of norms of rationality. For present purposes the methodology of those studies was influential in choosing measures of power, and they are discussed further in the next chapter.

Pfeffer and Leong (1977). These researchers studied the allocation of funds to social services by a sample of United Funds (co-operative charitable fund-raising bodies), and argued that the power of a member agency in the Fund was negatively related to the agency's dependence on the Fund (i.e. the proportion of that agency's funds derived from the Fund), but that the power of a member agency in a fund was positively related to the Fund's dependence on the agency (the proportion of that Fund's budget going to that agency):

> The individual agency's power within the United Fund is a function of its importance to the United Fund and its ability to articulate a credible threat of withdrawal. The ability to threaten withdrawal is determined by by the agency's ability to raise funds on its own outside the Fund ... the greater the amount of outside funds raised, the higher the allocation from the United Fund ... Our argument suggests that this causal relationship will be stronger (a) the smaller the proportion of the agency's budget received from the United Fund (the less dependent the agency is on the Fund), and (b) the larger the proportion of the United Fund's budget that goes to a given agency (the larger,

> and hence, the more important, the agency is to the Fund). (Pfeffer and Leong, 1977)

On the other hand, the researchers found no significant association between any demographic variable – such as ethnic population, incomes, and so on which might reasonably be expected to influence the distribution of charity funds – and allocation, and they suggested that 'the political model found empirical support'.

Provan et al (1980). In a replication and extension of Pfeffer and Leong (1977), Provan et al (1980) again found that the higher the proportion of non-United Fund resources obtained (and thus the greater the agency's power and the less its dependence on the Fund) the higher the allocation received. This study also found that community centrality was important to agencies in obtaining funds.

Implications of the Social Services Studies. It has been concluded of this set of studies:

> the two studies conducted so far of United Fund allocations to member social service agencies support the position of the importance of power and politics in the resource allocation process. The unimportance of measures which might serve as surrogates for community need provides a striking testimony to the very political nature of budget decision making when the standards of assessment and unclear and technologies are uncertain. (Pfeffer, 1981)

Related studies were concerned with resource allocation in the US school system.

Freeman and Hannan (1975). This work argued that the general norms of teacher/pupil ratios produced constant school class size, and that there would be a proportional change up or down in teacher numbers as the enrolments changed in school districts. On the other hand, they argued that the administrative personnel component would behave differently – with growing enrolments in a district, administrative personnel numbers would change in line with teacher numbers, but with declining school roles the power of the administrative staff was expected to lead to a less than proportional decline in their staff numbers, because the administrative staff enjoyed the hierarchical power of managing budget adjustments. In other words, they expected that in growing school districts all personnel types would adjust upwards, but in declining districts the administrative staff would protect their numbers through political power. This model was supported by their empirical results.

Freeman (1979). This work extended the Freeman and Hannan (1975) study to include enrolments, sources of funds, and tax inspections, to arrive at the conclusion that: change in enrolment had a ten times greater effect on administrative staff numbers in growing rather than declining districts; the change in funds had about twice the effect on administrator numbers in growing rather than declining districts; but that tax elections were more complex in their effects, since it seemed that 'districts exposed to outside scrutiny responded to relief from that scrutiny by becoming less responsive to changes in enrolments' (Freeman, 1979).

Hannan and Freeman (1978). This study involved a more complex analysis of the school district data, to examine two factors: the 'carrying capacity', or number of personnel that would be observed in equilibrium, and the time required for the system to adjust towards the equilibrium, and they suggested that the size of a personnel category was determined by: the availability of environmental resources; the size of competing components and the intensity of competition; and stable factors in the organisation and environment that favour the personnel category. They concluded:

> When enrolments are growing, the administrative staff appears to get only the remainder of the resource pie. However, when enrollments are declining, administration shifts to a more controlling position in the political struggle for resources. (Hannan and Freeman, 1978)

Of this set of studies of resource allocation in US education and social services, it has been suggested that:

> The studies of universities, United Funds, and school districts together provide support for the position that power and politics affect the allocation of budgetary resources within organizations. (Pfeffer, 1981)

Implications

This section of evidence has demonstrated the following points relating to the general notion that power and politics influence the allocation of budgetary resources: that there is some recognition of budgeting as a political 'game'; that budgeting in governmental organisations has been shown to be susceptible to political analysis; that a case may be made for suggesting that such an approach may be equally valid in the business as in the non-business organisation; that, in fact, budgeting in business organisations - both capital and operational - has been shown to exhibit signs of political behaviour; and that budgeting outcomes (in public sector organisations of various types) demonstrate not simply that political behaviour is significant to budgetary outcomes, but that these outcomes reflect the balance of power in organisations.

If one accepts that the potential role of power and politics in budgeting is thus substantiated, then the next stage is to question the extent to which this general model may be applied to budgeting for marketing. The question is therefore to what extent the signs and processes described above may be found in marketing budgeting, in seeking support for the information-structure-power model.

THE POWER AND POLITICS OF MARKETING BUDGETING

In fact, in examining the literature of marketing as it relates to resource allocation, there is little explicit recognition of the impact of power and politics. For this reason, the best that may be found are certain indicators of political behaviour and the importance of power differences to outcomes – commonly, however, not using those terms as descriptors.

Information in Marketing Budgeting

To begin, there would seem some parallels in marketing studies for the use of information as a power base, and for the manipulation of information in a political sense – though particularly, it will be noted, the latter rather than the former, which leads us to take information manipulation as a proxy for political behaviour (see pp. *300-308*).

Lowe and Shaw (1968). This study of the sources of bias in sales forecasting by managers in a large UK chain of retail stores concluded that biases resulted from the self-interest of managers and their attempts to influence outcomes like budget size.

Lowe and Shaw examined the sales budgeting process over two years in a retail chain of several hundred stores in the UK. Their initial premise was that while the budgeting process was the single most important decision and control routine, it was also true that:

> The budgeting mechanism, like the external market, is by no means perfect, embodying as it does, both complementary and competing objectives in a situation of 'bilateral monopoly' and incomplete information. Members of a management team must co-operate and <u>compete</u> to serve their own ends ... The competitive element concerns the desire for promotion and greater shares of scarce resources. (Lowe and Shaw, 1968)

The leverage of sales forecasts on budget outcomes was achieved through the impact of the forecast on anticipated cash flows and thus the funds 'available' for expenditure on such activities as marketing. It was noted by these researchers that:

> In the company we studied, projected net revenue fell short of an 'aspired' profit level and hence expenditure plans were reviewed. It resulted in adjustments to a number of departmental budgets ... For example the advertising and training budgets were cut. (Lowe and Shaw, 1968)

Thus, influence over sales forecasts may amount to influence over budgetary outcomes.

In the system studied, area managers made sales forecasts for each store, which were discussed with the Senior Marketing Officer to finalise the forecast. Bias, defined as 'the extent to which a forecaster adjusts his forecast due to his own personal interests and perceptions and independently of factors which might influence the final result', was found to stem from three sources: the reward system (leading to a downward bias), company practice and norms, and management insecurity (leading to upward bias). The reward system induced area managers to bias forecasts downwards in order to improve their future income. Company norms had been established in a period of 'top-down' sales forecasting, and although the latter system had been replaced with 'bottom up' forecasting, 'recent practice, and the norms established by it, continued to influence forecasting behaviour ... the desire to please head office had a considerable influence on forecasting' (Lowe and Shaw, 1968), and this tended to lead to unrealistically high forecasts. Management insecurity was found also to push sales forecasts upwards, as managers sought approval of superiors through promising improvements in performance. These researchers concluded:

> The three sources of bias identified have their base in the rational economic behaviour of individual managers who seek to achieve a balance between increases in future income and current security. These sources may be combined in an 'approval seeking' model of forecasting behaviour which may explain the apparently contradictory forces at work ... there are reasons for suggesting that biasing may be a common phenomenon in industry: the desire to please superiors in a competitive managerial hierarchy and competition to acquire a share of scarce resources seem likely to be widespread. (Lowe and Shaw, 1968)

Although biasing was anticipated by senior managers, attempts at counter-biasing were difficult, and to some extent avoided because biases were approved.

For present purposes the important point is that this study demonstrates the deliberate manipulation of marketing information to influence, among other things, budget size.

Briscoe (1972). This study was concerned with the sources and uses of marketing information in the Special Steels Division of British Steel, but some of the reported findings are particularly related to the information-budget relationship in marketing (and indeed the information-structure relationship considered below).

In budgeting for marketing activities at different levels (in centralised marketing departments, works-level commercial centres, and area sales offices, and the allocation within areas), the formal system was that each department drew up plans for expenditure on marketing variables in support of the annual sales forecasts, with these budgets being 'centrally resolved and coordinated by the Divisional Accountant'. This implied the need for marketing information – historical sales and marketing budgets, and how these related to results in sales, market shares and profitability. It was found that in the absence of such marketing information, budget allocations were achieved by precedent, in that the current year budget was determined by modifying the historical budget figure to account for any proposals put forward by product sales managers and divisional liquidity.

The main planning mechanism was a divisional committee covering marketing development, where it was found that 'with this type of activity, market information is used to plan how expenditures should best be allocated, but lack of detail and the difficulties of measuring the returns to expenditure in this area creates acute problems' (Briscoe, 1972). The conclusion was that:

> In consequence, in times of low profitability and liquidity, the budgets of the marketing services departments tend to be one of the first areas to suffer, because they currently cannot generate information to establish their value to the Division. (Briscoe, 1972)

Briscoe's other principal findings were: that annual sales forecasting by marketing services suffered from too much data being supplied by other departments; that new product planning was production-led for structural reasons because 'the mechanics for how marketing information can lead production planning are not at all clearly established'; that information was presented in the structure 'imposed by

257

the financial and production functions'; and that there was a somewhat limited input of marketing information to the formulation of corporate strategy.

While Briscoe's analysis was not explicitly political, the findings above would seem illustrative of the information-budget interaction and the politics of information, in the terms discussed earlier, in the case of a low-power, low-influence marketing organisation.

Cunningham and Clarke (1975). In a study of the working of product management, these writers adopted a perspective analogous to that taken in this present study, and suggested that:

> Academic work has focussed upon creating models of consumer behaviour and logical budgeting, investment and decision models designed to guide the product manager inexorably along the optimal path for achieving corporate objectives.   It is our contention that, though such work is an essential and necessary activity ... it is unlikely to provide an adequate answer because it ignores the realities of what is occurring within the system itself.   It is of little use making marginal improvements in data inputs into a system and discussing normative, theoretically optimum outputs, if there are important internal variables causing major disruptions to the data that is subsequently used for decision making by senior management. (Cunningham and Clarke, 1975)

Their empirical work 'hinged around the product manager's deviant behaviour in his organizational environment', and had two main elements: risk avoidance, and biased information handling by product managers, although the second area was extended to the related issue of biased target setting.

In the area of risk avoidance, the researchers found that with hypothetical perceived risks product managers tended not to terminate the risk situation but to reduce the amount at stake - mainly through 'organizational strategies' as suggested below:

Product Manager Responses to Risk	No. of Product Managers
1. Reduce the amount at stake -	
(a) reduce the investment	7
(b) reduce own or others' aspirations	10
(c) reduce the consequences by organisational strategies	28
2. Increase subjective certainty -	
(a) passive 'wait and see' policies	2
(b) active information seeking	30
3. Terminate the risk situation	0

The 'organizational strategies' envisaged included attempting to ensure that someone else took responsibility for success or failure. Perhaps of greatest note, however, is that in responding to risk situations, it seemed that product managers:

> identified so strongly with their brands that they tried to increase their influence in decision-making as risks increased, in order to counter the centralising influence of company policy on important decisions. (Cunningham and Clarke, 1975)

On the second, though related, question of biased information handling, the researchers reasoned that: product managers need to produce strong claims to promote their products, and in this sense optimistic data are 'allowed and encouraged by the organization'; product management requires product-related confidence and enthusiasm, so 'The role is one of selling product priority to other company departments'; and product management systems operate so the product manager is primarily concerned with objectives specific to his product and 'fights both within and outside the company to fulfil those objectives'. Thus it was suggested that:

> product managers will use information in a way favourable to their products and this will affect resource allocation in ways not always conducive to corporate objective achievement. (Cunningham and Clarke, 1975)

While recognising that the distortion of data may be conscious or unconscious, Cunningham and Clarke suggested that the means of distortion used by product managers included:

(1) generalising from the particular by estimating national advertising expenditure from a heavy regional campaign for test launching;

(2) selectivity by choosing figures relating to favourable brand characteristics and omitting less favourable data;

(3) rounding upwards distribution coverage of 76% to 80%;

(4) using unusual market segmentation to give brand leadership such as taking large pack size figures only;

(5) choosing favourable time periods to illustrate favourable sales just after a promotional campaign and ignoring the time immediately before when competitors were promoting their brand;

(6) unrealistically projecting sales by assuming linear

relationships between distribution outlets handling the product and the sales volume achievable. (Cunningham and Clarke, 1975)

Such distortion was over and above the unconscious manipulation of data by memory loss or selective recall of unrepresentative data that favour the brand.

These researchers found 'numerous' examples of deliberate biasing by product managers, of the type summarised in Table 9.2. The interactions also suggested two further significant factors in this area: first, although biasing was a 'delicate subject' it emerged that some biasing was considered legitimate by companies and individuals (e.g. in presentations to the sales department), while other forms of biasing were 'frowned upon' (e.g. in presenting forecasts and budget requests to management); but, second, information biasing was <u>expected</u> organisational behaviour and in this sense sanctioned:

biasing of reports to superiors by means of presentation style or selectivity of data was exactly the type of behaviour expected and desired from the aggressive work style of product managers ... The extent to which such biasing is important and leads to sub-optimal or wrong resource allocation decisions depends upon the interplay between the product manager and his superiors. (Cunningham and Clarke, 1975)

The third issue studied was the information manipulation exhibited in target setting for products. Here the initial

---

Table 9.2: Product Manager Information Biasing

Type of Biasing	Number of Product Managers
Biases of presentation	32
Biases of selectivity	12
Biases of safety margins	14
Biases of rounding up or down	3
Biases by actually changing data	4
	(N=33)

Source: Cunningham and Clarke (1975)

---

premises were: that product managers have a high degree of participation in target setting; that reward systems tend to be asymmetrical – the reward for doing better than expected is greater than the penalty for setting low targets; if superiors consistently raise targets product managers learn to set low targets in the first place; risk aversiveness will cause some product managers to 'never squeeze every last unit of sales out of their brands but always keep something in reserve for emergencies' (i.e. to create organisational slack); and optimistic target setting will be true of some product managers because of the prestige associated with managing a high sales volume, high budget brand. It was thus hypothesised that product managers would manipulate target setting to obtain the maximum rewards (where, it might be added, a variety of 'rewards' were at stake).

The target biasing found in the study is summarised in Figure 9.1. It was found that a variety of interesting causes for biasing or non-biasing behaviour emerged, and some two-thirds of the product managers disclosed some form of target biasing.

Figure 9.1: Biasing of Targets by Product Managers

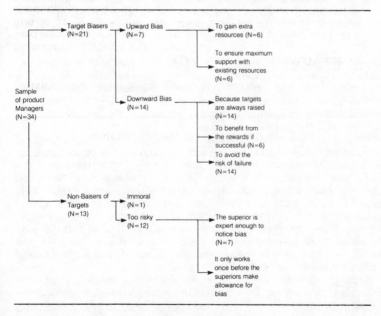

Source: Adapted by the Author from Cunningham and Clark (1975)

Of most particular note for present purposes was that those product managers who engaged in target raising mainly did so to benefit their products by obtaining an increased budget allocation. This behaviour was explained in various ways, for instance: it was easier to obtain money for advertising and promotion at the beginning of the year than to retain it later, because the company would expropriate any unused budgets as the year progressed, so the product managers requested more funds than 'needed' to allow for later expropriations; a similar problem was solved in another case by spending the bulk of the budget early in the year, leaving a bare minimum for later in the year which was less likely to be expropriated – the effect was that 'media spending was timed, not to relate to true market needs, but to cope with the company's own budget behaviour'. The researchers concluded that:

> As companies centralise, and allocate to higher management the important and risky decisions, so do product managers act to counter this by biasing both decision data and brand targets. The bias of style, presentation, emphasis and selectivity of data was widespread and was considered acceptable by both product managers and superiors alike. (Cunningham and Clarke, 1975)

Hanmer-Lloyd and Kennedy (1981). A qualitative study of marketing communications budgeting by seventeen major UK companies, carried out at Cranfield School of Management, uncovered a number of points related to the use of information to influence budgets, although the study did not take an overtly political stance.

First, it was noted that in bargaining for budgets, information access was restricted. Given the importance of continuous research data on advertising effectiveness, the researchers found that the use of market research data varied between companies, but also more significantly that this variation was not just due to the amount of information available, but to the 'attitude' of marketing management. For instance, in one case 'it was stated that access to one useful form of in-company data was not available because the file in which it was held stored other 'confidential' data' (Hanmer-Lloyd and Kennedy, 1981).

Second, these researchers found some evidence of the deliberate distortion of marketing information to manipulate budgeting systems. In modelling marketing budgeting processes (see pp. 74 – 76 above) it was found that most of the companies used bottom-up/top-down or top-down/bottom-up budgeting systems, but that anomalies arose in methods of calculating the marketing appropriation. The anomalies included undesirable short-term policies such as price-cutting and below-the-line at the expense of building long-term brand franchise, but that at the heart of this were:

1. Over optimistic volume forecasts to increase the marketing budget.
2. Over optimistic price increases to increase the marketing budget.
(Hanmer-Lloyd and Kennedy, 1981)

Third, these researchers further emphasised, in the determination of total marketing appropriations, the selectivity used by marketing and product managers in distorting information to obtain a budget:

It was apparent that a degree of subjective analysis existed. The most important reason given for this was the lack of relevant data. Having said that, it was also noted that some marketing personnel were 'selective' in their information gathering to help substantiate a particular viewpoint. (Hanmer-Lloyd and Kennedy, 1981)

Turning to their findings on the division and allocation of marketing budgets to different media, the researchers noted more obliquely that:

There was a limited, sometimes neglible, amount of research data on the various media options (except possibly television) and media mixes. Therefore decisions were often based on subjective criteria that existed within the person or the organisation. It was also noted that information availability did not always coincide with its use in making decisions. (Hanmer-Lloyd and Kennedy, 1981)

Wills and Kennedy (1982). In reporting qualitative research findings on marketing budgeting in large UK consumer goods companies, Wills and Kennedy (1982) sought to answer the question 'Is the influence of marketing men in determining the marketing budget on the wane?' since they found that 'there is a move to curtail the marketers' enthusiasm and to exert much tighter control on their activities. Today, boardrooms are setting marketing budgets by allocating the residual income after deducting operating costs and profit consideration'.

The Wills and Kennedy description of the 'negotiating structure' for marketing budgeting was considered earlier, but it is worth noting at this point that the cause-and-effect uncertainty surrounding marketing effectiveness was one of the reasons why companies appeared not to adopt task-related budgeting methods, but by implication the methods remaining are susceptible to influence through information manipulation. It was found that:

> The marketing budget becomes directly related in some way to sales and revenue forecasts. Among several consequences, over-optimistic volume forecasts are made, because the greater the volume and associated revenue forecast, the more convincing the case for a larger budget; and over-optimistic price increases are proposed, because this is seen as a legitimate way of boosting the revenue base against which the budget will be evaluated. (Wills and Kennedy, 1982)

Among their conclusions, these writers make the point that information distortion would appear apparent in marketing budgeting for at least two reasons:

> A degree of subjective analysis exists. The most important reason given is the lack of relevant data. Having said this, some marketing personnel are plainly 'selective' in gathering information to help substantiate a particular viewpoint. (Wills and Kennedy, 1982)

Implications. On the basis of the studies above, it would seem reasonable to suggest that there is evidence of a link between marketing information and budget outcomes through power and politics (although as will be seen in the next chapter there are difficulties in establishing whether that link is generally causal, and if so the extent, or indeed, the direction of causality). Evidence of political behaviour using marketing information would seem clear: in biasing sales forecasts and targets to manipulate marketing budgetary systems in a variety of settings. What emerges also, however, is marketing information control as a source of power – in one case more strictly the lack of control representing a lack of power – possibly as a reflection of a corporate struggle for control of the marketing budget. However, it is this latter question which leads us to the more obscure issue of the relationship between structure (our proxy for power) and the marketing budget.

Structure and the Marketing Budget

Explicit attention to the hypothesis that organisational structure directly influences marketing budgeting and its outcome is, in effect, absent from the literature. It was suggested early on that such analysis could be profitable:

> Advertising, sales, and market research expenditures, are special cases of 'the internal allocation of resources' treated in organization theory ... The analytical details of treating marketing as a problem in the internal allocation of resources are not well developed as yet, but research is going forward. (Howard, 1965)

In fact, research of the kind anticipated by Howard has not generally been forthcoming, and this perspective is still being identified as an important research question for marketing:

> In what ways is marketing decision making (the area of traditional interest in the marketing literature) affected by the organizational design of the marketing department and the organizational power of the department? (Nonaka and Nicosia, 1979)

However, from work in two areas some tentative evidence of that relationship may be deduced: from studies of product management, and from the Cranfield work on communications budgeting. In addition, the creation of organisational slack may in some instances be related to the marketing budget.

Product Management. By implication the studies above of information manipulation by product mangers are suggestive of the converse: that this structural form is particularly associated with political behaviour.

If we accept that the product management structure has been demonstrated to create a situation where task responsibility exceeds formal authority (e.g. Buell, 1975; Cunningham and Clarke, 1975; Venkatesh and Wilemon, 1976; 1980), then it seems reasonable to hypothesise that political behaviour will emerge, and in this sense the structural device is associated with politics to influence such outcomes as budgets for products. This argument was reflected by Cunningham and Clarke (1975) (see pp. *258-62* above), and for example in Haller's (1980) argument that the political environment for product management means that share-building, growth strategies tend to be recommended (with appropriate budget support) by product managers for reasons of personal career development. A compatible empirical finding by Schlackmann (1979) was that when companies move from a functional to a product base for structuring marketing, marketing research budgets tend to be reduced to improve individual products' apparent 'profit' performance. On a broader scale this last point is made by Corey and Star (1971) regarding the conflict between programmes and resource management in the matrix structure.

More recently the Cranfield work discussed below has added to this case specifically in the area of budgeting for communications. Wills and Kennedy (1982) reported the view that in the 1970s the product manager in large companies typically ran his product or brand as an independent entity, with plans and budget requests being passed upwards, and amalgamated at each hierarchical level until they reached the Board of Directors. These researchers concluded:

> Under such a system, the budgets inevitably became very large, and they frequently had to be cut back dramatically. Another disadvantage is that such budgets do not take into account the overall strategic decisions of the company, and the consequent differences in importance of each brand or product group. This lack of perspective among brand managers has been further exacerbated by rapid staff turnover. It was these problems that encouraged a change of structure from these large hierarchical marketing departments and a change in the budget process. (Wills and Kennedy, 1982)

The implication is that the size of budgets (or at the very least of budget requests) was a function of the existence and strengths of product management (a factor shown elsewhere to vary considerably between companies) and that changing the product management system changed budgeting behaviour. It may be hypothesised therefore that changing structure in marketing changes budgeting processes and thus outcomes.

The Cranfield MCRC Studies. In fact, the Cranfield work is concerned with more than simply the product management issue discussed above, and relates not simply to political behaviour but implicitly to the power of the marketing sub-unit in relation to general management and to other sub-units.

In particular, Hanmer-Lloyd and Kennedy (1981) and Wills and Kennedy (1982) reported on the competition between sub-units to control the marketing budget, where the 'functional areas can be criticised for arguing more for their "corner" than for the company as a whole' (Hanmer-Lloyd and Kennedy, 1981), in the forum provided by strong inter-departmental committees for strategic planning, product planning and promotional planning. Interestingly, they note that if committee reviews suggest that plans are not working, then:

> At this stage a certain amount of wider objectivity disappears and a promotion to boost sales and market share is initiated. At worst, or at the end of the year, a relatively easy option is to cut the advertising

budget - if there is one left.   (Hanmer-Lloyd and
Kennedy, 1981)

While this evidence would seem to link the power of the
marketing departments to the size of the mrketing budget, the
direction and nature of this relationship is less clear.   It
might be that the formally powerful marketing department led
to increased marketing budgets, and that senior managements
(and other powerful interests) have intervened to stop this
trend by diffusing the control of the marketing budget (and
thus the power of the marketing department). Equally validly
it might be argued that as marketing budgets have increased
(due   to   outside   factors   like   competition,   market
fragmentation, inflation, and so on) then their relative
importance to the company and their visibility in the company
have increased - causing intervention by senior management
through direct means, inter-departmental committees, and the
like.   In this latter situation it would be argued that the
marketing budget influences the structural characteristics
(and power) of the marketing department. None the less, the
Cranfield data do point to the existence of a marketing
structure/marketing budget relationship in which we are
interested.

A second structural aspect of marketing highlighted in
the Cranfield work is the emergence of trade marketing
departments, which deal directly with major retail
distributors, either under the control of the chief marketing
executive, or as part of a sales sub-unit independent of
marketing. It is noted of this trend that:

this has led to a jostling of authority over the budget
... Marketing may have authority over as little as 30%
of the volume sold, with the rest of the business going
via the small number of national accounts.   (Wills and
Kennedy, 1982)

Certainly in terms of budget control it was found that 'some
companies' sales' departments see this as a way of moving
funds out of the marketing budget into the sales budget'
(Hanmer-Lloyd and Kennedy, 1981).   Whether or not trade
marketing reduces the marketing department's budget, there
would seem some grounds justifying the claims that:

given the direction the trade is moving in this function
will increase in importance and is likely to require the
setting up of a budget.   The problem of the allocation
of this budget and its control is hindered by the
unclear   position   this   function   now   occupies.
(Hanmer-Lloyd and Kennedy, 1981)

In some ways, therefore, the departmentation of trade

marketing would also appear to suggest that power (conceived as structure) is related to budget.

Aaker and Carman (1982). In an attempt to study the reasons for organisational 'overadvertising', these researchers claimed that there were essentially two causes of 'excess' advertising expenditure: the first was the difficulty of modelling advertising response but also it was concluded that 'Undoubtedly, there are organizational pressures causing both the agency and the client to advertise more than might be optimal' (Aaker and Carman, 1982). In particular they suggested that the reward structure in organisations and the product management system produced a situation where there was no incentive to reduce advertising budgets but considerable incentive to increase them.

This is taken as a further indication of an emerging link between structure, process and marketing budgets.

Organisational Slack Creation Through Marketing Budgets.

Lastly, if we take the creation by managers of organisational slack as a political activity which is enacted through understating revenues and overstating costs, then it is notable that the marketing budget would seem to play a role of a kind in this political process:

> Marketing expenses result from many programs (for example, training, meetings, special promotions, and the like) which are viewed by management as niceties. These programmes appear on budgets, but the commitment of resources is contingent on progress made during the year in attaining the budget. (Schiff and Lewin, 1970)

Similarly, it has been reported that in order to project an image of growth 'management appears to have deliberately evened-out reported income by decisions to expense or defer advertising costs of new products' (Schiff and Lewin, 1968).

This suggests that in some cases the marketing department may enjoy only a symbolic position and may lack substantive power over the budget in certain circumstances, so that budget size reflects the political goals of the more powerful (see back to the British Steel Study by Briscoe, pp. 257-58).

Implications. Although in some ways inseparable from informational issues, there would seem some grounds for tentatively claiming that the structural characteristics of the marketing sub-unit are linked to marketing budget outcomes. This was seen in the literature of product management – where this structure appears to have a direct relationship with budget size – in the Cranfield MCRC research – which links marketing's structural power to budgets – and in the manipulation of marketing budgets by the powerful interests in the organisation.

Implications of the Empirical Evidence for Marketing Budgeting

As a preliminary test of the information-structure-power thesis as it may apply to marketing budgeting, this section sought to find in the literature of marketing evidence of the use of power and politics in resource allocation as a counterpart to the more general evidence cited in the previous section.

In considering the information-budget relationship in marketing it was possible to cite evidence of information and target biasing and distortion as methods of influencing marketing resource allocation, as well as information gaps reflecting a low degree of marketing department power over the marketing budget. In examining the structure-budget relationships rather less evidence was available, but it was possible to point to some evidence that the product management structure is related to budget size, and that the structural characteristics of the marketing sub-unit are linked (albeit in an ambiguous way) to the marketing budget. Finally, it was seen that the marketing budget may be simply a symbolic entity manipulated by non-marketing management to create organisational slack.

Although the evidence is fragmented and to some extent mixed, it is suggested that enough signs exist to justify our pursuit of greater insight into the power and politics of marketing budgeting.

However, first, following the logic of the earlier discussion, it is necessary to further test the power and politics/budget link in marketing, by considering the contingencies for the use of power, as they may relate to marketing budgeting.

POLITICAL CONTINGENCIES IN MARKETING BUDGETING

Following the structure of the earlier discussion of the contingencies for the use of power and politics (see pp. *199 - 206*), we may briefly consider the extent to which marketing budgeting as a decision area or process may typically be associated with certain contingencies, and the extent to which the situations surrounding marketing budget decisions may on occasion display such conditions.

Goal Uncertainty and Dissensus

The general commentary earlier (pp. *206-209*) suggested that goals in marketing are both uncertain and conflictual.

For example, Cunningham and Clarke (1975) in their study of product managers found that:

there is great certainty only about profit and sales volume objectives. Considerable uncertainty surrounds brand share, growth, distribution and brand development objectives, and some uncertainty is in existence about brand image ... Obviously, uncertainty exists in all facets of the company objectives but less so regarding the nature (or range) of objêctives than about their relative importance, company's acceptance level and current brand achievement. (Cunningham and Clarke, 1975)

Indeed, more specific to marketing budgeting: Turnbull (1974) studying marketing communications budgets in industrial companies noted that frequently objectives were not set and budget allocations were <u>ad hoc</u>; and Wills and Kennedy (1982) reported in the Cranfield work that:

The objectives ... tend to be very general, too open-ended to provide a firm base against which achievement can be monitored. In part, this generality is encouraged by a feeling that the achievement of promotional goals cannot be measured with any sort of accuracy. (Wills and Kennedy, 1982)

Similarly, Hanmer-Lloyd and Kennedy (1982) noted that 'One of the main problems in evaluating sales promotion activity is the lack of specific objectives set for promotion.'

It would seem that the general case for goal dissensus in marketing may in fact turn out to be typical of the marketing budgeting process.

Technology Uncertainty and Dissensus

It follows from the comments quoted above that goal uncertainty may be linked to technology dissensus.

For example, there was some suggestion in the empirical work describing marketing budgeting, which was reviewed in Chapter 2, that in companies where the use of decision rules or 'guidelines' is common, there is no external logic or rationale for the rules used (e.g. Lilien and Little, 1976) – or at least no rationale of which managers are aware or to which they will admit when questioned by researchers – and it has been found that managers 'are unsure of the basis on which the percentage used was originally arrived at or, indeed, of the rationale underlying the change of method' (Gilligan, 1977). It was argued earlier that these findings suggest that guidelines may be a political outcome, but that would only be possible because of the underlying difficulty of establishing the relationship between marketing expenditures and results, in whatever form.

Certainly, this element of uncertainty would appear consistent in studies over a wide time period. Early work by Taplin (1959) found that advertising was treated as a deduction from profit, because, while advertising was thought to have some effect on sales, there appeared to managers no way of knowing what that effect was. Another researcher explained the use of arbitrary rules of thumb in setting advertising appropriations, in the following terms:

> The reason for it seems to be uncertainty about what advertising contributes to the marketing mix ... if a company feels totally uncertain about quantifying the results of its advertising it has very sound reasons for confining its expenditure to an affordable amount ... Nor is it surprising that precise cause and effect relationships cannot be ascertained. Advertising results do not depend simply on the size of the appropriation. Other factors such as the media chosen for the campaign and the creative content influence the outcome but it is usually impossible to assign any one of them with a particular share of the credit or blame. (Eassie, 1972)

More recently the MIT work cited earlier (pp. *81 - 85*) found that in marketing and advertising budgeting 'these decisions are based on impressions rather than fact' (Lilien and Weinstein, 1981), the reason being that: 'At the heart of the problem of budgeting expenditures for advertising is the lack of understanding of the nature of the advertising response' (Lilien et al, 1976).

It will be recalled that these workers found that general reliance on simple heuristics in budgeting was not replaced by even the moderately more sophisticated objective and task method because 'it requires knowledge about how levels of expenditures and various communication response measures are related and how the latter are linked to the purchase behavior that is relevant' (Lilien et al, 1976).

An interesting side issue thrown up by Kennedy and Corkindale (1976) is the suggestion that as well as reflecting a lack of understanding of cause and effect, the common policy of setting the advertising appropriation as a fixed percentage of sales also creates and perpetuates uncertainty, since it obscures the sales response function and prevents a firm from learning the effect of changing the advertising/sales ratio.

The Cranfield workers concur, in this respect, with the earlier research, suggesting that marketing budgeting practice reflects a lack of marketing information, a lack of measurement of cause-and-effect, and constrasting criteria of allocation. Similar findings, it will be recalled, were noted in the Briscoe (1972) study of British Steel.

It seems reasonable again to suggest that the general case for technology dissensus in marketing decision making therefore be extended to marketing budgeting, and indeed may typify the marketing budgeting problem.

Conflict

Again following the earlier structure (pp. *199-206*) and to avoid repeating that argument, the existence of goal and technology dissensus or uncertainty increases the chances that the marketing budgeting process will be conflictual, as in the 'jostling for authority' over marketing noted above, and the more general case discussed that marketing decisions are typically conflictual (pp. *210-13*).

This would, of course, only be true given the existence of other contingencies, which are more likely to vary, i.e. to be present in some marketing budgeting situations but not others.

Resource Scarcity

It is argued that in the absence of resource scarcity, there would be no need for a political contest over resources, though this view might be superficial. Certainly, there have been suggestions that economic recessions have placed greater pressure on marketing budgets (Buell, 1982) and have imposed pressures to cut-back (Wilson, 1981), in ways which may be compared to the Hannan and Freeman (1978) argument that the use of power and politics is greater in time of resource decline. Even so, it is necessary to recognise that general economic conditions are not likely to affect all companies equally at any particular time.

Over and above this it is necessary also to recognise that scarcity is not simply an absolute – reflecting such factors as economic conditions, or corporate liquidity – but a relative variable, which may be subjectively or politically defined. It may be hypothesised, for instance, that even in times of organisational 'plenty' there will be those competing for a greater share of resources and growth in allocations, with what this implies for status and power; or that sensitivity to certain resources may be a politically-generated and manipulated variable – a manifestation, say, of the political activities of attacking others or image-building (Allen et al, 1979). It may be, for instance, that the propensity of senior management to intervene in marketing expenditure or expropriate marketing budgets reflects the organisational 'visibility' of those resources, which is created by others.

Importance of Outcome

Again, in the absense of a significant value being placed on

272

the marketing budget there would seem no likelihood of a political struggle emerging, but, equally, importance may be viewed both in absolute and relative terms.

In absolute terms one might be led to argue that the size of the resource allocation to marketing will relate positively to the use of power and politics – only large resource allocations are worth the political risks and effort.

However, this would be to ignore the incrementalism and precedent of budgets, and the interaction of power and politics. For example, the establishment of a new marketing budget (i.e. one by definition large in incremental terms) might attract far more political resistance than changes of a similar size in an established budget. Similarly, if one distinguishes power and politics in the way established earlier (pp. *176-179*), then the large marketing budget may be regarded as immutable – the evidence of the working of a powerful interest in the organisation – while the smaller marketing budget (reflecting a low-power marketing sub-unit) may be perceived as far more susceptible to political influence. Even then, it may be argued that this is to assume that the marketing resource allocation directly reflects the power of the marketing sub-unit, which it may or may not do. It may be that in some circumstances the marketing sub-unit's control over the 'marketing budget' is symbolic – as perhaps in the Schiff and Lewin (1970) study of the use of the marketing budget to create slack in the larger budgeting system – rather than substantive. At the very least this suggests that if it is possible to measure the power and politics of budgeting, we should expect relationships with resource outcomes to be non-linear.

One moves, thus, from taking importance as an absolute reflecting budget size and incremental change, to taking importance as subjective and possibly itself a political outcome. In the first instance – subjective importance – a small promotional budget, for example, might be perceived as highly important by a product manager, but far less so by others. Equally the definition of importance may reflect other situational attributes – the newness of marketing to a company, the method of financial reporting, and so on.

However, it is possible to argue that 'importance' may be a political outcome in the organisation reflecting both power – in structural and informational terms – and political behaviour. The structural location and departmentation of marketing and of other sub-units, and the ability to structure and control information about critical contingencies may both affect the ability, for example, of the marketing department to articulate a case for the importance of its resource allocation. In the same way, the ability of others to influence perceptions of the marketing

budget may determine the level of its importance to an
organisation.

It would seem, therefore, that one may accept a prime
facie case that marketing resource allocation is conflictual
in nature because of technology and goal dissensus, and that
the emergence of the use of power and politics is made more
likely by resource scarcity and the importance of outcome.

Interdependence and Relative Power Differences

Returning to the general model of political contingencies,
differentiation in response to environmental characteristics
leads to the creation of interdependent sub-units, and thus
to the definition of a potential for conflict between those
sub-units.

It was seen earlier that the departmentation of
marketing is variable between organisations - both in
absolute terms of the existence of a marketing department and
relative terms of the responsibilities and status of a
marketing department - reflecting, it is suggested in a
contingency approach to marketing organisation, variations in
such factors as environmental uncertainty.

This suggests that at one extreme there will be no
marketing sub-unit to become involved in political resource
struggles.

However, assuming the existence of a marketing sub-unit
of some form, the concept of centrality (relating to
workflow immediacy and pervasiveness), drawn from the
strategic contingencies' theory of intraorganisational power,
suggests the possibility of sub-unit variability in the
dimensions of interdependence which relate to the criticality
of a sub-unit's work to that of other sub-units and the
connectedness of a sub-unit's work to that of others.
Applying this to the marketing sub-unit - one may hypothesise
situationally-determined variations in that sub-unit's
centrality to others and, thus variations in power.   It
would seem reasonable to suppose, therefore, that there may
be relative power differences between marketing and others,
in some situations, which may be reflected by relatively
strong or relatively weak marketing departments.

Given the view of power and politics taken above, then
one would argue that where relative power differences exist,
the powerful will seek to have resource allocations
determined in their preferred direction (i.e. through power),
while the less powerful are likely to pursue their aims
through political influence attempts.

Turning from lateral to vertical relations it is
suggested by the contingencies paradigm (Pfeffer, 1981) that
the concentration of power (i.e. centralisation) reduces the
scope for the use of decentralised power (since none exists),
though presumably increasing the scope for political

behaviour to influence outcomes, while in the decentralised organisation there is more scope for the use of dispersed power and political behaviour.

In fact, this argument is somewhat contentious, and it might just as easily be argued that (apparent) centralisation disguises the power of the decentralised and <u>vice versa</u>. More comment is offered on this point shortly.

The suggestion is that both interdepartmental relative power, and centralisation/decentralisation provide contingencies for the use of power and politics, which may be applicable to the marketing budget situation.

Implications

Drawing on the more general model described earlier it is possible to construct a case for the conclusion that marketing budgeting has been shown to demonstrate both goal and technology uncertainty and dissensus, to the degree where the working hypothesis is that such conditions are inherent in marketing budgeting. This suggests, by default if nothing else, that marketing resource allocation may be regarded as potentially both conflictual and political in determination. The probability of such a manifestation of the use of power and politics may be increased in marketing budgeting in cases where resources are defined as scarce, where the outcomes are perceived as important and where relative power differences exist.

The implication is that certain of the contingencies for the use of power and politics in marketing resource allocation may be inherent in, and specific to, this area of decision, while other of the contingencies are specific to particular situations in which such decisions are made. It would seem, therefore, reasonable to suggest that there are further grounds thus provided for pursuing a political analysis of marketing budgeting.

CONCLUSIONS

To review briefly the contents of Part II, we have successively: first, considered an organisational perspective on marketing, in terms of the corporate environment for marketing and changing views of the corporate role of marketing and its organisational dimensions, leading to an emphasis of structure and information in understanding marketing decision making; second, concentrated on power and politics as key elements of organisational behaviour, which were described and contrasted as potential explanatory variables in analysing the outcomes of marketing decisions, under certain conditions or contingencies; third, described an information-structure-power theory of managerial marketing, which relies on information-structure interrelationships to explain the power level of the marketing department and its scope for political influence; and finally turned to the power and politics of marketing budgeting, where it was seen that power (in the structural sense adopted earlier) and politics (in the influence sense) have been recognised in the general literature of resource allocation, have been measured in both public and business organisational studies of resource allocation, and have been, to some extent, recognised in marketing budgeting studies; and it was suggested that the certain of the contingencies for the emergence of power and politics are specific to the marketing budgeting decisions and others may emerge in certain situations.

Conceptually, therefore, from the analysis of marketing budgeting in Part I and the organisational perspective developed in Part II, we have reached the position where marketing budgeting may be analysed (via the information-structure-power theorem) in the way summarised in Figure 9.2.

Figure 9.2: An Analytical Model of the Power and Politics of Marketing Resource Allocation

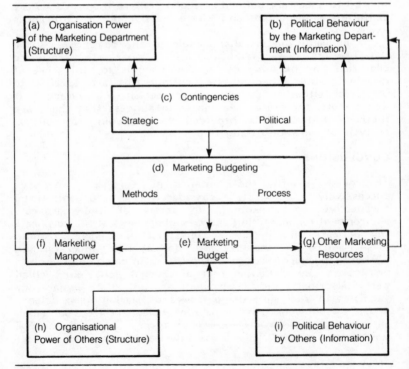

This model suggests that our starting point in analysing marketing budgeting should be with (a) the power of the marketing department, which is conceived here, for the reasons given above, as primarily structural, and (b) the political behaviour of the marketing department. The use of power and politics to influence resource outcomes is contingent, as in (c), in two senses: that the contingencies controlled by the marketing department are critical, and that the decision and situation characteristics are those where decisions are likely to be resolved by power and politics rather than in any other fashion. If the contingencies fulfil those last criteria, one may look at two aspects of (d) marketing budgeting in political terms: the methods and guidelines recognised and used; and the process of marketing budgeting. The outcomes of those methods and processes may be assessed in terms of: (e) the financial resources devoted to marketing; (f) the manpower controlled by marketing; and (g) other resources held by marketing, such as office space, facilities, and so on – in each case we should be concerned not just with absolute values but with incremental change. Qualifications to the thesis advanced are represented by (h) the organisational power of others within the organisation and outwith, and (i) political behaviour by others.

It is this model which we seek to evaluate in Part III of the book.

REFERENCES

Aaker, D.A. and Carman, J.M. (1982) 'Are You Overadvertising?', Journal of Advertising Research, 22 (4), 57-70

Allen, R.W., Madison, D.L., Porter, L.W., Renwick, P.A., and Mayes, B.T. (1979) 'Organizational Politics - Tactics and Characteristics of its Actors', California Management Review, 22 (1), 77-84

Bower, J. (1970) Managing the Resource Allocation Process, Harvard, Cambridge, Mass.

Briscoe, G. (1972) The Sources and Uses of Marketing Information in the British Steel Corporation (Special Steels Division), Centre for Industrial Economic and Business Research, University of Warwick

Buell, V.P. (1975) 'The Changing Role of the Product Manager in Consumer Goods Companies', Journal of Marketing, 39, 3-11

Collins, F., Munter, P. and Finn, D. (1983) 'Do Managers Play Games with Their Budgets?', Managerial Planning, 32 (1), 28-34

Corey, E.R. and Star, S. (1971) Organization Strategy: A Marketing Approach, Harvard, Cambridge, Mass.

Cunningham, M.T. and Clarke, C.J. (1975) 'The Product Management Function in Marketing', European Journal of Marketing, 9 (2), 129-49

Cyert, R.M. and March, J.G. (1963) A Behavioral Theory of the Firm, Prentice-Hall, Englewood Cliffs, N.J.

Eassie, R.W.F. (1972) Setting Area Appropriations, Southern Television, London

Freeman, J. (1979) 'Going to the Well: School District Administrative Intensity and Environmental Constraint', Administrative Science Quarterly, 24, 119-133

Freeman, J.H. and Hannan, M.T. (1975) 'Growth and Decline Processes in Organizations', American Sociological Review, 40, 215-228

Gilligan, C. (1977) 'How British Advertisers Set Budgets', Journal of Advertising Research, 17 (1), 47-9

Haller, T. (1980) 'Strategic Planning: Key to Corporate Power for Marketers', Marketing Times, 27 (3), 18-24

Hanmer-Lloyd, S. and Kennedy, S. (1981) Setting and Allocating the Marketing Communications Budget: A Review of Current Practice, Marketing Communications Research Centre, Cranfield School of Management, Beds.

Hannan, M.T. and Freeman, J.H. (1978) 'Internal Politics of Growth and Decline', in M.W. Meyer et al (eds.) Environments and Organizations, Jossey-Bass, San Francisco

Hills, F.S. and Mahoney, T.A. (1978) 'University Budgets and Organizational Decision Making, Administrative Science Quarterly, 23, 454-65

Howard, J.A. (1965) Marketing Theory, Allyn and Bacon, Boston, Mass.

Kennedy, S.H. and Corkindale, D.R. (1976) Managing the Advertising Process, Saxon House/Lexington, Farnborough

Lilien, G.L. and Little, J.D.C. (1976) 'The Advisor Project: A Study of Industrial Marketing Budgets', Sloan Management Review, 17 17-33

Lilien, G.L. and Weinstein, D. (1981) Do European Industrial Marketers Budget Differently? An International Comparison Via the Advisor Model, Massachusetts Institute of Technology, Working Paper 1222-81, Cambridge, Mass.

Lilien, G.F., Silk, A.V., Choffrey, J.M. and Rao, M. (1976) 'Industrial Advertising Effects and Budgeting Practices', Journal of Marketing, January, 16-24

Lowe, E.A. and Shaw, R.W. (1968) 'An Analysis of Managerial Biasing: Evidence from a Company's Budgeting Processing', Journal of Management Studies, 5 (3), 304-315

Mintzberg, H. (1983) Power In and Around Organizations, Prentice-Hall, Englewood Cliffs, N.J.

Nonaka, I. and Nicosia, F.M. (1979) 'Marketing Management, Its Environment and Information Processing: A Problem of Organization Design', Journal of Business Research, 7 (4), 277-301

Pfeffer, J. (1981) Power in Organizations, Pitman, Marshfield, Mass.

Pfeffer, J. and Leong, A. (1977) 'Resource Allocations in United Funds: Examination of Power and Dependence', Social Forces, 55, 775-90

Pfeffer, J. and Moore, W.L. (1980) 'Power and Politics in University Budgeting: A Replication and Extension', Administrative Science Quarterly, 25, 215-32

Pfeffer, J. and Salancik, G.R. (1974) 'Organizational Decision Making as a Political Process: The Case of a University Budget, Administrative Science Quarterly, 19, 135-51

Pondy, L..R. (1969) 'Varieties of Organizational Conflict', Administrative Science Quarterly, 14 (4), 499-505

Pondy, L.R. (1970) 'Toward a Theory of Internal Resource Allocation', in Zald, M.N. (ed.) Power in Organizations, Vanderbilt UP, Nashville, Tenn.

Provan, K.J., Beyer, J.M. and Kruytbosch, C. (1980) 'Environmental Linkages and Power in Resource-Dependence Relations Between Organizations', Administrative Science Quarterly, 25, 200-205

Schiff, M. and Lewin, A.Y. (1968) 'Where Traditional Budgeting Fails', Financial Executive 36 (5), 50-62

Schiff, M. and Lewin, A.Y. (1970) 'The Impact of People on Budgets', Accounting Review, 45 (2), 259-68

Schlackmann, W. (1979) 'The Participation Factor as a Key Factor in Integrating Professional Services Within the Modern Corporation', Admap, 15 (6), 292-7

Taplin, W. (1959) 'Advertising Appropriation Policy', Economica, 26, 227-39

Venkatesh, A. and Wilemon, D.L. (1976) 'Interpersonal Influence in Product Management', Journal of Marketing, 40, 33-40

Venkatesh, A. and Wilemon, D.L. (1980) 'American and European Product Managers: A Comparison', <u>Columbia Journal of World Business</u>, 15 (3), 67-74

Wildavsky, A. (1964) <u>The Politics of the Budgetary Process</u>, Little Brown, Boston, Mass.

Wildavsky, A. (1968) 'Budgeting as a Political Process', in D.L. Sills. (ed.) <u>International Encyclopaedia of the Social Sciences</u>, Macmillan, New York

Wildavsky, A. (1979) <u>The Politics of the Budgetary Process</u>, Little Brown, Boston, Mass.

Wills, G. and Kennedy, S. (1982) 'How to Budget Marketing', <u>Management Today</u>, February, 58-61

Wilson, C. (1981) 'When the Export Trade Get Tough', <u>Marketing</u>, 3rd June, 28-31

PART THREE

An Empirical Study of the Power and Politic of Marketing Budgeting

10

The Empirical Approach

INTRODUCTION

We start Part III having reviewed the state of knowledge of marketing budgeting and resource allocation, having traced the development of an information-structure-power model of corporate marketing, and having attempted to establish the validity of applying power/structural and political/ informational/processual concepts to the analysis of resource allocation in marketing. This Part of the book turns to the empirical study of marketing budgeting using the terms and perspective developed.

Chapters 11 and 12 review new empirical data on marketing organisation and budgeting, but, first, in this chapter we discuss the empirical approach taken. This discussion is necessary for valid interpretation of the present empirical results, and for those who may seek to undertake replicative works.

First, the chapter considers the conceptual problems inherent in studying such questions, before considering the specific research objectives. Attention then turns to the choice of data collection method and measurement devices used.

CONCEPTUAL RESEARCH PROBLEMS

While the model of the power and politics of marketing budgeting at which we arrived (Figure 9.2) identified a number of research variables to be operationalised, there are a variety of intervening problems of varying degrees of intractability which must be noted. In that these issues shape the empirical problem and interact with the methodological choices, as well as providing caveats to the interpretation of results, these questions require at least brief evaluation.

Measuring Power and Politics

It was noted by one analyst of this area that: 'the literature on power is not particularly large, and the empirical study of power and politics is unfortunately a rare event' (Pfeffer, 1981b). Pfeffer is, in fact, led to the conclusion that this shortfall suggests that:

> Power and politics are basic processes which occur in many organizations much of the time, and are empirically researchable and analyzable using a set of conceptual tools which are already largely in place. (Pfeffer, 1981b)

This is, however, to set aside the more pessimistic thought that it is the intractability of the research problems which has restricted the development of the empirical literature, as suggested for example by Pettigrew (1973) and Hickson et al (1981), or by the conclusion that 'research topics relating to organizational politics are fraught with more than the usual amount of sticky and methodological obstacles' (Porter et al, 1981).

Certainly, the literature would suggest that the operationalisation of power and politics provides some substantial difficulties, as does the actual measurement of the operational terms once they are defined.

It will be seen shortly (pp. *300 - 308*) that the first simplifying assumption made in this study is that power may be measured primarily in overt structural terms (although necessarily to some extent also as a perceived or reputational variable), while politics may be evaluated primarily in informational terms (although again in a secondary way as a perceived or experienced characteristic). Even so, there remain empirical barriers which cannot be ignored.

The Completeness of the Explanation of Outcomes by Power and Politics.

While it is central to the approach here that marketing resource allocations are hypothesised to result from organisational power and political behaviour in organisations, this can at best be no more than a partial explanation.

Generally while the use of power and political behaviour may explain part of decision making, or may even possibly be specific to certain types of decision, there is little basis in the received literature for suggesting that all situations are analysable in political terms (Pfeffer, 1981b) — although clearly the valid applicability of concepts of power and politics depends ultimately on the definition of those concepts, and it may be that the statement should contain the qualification 'usefully analysable'.

Pettigrew (1973), for example, made the point that it is necessary to ask the question how political is a particular decision - a conceptual approach to which was provided for marketing budgeting in the last chapter - bearing in mind, for example, Crozier's (1964) heated attack on Dalton for exaggerating the extent of power struggles and politics in managerial behaviour. Indeed, the strategic contingency theorists (Hickson et al, 1971; Hinings et al, 1974) expressed quite explicit reservations about attempts to explain all decisions in political terms. More recently, Porter et al (1981) suggested that the received theory is such that the actual ratio of political to non-political behaviour in an organisation remains a question soluble only empirically, and this point is taken.

In addition, one must note the implied need to question how political a particular organisation may be, which in this present study is taken as a further contingency for decisions to be analysed as political outcomes. There is some evidence, for example, that the propensity towards political behaviour varies between organisations (Butler et al, 1977; Hickson et al, 1981) as an attribute of those organisations.

These points together are suggestive of the earlier implications drawn from the community power literature (pp. *142 - 3*) that the underlying question remains not which powerful interests influence the marketing budget, but whether any powerful interests do so.

In this present study the view is that by analysing the contingencies surrounding the marketing resource allocation and the perceived politicisation of the organisation, we may attempt to distinguish between situations where the marketing budget is a political outcome, and those where it may be otherwise determined.

The Pervasiveness of Power and Politics. A second, converse, area of difficulty is provided not by the case above that power and politics offer only a partial explanation of outcomes, but by the argument that power and politics are so pervasive as to be impossible to isolate as decisional determinants.

For example, Pettigrew (1973) noted that the formal structures of power and legitimacy are problematic in this sense, because in the absence of clear evidence about what is legitimate, it is difficult to be certain as to what is political and what is not - leading to the related problem of the attribution of power use and political behaviour by observers to others, which is considered separately below (pp. *292-94*).

On the question of pervasiveness, it will be recalled that Pfeffer (1981b) argued that in the empirical study of decision making processes from a political perspective, it is necessary to accept, firstly, that the rules, procedures and policies of an organisation are determined by the balance of power, and by implication possibly by the successful use of political influence, and thus represent the legitimation of the political structure; and secondly, that 'rational' decision procedures and planning may be part of the ritualised ideology or symbolism of management, which are used to legitimate and obscure the choices made.

The first aspect of the pervasiveness/legitimation argument is met in this study by looking to formal structure as _prima facie_ evidence of the power of the marketing sub-unit, relying on the proposition that structure provides evidence of the balance of power. Indeed, this proposition has its source in Pfeffer's (1981b) case, stated above, that the study of organisational phenomena, such as rules and procedures, and how they benefit different interest groups, provides a mechanism for implying power differences, on the grounds that such characteristics may be taken as indicators of the success of different interest groups in gaining legitimation of their relative positions and resource claims.

The second pervasiveness/legitimacy point, relating to the substantive or symbolic nature of structure and procedure is attacked by analysing separately the issues of power and formal control, and political behaviour and level of influence, over resource outcomes - a perspective which implicitly accepts the possibility that 'rational' budgeting methods may serve political interests.

Interrelatedness of the Variables. A further difficulty implied by the argument above is that both the independent variables for study - power and politics - and the dependent variables of resources (as well as the intervening independent variables) are interrelated to the degree that their separation may be misleading and, perhaps most damaging, the direction of causality is further obscured.

For instance, if it is to be argued that structure is both a source of power and the outcome of political processes (Pfeffer, 1978), then the problem is whether structure should be taken as a dependent or independent variable. Similarly, the argument that power is gained by those who absorb critical uncertainties, is made more complex by the proposal that the definition of criticality is itself a socially-determined or political outcome (Pfeffer and Salancik, 1978).

Just the same case may be made for the information system - it is influenced by the power distribution in the organisation, but itself also affects that distribution (Keen, 1979; Markus, 1980); while similarly the budget itself may also be represented as both a dependent determined by power and political behaviour, but also as a source of power in acting as a symbol of a powerful interest and providing the resources for reward, coercion, and so on.

The interrelatedness of the variables and the potentially complex pattern of causalities remains a problem which may be recognised (as in Figure 9.2) but not solved, and these issues emerge again in interpreting the results of the empirical study.

Access. It must also be noted that the empirical study of the processes and results of power and politics in organisations is accompanied by problems of research access which are greater, more subtle, and more covert, than is usual, even in social research. We discuss later the access problems associated with, for instance, the confidentiality of company cost and profit data, but the access problems associated with power and politics go far beyond this.

To begin with, there is the literal problem of access to organisations to collect data, which are shared by all such research, but which are exacerbated by **ideological resistance** to notions of power and politics in management and business organisations.

The effect is that the generally negative connotations of political behaviour are such that organisational members may deny its existence – if not to themselves, certainly to researchers. It is suggested that:

> Political aspects of behavior in organizations ... are something that organizations (qua organizations) tend to deny in their own operations, or at least tend to deny that it affects any crucial decision making; likewise, individuals tend to deny that they themselves engage in it, even though they (just as organizations) may acknowledge – indeed strongly aver – that it is practised by others. It is a topic that is highly sensitive, strongly hidden from public view insofar as the organization is willing to attribute behaviour to itself (him/herself), generally socially 'undesirable', and about which there is a great defensiveness ... It is, in a phrase, the 'dark side' of organizational behavior. (Porter et al, 1981)

The suggestion made by Porter et al, citing support from Madison et al (1980), is that direct measurements of political behaviour are doomed, other than in the form of attribution of behaviour by observers or participants.

Attention turns in a moment to the issue of attribution, but to some extent the problem identified above may be reduced by the use of covert or indirect techniques to deduce or imply the use of power and political behaviour – for example, Pettigrew's (1973) observational approach, or the scaling techniques used in the strategic contingencies' research. The problem is eased also by the use of relatively objective indicators of power – such as committee representation or budget increment size in the university and social services research discussed earlier (pp. *250 - 254*), or such as the formal structural characteristics which are used in this study.

To some extent, however, the use of indirect measurements is merely to transfer attribution from the respondent to the researcher - at least in the interpretation stage, if not in the design and construction of methodology in the first place - for instance, in the hypothesised relationship between an 'indicator' of power and power itself.

For example, as noted earlier, Bell and Newby (1971) in evaluating studies of community power drew attention to the argument that the measurements and techniques chosen by a researcher may imply the results expected and, indeed, the results obtained. They contrasted, for instance, sociological perspectives - based on reputational measures of pyramidal power, which they took to reflect an elitist or stratificationist ideology - and a political science perspective - relying on decision or issue analysis, leading to a factional or coalitionist view of power, reflecting a pluralist ideology.

To some degree these issues remain intractable, in the sense that any social science research design implicitly incorporates the frame of reference represented by the received theory and the researcher's interpretation of that theory. On the other hand, the problem may be partly overcome by a focus on a specific decision, and to some extent by using a variety of measurements of both power and politics in an attempt to follow the logic of Pettigrew's (1973) 'validation through convergence' - which represents an accepted attempt to solve this problem.

None the less, in the final analysis the imposition of a framework of measurement implies ideologically-based assumptions which should be noted as the context for interpreting the findings.

A related aspect of access problems is that the use of power and politics is likely to be **hidden** - perhaps because it is perceived by organisational members as socially undesirable, as argued above, but also for a number of other reasons.

For example, Pfeffer (1981b) argues that success in the use of power frequently relies on the unobtrusiveness with which it is used, both in the sense that those organisational participants involved may seek to display signs of legitimacy through the 'rational' justification of decisions and the use of analytical methods that provide support for their preferred courses of action, and also in the sense that politically-based decision processes may be protected through the function of institutionalised organisational secrecy (Pfeffer, 1978).

Similarly, Hedberg <u>et al</u> (1979) noted the problem in

relying on participants' perceptions of power, when studying power in relation to outcome, since 'People have a natural tendency to rationalize and legitimize after the fact'.

In some studies this barrier has been overcome by adopting an observational or case study methodology (e.g. Crozier, 1964; Pettigrew, 1973), while in others by seeking to correlate tangible, purportedly objective, indicators of power with decision outcomes (e.g. as in the university and social services studies discussed earlier (pp. 250-254)). In this present study the approach largely follows that taken by the latter works, in attempting to relate structure and information control to budgetary processes and outcomes, although it is unlikely that the secrecy barrier is fully overcome.

A yet subtler aspect of access comparable to secrecy relates to what has been called 'power beyond decision making' (Hickson et al, 1981), in their finding that:

> This notion of power beyond decision making, then, brings into focus the difference between power and the experience or exercise of power. It warns us not be misled by the latter since power can be exercised in many ways that are not easily recognised as acts of dominance. (Hickson et al, 1981)

In straightforward terms it may simply be that at least some organisational participants are unaware of the use of power and politics.

In support of such a view, Perrow (1970), for example, described the 'engineering' of decisions by organisations rather than the blatant use of political strength, and we are returned to the well-known Bachrach and Baratz view of the 'hidden face of power' or power through 'non-decision making' and the 'hidden agenda' as forms of infuence:

> of course, power is exercised when A participates in the making of decisions that affect B. Power is also exercised when A devotes his energies to creating or reinforcing social and political values and institutional practices that limit the scope of the political process to public consideration of only those issues which are comparatively innocuous to A. To the extent that A succeeds in doing this, B is prevented for all practical purposes, from bringing to the fore any issues that might in their resolution be seriously detrimental to A's set of preferences. (Bachrach and Baratz, 1970)

It may be that this represents one of the more intractable problems faced, and it is approached only in the 'black box' assumption - that we can measure certain inputs and surrounding conditions (contingencies, power indicators, and so on) and certain outputs (budgets, resources, and the like) but are left largely to deduce what we can of the intervening processes. This, in turn, is challengeable on the grounds that the results or outputs of management decision making may be symbolic rather than substantive (Pfeffer, 1981a), suggesting at the very least that the outputs referred to above require evaluation with some care.

It would seem, thus, that access in the context of studying power and politics poses both straightforward, literal problems of gaining a way into organisations and obtaining respondent cooperation once there, but also subtler and potentially more intractable difficulties associated with ideological issues and the hidden nature of political behaviour extending to 'power beyond decision making'.

Attribution. A further barrier to validity is reliance – consequent upon the issues already mentioned – on the attribution by one organisational observer or participant of motives and forms of behaviour to other participants. It has been noted that:

> to the extent that self-interest objectives are not acknowledged by the actor, the question of whether an upward influence behavior is <u>designed</u> to advance or protect self-interests at the expense of theirs is one of attribution. Regardless of the 'true' intent of the actor, if the observer characterizes the behavior as political, it <u>is</u> political to the observer ... While all behavior is potentially observable, the actor's intent is solely one of attribution (by self or other). (Porter <u>et al</u>, 1981)

On the one hand we have the problem that observers or respondents are making evaluative judgements as to the goals of others, while on the other hand they are at the same time attributing hidden, unsanctioned forms of behaviour to them in pursuit of their goals. Such data might well validly measure one participant's perceptions of his organisational environment but not necessarily the actual goals and behaviour of the other participants concerned. It should be noted, of course, that while Porter <u>et al</u> were concerned with attribution by organisational participants, just the same issue is relevant to empirical observation from outwith the organisation, and the more fundamental question is whether behaviour characterised by a researcher as political, which in Porter's terms therefore <u>is</u> political to that researcher, is in fact political in any other sense.

As suggested by Pfeffer (1981b) possibly the most insoluble problem of all is evaluating the impact or result of power and politics, which strictly would require the following: first, knowledge of what would have happened in the absence of the use of power and politics; second, knowledge of the actual intentions of the actors exercising power; and third, knowledge of the effect of the actions taken – which presupposes both an answer to the first question as well as identification of what those actions are. The implication is a need for control measurements of a type unlikely to be readily available.

Returning to the observer/participant issue, Patchen (1974) noted the problems in assessing influence in organis- ations which relate to disagreements among participants in the same organisation, and he suggested that general or global questioning is of limited value in assessing influence. Patchen points out that people at different hierarchical levels are likely to have different perceptions of the influence associated with each level (an argument quantified in the well-known Tannenbaum Control Graph discussed later, pp. *307-308*), but that there are essentially two sources of variation in such judgements about influence: first, the nature of the contributions made by various people to the overall decision varies considerably, so different respondents may have in mind different contributions; and, second, the process of decision making is often one of 'accommodation', with the effect that the relative influence of different participants in joint decision making may be impossible to observe. Patchen thus concludes that global measures of influence may be useful where large influence differences exist, but that where many people and levels are involved, there is a need to go beyond the general question to study specific actions and the reactions they elicit, in order to assess the relative importance and influence of each person in a specific decision.

It is, in fact, implicit in other observers' comments that attribution is a fundamental flaw in linking actions taken and results achieved. For instance, March (1966) raised the issue of the difficulty of distinguishing power or force from chance; while Dahl (1957) commented on the existence of 'chamelons' and 'satellites' – i.e. individuals who forecast outcomes and agree with or follow the lead of the powerful; and Pfeffer (1981b) similarly notes the difficulty of distinguishing power from foresight. Indeed the latter writer, in evaluating reputational measures of power, draws attention to the fact that while they are frequently accepted as valid in the literature of organisational behaviour, they have aroused controversy, of the type discussed earlier, in the literature of community power (and it is certainly self-evidently the case that to ask departmental managers to rank departmental power is to assume that a system of differentiated power actually exists).

While the problem appears unavoidable, and is approached in this study through scaling, the use of indirect questions, and the use of multiple measurements, Pfeffer (1981b) concludes optimistically that the measurement of power is subtle rather than wholly intractable, and he proposes a matrix for identifying political actors, and the multiple measurement of the determinants, consequences and symbols of power. Similarly, Hedberg et al (1975) suggested the need for empirical approaches at three levels: the influence of participants over outcomes; the participation in decision making; and, the existence of interpersonal influence – each level being associated with a number of specific empirical tools (pp. *307-308*).

Thus, while attribution – by respondent and researcher – poses substantial problems, as recognised here, there is some precedent for the view that the available techniques offer a way forward, though admittedly without truly overcoming the problems of attributed goals and behaviour and the lack of suitable control measurements.

Studying the Marketing Organisation and Marketing Information

While problems exist in studying the structural variables of the marketing organisation – its departmentation, location, responsibilities, and so on – and the marketing information system characteristics, they are somewhat less than in the case of power and politics.

In fact, this element of the work is largely replicative and draws on the tools developed in earlier marketing research (see pp. *300 - 308* below for a discussion of the measurement devices used).

Studying the Marketing Budget

The major dependent variable in the study is the resources allocated to marketing – primarily financial, but also manpower and other facilities – and there are rather more problematic issues relating to this than was the case with the intervening variables of organisation structure and information or budgeting processes.

First, there is a particular problem of **access**. Budgetary data are typically surrounded by secrecy and confidentiality within commercial organisations, for a variety of reasons – some, indeed, political but others not. Given the methodology used here, access to budgetary data was more limited than it might otherwise have been, with the secondary effect that questions about budget sizes are likely to have adversely affected response rates and thus threatened sample completeness.

Second, it is clear from the literature discussed

earlier that there is little consensus on the **form or content** of the marketing budget. At one level it is clear that some organisations do not have a specific marketing budget, or even a near-equivalent, but over and above this the operational definition of the budget would appear highly variable between organisations.

In fact, the study does not pursue the question of the precise content of an organisation's marketing budget, partly on the grounds that the existence and form of the budget is taken itself as a political outcome, which is significant as an outcome representing the institutionalisation of the prevailing balance of sub-unit power, but also because of the possibly symbolic rather than substantive nature of that budget outcome. The latter point suggests that we should be more interested in responsibilities, influence and control - i.e. process - than the precise formulation of budget structure.

A last factor relates to **external influences** over the marketing budget - particularly such as advertising and sales promotion and marketing research agencies and consultants, or, more broadly, powerful distributors and customers (Piercy, 1984). These influences were not intended to be included in the study, although they did in fact emerge in certain of the companies studied as significant not merely to budgeting but to the whole nature and form of corporate marketing, in just the way that would be expected from the contingency view of marketing organisation (pp. *119-29* above). These factors are subsumed under the measurement of environmental uncertainty, although they emerge explicitly at various points in discussing the survey results.

Implications

It may be seen that a variety of problems were faced in designing the empirical element of this study, relating particularly to the measurement of power and politics. These problems are important in that they shaped the methodology and thus the measurement devices available, but also because they provide important qualifications to the empirical findings advanced, and emerge in the discussion and interpretation of those findings.

METHODOLOGICAL RESEARCH PROBLEMS

The data collection approach is detailed in Appendix A, together with the survey documentation and response statistics. Broadly, the main study involved a postal questionnaire survey of medium-sized UK manufacturing companies, where responses were provided by chief marketing executives. The methodology chosen imposed certain limitations which should be recognised.

Representativeness

There is some controversy surrounding the representativeness of studies of power and politics generally. In terms simply of sample size, a large proportion of the available literature is based on small studies, relying on the intensive study of a limited number of situations. Indeed, Hickson et al (1981) commented that the literature of power is, in fact, largely drawn from samples which are restrictive, often no more than single cases, and resulting in caricatures.

There is some debate concerning the choice between 'qualitative' (typically small sample and often case-oriented) studies and 'quantitative' (typically larger) studies (e.g. Downey and Ireland, 1979).

This present study used a questionnaire study of a relatively large number of companies rather than restricting the approach to a small number of intensive case studies. This approach was taken because of: the essentially exploratory nature of this present work and the relative infrequency of marketing budget decisions in organisations; the need to evaluate the theory developed in as representative a way as possible, in terms of different marketing organisations; the need to study a variety of contingencies surrounding the dependent variable of marketing budgeting; and the need to pursue the goal of contrasting the politicisation of marketing budgeting in different organisations which are distinguished by their internal characteristics and by the environments in which they operate.

However, while representativeness in this sense may be achieved to a greater extent than in small sample studies, any such gains are made only at the cost of other sacrifices inherent in the data collection method used.

Response Rate

It is characteristic of postal surveys that response rates are relatively low, inducing biases of respondent self-selection and sample incompleteness. Indeed, for the reasons discussed earlier, the nature of the variables studied itself introduces further uncontrollable response rate bias. In fact, the total response rate is regarded as broadly acceptable for the reasons detailed in Appendix A. None the less, it will be seen that the response rate remained a substantial problem in interpreting the survey results.

Respondents

The methodology used involves respondent problems in two ways. First, there is little or no control of the respondents' behaviour in providing data, as to their effort, understanding, identity, and so on. Second, respondents are inevitably asked to make judgements – the data are explicitly or implicitly subjective – or to make attributions (see pp. 292-94 above). Where possible the subjectivity is minimised – for instance, in looking for relatively objective indicators of variables – but it remains inherent to this research design (as to most others) and should be recognised.

Indeed, this study also shares with most others of its type the limitation of relying on data from a single respondent in each participating company, a methodology, analysed and criticised by Phillips (1981). In addition, it should be noted that the data collected are facts and perceptions reported by marketing executives, and they may be expected to reflect their selective perceptions and departmental identifications (e.g. Dearborn and Simon, 1958). It may be that our results should be interpreted thus as referring to the perceptions of a sample of chief marketing executives rather than to organisational characteristics, but the approach is defended in terms of the essentially exploratory nature of the study.

Sampling Precision

In fact, as shown in Appendix A, the available sampling frames did not allow a precise sampling of firms with marketing departments (again, a problem found by others, e.g. Hayhurst and Wills, (1972)). The implication is that many respondents did not participate – or did not do so as fully as would have been desirable – because their organisations had no marketing departments. A fuller analysis of this question is provided in Appendix A and Chapter 11 (pp. 314-318). This has two further implications. First, the study results are largely restricted to those firms with some degree of marketing departmentation however minimal that departmentation might be. Second, more interestingly, what may be termed the 'real' response rate is thus quite high. The study therefore claims to be reasonably representative of medium-sized manufacturing firms with some degree of marketing departmentation.

With these limitations recognised, we may turn to examine the objectives which were pursued.

RESEARCH OBJECTIVES

The debate developed in Part III of this book, and its

sources in the earlier work <u>Marketing Organisaation: An Analysis of Information Processing, Power and Politics</u> (Piercy, 1985), led to a number of research objectives for the exploratory work which is reported here. These objectives may be grouped into those concerned with clarifying and describing the structural and processual characteristics of marketing organisation; and those concerned with applying the frame of reference provided by organisational power and politics to the analysis of structure, process and resource outcomes in marketing.

The Structural Characteristics of the Marketing Organisation

The **first** objective was to examine and describe the organisation of marketing, in the sample of companies selected, in terms of departmentation characteristics, the integration and unification of marketing functions, and specialist roles, and the responsibilities of the chief marketing executive.

In the earlier work (Piercy, 1985) such variables were taken from the received literature as the key attributes associated with the development of corporate marketing as a formalised, specialised functional activity, but it was argued that high variability on such criteria was to be expected, since the contingency view of the marketing organisation, which was developed in that work, implies that different contingencies will create different burdens and hence different structural responses.

The Corporate Status of the Marketing Department

The **second** objective was to evaluate the standing of the marketing department in the organisation in terms of factors related to status and control or pervasiveness, rather than simply structure and formal authority. This involved the study of such factors as: the status of the chief marketing executive compared to other functional heads; the representation of marketing on the board of directors; the perceived ranking of marketing compared to other departments; the influence of the marketing department over those activities considered critical to the success of a particular organisation; and the recognition of the marketing paradigm, i.e. the orientation of the firm.

In the first instance these variables were studied to give insight into the contemporary standing of the marketing department, but it follows from the logic advanced earlier that such variables may also act as significant indicators of organisational power.

Resource Allocation in Marketing

A **third** objective, given our present focus was to identify and describe the resources allocated to marketing, together with the processual characteristics associated with those allocations. We sought to evaluate marketing resource outcomes in financial budgets, manpower levels and other resources. Attention was also focused on the budgeting methods used, the type of budgeting process, the intervention of top management in determining marketing budgets, and the influence of other functional units in marketing budgeting.

The measurements provide insight at a descriptive level into our major area of interest, in developing a focus on marketing resources, but further serve as the intervening variables in the later analysis.

The first three objectives are thus primarily descriptive, and serve three main purposes: to clarify the characteristics of the companies included in the study, to replicate measurements of organisational and budgeting variables from other studies, and to provide a foundation for applying the concepts of power and politics discussed as the major themes of the earlier work.

Discussion of the findings relevant to these descriptive objectives is presented in Chapter 11. The following goals are concerned with developing a political analysis of resource allocation from that descriptive foundation.

Power, Politics and Resources

It is at this point where we come to the central interest - the measurement of the power of the marketing department, political behaviour, the surrounding strategic and political contingencies, and their relationship with resource allocation processes and outcomes.

The **fourth** objective was to measure the power of the marketing department, including positional, participative and perceptual dimensions, and to investigate the relationship between power (as it is was thus operationalised), and the political and contingency measurements discussed below.

The **fifth** objective was to measure the politicisation of resource allocation in marketing, which is conceived here as primarily informational - in terms of information access, restriction and control and in influence over the critical sales forecasting process - and as subjective or perceptual, and to investigate the relationship between political control or politicisation and the power of the marketing department, in the context of the contingency measurements discussed below.

The **sixth** objective was to measure the strategic and political contingencies discussed earlier (pp. *199-214*), as factors surrounding the use of power and politics to determine resource outcomes.

The **seventh**, and final, objective was to investigate the relationship between power, politics, and strategic and political contingencies, and the outcomes of process control and resource allocation, together with the implications for corporate performance.

It is in this analysis that we seek to model process and resource outcomes as at least partially explained by differences in power and political behaviour, in attempting to evaluate the model of the power and politics of marketing resource allocation. The discussion of these later, analytical issues is presented in Chapter 12.

However, before proceeding to the empirical evidence, some attention should be given to the research design adopted.

RESEARCH DESIGN

Data Collection

The data presented were collected in a postal survey carried out in the period April to September, 1984, following a number of exploratory interviews with marketing executives. The survey methodology and background statistics and documentation are presented in Appendices A and B.

Measurement of Variables

Taking the model presented in Figure 9.2, the variables were measured in the ways discussed below, and a summary of the operationalisation of the model is given in Figure 10.1.

Organisational Power of the Marketing Department. In view of the structural conception of power advanced here, the power of the marketing department was taken to be indicated firstly by a series of structural variables: (a) the degree of integration of the key activities of sales, distribution, customer service, trade marketing, advertising, exporting, and marketing research in the marketing department; (b) the number of employees in the marketing department, compared to the number of employees carrying out 'marketing' tasks outside the control of the marketing department; (c) the representation of the marketing department on the board of directors; (d) the scope and degree of marketing department responsibility for key areas of market-related but also strategic or corporate decision making; and (e) the control of critical success factors.

In addition, measurements included the perceptual variables: (f) the status of the chief marketing executive compared to the chief production executive, the chief finance/accounting executive, and, where applicable, the chief sales executive; (g) the perceived power of the

Figure 10.1: The Power and Politics of Marketing Budgeting

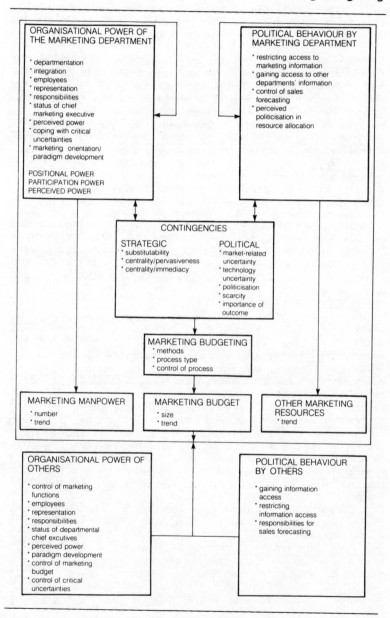

marketing department compared to other functional departments; and (h) the orientation of the firm (production, sales or marketing) as an indication of the level of marketing paradigm development.

These measurements were scored and combined in the way shown in Appendix C to produce indicators of the organisational power of the marketing department.

Political Behaviour. Political behaviour was taken for these present purposes as largely informational in nature and was assessed by the following indicators: (a) the control and restriction of access of other departments to marketing information sources by the marketing department; (b) the success of the marketing department in gaining access to important information held by other departments; (c) the formal responsibility of the marketing department for sales forecasting, compared to the sharing of control of this process with other departments.

In addition, perceived political behaviour particularly related to marketing budgeting was measured in terms of: (d) the perceptions of how 'political' is obtaining a financial budget manpower and other resources, i.e. the politicisation of resource allocation.

Again, these individual indicators were combined as shown in Appendix C, to produce indices of political behaviour by the marketing department in gaining resources of different kinds.

Contingencies. First, the measurements used earlier by the strategic contingencies' theorists (see pp. *156-60*) were adapted in the following ways: (a) substitutability (subsuming for these purposes the replacement of an uncertainty coping by routinisation) was indicated by the rating of the ease with which marketing department personnel could be replaced by personnel from other departments, by external recruitment, or by using outside agencies; (b) centrality/pervasiveness was indicated by the perceived connectedness of the marketing department to the finance, production and R&D departments, and the perceived level of influence of marketing over those departments; and (c) centrality/immediacy was taken to be shown by the impact of the marketing department on the despatch of goods from the factory.

Second, the political contingencies associated with the use of power and politics (as discussed earlier (pp. *200-14*)) were assessed using the following measurements: (d) market-related uncertainty was indicated by two factors, first the perceived predictability of demand, and second, the perceived ability of the firm to influence demand; (e) technology uncertainty in marketing was indicated by the perceived ability to assess the effectiveness of marketing actions; (f) the rating of the importance to success of political activities defined as selective information use, image building, attacking or criticising other departments, gaining informal support, praising others to make them allies, cultivating the influential, creating obligations and favours 'owed', and knowing the 'rules' and using them, i.e. the politicisation of the company; (g) resource scarcity was indicated by the profit to sales ratio over three years, and by the perceived impact of the recession on the company's main interests; and (h) importance of outcome was indicated by the marketing budget to profit ratio.

Marketing Budgeting Processes.

Descriptively the marketing budgeting activity was studied in two ways: (a) budgeting methods were measured by directly asking which of the traditional and more sophisticated methods of budget-setting were used for advertising and sales promotion; and (b) budgeting processes were evaluated by asking respondents which of the recognised models of budgeting processes (bottom-up, top-down/bottom-up, or bottom-up/top-down), if any, was the closest to their company's approach.

In addition the control of marketing budgeting by the marketing department was measured in three ways: (c) perceived control of the budget by higher management and the size of adjustments made to budget size by higher management; (d) the degree of participation of the marketing department in marketing budget decision making; and (e) the perceived degree of influence of other departments in determining the size of marketing budgets.

Resource Allocation Outcomes.

The results of budgeting processes and the allocation of resources to the marketing department were evaluated as: (a) the size and trend of the marketing budget for advertising, promotion, and other expenses, and in total, over three years; (b) the size and trend of the employee number in the marketing department over three years; (c) the trend in the other resources (equipment, offices, space, buildings, etc.) taken up by the marketing department over three years.

Organisational Power of Others.

This was taken to be indicated by the following measurements: (a) the organisation of key marketing activities outwith the marketing department (i.e. non-integration, see above); (b) the number of employees carrying out marketing tasks outwith the marketing department (see above); (c) the relative responsibility of others for key marketing and corporate decisions (see above); (d) the perceived status of senior executives in production, finance/accounting and sales, relative to the chief marketing executive (see above); (e) the perceived power of non-marketing departments (see above);

(f) the orientation of the firm (see above);   (g) control of
the marketing budget (see above);   and (h) control of
critical success factors (see above).

Political Behaviour by Others.   This was taken to be
indicated by the the following measurements: (a) access to
marketing information gained by other departments (see
above);   (b) control of access for the marketing department
to non-marketing information exerted by other departments
(see above);   (c) responsibilities for sales forecasting
(see above).

Discussion.   The measurement philosophy is essentially
one of adaptation from the measurement devices developed by
others and in some cases the replication of the measurements
taken by them.

In approaching **organisational power** we start from
the proposition that power may be measured directly and
indirectly (Simon, 1958), and in this study the goal was to
take a primarily structural approach and to seek the type of
relatively objective measurement used in the university and
social   services   budgeting   studies   discussed   earlier
(pp. 250-55).

It is for this reason that we looked at the overt
departmentation, integration, relative employee number, and
responsibilities   indicators,   as   relatively   objective   facts,
from which power characteristics could be implied.   This
form of approach is that advocated by Pfeffer (1981b) in his
suggested   indicators   of   power   in   organisational   contexts.
In this area it should be noted that the key marketing and
corporate responsibility measurement was partly a replication
of the instrument used by Hayhurst and Wills (1972) in their
study of large UK marketing organisations.   It was reasoned
further, however, that the significance of formal control or
responsibility for an activity should be weighted according
to   the   importance   of   that   activity   to   the   company's
performance.   For this reason respondents were also asked to
identify the critical success factors for their main markets
and the departments mainly responsible for those factors, to
allow   the   assessment   of   the   relative   control   of   critical
uncertainties.

However, the Pfeffer (1981b) logic is to look also for
other   power   indicators   than   simply   the   structural   or
positional,   in   a   similar   way   to   the   multiple   measurement
philosophy adopted by others (e.g. Pettigrew, 1973; Hinings
et al, 1974), accepting that this renders the work
essentially   exploratory.   Using the Hickson et al (1971)
terms, in addition to positional and participative power,
which may be measured relatively objectively, we were also
concerned with perceived power.   For this reason we looked
also, firstly, at the perceived status of the chief marketing

executive, again replicating a form of questioning tested and used by Hayhurst and Wills (1972). Secondly, we examined the perceived power of departments, adapting from the questioning technique used by Perrow's (1970) work on departmental power in industrial firms. Thirdly, we examined the perceived 'orientation' of the firm as a measure of the development and strength of the marketing paradigm in the firm (see pp. 2 - 13 above). In this last case, the measurement device was a direct replication of that tested and used by Hooley et al (1984).

The evaluation of **political behaviour** was rather more problematic. Throughout the conceptual formulation process in the earlier parts of the book, one theme was that information in marketing lay at the heart of power and politics. For this reason the first political measurements related to the degree of success of the marketing sub-unit in gaining access to: firstly, various pieces of 'marketing' information (product costs, marketing costs); secondly, financial data (company profitability, company-wide budgets) thirdly, data relating to other sub-unit operations (production schedules, R&D projects); and fourthly, corporate information (investment plans, corporate plans). The information items were chosen following interviews with senior marketing executives in a number of companies as reasonably representative of that type of information which is: typically defensible with barriers of secrecy and confidentiality; important to at least symbolic involvement in strategic decision-making; and of a type that a marketing manager could claim was significant to marketing decision making, but over which others could wield political jurisdiction.

Correspondingly, we also attempted to measure the degree of success of the marketing department in restricting the access of other sub-units to key items of marketing information chosen on a similar basis (market studies, customer reports, sales plans, marketing plans, marketing budgets, new product plans, and other marketing research reports). Again, the reasoning was that these items are potentially politically important on the grounds that they are: defensible with organisational secrecy; potentially (at least symbolically) important to decision making participation; and ambiguous in jurisdiction.

In addition, sales forecasting was taken as a key informational activity, which is linked to the absorption of whatever demand-related uncertainty may exist, or may be perceived, in a company's markets. Here we attempted to identify the sub-unit formally responsible for sales forecasting (marketing or otherwise) and the degree of shared responsibility of sub-units in producing sales forecasts and the balance between the two.

Thirdly, we measured directly the perceived

politicisation of resource allocation related to financial budgets, manpower, and other resources for marketing.

The **contingency** element was approached in two ways to represent the 'strategic contingencies' model of power differences and the 'political contingencies' or conditions for the emergence of the use of power and politics (see pp. *199-206* above). These frameworks are taken together because while one relates strictly to the explanation of sub-unit power differences and the other relates to the circumstances under which power and politics are likely to be used to resolve conflict and to determine outcomes, they are linked by the concept of uncertainty.

The strategic contingencies for the analysis of intraorganisational power were evaluated by replicating as closely as possible certain of the measurements developed and tested by Hinings et al (1974). This was true in the case of the measurement of: substitutability (the ease of replacing marketing department personnel); pervasiveness (the number of connections between marketing and other sub-units, and the influence of marketing over those other sub-units); and immediacy (the impact of the marketing department on the despatch of goods).

The contingencies for the emergence of political decision making were evaluated following Pfeffer's (1981b) paradigm: market-related uncertainty with which the organisation must cope (the ability to predict demand and the ability to change or influence the market); technology uncertainty (the ability to trace sales results to specific marketing actions like advertising and promotion); and the scarcity and importance of the resources at stake.

While accepting that uncertainty may be taken either as an 'objective property of the environment or a property subjectively interpreted by key decision makers' (Gordon and Narayanan, 1984), we take the view here, consistent with the theoretical positions of Angyal (1941) and Weick (1969) that uncertainty should be taken as a subjective or perceived variable in the process of 'environmental enactment'. This view is consistent too with the argument that the structuring actions taken by an organisation in responding to its environment are more closely related to perceptions of that environment than to objective measurements environment (Downey et al, 1975; Galbraith, 1973). Precedent in the empirical marketing literature for this decision is found in Nonaka and Nicosia (1979).

However, following the Butler et al (1977) and Madison et al (1980) logic, we also attempted to distinguish the perceived degree of company politicisation as a contingency for the use of political behaviour, using the Allen et al (1979) framework of political influence acts.

Marketing budgeting was evaluated at two levels — the description of budgeting methods and the budgeting process mode, and the analysis of the control of the marketing department over budgeting compared both to top management and to other sub-units.

The description of marketing budgeting methods (for advertising and sales promotion) was a replication of the measurement instrument developed and tested by Hooley et al (1984), which was in turn developed from the measurements taken by others over a substantial time period (see pp. *78-80*). A second question asked respondents to classify the marketing budgeting process in the company into a bottom-up, top-down/ bottom-up, or bottom-up/top-down decision process (or to describe how their approach differed from these). This classification was adapted from Hanmer-Lloyd and Kennedy (1981), and the operational descriptions of these process-types were developed from their MCRC work at Cranfield.

The analysis of the control of the budgeting process by the marketing department was adapted conceptually from Tannenbaum's (1968) 'Control Graph' measurements, and the Aspiration-Outcome-Gradient and Influence-Power-Sharing-Continuum measurements proposed by Hedberg et al (1975). These last writers proposed three measures of power: first, the Aspiration-Outcome Gradient – which attempts to rate sub-unit power as the gradient from sub-unit's aspirations in terms of its expressed initial preferred income to the final decision outcome which was based on Abell's (1975) suggestion that sub-unit power can be assessed by measuring its effect over critical phases of decision making and thus over outcomes; second, the Influence-Power-Sharing-Continuum (Heller, 1971), which attempts to evaluate the degree of perceived influence and power sharing, where a Decision Centralisation Score (DCS) indicates the degree to which the superior A allows the subordinate to participate in a decision or the degree to which A incorporates the subordinate's view in the outcome of decisions; and third, the Control Graph (Tannenbaum, 1968) which evaluates power as interpersonal influence by asking respondents to scale the amount of influence they (and others) exert.

The proposal made by Hedberg et al was that these measures used in conflictual decision situations would reveal three distinctive manifestations of organisational power: the 'structural power' of bargaining parties (organisational units or alliances) as measured by the outcome of decisions against their original ambitions (the Aspiration-Outcome-Gradient); inter-level power within organisational units taken as different degrees of control over information relevant to the decision (the Influence-Power-Sharing-Continuum); and the intra-level power across organisational units (the Control Graph).

This schema was developed in the context of implementing computerised management information systems, which is a related but somewhat different interest to that pursued here. Accordingly, the measures were adapted to meet our present needs, and indeed the restrictions imposed by the fieldwork methodology.

First, we measured the amount by which budget requests were usually adjusted by top management as an approximation of the Aspiration-Outcome-Gradient, in the sense that large budget request cuts were taken to be indicative of low marketing sub-unit control over budgeting. Second, we adapted the Influence-Power-Sharing Continuum concept to evaluate the style of marketing budget decision making existing between the marketing sub-unit and top management, changing the original scale to run from 'It is Marketing Department decision' to 'The marketing budget is set by top management'. Third, we used the measurement framework of the Control Graph, but in the context of evaluating the influence over the marketing budget of other non-marketing sub-units, rather than simply hierarchical levels. Although the measurement is thus somewhat different to Tannenbaum's original Control Graph concept, which was concerned with vertical rather than lateral power relationships, the adapted version does retain the implicit capacity to distinguish both variations between the points of focus in the relative power or control they wield (the slope and shape of the curve) and also in the 'amount' of power available to be wielded (the average height of the curve).

While interest has generally been in the influence of such factors as participation on the total amount of control, our interest here was more simply in the amount of sub-unit power over the marketing budget in different organisations (for example, compared to top management) and the source of non-marketing sub-unit influences.

The **decision outcomes** of concern here were measured by direct questioning as to marketing resources in terms of: the size of the financial marketing budget for three years, indicating its division into advertising, sales promotion, and other expenses; the number of employees in the marketing sub-unit over three years; and the trend in the other resources (offices, space, buildings, etc.) taken up by the marketing department in the previous three years.

The **organisational power of others** and **political behaviour by others** were evaluated essentially as residuals of the power and politics measurements applied to the marketing sub-unit.

CONCLUSIONS AND SUMMARY

This chapter has attempted to summarise the empirical approach adopted to study the power and politics of marketing budgeting as the context for interpreting the present results and developing replicative works.

First, it was necessary to recognise a variety of conceptual problems which exist in this type of research, and which exhibit varying degrees of intractability. These points reveal the underlying assumptions of the research and the qualifications necessary to the interpretation of its findings.

In particular it was noted that the measurement of power and the evaluation or detection of political behaviour (even once definitions or operational descriptions of these phenomena are proposed) pose problems in terms of: the incomplete explanation of outcomes the phenomena provide (an argument partly countered by the contingency approach taken here); the pervasiveness of the phenomena and the dangers inherent in taking too wide a view of them (see Chapter 7 for the more limited concepts of power and politics pursued here); the potentially ambiguous interrelatedness of the variables to be studied; the barriers posed by various aspects of access to the phenomena (countered here to some extent by attempting to incorporate indirect indicators into the research design in addition to direct measurements); and the related issue of attribution by respondents of motives and behaviour to others.

While problems exist too in studying marketing organisation and budgeting which are similar - access, attribution, definition, and so on - they are by comparison relatively straightforward, although providing certain further limitations to the study.

In a somewhat different way, the choice of methodology makes certain gains in representativeness compared to other designs, but inevitably at certain costs - specifically in terms of response rate, respondent control and objectivity, and sampling precision.

The theory and argument developed through Parts I and II of the book was then formulated into a series of research objectives.

This led to the operationalisation of our model of power and politics in marketing budgeting, which proposed measures of: the organisational power of the marketing department (and of others); political behaviour by the marketing department (and by others); contingencies (in the sense, first of centrality and coping, i.e. 'strategic contingencies' and second, of conditions of uncertainty and politicisation - i.e. 'political contingencies' - that surround the emergence of power and politics to resolve decisional issues); marketing budgeting methods, processes and control; and outputs in terms of financial budgets, manpower and other resources.

REFERENCES

Abell, P. (1975) Organizations as Bargaining and Influence Systems, Heinemann, London

Angyal, A. (1941) Foundations for a Science of Personality, Harvard University Press, Cambridge, Mass.

Bachrach, P. and Baratz, M.S. (1970) Power and Poverty: Theory and Practice, Oxford UP, London

Bell, C. and Newby, H. (1971) Community Studies, Allen and Unwin, London

Crozier, A. (1964) The Bureaucratic Phenomenon, Tavistock, London

Dearborn, D.C. and Simon, H.A. (1958) 'Selective Perception: A Note on the Departmental Identifications of Executives', Sociometry, 28, 140-44

Downey, H. K. and Ireland, R. D. (1979) 'Quantitative Versus Qualitative: Environmental Assessment in Organizational Studies', Administrative Science Quarterly, 24, 630-637

Downey, H., Hellriegel, D. and Slocum, J. (1975) 'Environmental Uncertainty: the Construct and its Application', Administrative Science Quarterly, December, 613-29

Duncan, R.B. (1979) 'Qualitative Research Methods in Strategic Management', in D.E. Schendel and C.W. Hofer (eds.) Strategic Management: A New View of Business Policy, Little Brown, Boston

Galbraith, J.R. (1973) Designing Complex Organizations, Addison-Wesley, Reading, Mass.

Gordon, L.A. and Narayanan, V.K. (1984) 'Management Accounting Systems, Perceived Environmental Uncertainty and Organization Structure: An Empirical Investigation', Accounting Organizations and Society, 9 (1), 33-47

Hanmer-Lloyd, S. and Kennedy, S. (1981) Setting and Allocating the Marketing Communications Budget: A Review of Current Practice, Marketing Communications Research Centre, Cranfield, Beds.

Hayhurst, R. and Wills, G. (1972) Organizational Design for Marketing Futures, Allen and Unwin, London

Heller, F. (1971) Managerial Decision Making, Allen and Unwin, London

Hedberg, B., Edstroem, A., Muller, W. and Wilpert, B. (1975) 'The Impact of Computer Technology on Organizational Power Structures', in E. Grochla and N. Szperski (eds.) Information Systems, de Gruyter, Berlin

Hickson, D.J., Hinings, C.R., Lee, C.A., Schneck, R.E. and Pennings, J.M. (1971) 'A Strategic Contingencies' Theory of Intraorganizational Power', Administrative Science Quarterly, 16, 216-29

Hickson, D.J., Astley, W.G., Butler, R.J. and Wilson, D.C. (1981) 'Organization as Power', in L.L. Cummings and B.M. Staw (eds.) Research in Organizational Behavior, Jai Press, Greenwich, Conn.

Hinings, C.R., Hickson, D.J., Pennings, J.M. and Schneck, R.E. (1974) 'Structural Conditions of Intraorganizational Power', Administrative Science Quarterly, 19, 22-44

Hooley, G.J., West, C.J. and Lynch, J.E. (1984) Marketing in the UK - A Survey of Current Practice and Performance, Institute of Marketing, Cookham, Berks.

Keen, P.G.W. (1979) Information Systems and Organizational Change, Working Paper 1087-9, Massachusetts Institute of Technology, Cambridge, Mass.

Madison, D.L., Allen, R.W. Porter, L.W., Renwick, P.A. and Mayes, B.T. (1980) 'Organizational Politics: An Exploration of Managers' Perceptions', Human Relations, 33, 79-100

March, J.G. (1966) 'The Power of Power', in D. Easton (ed.) Varieties of Political Theory, Prentice-Hall, Englewood Cliffs, N.J.

Markus, M.L. (1980) Power, Politics and MIS Implementation, Working Paper 1155-80, Massachusetts Institute of Technology, Cambridge, Mass.

Nonaka, I. and Nicosia, F.M. (1979) 'Marketing Management, Its Environment and Information Processing: A Problem of Organization Design', Journal of Business Research, 7 (4), 277-301

Patchen, M. (1974) 'The Locus and Basis of Influence in Organizational Decisions', Organizational Behaviour and Human Performance, 1 (11), 195-221

Perrow, C. (1970) 'Departmental Power and Perspective in Industrial Firms', in M.N. Zald (ed.) Power in Organizations, Vanderbilt UP, Nashville, Tenn.

Pettigrew, A. (1973) The Politics of Organizational Decision Making, Tavistock, London

Pfeffer, J. (1978) 'The Micropolitics of Organizations', in M.W. Meyer et al (eds.) Environment and Organizations, Jossey-Bass, San Francisco

Pfeffer, J. (1981a) 'Management as Symbolic Action: The Creation and Maintenance of Organizational Paradigms', in L.L. Cummings and B.M. Staw (eds.) Research in Organizational Behavior, Jai Press, Greenwich, Conn.

Pfeffer, J. (1981b) Power in Organizations, Pitman, Marshfield, Mass.

Phillips, L.W. (1981) 'Assessing Measurement Error in Key Informant Reports: A Methodological Note on Organizational Analysis in Marketing', Journal of Marketing Research, 18, November, 395-415

Piercy, N. (1984) 'The Impact of New Technology on Services Marketing', Services Industries Journal, 4 (3), 193-204

Piercy, N. (1985) Marketing Organisation: An Analysis of Information Processing, Power and Politics, Allen and Unwin, London

Porter, L.W., Allen, R.W. and Angle, H.L. (1981) 'The Politics of Upward Influence in Organizations', in L.L. Cummings and B.M. Staw (eds.) Research in Organizational Behavior, Jai Press, Greenwich, Conn.

Simon, H. (1958) 'Notes on the Observation and Measurement of Power', Journal of Politics, 15, November, 503

Tannenbaum, A. (1968) <u>Control in Organizations</u>, McGraw-Hill, New York

Weick, K. (1969) <u>The Social Psychology of Organizing</u>, Addison-Wesley, Reading, Mass.

11

The Status Quo of Marketing
and Marketing Budgeting

INTRODUCTION

This chapter sets out the descriptive findings of the survey described in Appendices A and B, concerned with the organisation of marketing and with marketing resource allocation in a sample of medium-sized UK manufacturing firms. The second stage is to proceed from this foundation to an analysis of the power and politics of marketing in Chapter 12, to evaluate in the same organisations the model of marketing budgeting which was formulated earlier and summarised in Figure 10.1.

THE DEPARTMENTATION AND RESPONSIBILITIES OF MARKETING

Departmentation

The first of the research objectives stated in Chapter 10 was to examine the major organisational characteristics of marketing in companies, although even this apparently modest aim was not straightforward. In evaluating the survey response rate in Appendix A, the point was made that the sampling methodology was unavoidably relatively crude and inevitably the sampling frame included many firms which did not have any type of formal marketing department.

The initial suggestion of the data in Table 11.1 is that in a random sample of medium-sized UK manufacturing organisations only a minority of companies had formally organised marketing activities (even when taking a liberal interpretation of what constituted a 'marketing' department to include any sales organisation that incorporated 'non-sales' marketing responsibilities. It is clear, however, that such a finding must be placed in the context of the characteristics of the sample of companies studied.

In particular two factors must be taken into account. Firstly, the sample in this study was heavily biased towards medium-sized firms and under-represented the very large organisations frequently studied by others. For example,

Table 11.1:   The Departmentation of Marketing

Firms with <u>no</u> marketing department* (i.e. no formally organised marketing operations)	55
Firms with a marketing department*	45 (N=284)

* The departmentation of marketing includes departments with such titles as Marketing Department, Marketing and Sales Department, Sales and Marketing Department, Marketing Development, and Sales Department (but only in those cases where the department was responsible for other marketing functions such as advertising and marketing research).

Table 11.2:   Marketing Departmentation and Company Size

	Marketing Department		
	Yes	No	
	%	%	
Company Size (Employees)			
Less than 250	74	26	(N=46)
250-500	98	11	(N=44)
500-1000	89	11	(N=36)
More than 1000	92	8	(N=24)
Company Size (Sales Revenue)	%	%	
Less than 5M	70	30	(N=23)
5M- 10M	82	18	(N=38)
10M- 20M	83	17	(N=30)
20M- 50M	96	4	(N=23)
More than 50M	89	11	(N=18)

consider three of the widely cited studies comprising what is probably the major contribution to the current state of knowledge of marketing organisation in the UK.

In their study Hayhurst and Wills (1972) attempted to sample from only the largest firms in the UK, although it is not clear from their reports that this effect was actually achieved. Because of the way in which the Hayhurst and Wills survey is reported, direct comparisons between their sample and that in the present survey are problematic. However, it is known that Hayhurst and Wills sampled from the 2,400 largest firms in the UK - i.e. those with sales greater than £0.75M at the time. If we work from the fact that there are of the order of 120,000 manufacturing firms in the UK (itself a crude figure - see Appendix B), then the Hayhurst and Wills sampling frame accounted for approximately the largest 2% of UK manufacturers. On the same basis the largest 2% of firms in employee number terms are those with more than 500 employees (from Appendix B). This suggests at the very least that the Hayhurst and Wills study is restricted to firms with more than 500 employees, while this present study has only 17% of its sample in a comparable size category. For present purposes it is assumed that the Hayhurst and Wills work in effect describes only large companies, while this present survey is concerned essentially with medium-sized businesses.

More recently, in their survey Hooley et al (1984) sampled from the mailing list of Marketing magazine, which included the entire membership of the UK Institute of Marketing - producing a sample almost certain to be heavily influenced by larger organisations, but conversely also including many smaller firms. Since we are again to compare this present survey with the Hooley et al work, it should be noted that, in fact, some 41% of their sample were organisations with less than 100 employees and 21% had more than 1000 employees, both of which categories fall outside the scope of this presently reported study, so a valid comparison between the findings of this survey and the Hooley et al work should be restricted to the central 38% of their sample - a comparison not facilitated by the way in which Hooley et al reported their findings.

Heidrick and Struggles (1985), who attempted to profile the chief marketing executive in the UK, again sampled from the largest organisations in the UK, with the effect that their total sample of 260 contains no companies with sales of less than]50 millions, so there is, in effect, no overlap between the two surveys.

The effect, therefore, is that this present study is concerned with a size of organisation either excluded by others or subsumed in their reports with far larger companies. By implication to compare this present study's findings with those of the other empirical works cited, is to compare medium-sized companies with larger firms.

The second factor which should be taken into account is the implication of the response rate achieved in this present study, and in particular the distribution of non-responses both between companies and between items of the research instrument. For example, Table 11.1 suggests that 55% of the 284 companies which provided some data did not have any marketing departmentation - i.e. there were no separate or explicit marketing functions identified as such. On the other hand, Table 11.2 describes the 130-150 respondents who provided 'full' responses, and while suggesting that the formalisation of marketing organisational arrangements is related positively to company size, also provides a very different picture of the level of departmentation - i.e. 85% of the sample rather than 45%.

In fact this is somewhat misleading and suggests that some care is needed in interpreting the figures. In essence, the descriptive data in this chapter refer to the 128 companies with marketing departments (defined as indicated in Table 11.1) plus some 20 cases where there was no marketing department but there was some identifiable level of 'marketing' expenditure or there was some locus of 'marketing' responsibility identified by respondents - e.g. the chief executive controlled advertising and promotion, or the sales director carried out this function but with no specialised employees outside the sales force, or more commonly there was a chief marketing executive operating in a staff role with no department or specialised employees reporting to him. Where significant differences were found between the non-departmented respondents (N=22) and the departmented respondents (N=128) attention is drawn to this fact, although otherwise it is not further reported. It should be noted that this does imply that more firms have CMEs than have marketing departments in various of the tabulations in this chapter.

Returning to the main argument, from the first of the factors above, Table 11.2 suggests, as noted, that the departmentation of marketing is predictably related positively to company size, although not to a significant extent when tested in crosstabulations with a Chi-square statistic (for employee numbers Chi-square = 4.7 with 2 d.f. and for sales turnover Chi-square = 5.8 with 3 d.f.).

In fact, in pursuing the relationship of relative marketing department size to company size (in employees), the function takes the form $y = ax^{-b}$ so that with a double log transformation R = -0.53, a = 5.00 and b = -0.68. This suggests that because of the 'critical mass' required to establish any form of marketing department - i.e. there may be only one or two marketing employees in firms varying from 50 to 500 employees - the relative marketing department size is large in small firms and reduces rapidly to approach a base value for larger businesses. The qualification must be expressed that it would be expected that a sample of medium-sized firms would show a lower level of departmentation than a sample biased towards larger firms (e.g. as in Pugh, 1970). None the less, it must be noted that the level of departmentation is found surprisingly low, in the sense that in a random sample of medium-sized manufacturing companies some 55% had no identifiable marketing department or explicit marketing representation, while in the companies studied in some detail (i.e. even in a sample heavily biased towards marketing-active firms) there were some 15% with no measurable marketing departmentation.

Closely related to the actual departmentation of marketing are the issues of the integration of functions within that department, and its size, to which attention turns next.

Integration of Marketing Functions

Table 11.3 shows the degree to which the supposedly 'marketing' functions were formally organised in the companies studied, and, rather more significantly, the extent to which they were integrated into the marketing department or organised separately from it.

On the face of it: if they are organised at all, advertising and marketing research would appear normally to be marketing department functions; trade marketing and sales are organised in marketing in two-thirds of the firms, although 25% do not recognise a trade marketing function, and perhaps most importantly nearly 40% organised sales separately from marketing; while the functions of customer service, exporting and distribution were part of marketing only in a minority of companies - most usually being organised separately from marketing, rather than not being organised at all.

It would seem that marketing departments in companies of this type demonstrate a fairly low degree of formal or structural integration of marketing functions compared to the 'integrated marketing concept' of the received theory and the unification of marketing functions which this implies. Further insight into this aspect of departmentation is gained from analysing the distribution of employees working in 'marketing' functions, and the responsibilities of the chief marketing executive.

Size of Marketing Departments

The distribution of marketing department size in the responding companies is shown in Table 11.4, with a comparison with Hayhurst and Wills (1972) study.

Hooley et al (1984) suggested that, in their broad

Table 11.3: Integration of Marketing Functions

Marketing functions	Organised as part of the Marketing Department %	Organised separately from the Marketing Department %	Not organised as separate functions %	
Sales	59	37 *(14)	4 * (6)	(N=148)
Distribution	27	57 * (5)	16 * (12)	(N=145)
Customer service	45	40 *(13)	15 * (5)	(N=146)
Trade marketing	63	12 * (2)	25 * (15)	(N=145)
Advertising	81	9 * (5)	10 * (12)	(N=145)
Exporting	38	40 * (4)	22 * (12)	(N=144)
Marketing research	77	4 * (4)	18 * (14)	(N=146)

*These categories include the number of cases indicated in brackets which were classified in the present study as having no marketing departmentation.

sample of companies, in product and sales oriented companies the marketing department was typically small - one or two people - while in the marketing oriented firm there were typically seven or eight posts, but they did not go further in quantification or comparison with company size. In this present study, it should be noted that cases of the former type - where there is only one marketing 'person' - the CME - the firms concerned are classified as having no marketing department.

It should also be noted that the recent survey by Heidrick and Struggles (1985), which has gained some considerable attention, suggests that UK chief marketing executives 'typically' control departments of 30 people, although the authors accept that total department size varies considerably and that more than 50% of CMEs have a total department size of less than 50 people. In fact, as noted above, the Heidrick and Struggles (1985) study is heavily biased towards very large companies.

Hayhurst and Wills provided the figures shown in Table 11.4 for all marketing personnel and for all marketing personnel other than members of the sales force. Comparing the two surveys, in total department size it may be seen that in the Hayhurst and Wills large company figures some 43% of departments had less than 20 personnel, and there were substantially fewer large marketing departments with more than 50 employees in the present survey of medium-sized firms.

It seems that, as would be expected, there are far fewer large marketing departments and rather more small units in the medium-sized company sample as compared to the broader Hayhurst and Wills sample. This would appear reasonable since we have already suggested a significant relationship between company size and marketing departmentation and departmental size. However, it is of some note that if we exclude sales personnel the situation in the two sets of figures is very similar: in the broader 1972 sample 81% of marketing units excluding sales had less than 20 employees and 10% more than 20, while in the 1985 medium-sized company sample 84% were below 20 employees and 16% had more than 20. Accepting that differences in total department size reflect company size differences between the samples, and that the relative manpower to company size function is not linear (see pp. *317-18*) the latter comparison excluding sales employees is the more intriguing. Examining non-sales marketing employment suggests that: (a) the two samples show the same proportions below 20 employees and (b) the medium-size companies actually had significantly fewer departments in the smallest category ($\alpha = 0.01$). There would seem some grounds for at least hypothesising growth in non-sales marketing employment in the 15 years separating the two studies. This is all the more surprising given the reduction in sales

Table 11.4: Marketing Department Size

All Marketing Department Employees	This Survey (1985) %	Hayhurst and Wills (1972) %
1-5	26	25
6-10	18	18
11-20	26	20
21-50	18	29
More than 50	12	
	(N=127)	(N=553)

Marketing Department Size Excluding Sales Force	This Survey (1985) %	Hayhurst and Wills (1972) %
1-5	45	72
6-10	16	9
11-20	23	6
21-50	11	4
More than 50	5	
	(N=128)	(N=553)

employment through the 1970s, since Census data suggest a fall in sales employment of some 8.5% between 1971 and 1981 figures.   By implication, the evidence would seem to suggest that there may have been some entrenchment of the marketing department, albeit that this remains a somewhat tentative suggestion given what was noted earlier regarding the marketing department size/company size function.

Pursuing the question of employment in marketing and the integration characteristics considered earlier, one useful comparison is between the number of personnel working in 'marketing' functions within marketing departments and those similarly working in 'marketing' functions outwith marketing departments in the way shown in Table 11.6.   Perhaps the clearest link between the notions of the integration of marketing functions and marketing department size is shown by comparing the total employment of people in marketing functions within and outwith marketing departments, as in Table 11.5.

In the **sales** area, it may be seen that (in Table 11.6) the majority of companies organised sales and marketing together, but that in some 40% of cases the activities were separated.   The lack of a specialised sales function in either location in a small number of companies was explained by respondents as due to such factors as: small company size, when senior general managers typically handled sales personally, and own-label brand production where negotiations were carried out only at a senior general management level with retailers.   However, examining Table 11.5 suggests also that the separated sales organisations were mainly the larger ones, which could be compatible with the suggestion made elsewhere that the tendency is for small sales operations to be organised with marketing, and for larger sales organisations to either be disintegrated from marketing or to include marketing within sales rather than vice versa.

As far as **advertising** is concerned, some 40% of the companies had no specialist employees, but where they did exist they were almost wholly in the marketing department.

Product management was used by two-thirds of the companies in the study, almost always within the marketing department and in groups of less than five employees. Perhaps the most surprising fact is that product management in 11% of the companies was separated from the marketing department but this was largely accounted for by the use of a 'product planning' structure in certain of the industrial product firms.

Customer service had specialised employees in 80% of the companies, most frequently in the marketing department, but in one-third of cases outside.   Those customer service organisations outside the marketing department tended to be the larger ones, while most within the marketing department were small.

Table 11.5: Marketing Functions In and Out of the Marketing Department*

Employees in the Marketing Department

	1-5 %	6-10 %	11-20 %	More than 20 %	
Sales	43	21	19	17	(N=77)
Advertising	95	1	3	1	(N=73)
Product management	82	6	9	3	(N=79)
Customer service	74	13	8	5	(N=61)
Distribution	72	16	6	6	(N=32)
Marketing research	96	2	1	1	(N=83)
Marketing planning	97	1	1	0	(N=77)
Marketing services	88	7	3	2	(N=88)
Exporting	91	9	0	0	(N=45)
Other	58	21	15		(N=33)

Employees Separate from the Marketing Department

	1-5 %	6-10 No.	11-20 No.	More than 20 No.	
Sales	2	18	24	56	(N=50)
Advertising	71	29	0	0	(N=7)
Product management	79	21	0	0	(N=14)
Customer service	44	19	16	21	(N=43)
Distribution	35	25	14	26	(N=55)
Marketing research	75	25	0	0	(N=4)
Marketing planning	89	11	0	0	(N=9)
Marketing services	73	13	7	7	(N=15)
Exporting	63	30	2	5	(N=43)

*Excludes cases where no personnel are employed under a Chief Marketing Executive in specialist marketing roles.

Table 11.6:   Marketing Employment

	Personnel in this function are within the Marketing Department %	Personnel in this function are outside the Marketing Department %	No personnel are employed in this function %
Sales	59	38 *(3)	3 *(2) (N=131)
Advertising	56	5 *(2)	39 *(11) (N=131)
Product management	60	11 *(2)	29 *(8) (N=131)
Customer service	47	33 *(3)	20 *(3) (N=131)
Distribution	24	42 *(3)	34 *(7) (N=131)
Marketing research	63	3 *(1)	34 *(10) (N=131)
Marketing planning	59	7 *(1)	34 *(11) (N=131)
Marketing services	67	12 *(1)	21 *(9) (N=131)
Exporting	34	56 *(3)	10 *(6) (N=131)
Other	26	-	74 *(12) (N=129)

* These categories include the number of cases indicated in brackets which were classified in the present study as having no marketing departmentation.

Table 11.7:   Marketing Department Integration Differences

Level of Integration of Marketing Functions	%
1. Advertising and Marketing research	51
2. Advertising, Marketing research, Trade marketing and Sales	21
3. Advertising, Marketing research, Trade marketing, Sales, Customer service, and Exporting	13
4. Advertising, Marketing research, Trade marketing, Sales, Customer service, Exporting, and Distribution	15
	(N=102)

Distribution as a specialised employment area was organised in two-thirds of the companies, and was most frequently separated from marketing. Again small distribution groups tended to be organised with marketing and larger ones separately.

Marketing research, marketing planning and marketing services employed individuals in two-thirds or more of the companies, in almost every case as part of the marketing department. In each case, the number employed was normally small, falling in the 1-5 employee category.

Exporting was organised as a staffed, specialist function in the vast majority of the companies studied, but was normally outside the marketing department. Again small groups of export specialists tended to be employed within marketing and larger numbers were organised separately.

While the suggestion remains tentative, if one accepts that the integration of certain key functions into a marketing department reflects size - since in the cases of sales, customer service, distribution and exporting, small employee numbers tended to be integrated with marketing while larger groups were organised separately from marketing - then one possible implication is that company growth is associated with the disintegration of 'marketing' in the way hypothesised earlier (Piercy, 1985).

Whatever the underlying causes, generally the marketing specialisms in the companies studied appeared to exhibit varying levels of integration, in the way shown in Table 11.7. Although a relatively crude analysis, it would seem that: in half the companies marketing is simply organised as advertising and marketing research; in a further 20% trade marketing and sales are included; but only in a relatively small number of cases are customer service, exporting, and distribution integrated into the marketing department. This measure crosstabulated with product-markets suggests that significant differences exist between the latter in terms of integration of marketing functions (Table 11.8). Perhaps the most surprising finding is that the highest degree of integration is most frequent in industrial goods firms and the lowest level of integration is more frequently found in consumer goods firms. It may be that it is the converse should be noted - the disintegration of marketing functions is commoner in consumer goods firms. While the comment is somewhat speculative this finding is compatible with the suggestion that where marketing activities are (expected to be) more important to a company - or at least more visible - then there is a tendency for those functions not to be integrated into the marketing department. Similarly, Table 11.9 suggests that high integration is negatively related to company size, which is compatible with other evidence suggesting that increased company size is related to the disintegration of marketing functions from the marketing department.

Table 11.8: Integration by Product-Market

Level of Integration of Marketing Functions	Product Markets	
	Consumer Goods %	Industrial Goods %
1. Advertising and Marketing research	60	42
2. Advertising, Marketing research, Trade marketing and Sales	15	29
3. Advertising, Marketing research, Trade marketing, Sales, Customer service, and Exporting	16	7
4. Advertising, Marketing research, Trade marketing, Sales, Customer service, Exporting, and Distribution	9	22
	(N=55)	(N=45)

(Chi-square = 36.3 with 3 d.f., = 0.01)

Table 11.9: Integration by Company Size

Level of Integration of Marketing Functions	Company Size		
	Less than 250 employees %	250-500 employees %	More than 500 employees %
1. Advertising and Marketing research	42	48	62
2. Advertising, Marketing research, Trade marketing and Sales	16	26	19
3. Advertising, Marketing research, Trade marketing, Sales, Customer service, and Exporting	19	10	13
4. Advertising, Marketing research, Trade marketing, Sales, Customer service, Exporting, and Distribution	23	16	6
	(N=31)	(N=31)	(N=32)

(Chi-square = 19.9 with 6 d.f., = 0.01)

Responsibilities of the Chief Marketing Executive

Following the logic advanced by Hayhurst and Wills (1972) it
is possible to argue that a fuller impression of corporate
marketing development may be gained by examining the
responsibilities of the chief marketing executive (CME), and
examining both the spread of those responsibilities and their
level, rather than restricting consideration to formally
integrated functions and manpower. This survey partly
replicated a number of questions used by Hayhurst and Wills,
and the findings are summarised in Table 11.10.

For the purposes of analysis and comparison, these
responses are divided into functional responsibilities for:
product policy, pricing, marketing communications, marketing
planning and information, staffing, and corporate planning
and strategy (and the former measures are summed into
marketing mix responsibilities). Throughout these
comparisons, however, it must be borne in mind that the
Hayhurst and Wills findings relate to a sample of large
companies while the 1985 figures describe medium-sized
businesses. It should also be noted that this analysis
revealed no clear sign of responsibility levels being related
to size and no significant differences emerged on the basis
of size (either on the basis of employees or sales revenue).
However, it did emerge that there were significant
differences between product-market types in examining
marketing mix responsibilities and strategy responsibilities
as shown in Table 11.11. Broadly, marketing mix
responsibilities are highest with fast moving consumer goods
and lowest in industrial capital goods firms.

In the case of **product policy**, the data are shown in
Table 11.12. In the most directly equivalent categories –
product planning and packaging design in this survey, and new
product policy and packaging in the Hayhurst and Wills (1972)
work, no difference emerges. In both surveys in product
planning just under a quarter of the sample claimed full and
sole responsibility for this area, three-quarters had some
degree of shared or participative responsibility and a small
number had no responsibility; similarly in both surveys
around 30% had sole responsibilities for packaging and the
majority had shared responsibilities (although in the 1985
survey rather fewer had no responsibility at all). In the
area of **pricing policy**, the data are summarised in Table
11.13, where the broad comparison suggests that the CMEs in
the 1985 survey of medium-sized companies had a somewhat
lower degree degree of responsibility for pricing than was
the case in the 1972 survey of large firms: the proportion
with sole responsibility for pricing was 36% rather than 20%,
and the proportion with no responsibility (although small)
was double.

Table 11.10: Chief Marketing Executive Responsibilities

Responsibility areas	Full and sole responsibility %	Major responsibility but shared with others %	Equal responsibility with others %	Some responsibility but less than others %	No responsibility %	
Advertising	57	31	4	1	7	(N=134)
Sales promotion	52	25	11	8	4	(N=134)
Price setting	20	38	20	10	11	(N=134)
Discount structures	27	25	14	20	14	(N=133)
Product planning	24	36	25	10	5	(N=134)
Field sales force operations	44	10	4	19	23	(N=133)
Negotiations with distributors/retailers	32	17	8	21	22	(N=130)
Sales forecasting	43	28	10	13	6	(N=133)
Marketing research	61	24	6	2	7	(N=133)
Marketing planning	53	31	7	4	5	(N=133)
Product design	15	30	27	17	11	(N=133)
Packaging design	27	30	16	14	13	(N=129)
Warehousing	7	4	5	25	59	(N=128)
Transport of finished goods	6	5	6	23	60	(N=132)
R & D strategy	5	27	30	25	13	(N=133)
New product launches	44	39	11	2	4	(N=132)
Investment appraisal	1	16	42	24	17	(N=134)
Diversification studies	3	22	46	13	16	(N=134)
Marketing staff selection	57	28	7	3	5	(N=133)
Marketing training	57	25	9	4	5	(N=134)
Corporate planning/strategic planning	4	35	38	14	9	(N=134)

Table 11.11: CME Responsibilities by Product-Market

	Product Markets				Total
	Fast moving consumer goods	Consumer durables	Industrial consumable	Industrial capital	
	%	%	%	%	%
Marketing mix responsibilities					
Low	11	28	37	35	30
Medium	49	41	20	11	34
High	40	31	43	16	36
	(N=37)	(N=29)	(N=30)	(N=23)	(N=119)

(Chi-square = 18.8 with 6 d.f., = 0.05)

	Fast moving consumer goods	Consumer durables	Industrial consumable	Industrial capital	Total
	%	%	%	%	%
Strategy responsibilities					
Low	13	26	28	42	26
Medium	23	55	38	19	33
High	64	19	34	39	41
	(N=39)	(N=31)	(N=32)	(N=31)	(N=133)

(Chi-square = 22.3 with 6 d.f., = 0.01)

Table 11.12: CME Product Policy Responsibilities

	Full and sole responsibility	Major responsibility but shared with others	Equal responsibility with others	Some responsibility but less than others	No responsibility	
	%	%	%	%	%	
This Survey (1985)						
Product planning	24	36	25	10	5	(N=134)
Product design	15	30	27	17	11	(N=133)
Packaging design	27	30	16	14	13	(N=129)
New product launches	44	39	11	2	4	(N=132)
	Full responsibility		Shared responsibility		No responsibility	
	%		%		%	
Hayhurst and Wills (1972)						
New product policy	23		74		3	(N=488)
Packaging	28		47		24	(N=410)

Table 11.13: CME Pricing Policy Responsibilities

	Full and sole responsibility	Major responsibility but shared with others	Equal responsibility with others	Some responsibility but less than others	No responsibility	
This Survey (1985)	%	%	%	%	%	
Price setting	20	38	20	10	11	(N=134)
Discount structures	27	25	14	20	14	(N=133)
Hayhurst and Wills (1972)	Full responsibility		Shared/responsibility		No responsibility	
	%		%		%	
Pricing	36		59		5	(N=531)

In the area of **marketing communications**, the data are summarised in Table 11.14. In advertising and promotion CME responsibility seems lower in the 1985 survey with fewer CMEs holding sole responsibility and rather more having no responsibility at all. The other figures are not comparable across the surveys, but we can note that in the managing the sales force, the CME in 23% of companies in the 1985 survey of medium-sized firms had no responsibility and in only 44% of the companies was the CME fully responsible for the sales force.

Turning to the area of **distribution** management, CME responsibilities are shown in Table 11.15. In the physical distribution function, the 1985 CMEs appeared to have a substantially lower level of responsibility – far fewer had full responsibility and far more had no responsibility in the 1985 survey as compared to the 1972 study. Negotiations with channel intermediaries were not included in the 1972 study, but in the 1985 study some 46% of CMEs shared responsibilities for this function, while one-third had sole responsibility and one-fifth had no responsibility at all.

The responsibilities for **planning and information** are summarised in Table 11.16. In terms of marketing research responsibilities, the profile of the two surveys is essentially similar – i.e. approximately two-thirds the CMEs had sole responsibility and one-third shared responsibilities. However, it appeared that responsibilities for sales forecasting were lower in the 1985 survey – 43% of CMEs having sole responsibility compared to 58% in 1972.

The position relating to marketing **staffing and training** is shown in Tables 11.17 where it seems that the profile is almost identical in the two studies.

Finally, the 1985 survey examined the involvement of the CME in various aspects of **strategic planning** with the results shown in Tables 11.18. In this area, while relatively few CMEs had sole responsibility for strategic functions, the great majority did share some degree of responsibility for such issues as corporate planning and supporting functions.

Clustering Companies by CME Responsibilities

To reduce the data, the CME responsibility measures were factor analysed in the way shown in Table 11.19, leading to the identification of five significant factors or types of CME responsibility, as summarised in Table 11.20: 'selling' – where the CME had highest responsibilities for the sales force, sales promotion, channel negotiations, prices and discounts and sales forecasting; 'product policy' responsib- ilities, where scores were relatively high on product and packaging design, product planning, new product launches

Table 11.14: CME Marketing Communications Responsibilities

This Survey (1985)	Full and sole respons- ibility %	Major respons- ibility but shared with others %	Equal respons- ibility with others %	Some respons- ibility but less than others %	No respons- ibility %	
Advertising	57	31	4	1	7	(N=134)
Sales promotion	52	25	11	8	4	(N=134)
Sales force	44	10	4	19	23	(N=133)

Hayhurst and Wills (1972)	Full respons- ibility %	Shared respons- ibility %	No respons- ibility %	
Advertising and promotion	62	36	2	(N=520)
Public relations	39	52	9	(N=481)

Table 11.15: CME Distribution Responsibilities

	Full and sole responsibility	Major responsibility but shared with others	Equal responsibility with others	Some responsibility but less than others	No responsibility	
	%	%	%	%	%	
This Survey (1985)						
Negotiations with distributors/ retailers	32	17	8	21	22	(N=130)
Transport	6	5	6	23	60	(N=132)
Warehousing	7	4	5	25	59	(N=128)

	Full responsibility	Shared responsibility	No responsibility	
	%	%	%	
Hayhurst and Wills (1972)				
Physical Distribution	23	41	36	(N=459)

Table 11.16: CME Planning and Information Responsibilities

	Full and sole responsibility %	Major responsibility but shared with others %	Equal responsibility with others %	Some responsibility but less than others %	No responsibility %	
This Survey (1985)						
Marketing planning	53	31	7	4	5	(N=133)
Sales forecasting	43	28	10	13	6	(N=133)
Marketing research	61	24	6	2	7	(N=133)
	Full responsibility %		Shared responsibility %		No responsibility %	
Hayhurst and Wills (1972)						
Sales forecasting	58		40		2	(N=537)
Marketing research	64		35		1	(N=487)

335

Table 11.17: CME Marketing Staffing Responsibilities

	Full and sole responsibility	Major responsibility but shared with others	Equal responsibility with others	Some responsibility but less than others	No responsibility	
	%	%	%	%	%	
This Survey (1985)						
Staff selection	57	28	7	3	5	(N=133)
Training	57	25	9	4	5	(N=134)

	Full responsibility	Shared responsibility	No responsibility	
	%	%	%	
Hayhurst and Wills (1972)				
Staff selection and training	58	40	2	(N=503)

Table 11.18: CME Strategic Responsibilities

	Full and sole responsibility	Major responsibility but shared with others	Equal responsibility with others	Some responsibility but less than others	No responsibility	
	%	%	%	%	%	
R & D strategy	5	27	30	25	13	(N=133)
Investment appraisal	1	16	42	24	17	(N=134)
Diversification studies	3	22	46	13	16	(N=134)
Corporate planning/ strategic planning	4	35	38	14	9	(N=134)

and R & D strategy; a type of 'marketing services' responsiblity, covering marketing research, marketing planning, and staff functions; 'corporate strategy' responsibilities for diversification studies, investment appraisal and corporate/strategic planning; and a 'physical distribution' responsibility factor, covering transport of finished goods and warehousing. The company cases were then clustered on the basis of the factor scores, with the result shown in Table 11.21.

The clustering suggests a number of significantly different types of marketing organisation role or function, on the basis of CME responsibilities: the 'integrated/full service marketing organisation' which ranked relatively high on all responsibility factors - with notably high scores on selling, product policy, and marketing services responsibilities, and relatively high scores on corporate strategy and physical distribution responsibilities; the 'strategy/services marketing organisation' with high scores on product policy, corporate strategy and marketing services responsibilities, but relatively low on the others; the 'sales-oriented marketing organisation' which ranks high on selling responsibilities, but relatively low on the other factors; and the 'limited/staff role marketing organisation' which ranked lowest on all responsibility factors.

In terms of the other variables already discussed, these marketing organisation types would appear to differ in various respects as below:

Full service marketing organisations - rated highly on the integration of manpower and functions and have relatively large departments, but were low on manpower growth; they ranked high on departmental rank and increase in that rank, but were represented fairly evenly in all product-markets (with the possible exception of fewer industrial capital goods firms).

Strategy/services marketing organisations - ranked low on the integration of manpower and were relatively small departments, but were high on board representation, departmental rank and rank change, and were found in larger firms and mostly in fast-moving consumer goods markets.

Selling-oriented marketing orientations - rated relatively high on integration, particularly of manpower, being typically large departments, and on representation. These were the highest perceived rank departments, and seemed to operate particularly in consumer durable markets.

Limited/staff role marketing organisations - ranked low on the integration of functions and manpower and were small departments, as well as being low on representation and rank, and were found particularly in industrial capital goods marketing firms and the smaller firms in the study.

This analysis and the one preceding it suggest some diversity in the role played by the CME and distinctly

Table 11.19:   Factor Analysis of CME Responsibilities*

	Factor 1	Factor 2	Factor 3	Factor 4	Factor 5
V43 Field sales force operations	.88				
V44 Negotiations with distributors/retailers	.85				
V41 Discounts structures	.83				
V45 Sales forecasting	.71				
V39 Sales promotion	.69				
V40 Price setting	.67				
V48 Product design		.83			
V49 Packaging design		.79			
V42 Product planning		.72			
V53 New product launches		.58			
V52 R&D strategy		.52			
V57 Marketing training			.85		
V56 Marketing staff selection			.79		
V46 Marketing research			.74		
V47 Marketing planning			.69		
V55 Diversification studies				.80	
V54 Investment appraisal				.78	
V58 Corporate planning/strategic planning				.73	
V50 Warehousing					.92
V51 Transport of finished goods					.91

*Varimax rotation in 6 iterations. Coefficients less than 0.5 are suppressed. The 5 factor solution produces an eigenvalue of 1.23 and accounts for 76% of variance, subsequent factors produced eigen values below 1.00 and the 5 factor solution was accepted by the Kaiser criterion.

Table 11.20: CME Responsibilities Factors Extracted

	Factor 1	Factor 2	Factor 3	Factor 4	Factor 5
	SELLING	PRODUCT POLICY	MARKETING SERVICES	CORPORATE STRATEGY	PHYSICAL DISTRIBUTION
	V43 Field sales force operations	V48 Product design	V57 Marketing training	V55 Diversification studies	V50 Warehousing
	V44 Negotiations with retailers/ distribution	V49 Packaging design	V56 Marketing staff selection	V54 Investment appraisal	V51 Transport of finished goods
	V41 Discount structures	V42 Product planning	V46 Marketing research	V58 Corporate planning/ Strategic planning	
	V45 Sales forecasting	V53 New product launches	V47 Marketing planning		
	V39 Sales promotion	V52 R & D strategy			
	V40 Price setting				
% of VARIANCE EXPLAINED	43.0	12.7	8.4	6.1	5.9
EIGENVALUE	9.0	2.7	1.8	1.3	1.2

*Factor scores were obtained by summing the tables of variables with loadings higher than 0.5.

different types of marketing department in the companies
studied.   In the later part of this study these differences
are represented as power differences which may be related to
processual and resource outcomes.

Summary: Marketing Departmentation and Responsibilities

In brief, a number of points emerge from the descriptive data
discussed above.

The formal **departmentation** of marketing was found
only in some 45% of the first sample of nearly 300
medium-sized companies, although adopting a liberal
interpretation of what constituted that departmentation.
However, of the 150 companies providing fuller data, 85% had
some form of formalised marketing organisation and this was
positively related to company size.   The qualitative evidence
available explained the lack of marketing departmentation as
being related to such factors: small company size; the lack
of formal marketing activities, e.g. in textile companies
producing own-label goods for retailers;   the lack of
specialisation in marketing, because the activity involved
all managers, e.g. in a multinational corporation chemicals
division;   and a high degree of marketing concentration,
where marketing or selling amounted to no more than
management negotiation with major customers, e.g. selling
interior trim to the automotive industry, and where decisions
on advertising, promotion, and the like, were made directly
by the chief executive.

Accepting the caution necessary in commenting on the
sample in question, it is suggested that the departmentation
of marketing is rather lower than might have been expected in
such a sample.

Turning to the **integration** of functions within
marketing departments, it was found that of a list of major
'marketing' functions, typically only a few were integrated
into a marketing organisation in the companies studied.
Some 50% of marketing departments had functional
responsibility only for advertising and marketing research,
and a further 20% also integrated trade marketing sales.
Only one-sixth of the firms displayed high levels of
functional integration.

In terms of **manpower**, or marketing department size,
it was found that the marketing departments studied were
mainly small (less than 10 non-sales employees), although
there were some of the signs that non-sales marketing
employment was as high in these medium-sized companies in
1985 as had been found in large companies in 1972 by Hayhurst
and Wills.   Considering the allocation of specialist
personnel to the marketing department, specialist roles were
in marketing departments in only 60% of cases for sales,
advertising, product management and marketing research,

Table 11.21:   CME Responsibility Clusters

	Clusters*				All Companies
	1 Integrated/ full service marketing organisations	2 Strategy/ services marketing organisations	3 Selling- oriented marketing organisations	4 Limited/ staff role marketing organisations	
CME Responsibility Factors					
Selling	4.80	3.07	4.15	1.91	3.63
Product policy	4.20	4.08	2.99	2.34	3.41
Marketing services	4.84	4.68	4.01	3.39	4.23
Corporate strategy	3.42	3.29	2.68	1.94	2.85
Physical distribution	2.68	1.44	1.59	1.14	1.71
	(N=31)	(N=34)	(N=39)	(N=28)	(N=132)
Marketing Department Characteristics					
**Integration of functions	4.32	3.64	4.18	3.37	3.80
**Integration of manpower	3.89	1.77	3.53	2.44	3.03
Number of marketing department employees (mean)	52	20	174	10	67
Marketing employees/total employees % (mean)	13.7	2.5	5.3	3.4	6.1
**Marketing manpower trend	2.41	3.28	3.06	3.46	3.05
**Board representation	3.40	3.15	3.55	2.44	3.10
**Marketing department perceived power rank	4.36	4.29	4.44	3.09	4.13
**Marketing department perceived rank change	3.88	3.73	3.83	2.69	3.62
Company Size					
Employee number (median)	320	640	340	300	365
Product-Markets	%	%	%	%	%
Fast moving consumer goods	29	56	21	14	30
Consumer durables	26	18	31	18	22
Industrial consumables	29	12	31	25	26
Industrial capital goods	16	14	17	43	22

* Extracted using Ward's method of hierarchical clustering.   ** These factors are normalised to a 5 point scale (see Appendix C).

planning and services, in half the cases for customer service and in only a minority of cases for distribution and exporting.

In examining **CME responsibilities** the outstanding finding was that responsibilities were largely participative and shared. Full and sole responsibility was claimed in only approximately half the cases for advertising, sales promotion, marketing research, and marketing staffing and training, and in other areas only a minority of CMEs claimed full responsibility. The findings were broadly similar to those in the 1972 Hayhurst and Wills study of larger companies. Factoring the responsibility measurements and clustering the companies around the resulting CME responsibility factors suggested that it was possible to identify a number of distinctive and differentiated marketing organisational roles: the integrated/full service marketing organisation; the strategy/services marketing organisation; the selling-oriented marketing organisation; and the limited/staff role marketing organisation. These groups of firms differed in terms of a number of marketing departmentation, corporate, and product-market characteristics.

These findings suggest that the corporate position of marketing was weak in many of the companies in the study in terms of: the frequency of marketing departmentation, the integration of 'marketing' functions and specialist personnel into the marketing organisation, and the essentially shared responsibilities of the CME in respect of the elements of the marketing programme. Perhaps the most significant finding is the high differentiation in the corporate position of marketing between the companies.

THE CORPORATE STATUS OF MARKETING

The second research objective of the study was to evaluate the standing or status of the marketing department, in terms of such factors as: the perceived status of the CME, the representation of marketing on the board of directors, the perceived power of the different functional departments, the control of critical functions, and the marketing orientation or otherwise of companies, again within the context of the other studies cited above.

Chief Marketing Executive Status

Table 11.22 shows the perceived status of the CME compared to the chief production executive in the 1985 study and the corresponding figures from the Hayhurst and Wills (1972) survey of large companies. Although there are small differences a Chi Square test suggests the two sets of figures are not significantly different. It apparently

Table 11.22: CME Status vs. Production

	Hayhurst and Wills (1972) %	This Survey (1985) %
CME compared to the Chief Production Executive		
The CME has lower status	10	13
Equal status	60	59
The CME has higher status	30	28
	(N=503)	(N=134)
	(Chi-Square = 1.06 with 2.d.f.)	

Table 11.23: CME Status vs. Finance and Sales

	CME compared to the chief finance/ accounting executive %	CME compared to the chief sales executive %
The CME has lower status	17	15
Equal status	65	49
The CME has higher status	18	36
	(N=136)	(N=112)

is the case, thus, that CMEs are perceived in most of these medium-sized companies, i.e. two-thirds, as equal in status to the chief production executive, while in more than a quarter the CME has higher status, in a very similar pattern to the earlier study of larger firms.

The 1985 survey also asked the same question with respect to the chief finance/accounting executive and the chief sales executive, with the results shown in Table 11.23. In comparison with the chief accountant, again two-thirds of CMEs were rated as equal in status, but rather more were rated lower and somewhat fewer as higher in status.

In comparison with the chief sales executive the position was rather different. In half the companies the CME was rated as equal in status to the head of sales. However, in just over one-third of the firms the CME had higher status that the chief sales executive - which includes both situations where marketing and sales were in separate departments and where they were organised together.

Perhaps most interesting is the fact that in some 15% of the firms the CME had lower status than the head of the sales function. In fact, Table 11.24 suggests that where marketing and sales are organised together the most common position is that the CME has higher status, while in one-third cases the CME and head of sales are equal. Where sales and marketing are organised separately, in 60% of cases the two executives are seen as equal in status, and other cases are divided equally between the CME having lower or having higher status than the head of sales.

Board Representation of the Marketing Department

In terms of representation on the board of directors shown in Table 11.25, the most usual position, i.e. in two-thirds of the companies, is where the marketing department has one board representative (normally the CME), while the average board size is approximately six directors.

Although in some 27 firms there was no marketing representative on the board of directors (which includes those firms with no marketing department), in the vast majority of cases a significant proportion of board membership was made up by one or more marketing representatives. In fact, three-quarters of the companies fell into the category between board membership of one in eight and one in three. Higher levels of representation were found, but relatively infrequently. It would seem, then, that typically the CME is seen in these companies as equal in status (or higher) than the heads of production and finance, and that typically marketing is represented to a greater or lesser extent on company boards (although it is perhaps most interesting that, in some one-third of the companies that representation was relatively low or wholly absent).

Table 11.24: CME Status vs. Sales and Integration

	Integration Sales is in the marketing department %	Sales is organised separately from the marketing department %	All companies %
CME Compared to the Chief Sales Executive			
The CME has lower status	12	20	15
Equal status	38	60	49
The CME has higher status	50	20	36
	(N=58)	(N=51)	(N=112)

Table 11.25: Board Representation of Marketing

Marketing representatives/ Total Board membership	%
No representative	19 *(8)
Less than 20%	36 *(3)
20-30%	34 *(4)
30-40%	9 *(3)
More than 40%	3 *(2)
	(N=143)

*These categories include the number of cases indicated in brackets which were classified in the present study as having no marketing departmentation.

The Perceived Power of Departments

Respondents were also asked to rate the power of the different departments in the firm, with the results shown in Table 11.26. Perhaps the most interesting question is to ask which is perceived as the most powerful department in a company, and these data are shown in Table 11.27.

The suggestion is that in nearly half of the companies, the most powerful department is marketing. The Chi Square statistic suggested a significant change ($\alpha = 0.01$) over the past three years where: marketing has increased in power (in the sense of being perceived as the most powerful department in more companies) and at the same time the position of production has deteriorated markedly and the position of finance has improved – suggesting that the major corporate rivals are now marketing and finance in most cases, rather than marketing and production.

None the less, although the position of marketing has improved overall, it may be said conversely that marketing is the most powerful department in only a little more than 40% of the companies, while in more than a quarter finance dominates and in 20% production remains in the leading position.

The Control of Critical Functions

In addition, respondents were asked to rate the 'critical success factors' for their business in its major market and then to identify the department mainly responsible for those factors, producing the findings shown in Table 11.28. (The control of information is considered separately in the next section). The responses suggested that the most important competitive factors were seen as new product development, market standing, aggressive selling and promotion, and prices.

If we accept the qualification that, as we noted earlier, respondents from the marketing area are likely to perceive company problems primarily in marketing terms, then these rankings are not necessarily a valid listing of the actual critical success factors for companies. However, what is gained is a further insight into the status of marketing in companies, by attempting to identify which department controlled those factors seen by executives as the most important to corporate success. The global figures in Table 11.28 indicate that the critical factors of market standing and aggressive selling and promotion were seen as predominately under the control of marketing (although in 15% of cases sales and promotion were controlled by others, in the form of separated sales departments). However, similarly, in three-quarters of firms prices were seen as within the control of marketing. This said, in the case of

Table 11.26: Perceived Power of Departments

The present ranking of Departments in power	Marketing %	Production %	Finance %	R & D %	Other %
1st	49	20 *(3)	26 *(6)	8 *(2)	30 *(1)
2nd	29	35 *(2)	26 *(4)	8 *(1)	22 *(1)
3rd	12	28 *(4)	34 *(2)	23 *(3)	16 *(1)
4th	6	16 *(3)	12 *(1)	48 *(3)	16 *(1)
Lower	4	1	2	13	16
	(N=127)	(N=126)	(N=130)	(N=101)	(N=32)

The rankings of departments in power three years ago	Marketing %	Production %	Finance %	R & D %	Other %
1st	38	37 *(6)	23 *(3)	8 *(1)	36 *(1)
2nd	16	38 *(3)	36 *(5)	8 *(1)	16 *(2)
3rd	31	18 *(3)	29 *(2)	22 *(4)	24 *(1)
4th	12	7	11 *(1)	49 *(2)	16
Lower	3	-	1	13	8
	(N=104)	(N=108)	(N=108)	(N=86)	(N=25)

*These categories include the number of cases indicated in brackets which were classified in the present study as having no marketing departmentation.

Table 11.27: The Most Powerful Department

	The most powerful department three years ago %	The most powerful department now %
Marketing	33	44
Production	33 *(6)	19 *(3)
Finance	21 *(3)	24 *(6)
R & D	6 *(1)	6 *(2)
Other	7	7 *(1)
	(N=120)	(N=141)

(Chi-Square = 16.4 with 4 d.f.)

*These categories include the number of cases indicated in brackets which were classified in this study as having no marketing departmentation.

Table 11.28: The Control of Critical Success Factors

(a) The Ranking of Critical Success Factors

Factors	Ranking				
	1st %	2nd %	3rd %	4th %	
Legal factors and patents	-	1	5	94	(N=65)
New product development	24	13	14	49	(N=85)
Market standing	23	14	17	46	(N=90)
Aggressive selling and promotion	23	14	13	59	(N=92)
Reliable delivery and spares	7	26	15	52	(N=82)
Prices	23	17	16	44	(N=96)
Customer service	11	19	25	45	(N=91)
Distribution network	4	6	6	84	(N=72)
Brand image	14	19	15	52	(N=79)

(b) The Control of Critical Success Factors

Factors	Controlled mainly by:					
	Marketing %	Production %	R & D %	Finance %	Other %	
Legal factors and patents	15	4	16	41	23	(N=73)
New product development	36	5	55	-	4	(N=92)
Market standing	88	5	2	1	4	(N=92)
Aggressive selling and promotion	84	1	-	-	15	(N=102)
Reliable delivery and spares	18	64	-	-	18	(N=90)
Prices	72	3	2	11	12	(N=104)
Customer service	49	19	2	-	30	(N=99)
Distribution network	39	19	2	1	39	(N=85)
Brand image	87	2	4	-	9	(N=84)

the most highly rated competitive factor - new product development - the situation is that only one-third of respondents saw this as controlled by marketing, and in almost two-thirds of cases new product development was controlled by R & D and production departments.

However, if one raises the question of not simply which department typically controls the company's critical success factors, but which department controls them when they are the most important factors to a particular company - the results are as in Tables 11.29 to 11.35.

In the area of **new product development** (NPD), the factor most frequently ranked first by companies as a critical success factor, it was found that overall in 55% of cases this factor was controlled by R & D and in 36% by marketing. However, Table 11.29 suggests further that not simply does R & D typically control new product efforts, but that this is particularly the case when NPD is the first or second most important factor to the company, and this area is more likely to be controlled by marketing, production or others only when NPD itself is of lower importance to the company.

Following the same logic in the case of **prices**, the factor second most commonly perceived as the most important critical success factor by companies, is shown in Table 11.30. While the majority of respondents maintained that prices were controlled by marketing, we again see that this was less often the case when pricing was the first or second most important success factor to the company. Although less marked than with new product development, it seems that when this factor is most important to a company, control is more often held by non-marketing departments, and control vests in the marketing department rather more often (indeed in most companies) when pricing is less important to the company.

Table 11.31 shows the same comparison for **market standing** although in this area marketing is seen almost uniformly as controlling this critical success factor, regardless of its importance to the company. Indeed, much the same can be said of the control of **selling and promotion** (Table 11.32) - this was seen predominately as controlled by the marketing department, regardless of the rank of this factor in criticality to the company. The only exceptions shown - control of selling and promotion by 'Others' - arose where there was a sales department separate from marketing.

Moving down to the critical success factors which (from Table 11.28) were far less frequently seen as the most critical, in the case of **brand image**, this factor was seen as controlled by marketing regardless of its rank to the company, as shown in Table 11.33. In the case of **customer service**, shown in Table 11.34, marketing department control was higher when this factor was more important. In the case

Table 11.29: Control of New Product Development

Ranking of New Product Development	Controlled mainly by:					
	Marketing %	Production %	R & D %	Finance %	Other %	
1st	22	-	88	-	-	(N=18)
2nd	27	-	73	-	-	(N=11)
3rd	42	8	50	-	-	(N=12)
Lower	38	6	54	-	2	(N=39)
Total (All Ranks)	36	5	55	-	4	(N=92)

Table 11.30: Control of Prices

Ranking of Prices	Controlled mainly by:					
	Marketing %	Production %	R & D %	Finance %	Other %	
1st	64	-	-	18	18	(N=17)
2nd	57	14	-	22	7	(N=14)
3rd	80	7	1	13	-	(N=15)
Lower	75	1	2	5	18	(N=40)
Total (All Ranks)	72	3	2	11	12	(N=104)

Table 11.31: Control of Market Standing

Ranking of Market Standing	Controlled mainly by:					
	Marketing %	Production %	R & D %	Finance %	Other %	
1st	95	-	-	-	5	(N=20)
2nd	77	15	8	-	-	(N=13)
3rd	92	8	1	-	-	(N=12)
Lower	87	3	-	-	10	(N=31)
Total (All Ranks)	88	5	2	1	4	(N=92)

of control of delivery and spares (Table 11.35), this function is infrequently controlled by the marketing department, regardless of its importance to a company. What does seem apparent is that this factor is mostly controlled by the production department - and most particularly when it is highly important to the company.

Bearing in mind the qualifications that we are dealing with subjective measurements, and that views may be biased by a marketing perspective, certain points should be noted. First, in the areas rated highest as critical success factors - new product development and prices - it seems that control of these factors by the marketing department is negatively related to the importance of the factor to the company. In the next two most important success factor categories - market standing and selling and promotion - control was primarily in the hands of the marketing department regardless of the rank of the factor, although there were some intrusions on this control from separated sales departments. In the more minor critical success factors: brand image was controlled by the the marketing department relatively uniformly regardless of its rank in importance to the company; customer service was controlled by the marketing department where it was of high importance, and less so when it was not; and delivery and spares reliability was controlled mainly by the production department when it was an important factor and then shared between production and a specialist department, when this factor was less important.

On the face of things, the picture seemed mixed, but it should be noted that it is predictable that marketing departments would commonly claim responsibility for such factors as market standing, selling and promotion and brand image, and this is indeed the case. However, in other areas which might be seen as more 'up for grabs' between departments because of their interdisciplinary nature - new product development, pricing, customer service and delivery - here marketing department control shows some signs of being negatively related to the importance of these factors to a company, and it must be borne in mind that this latter category contains what were recognised as the two most important critical success factors - new product development and prices. For present purposes these comparisons suggest that the marketing department's real standing or pervasiveness may be rather lower than is suggested by the formal status of the CME (or, indeed, the acclaim for marketing orientation discussed below).

The Marketing Paradigm

Respondents were also asked to identify the 'orientation' of their companies, replicating the question wording used by Hooley et al (1984), with the results shown in Table 11.36.

Table 11.32: Control of Selling and Promotion

Ranking of Selling and Promotion	Controlled mainly by:					
	Marketing %	Production %	R & D %	Finance %	Other %	
1st	95	–	–	–	5	(N=21)
2nd	75	–	–	–	25	(N=12)
3rd	83	–	–	–	17	(N=12)
Lower	78	1	–	–	22	(N=41)
Total (All Ranks)	84	1	–	–	15	(N=102)

Table 11.33: Control of Brand Image

Ranking of Brand Image	Controlled mainly by:					
	Marketing %	Production %	R & D %	Finance %	Other %	
1st	90	–	–	–	10	(N=10)
2nd	100	–	–	–	–	(N=15)
3rd	91	–	9	–	–	(N=11)
Lower	82	3	–	–	15	(N=34)
Total (All Ranks)	87	2	4	–	7	(N=84)

Table 11.34: Control of Customer Service

Ranking of Customer Service	Controlled mainly by:					
	Marketing %	Production %	R & D %	Finance %	Other %	
1st	50	25	–	–	25	(N=8)
2nd	69	12	–	–	19	(N=16)
3rd	56	11	6	–	28	(N=18)
Lower	29	31	–	–	40	(N=45)
Total (All Ranks)	49	19	2	–	30	(N=99)

Table 11.35: Control of Delivery and Spares

Ranking of Delivery and Spares	Controlled mainly by:					
	Marketing %	Production %	R & D %	Finance %	Other %	
1st	20	80	-	-	-	(N=5)
2nd	11	72	-	-	17	(N=18)
3rd	-	82	-	-	18	(N=11)
Lower	18	61	-	-	21	(N=38)
Total (All Ranks)	18	64	-	-	18	(N=90)

Table 11.36: Company Orientation

	Hooley et al (1984) %	This survey (1985) %
Product Orientation - make what we can and sell to whoever will buy	13	14 *(7)
Selling Orientation - place major emphasis on advertising and selling to ensure sales	26	15 *(2)
Marketing Orientation - place major emphasis on prior analysis of marketing needs, adapting products to meet them, if necessary	61 (N=1632)	71 *(9) (N=129)

(Chi-Square = 12.21 with 2 d.f.)

*This category includes the number of cases indicated in brackets which were classified in the present study as having no marketing departmentation.

In fact, there would seem a significant difference between the two sets of figures ($\alpha = 0.01$), suggesting that an even higher proportion of this sample perceived their companies as marketing rather than selling oriented. It must be remembered, however, that the Hooley et al (1984) sample contains a high proportion of small firms (which might be expected to be less 'marketing oriented') and the way in which their figures are reported does not permit a comparison between similar sized companies. It should also be pointed out that the sample in both the surveys referred to, is likely to be skewed significantly towards 'marketing-oriented' companies, and it is necessary to avoid generalising from these samples to the larger population.

It would seem, however, that the marketing paradigm is widely accepted in this sample of companies, though we may seek in the next chapter to question the relationship between the paradigm strength and corporate behaviour.

In terms of distinguishing between marketing oriented firms and others, the high proportion of the sample of firms claiming to be marketing oriented posed difficulties. The data available on the relationship between marketing orientation and other company characteristics suggested that: (a) there was no evidence to suggest that the marketing oriented firms spent significantly more on marketing budgets (either in absolute terms or in budget/sales ratios) than did the other firms; (b) there was only a limited suggestion that marketing oriented firms were significantly more profitable than other firms (a claim advanced by Hooley et al, (1984)); (c) there was no evidence that marketing orientation was associated with company size (within the somewhat limited size range of this sample); (d) there was a limited amount of evidence that marketing orientation related positively to marketing department size – though this is significant ($\alpha = 0.05$) only at the top end, where most of the largest (50 people or more) marketing departments existed in marketing oriented companies. Interestingly, excluding sales employees from this comparison removed the relationship, implying that marketing oriented firms are more likely to integrate sales and marketing; and (e) there was little evidence to support the claim that marketing departments were more powerful in marketing oriented companies. In comparing company orientation to perceived marketing department power the data suggested the expected relationship – marketing departments in marketing oriented firms are more likely to be perceived to be the most powerful – but the relationship was not significant to any acceptable level.

Summary: The Corporate Status of Marketing

We have attempted to evaluate the corporate status of

marketing in a number of ways: by examining the perceived status of the CME in comparison to other executives; by examining the representation of the marketing department on company boards; by asking overtly which departments are the most powerful; by studying the control of critical success factors by different departments; and finally by examining company orientation.

On the first criterion: the **status of the CME** compared to the head of production would appear broadly similar to the findings of Hayhurst and Wills (1972) – in almost 60% of cases the two were seen as equal, in 13% the CME had lower status and in 28% the CME had higher status. We also compared the CME's status to that of the chief finance/accounting executive with essentially the same result. It was only in comparison with the chief sales executive that a significant difference emerged – 15% of CMEs had lower status, 49% were equal, and 36% of CMEs had higher status – which is explained by the varying policies found relating to the integration of sales with marketing and thus the relative positions of marketing and sales heads.

On the second criterion: three-quarters of the marketing departments have some **board representation** – most commonly restricted to one person – on boards averaging a membership of six, although some 20% had no board representation at all.

On the third criterion: **perceived departmental power**, the marketing department was perceived as the most powerful in some 44% of companies, the rest mainly being divided between finance and production. In considering 'who leads the company?', it emerged that the perceived power of marketing had typically increased significantly, and that this has been at the expense of production departments, suggesting the major corporate rival to marketing typically now to be the finance department.

Fourth, in considering the **control of critical success factors**, while it seemed that many of the critical factors considered by respondents were frequently controlled by marketing, in the two most highly rated areas – new product development and prices – as well as certain of the more minor success factors, the frequency of control by the marketing department was negatively related to the rating of the factor in a company, i.e when these factors were highly important other departments were more likely to control them, when they were relatively unimportant, the marketing department was more likely to control them. While the marketing department controlled a number of strictly 'marketing' areas, the picture elsewhere is of control being held by others.

Finally, in considering the **marketing paradigm**, more than 70% saw their companies as 'marketing oriented', suggesting among other things that marketing orientation exists as a separate entity to responsibility, the status of marketing specialists and control of critical success factors. Indeed, if one follows the logic of distinguishing marketing 'philosophy' or strategic development from marketing management of mix areas (see Chapter 1), then this differentiation is not unreasonable.

Our view of the corporate status of marketing is therefore mixed, depending on the criterion used, again suggesting some diversity. In the next chapter these factors are balanced in evaluating the power of the marketing department.

INFORMATIONAL BEHAVIOUR IN MARKETING

One topic not so far considered is the use of information in marketing, and particularly the control of critical information sources and processing. At the present stage this issue is most relevant to what has been said regarding the corporate status of the marketing department and the control of critical success factors, but these issues emerge in the next chapter in the context of political behaviour. We consider here the questions of information access and restriction, and sales forecasting control and influence.

Information Access and Restriction

Table 11.37 shows the access to various types of corporate information which was claimed by the marketing departments in the study. It may be seen that the distribution of responses is heavily skewed towards one end of the scale, since most respondents claimed total access to the listed information types. This is most clearly the case with product and marketing costs where virtually all claim total access - in spite of the comment appended to the survey by one managing director to the effect that 'the Marketing Department has no right to such information and I would never permit them to have it'.

In the case also of company profitability and R & D projects, some 70% of respondents claimed total access, and it is only in such areas as corporate budgets, investment plans, production schedules and corporate plans, that there is a wider distribution of responses.

The corollary measurement to the information access enjoyed by the marketing department, is the degree to which the marketing department restricts the access of other departments to marketing information and the data collected here are shown in Table 11.38.

Interestingly, while the overwhelming majority of respondents claimed total access to information held by other departments, in each case the majority of respondents failed to offer equally unhindered access to marketing information

Table 11.37:   Marketing Department Information Access*

Corporate Information	Marketing Department Access to Information Held by Other Departments					
	None %	Limited %	Some %	Most %	Total %	
Product costs	5	–	6	4	85	(N=133)
Marketing costs	4	–	1	1	94	(N=133)
Profitability of company operations	4	2	7	14	73	(N=133)
Company wide budgets	6	2	12	22	58	(N=133)
Investment plans	8	5	15	18	53	(N=133)
Production schedules	3	5	15	16	61	(N=131)
R&D projects	3	4	6	18	69	(N=131)
Corporate plans	7	6	9	21	57	(N=133)

*Includes all cases where a Chief Marketing Executive exists.

Table 11.38:   Marketing Department Information Restriction*

Marketing Information	Access of Other Departments to Marketing Information					
	None %	Limited %	Some %	Most %	Total %	
Market studies	3	7	28	22	40	(N=139)
Customer reports	2	11	25	21	41	(N=140)
Sales plans	2	9	19	19	51	(N=138)
Marketing plans	4	7	21	22	46	(N=139)
Marketing budgets	9	12	21	19	39	(N=138)
New product plans	3	8	19	24	46	(N=138)
Other marketing research	5	11	28	20	36	(N=127)

*Includes all cases where a Chief Marketing Executive exists.

to other departments.   This restriction of information was most marked with marketing research, marketing budgets, market studies, and customer reports, but it is still significant in the case of marketing and sales plans.

Clearly, some caution is needed in the interpretation of such measurements - which are measures of perceptions rather than actual information flows.

None the less, if it is accepted that the same limitation applies to both measurements, then there would seem some grounds for suggesting that the marketing departments in the study manage information flows and attempt to restrict them - and indeed succeed in doing so.

Sales Forecasting

It was argued earlier that sales forecasting is a critical information function associated with absorbing the uncertainty of the market environment and a number of measurements were taken in this area.

As noted earlier (Table 11.16 above), the responsibilities of the CME for sales forecasting suggested that some 43% claimed full and sole responsibility, with the majority holding some degree of shared or participative responsibility.

More explicitly, respondents were asked which department was formally responsible for the sales forecasting function, with the results shown in Table 11.39.   These data suggest that in the vast majority of cases formal responsibility for sales forecasting was vested in the marketing department, the only major exception being where there was a separate sales department responsible for this function.

However, it is necessary to recognise that formal control or authority over sales forecasting may give an incomplete picture, and respondents were also asked about the influence of other departments over sales forecasting, as shown in Table 11.40.   This suggests that although the marketing department is seen most commonly as the sub-unit with full and sole responsibility for sales forecasting, in the majority of cases there is some sharing of that responsibility with other sub-units - most notably with finance where nearly two-thirds of companies see some finance department influence, and with production where some 45% have an involvement.

It would seem therefore that while formal control of sales forecasting is normally a marketing department power, there are a number of dilutions of that authority through the influence of others.   We return to this question in considering political behaviour in Chapter 12.

Table 11.39: Formal Control of Sales Forecasting

Department formally responsible for
sales forecasting

	%
Marketing	78 **(12)
Finance/Accounting	1
Productions	1
R & D	1 *(1)
Corporate Planning	
Other+	18 *(5)
	(N=141)

*These categories include the number of cases indicated in brackets which were classified in the present survey as having no marketing departmentation.
**This category includes the number of cases indicated in brackets where a chief marketing executive existed but no marketing departmentation.
+This category was mainly sales departments.

Table 11.40: Sales Forecasting Influences

	Full and sole responsibility %	Major responsibility but shared with others %	Equal responsibility with others %	Some responsibility but less than others %	No responsibility %	
Marketing	39 **(4)	41 **(9)	6	11 **(1)	3 **(2)	(N=139)
Finance/Accounting	1	8 *(2)	15 *(3)	32 *(5)	44 *(6)	(N=139)
Production	1	6 *(2)	10 *(3)	29 *(4)	54 *(7)	(N=137)
R & D	2 *(1)	4 *(3)	6 *(1)	18 *(2)	70 *(6)	(N=128)
Corporate Planning	2	10 *(3)	12 *(2)	17 *(3)	59 *(6)	(N=123)
Other+	4	21 *(1)	3	9	63 *(4)	(N=70)

*These categories include the number of cases indicated in brackets which were classified in the present study as having no marketing departmentation.
**This category includes the number of cases indicated in brackets where a chief marketing executive existed but no marketing departmentation.
+This category was mainly sales departments.

Summary: Informational Behaviour in Marketing

The evidence available suggests that information flows may well be 'up for grabs' in the way earlier hypothesised, on the grounds of the information access gained by marketing departments, but particularly in the restriction of marketing information flows to other departments.   While sales fore-casting is seen as primarily a marketing department responsibility, in formal terms, this function is seen as subject to influence from others – particularly in finance and production departments.   These measures provide the basis for studying informational power and political behaviour in the next chapter.

MARKETING BUDGETS AND BUDGETING

The third research objective was to identify and describe the resources allocated to marketing, together with the pro-cessual characteristics associated with those allocations.

Resource Allocations to Marketing

The **marketing expenditure** levels of the companies in the survey are shown in Tables 11.41 to 11.43, suggesting that throughout the period studied, advertising budgets and sales promotion budgets in this sample of medium-sized companies were most commonly less than £50K and total marketing budgets were normally less than £250K.

Clearly a major factor unaccounted for was the constitution of the 'Other Marketing Expenses' category reported by companies.   In some firms this was a large category of expenditure, including salaries and other major cost items, while in others this category was small or non-existent.   Although further detail is not available, it does seem that we are confirmed in the expectation expressed earlier that firms vary greatly in their definition of the marketing budget.

In relating expenditure to sales, the results in Tables 11.44 to 11.46 show that: most commonly advertising was less than 0.25% of sales and in the majority of firms it was less than 0.5% of sales;   the same was true of sales promotion. As far as the total marketing budget was concerned the commonest expenditure level was less than 1% of sales and the majority of firms spent less than 2% of sales on marketing (bearing in mind, of course, that we have noted that firms have very different definitions of the components of that budget).

In terms of **other marketing resources**, the findings are shown in Table 11.47, where the commonest response was that the workspace and other resources of the marketing department had not changed in the previous three years, and of the rest almost 40% had claimed additional resources and

Table 11.41: Company Advertising Budgets

Advertising Budget Size	This Year	Last Year	The Year Before Last
	%	%	%
Less than £10K	29	32	33
£10K-£50K	27	26	28
£50K-£250K	23	22	20
£250K-£1M	12	11	11
More than £1M	9	9	8
	(N=99)	(N=89)	(N=84)

Table 11.42: Company Sales Promotion Budgets

Sales Promotion Budget Size	This Year	Last Year	The Year Before Last
	%	%	%
Less than £10K	28	34	38
£10K-£50K	23	21	21
£50K-£250K	31	30	27
£250K-£1M	11	7	6
More than £1M	7	8	8
	(N=97)	(N=87)	(N=82)

Table 11.43: Total Company Marketing Budgets

Total Marketing Budget	This Year	Last Year	The Year Before Last
	%	%	%
Less than £100K	31	30	33
£100K-£250K	20	25	25
£250K-£500K	17	17	18
£500K-£5M	25	21	19
More than £5M	7	7	5
	(N=103)	(N=92)	(N=92)

Table 11.44: Advertising Budget/Sales Ratios

Advertising Budget/Sales	This Year	Last Year	The Year Before Last
	%	%	%
0 - 0.25%	40	37	44
0.25% - 0.50%	18	17	10
0.5% - 1%	11	15	14
1 - 2.5%	15	18	15
More than 2.5%	16	14	17
	(N=95)	(N=85)	(N=80)

Table 11.45: Sales Promotion Budget/Sales Ratios

Sales Promotion Budget/Sales	This Year	Last Year	The Year Before Last
	%	%	%
0 - 0.25%	41	46	49
0.25% - 0.5%	13	11	9
0.5 - 1%	16	11	14
1 - 2.5%	15	18	17
More than 2.5%	15	14	11
	(N=93)	(N=83)	(N=78)

Table 11.46: Marketing Budget/Sales Ratios

Marketing Budget Sales	This Year	Last Year	The Year Before Last
	%	%	%
0-1%	35	32	35
1-2%	22	20	16
2-5%	20	24	21
5-10%	15	13	18
More than 10%	8	11	10
	(N=98)	(N=87)	(N=80)

only 14% had experienced declining resources.

In terms of **marketing manpower**, the trend is shown in Table 11.48, suggesting some increase in marketing department size. In fact, the averages are as follows:

	This Year	Last Year	Year Before Last
Median No. of Employees	12	9	8

In fact, following the trend shown in Table 11.49, it would seem that on the one hand the proportion of very small departments (1-5 employees) has fallen (38% to 31%) but at the same time so has the number of large departments (more than 20 employees) - from 34% to 27% with the result that the 11-20 employee marketing department has become more common (11% to 24%). Following the earlier comments on functional specialisations (pp. *318-326*) this is thought to reflect the disintegration of sales personnel from larger marketing organisations, but also an underlying growth in non-sales marketing department employment. This said, the data in Table 11.48 suggest that while the commonest department size remains the 1-5 employee category, the proportion of total company employment represented by the marketing department shows considerable divergence - suggesting among other things that perhaps the importance of the marketing department may also vary considerably between companies. It is clear too though that as would be expected the marketing department employment ratio differs significantly ($\alpha = 0.05$) between companies of different sizes, as demonstrated in Table 11.49 - a question discussed earlier (pp. *317-318*).

Marketing Budgeting Methods

Table 11.50 shows the data describing the budgeting methods for advertising and sales promotion in the companies studied. The budgeting methods listed in Table 11.50 were reduced into the broad categories of 'affordability', 'rules of thumb', 'objective and task' and 'modelling', suggesting the picture that affordability and rules of thumb are used by more than one-third of companies, the objective and task approach by 40%, and competitive analysis and modelling only by very small numbers.

In comparing budgeting methods used for advertising and sales promotion, the only noticeable difference was that the objective and task approach appeared to be used more for sales promotion than for advertising, but this difference was not large enough to be significant at an acceptable level.

In comparing this study with the earlier works concerned with larger companies (as far as is possible giving the different questions used) in this sample: significantly fewer firms used the '% of expected sales' method, affordability, target share of industry and computer modelling, and

Table 11.47:   Other Marketing Resources

Change in the last three years
in work-space and other resources
taken up by the marketing department

	%
Increased 100% or more	6
Increased 75-100%	4
Increased 50-75%	3
Increased 25-50%	10
Increased up to 25%	16
No change	47
Decreased up to 25%	9
Decreased 25-50%	4
Decreased 50-75%	1
Decreased 75-100%	-

Table 11.48:   Marketing Manpower Levels

	This Year	Last Year	The Year Before Last
	%	%	%
Marketing manpower			
1-5 employees	31	36	38
6-10	18	18	17
11-20	24	15	11
21-50	16	19	21
More than 50	11	12	13
	(N=117)	(N=117)	(N=116)

Table 11.49: Marketing Manpower/Total Employees

Marketing employees/ Total employees %	Company size (employees)			Total
	1 - 250 employees %	250 - 500 employees %	More than 500 employees %	%
Less than 1%	7	34	41	28
1 - 2%	15	22	21	19
2 - 5%	29	22	21	24
5 - 10%	20	12	11	14
More than 10%	29	10	6	15
	(N=41)	(N=41)	(N=47)	(N=129)

(Chi Square = 21.0 with 8 d.f.)

Table 11.50: Marketing Budgeting Methods

Budgeting Method Used	Advertising %	Sales Promotion %
% of past sales	6	5
% of current sales	5	2
% of expected sales	25	24
what we can afford	34	32
target share of total industry	2	2
objective and task method	41	47
agency proposal	4	3
computer model	1	1
other	2	2
	(N=130)	(N=130)

significantly more used the objective and task method.

In comparing the budgeting methods used with other variables, a number of points are noted.

Affordability. In the companies studied these approaches were used particularly with industrial capital goods, and were associated with companies making a loss or little or no profit. Similarly, affordability approaches were associated particularly with small firms (measured both in sales revenue and company employees). Affordability was also associated more with small marketing budgets and less with large budgets (taking budgets both in absolute terms and as a ratio to sales). The use of affordability was also apparently associated with lower ranking of marketing department power, and with increasing general management control over the marketing budget (in the top-down process mode rather than bottom-up, and in direct management intervention).

Rules of Thumb. Percentage of sales approaches were particularly common in fast-moving consumer goods firms, though their use was also associated with smaller businesses, in terms of both lower sales and employee numbers. It follows the percentage methods were also associated with smaller marketing budgets, both in absolute money terms, but also more significantly in the marketing budget/sales ratio. The use of percentage methods was marginally more common when the perceived power of the marketing department was high. However, the use of percentage methods would also appear to be associated with high management control and finance department influence over marketing budgets, and more with the top-down mode of budgeting process. The percentage approach was also more associated with budget adjustments downward rather than budget adjustments upwards.

Competitive. The use of target share of total competitive spending was reported only by a small number of companies, which were in fact all in the fast-moving consumer goods field. The target share method was thus found to be associated with larger companies with larger budgets and higher than average profitability, and where the marketingg department had high perceived power and high control over the budgeting process.

Objective and Task. The objective and task model was used more by fast moving consumer goods firms with high sales and was associated with a high marketing budget/sales ratio, and with higher perceived power of the marketing department. The objective and task methodology was associated with high marketing department budget control – particularly with the bottom-up and bottom-up/top-down budgeting processes; more with budget increases and preservation than adjustments downward; and with low general management control and finance department influence over marketing budgets.

Modelling. Very few companies reported this level of sophistication on marketing budgeting methods, and they were the largest companies in size and marketing budgets, though modelling was associated also with high marketing department perceived power. However, model use was also associated with budget adjustments downwards and high finance department influence over marketing budgets.

The Marketing Budgeting Process

In addition to budgeting methods, the study asked respondents to classify their budgeting process in the way shown in Table 11.51. The majority of firms fell into the intermediate category (bottom-up/top-down), while less than 10% of firms reported a bottom-up process. Only a small number of firms fell into the 'other' category, and these were mainly those who described a 'top-down' budgeting process, where decisions were made by top management with little or no marketing department involvement in that process - indeed this category was primarily firms with no marketing department. In terms of relationship with other company characteristics, the following picture emerged.

Bottom-Up and Bottom-Up/Top-Down Budgeting Processes. These budgeting systems were associated with higher levels of profitability, higher sales, larger companies, and larger marketing budgets (in absolute money terms but particularly in marketing budget/sales ratios), and with lower levels of general management control and finance department influence over marketing budgets.

Top-Down/Bottom-Up and Top-Down Budgeting Processes. Conversely, these budgeting process modes were associated with lower profitability, lower sales, smaller companies, and lower marketing budgets (in money and budget/sales ratios), with high general management control and finance department influence over marketing budgets.

Marketing Budget Adjustments by Management

Table 11.52 shows that marketing budget requests or bids were adjusted by management in slightly over half the cases studied, and that in the overwhelming majority of companies this involved adjustment downward. These different degrees of management intervention were associated with other factors in the following ways.

Table 11.51:   The Marketing Budgeting Process

Budgeting Processes

	%
Bottom-up decision process - managers of the sub-units in marketing (e.g. product managers, advertising managers, etc.) work out how much money they need to achieve their objectives and these amounts are combined to establish the total marketing budget	7 *(1
Bottom-up/top-down decision process - managers of the sub-units in marketing submit budget requests, which are coordinated by the chief marketing executive, and presented to top management, who adjust the total budget size to conform with overall goals and strategies	60 *(6)
Top-down/bottom-up decision process - first, the total size of the marketing budget is established by top management, and then the budget is divided up between marketing centres (such as products and markets)	27 *(5)
None of these are even approximately correct	7 *(7)
	(N=141)

*These categories include the number of cases indicated in brackets which were classified in the present study as having no marketing departmentation.

Table 11.52:   Marketing Budget Adjustments

Adjustment to Budget Requests by Higher Management	%
Increased 25-50%	2
Increased 0-25%	2
No change	46
Decreased 0-25%	39
Decreased 25-50%	10
Decreased 50-75%	1
	(N=107)

Upward Budget Adjustment. Very few responses were available, but management increasing marketing budgets appeared to be associated with high sales and larger companies, and large marketing budgets (in money and ratio to sales).

No Budget Adjustment. The clearest contrast is between cases where budgets were preserved or protected from revision and those where general management reduced marketing budgets. No budget adjustment tended to be associated with: higher profitability; lower sales and smaller companies; higher budget/sales ratios; high marketing department rank; and low management control and finance department influence over marketing budgets.

Downward Budget Adjustment. Conversely, situations where general management adjusted marketing budgets downwards were associated with: lower profitability; higher sales and larger companies; lower budget/sales ratios; lower marketing department rank; and high management control and finance department influence over marketing budgets.

General Management Budget Control

Table 11.53 shows responses on the degree to which the marketing budget was perceived as a marketing department decision at one extreme, and a purely top management decision, at the other extreme, i.e. low general management control through to high general management control over the marketing budget. The overall suggestion was that in nearly 50% of companies general management influence is relatively low, although in some 40% their influence is high. Distinguishing these degrees of management control suggested the following picture.

Low Management Budget Influence. A low level of management influence over marketing budgets was associated with: high profitability, and large marketing budgets (in money and ratio terms); high marketing department rank and low finance department rank and low finance department influence.

High Management Budget Influence. Higher levels of management influence over marketing budgets were associated with: lower profitability; smaller marketing budgets (in money and ratio terms); low marketing department rank; and high finance department influence over the marketing budget.

Finance Department Influence over Marketing Budgets

Table 11.54 shows the perceived influence of other departments over the marketing budget, suggesting that the

Table 11.53:   Marketing Department Budget Determination

Marketing Department Influence Over
Marketing Budget Size

	%
It is a Marketing Department decision	9
The budget is a Marketing Department responsibility but in consultation with others	40 *(2)
There is prior consultation with others	12 *(2)
The marketing budget is a joint decision with others	16 *(2)
The marketing budget is set by top management	23 *(9) (N=137)

*These categories include the number of cases indicated in brackets which were classified in the present study as having no marketing departmentation.

Table 11.54:   Influence of Other Departments Over the Marketing Budget

Departments	A very great deal	A great deal	Quite a bit	Some	Little or none	
	%	%	%	%	%	
Finance/Accounting	8 *(2)	21 *(9)	20 *(1)	29	30 * (3)	(N=133)
Production	-	1 *(2)	4	12 *(2)	109 *(11)	(N=131)
R & D	1 *(1)	3 *(2)	3 *(2)	15 *(2)	97 * (7)	(N=125)
Corporate Planning	5 *(1)	14 *(5)	12 *(2)	16 *(2)	64 * (5)	(N=122)
Others	13 (1)	3	13 (1)	9	63 * (3)	(N=64)

*These categories include the numbers of cases indicated in brackets which were classified in the present study as having no marketing departmentation.

major source of such influence was the finance department. In relation to other factors, the following picture emerges, regarding finance department influence over the marketing budget.

High Finance Department Influence. A higher perceived level of finance department influence over the marketing budget was associated with: lower profitability; lower sales levels; smaller companies; a small marketing budget size and low ratio of marketing budget to sales; and a low marketing department power rank.

Low Finance Department Influence. Lower perceived levels of finance department influence over the marketing budget were associated with: higher levels of profitability; higher sales levels; larger companies; larger marketing budgets; and high marketing department power rank.

These patterns of the marketing budgeting activity are summarised in Table 11.57 below.

The Politicisation of Marketing Budgeting

In addition to measures of control and influence, which are implicitly political judgements, respondents were also asked for their explicit evaluations of how political they considered resource allocation for marketing to be, with the results shown in Table 11.55. These data suggested that in each case - marketing budgeting, manpower increments, and gains in other resources - one-third of the respondents did not see these processes as political at all. By implication, however, two-thirds of the respondents did see some political element to the resource allocation process, offering support for the frame of reference pursued here.

Respondents were also asked to evaluate the more general notion of politicisation, in rating the importance of a number of political influence acts to success in gaining resources in their companies, and the results of these questions are summarised in Table 11.56. It seems that information selectivity was rated most highly as a political act, followed by seeking informal support for proposals. In the case of most of the other political influence acts cited - using image in the company, 'cultivating' the influential, and knowing the 'rules' and using them - respondents were roughly equally divided between the levels of importance attached to these acts. With the political acts of attacking or criticising other departments, praising others to gain support, and creating obligations and favours, the majority of respondents rated these low in importance.

These two sets of measures lead some support to the proposal that marketing resource allocation processes exist in a political context, and this is pursued in Chapter 12.

Table 11.55: Perceived Politicisation of Resource Allocation in Marketing

	Degree of Perceived Politicisation					
	Highly Political				Not political at all	
	1 %	2 %	3 %	4 %	5 %	
Financial budgeting for marketing	12	15	18	22	33	(N=132)
Gaining manpower for marketing	19	15	17	19	30	(N=119)
Gaining office-space, etc., for marketing	13	20	15	18	34	(N=119)

Table 11.56: Corporate Politicisation - Political Acts

	Importance to Success in Negotiations					
	Very Important				Not Important	
	1 %	2 %	3 %	4 %	5 %	
Information selectivity	49	27	9	8	7	(N=116)
Gaining informal support for proposals	28	29	26	7	10	(N=116)
Departmental image in the company	13	28	21	16	22	(N=117)
Knowing and using the 'rules'	18	22	24	10	26	(N=115)
Cultivating the influential	14	19	18	17	32	(N=115)
Praising others to gain support	3	6	18	18	55	(N=114)
Creating obligations and favours	1	4	10	10	75	(N=114)
Attacking/criticising other departments	-	2	8	15	75	(N=116)

Summary :   Marketing Budgets and Budgeting

First, we examined the levels of marketing expenditure in the companies studied.   The data suggest that for this sample of companies median expenditures in the 1984 financial year were 40K on advertising, £50K on sales promotion and £245K on the total marketing budget, representing median ratios to sales of 0.35%, 0.42% and 1.69% respectively.   Similarly, the median number of marketing department employees was 12, although the most common marketing department size was in the 1-5 employee category.   In terms of trends: total marketing expenditure appeared to have declined in the most recent year; while the median employee number had grown through the three years studied, there had been a reduction in the proportion of very small departments and also the proportion of very large departments – suggesting that several effects may be combined, such as growth in marketing employees in some companies, decline of sales employment members, and possibly the separation of sales from marketing in larger operations (although conceivably also the integration or reintegration of marketing and sales in smaller firms);   in terms of other resources for the marketing department, almost half of the firms reported no change over the three years, while 39% reported increased resources and only 14% had faced declining resources.

Perhaps the clearest points emerging were: the relatively small size of most corporate marketing operations and the high degree of variability between companies in different situations.

Second, we turned to the corporate marketing budgeting practices found in companies in terms of: budgeting methods; the budgeting process;   the adjustment of marketing budgets by general management;   the control of marketing budget setting by general management;   and the influence of other departments over the size of the marketing budget.

In terms of budgeting methods it was seen that practices remained dominated by concepts of 'affordability' and 'rules of thumb', like percentage of sales ratios, although a high proportion were using the 'objective and task' methodology. Very few firms reported the use of competitive analysis or modelling to determine budgets.

In examining the marketing budgeting process, a few firms reported a bottom-up mode, some 60% reported the middle ground of the bottom-up/top-down process, 26% reported the top-down/bottom-up mode, and a small number reported what amounted to a top-down budgeting mode.

In evaluating the adjustment by general management of marketing department budgets, in nearly half the cases no change was reported, but where changes did occur these were predominately decreases.   Correspondingly, looking at the degree of management control over the marketing budget, the

Table 11.57: Patterns of Marketing Budgeting Activities

	Budgeting Process			
	Bottom-up	Bottom-up/top-down	Top-down/bottom-up	Other (top-down)
Budgeting methods	Objective and Task Target Share (Percentages)	Objective and Target share Modelling (Percentages)	Affordability (Percentages)	Affordability (Percentages) Agencies
Marketing budget size	Large	Large	Small	Small
Marketing budget/sales %	High	High	Low	Low
Marketing department power rank	High	High	Low	Low
Management budget control	Low	Low	High	High
Finance department influence	Low	Low	High	High
Budget adjustment	No change	No change	Decrease	Decrease
Company size	Large	Large	Smaller	Smaller
Sales	Large	Large	Smaller	Smaller
Profitability	High	High	Lower	Lower

picture was very mixed: in 50% management influence was low, in 40% it was high. Influence of other departments over marketing budgets was mainly associated with the finance department, although again the picture was of very different situations in different companies.

In attempting to relate together these various aspects of marketing budgeting practices, a crude analysis provides the picture given in Table 11.57.

Lastly, it was seen that there is some support for claiming that resource allocation processes were perceived as political in the majority of the firms, and that a number of political influence acts were seen as significant to success in gaining resources.

SUMMARY AND CONCLUSIONS

The goal in this chapter was to describe the general findings of the empirical work, to provide a foundation for the analysis of the power and politics of marketing budgeting in Chapter 12.

First, we examined the **departmentation of marketing and the responsibilities of the chief marketing executive** and the marketing sub-unit in organisations with the following results:

(a) Formal departmentation existed in less than half the companies in the original sample, although there are problems in interpreting the representativeness of this proportion.

(b) Where marketing departments did exist, in one form or another, the level of integration of the 'marketing' functions within those departments was typically relatively low, and only one in six exhibited what can be regarded as a high degree of integration.

(c) Marketing department size was typically small, particularly in terms of non-sales marketing employment, although size had increased in these companies through the period studied.

(d) The responsibilities for marketing decisions were typically shared between the CME and other executives, both for marketing mix variables and for involvement in other management issues, and provided a mechanism for dividing firms by the role of the marketing organisation according to whether they were primarily concerned with 'selling' or 'strategy/services' or whether they were 'integrated full service operations' or took a 'limited/staff' role.

It would seem therefore that at the very least there is a high degree of variability between the organisations studied in the structural arrangements for marketing. This issue will be approached in the next chapter as an aspect of the positional power of marketing.

Second, we examined the **corporate status of marketing** in terms of perceived CME status versus other executives; board-level representation of the marketing department; the perceived power of different functional sub-units; and the support for the notion of the marketing concept or marketing orientation. The findings advanced here may be summarised.

(a) In CME status the position versus the chief production executive was broadly similar to that found in the 1972 Hayhurst and Wills study of large companies – in 60% of firms the two were perceived as equal, while in 13% the CME had lower status and in 28% higher status than the head of production – and a similar position existed versus the chief accounting/finance executive, although rather fewer CME's had higher status and rather more had lower status versus the head of finance, and although the position of the CME versus the head of sales was slightly different this was largely explained by variations in the location of sales within or outwith the marketing department.

(b) The majority of marketing departments had some board-level representation – although 20% had none – and this was typically one member of a board of six directors.

(c) The marketing department was perceived as the most powerful in almost half the companies, and this rank had typically increased over the last three years at the expense of the production function, leaving the finance department as the most significant corporate rival.

(d) Analysing critical success factors by their ranked importance to corporate success and their control by different functions, suggested that in the most highly rated areas of new product development and pricing (as well as some more minor factors), control by the marketing department was negatively related to the importance of the success factor, suggesting that while the marketing department controls a number of strictly 'marketing' factors, the control of the most critical success factors when they are most critical was held by others.

(e) The concept of marketing orientation was supported by some 70% of companies, suggesting that this paradigm exists (either substantively or symbolically) independently of other factors.

(f) There were some signs of marketing information restriction activities and outside influences over the sales forecasting control of the marketing department.

These issues again display high variability between the organisations studied and fit into our model in terms of perceived power (status and ranking of departments), representation (board membership), coping with critical contingencies (control of critical success factors and information manipulation), and paradigm development (marketing orientation) in Chapter 12.

Third, we turned to **marketing budgets and budgeting practices,** and made the following observations.

(a) That the allocation of resources to marketing is limited in most of the companies in financial and in manpower terms, and that there are some signs of pressures reducing financial allocations.

(b) The budgeting methods found remained dominated by the unsophisticated affordability, and rule-of-thumb approaches, and although a relatively high proportion used the 'objective and task' approach, the use of more sophisticated methods was very limited.

(c) In budgeting processes the majority of firms used the bottom-up/top-down mode, although more than a quarter reported the top-down/bottom-up mode, and small numbers reported the extremes of bottom-up and top-down process modes;

(d) adjustments to marketing budget requests by top management occurred in half the cases and these adjustments were mainly downwards.

(e) The reported degree of management control or influence over the marketing budget varied throughout the spectrum from budget setting as wholly a marketing department decision at one extreme, to being a wholly top management decision at the other extreme.

(f) Influence over the marketing budget by other functional sub-units came mainly from the finance area, and again varied substantially between organisations.

(g) Relating the various aspects of budgeting together in a crude fashion appeared to give a picture where budgeting processes and methods could be associated with perceived power, management intervention, finance department influence, and company characteristics, in a way supportive of the logic advanced here, and which is pursued in Chapter 12, where we attempt to relate resource allocation processes and outcomes to measures of marketing department power and political behaviour in a number of surrounding conditions of strategic and political contingencies.

(h) Lastly, there was some explicit support for the notion that marketing budgeting processes should be seen as political in nature, and that political influence acts were significant to success in gaining resources.

With this examination of marketing structure, status and resource allocation in the sample of medium-sized companies provided (and further details of the characteristics of that sample are provided in Appendix B), it is now possible to proceed to an analysis of structure, process and outcomes using the frame of reference provided by the earlier examination of power and politics.

REFERENCES

Hayhurst, R. and Wills, G. (1972) Organizational Design for Marketing Futures, Allen and Unwin, London.

Heidrick and Struggles (1985) Chief Marketing Executive in the United Kingdom 1984, Heidrick and Struggles, London

Hooley, G.J., West, C.J. and Lynch, J.E. (1984) Marketing in the UK - A Survey of Current Practice and Performance, Institute of Marketing, Cookham, Berks.

Piercy, N. (1985) Marketing Organisation: An Analysis of Information Processing, Power and Politics, Allen and Unwin, London

Pugh, D. (1970) 'The Structure of the Marketing Specialisms in Their Context', British Journal of Marketing, Summer, 98-105

12

The Power and Politics of Resource Allocation in Marketing

INTRODUCTION

The last chapter presented a number of descriptive findings relating to the organisation of marketing, and to practices in the allocation of resources to marketing, in the sample of medium-sized companies studied. This material met the descriptive objectives of the research (pp. *297-99*), but it is now possible to build on that foundation to pursue the key issues of the relationships between power and politics, budgeting processes and resource outcomes in marketing. To pursue these goals we adopt the frame of reference of the information-structure-power model of marketing developed in Part II and the deduced model of marketing budgeting described in Figure 9.2, which led in turn to the operationalisation of variables described in Chapter 10.

This present chapter examines in turn the results* obtained with the measurements of power and politics, their interrelationships, and their relationships with budgeting processes and resource outcomes. In this way we seek to evaluate the components of our model of resource allocation in marketing, although it would be somewhat unrealistic to see this as a complete testing of the model, given the relatively limited, exploratory nature of the research project.

Finally, having explored the relationship between power, politics, process and marketing resource outcomes, we turn to examine the implications for corporate performance, in terms of profitability and sales growth.

THE MEASUREMENTS

The measurements used in this part of the study and referred to in this chapter are detailed in Appendix C.

Firstly, in the case of power and politics a number of points may be made regarding the relationships between the variables measured. Ignoring very low correlation coefficients (i.e. less than R=0.30), correlations where the number of cases is small (i.e. less than 40), the more obvious artificial relationships (e.g. between an index and its constituents), and avoiding the repetition of correlation coefficients in discussing variables in turn, a number of significant points may be noted.

POWER AND THE MARKETING DEPARTMENT

Discussion of Intercorrelations

Integration of marketing functions and personnel. As discussed in Chapter 11 (pp. *318-26*), one prime element of positional power is the integration of functions and specialist personnel into a marketing department, and the relationships between the measurement of integration and other variables are shown in Tables 12.1 and 12.2.

From Table 12.1, it is worth noting that while it would be expected that the integration of functions would correlate positively with the integration of personnel and thus with the relative manpower allocation to marketing, this element of positional power is also related to participative power in the level of CME shared responsibilities, and to the control of critical functions – particularly sales forecasting control and influence. In turn this suggests that integration is therefore, quite reasonably, positively related to the strategic contingencies of connectedness, immediacy and influence.

Similarly, in Table 12.2, while it appears that the integration of personnel within the marketing department is significantly related to the integration of functions and relative marketing manpower as well as to the control of certain critical factors, this aspect of integration or positional power is also positively related to participative power in terms of CME responsibilities, and to politics in terms of sales forecasting influence, as well as to the strategic contingency of immediacy.

However, this aspect of positional power is also negatively related to one aspect of information restriction, suggesting that, in this case at least, higher positional power is associated with a lower level of political behaviour in restricting the access of others to information. Such a finding sits quite reasonably with the earlier argument that those who have power may not need to indulge in political behaviour, or may have gained a position where their political behaviour in such areas as information control has become institutionalised and legitimised. Equally, however, it is conceivable that the formally powerful marketing department may not be in a position to deny others access to marketing information (in the sense that institutionalised power may have too high a profile in a company to permit overt political behaviour).

Table 12.1: Simple Correlations with Integration of Functions in the Marketing Department

	POW1 - Integration of functions in the marketing department
POWER	
POW2 - Integration of specialist personnel	.34
POW3 - Relative marketing manpower	.52
POW7 - CME marketing mix responsibilities	.44
POW9 - CME total responsibilities	.44
POW16 - Control of sales forecasting	.34
V154A - Control of critical success factors (distribution)	.40
POLITICS	
V75A - Sales forecasting influence	.33
STRATEGIC CONTINGENCIES	
STRCON5 - Connectedness (all departments)	.31
STRCON6 - Immediacy	.35
STRCON7 - Influence over other departments	.34

It should also be noted, however, that the integration of personnel is negatively related to advertising budget size and to the trends in both 'other' marketing expenditure and the total marketing budget, which might at first sight overturn one of the basic tenets of the thesis here - that power relates directly to budgets. There is, in fact, a significant correlation ($R=0.51$, with a double-log transformation) between marketing manpower level and 'other' budget size, suggesting that this budget component is likely to contain a significant element of manpower-related expenditure. This may suggest, in turn, that once personnel are integrated into the marketing department, the rate of change in 'other' budget level declines, while in the process of increasing integration the rate of budget change is high and positive. By implication, if nothing else, this would

---

Table 12.2: **Simple Correlations with Integration of Personnel in the Marketing Department**

	POW2 – Integration of personnel in the marketing department
POWER	
POW3 – Relative marketing manpower	.70
POW9 – OME total responsibilities	.32
V150A – Control of critical success factors (selling)	.43
V151A – Control of critical success factors (delivery)	.49
V153A – Control of critical success factors (customer service)	.56
V154A – Control of critical success factors (distribution)	.58
POLITICS	
V72A – Information restriction (new product plans)	-.30
POL4 – Sales forecasting influence	.32
STRATEGIC CONTINGENCIES	
STRCON6 – Immediacy	.38
RESOURCES	
RES1 – Advertising budget this year	-.32
RES2 – Advertising budget last year	-.33
RES3 – Advertising budget year before	-.32
RES12 – Other marketing budget trend	-.35
RES16 – Marketing budget trend	-.35

---

suggest that integration is far from being a constant in the companies studied and this would help to explain the negative correlation between integration (power) and budget trends.

However, more interesting is the negative relationship between this measure of integration and absolute advertising budget size. In fact, if POW2 (integration of personnel into the marketing department) is divided into its components, the correlation coefficients are as in Table 12.3. The ratio of the number of specialist jobs in

Table 12.3: Simple Correlations Between Integration and Budget Size

	POW2 - Integration of specialist personnel in marketing department (POW2 = INMTG/OUTMTG)	INMTG - No. of 'marketing' jobs in the marketing department	OUTMTG - No. of 'marketing' jobs outwith the marketing department
RES1 - Advertising budget this year	-.32	.33	.61
RES2 - Advertising budget last year	-.33	.35	.63
RES3 - Advertising budget year before	-.32	.46	.59
RES5 - Sales promotion budget this year			.46
RES6 - Sales promotion budget last year			.46
RES7 - Sales promotion budget year before			.44
RES9 - Other marketing budget this year			.63
RES10 - Other marketing budget last year			.60
RES11 - Other marketing budget year before			.57
RES13 - Marketing budget this year			.57
RES14 - Marketing budget last year			.57
RES15 - Marketing budget year before			.54

marketing to the number of such positions outside the marketing department, correlates negatively with advertising budget size, suggesting the situation where 'marketing' roles being separated from the marketing department (i.e., POW2 is lower) is associated with larger advertising budgets and vice versa.

To some extent this relationship inevitably reflects company size – though singly these variables show no clear correlation with the company size in the relatively limited size range covered by the study. This said, what is most surprising is the existence of relatively high positive correlations between the number of 'marketing' jobs separated from the marketing department (OUTMTG) and all absolute budget sizes, suggesting that the greater the disintegration of the marketing department the higher the level of marketing expenditure, or indeed vice versa but equally significant – the higher the level of marketing expenditure the greater the disintegration of the marketing department.

In this sense, one explanation of this result lies in the lack of integration, or even disintegration, of marketing where large corporate expenditures are involved – and thus by implication generally in larger companies. At the very least, it seems that one of the clearest relationships is between the number of marketing roles outside the marketing department and absolute marketing budget sizes. It will be seen shortly that this relationship is of some predictive significance – however, it must be noted that the relationship is associated among other things with company size, since controlling for company size significantly reduces, though does not remove, the relationship.

Marketing Manpower. Turning to the more strictly marketing manpower-related variables, Table 12.4 suggests that the relative size of the marketing department – a positional power indicator – correlates positively with integration, as already noted, but also with measures of participative power (responsibilities and representation on the board), perceived power (departmental rank) and control of sales forecasting. Correspondingly, there are positive relationships with the political variable of sales forecasting influence, the strategic contingencies of immediacy and influence and the political contingency of importance, providing support for the notion of some consistency between the different dimensions of power and key strategic and political contingencies. It follows from this that there should be a negative correlation with the sales forecasting influence of others. The negative correlation with manpower trend suggests reasonably that relatively large departments are experiencing lower growth rates compared to smaller departments. Perhaps more significantly those larger departments are also associated with lower budget trends,

Table 12.4: Simple Correlations with Relative Marketing Manpower

Manpower	POW3 – Relative Marketing
POWER	
POW4 – Marketing manpower trend	-.35
POW6 – Marketing's board representation	.38
POW7 – CME marketing mix responsibility	.46
POW9 – CME total responsibility	.45
POW14 – Marketing department perceived power rank	.33
POW16 – Control of sales forecasting	.41
POLITICS	
POL4 – Sales forecasting influence	.47
STRATEGIC CONTINGENCIES	
STRCON6 – Immediacy	.46
STRCON7 – Influence over other departments	.41
POLITICAL CONTINGENCIES	
POLCON13 – Importance (year before)	.30
POLITICS OF OTHERS	
OTHPOL4 – Others' influence over sales forecasting	-.35
RESOURCES	
RES16 – Marketing budget trend	-.32

again possibly suggesting that the smaller, growing department is associated with a higher growth in budget.

The data in Tables 12.5 and 12.6 suggest negative relationships between absolute and relative marketing manpower trends and measurements of power, politics and political contingencies, and positive relationships with trends in budget and other resources. Here again, the most likely explanation is that those which are growing slowest are departments which have already grown, and vice versa, but also that this aspect of marketing department power is lower when resource scarcity is high.

Representation. Examining the data in Table 12.7, as noted earlier, board representation is correlated positively with relative manpower size, but it exhibits the same direction of correlation with measures of CME responsibilities and sales forecasting control (participative power). Representation also correlates positively with the politics of sales forecasting influence, and with the strategic contingency of immediacy.

Table 12.7: Simple Correlations with Representation

POW6 - Marketing's
board representation

POWER

V40	- CME responsibilities (price setting)	.32
V41	- CME responsibilities (discounts)	.31
POW16	- Control of sales forecasting	.34

POLITICS

V75A	- Sales forecasting influence	.36

STRATEGIC CONTINGENCIES

STRCON6	- Immediacy	.33

Table 12.5: Simple Correlations with Marketing Manpower Trend

	POW4 - Marketing Manpower trend
POWER	
POW5 - Relative marketing manpower trend	.68
POLITICAL CONTINGENCIES	
POLCON7 - Scarcity (this year)	-.37
POLCON8 - Scarcity (last year)	-.42
POLCON9 - Scarcity (year before)	-.30
POLCON12 - Importance (last year)	-.44
POLCON13 - Importance (year before)	-.33
RESOURCES	
RES16 - Marketing budget trend	.41
RES21 - Other resources trend	.53

Table 12.6: Simple Correlations with Relative Marketing Manpower Trends

	POW5 - Relative Marketing manpower trend
POWER	
V4A - Integration of functions (distribution)	-.30
V5A - Integration of functions (customer service)	-.35
V7A - Integration of functions (advertising)	-.44
POW7 - CME marketing mix responsibilities	-.34
POW9 - CME total responsibilities	-.33
V155 - Control of critical success factors (brand image)	.37
POLITICS	
POL1 - Information access	-.38
RESOURCES	
RES21 - Other resources trend	.39

CME Responsibilities. It has already been seen that the CME responsibilities indicators relate positively to the integration of functions and relative manpower size. Table 12.8 shows that the responsibility measures of participative power correlate positively with the perceived power measures of status and rank, as well as with sales forecasting control. The same applies to the political variables of information access and sales forecasting influence and corespondingly there are negative correlations with the politics of other departments in information control and sales forecasting influence.

Similarly, there are positive correlations between CME responsibilities and the strategic contingencies of connectedness, immediacy and influence. Somewhat more surprising are the negative correlations with the political contingencies of uncertainty and scarcity. The implication in the first case is that CME responsibilities correlate positively with the ability to predict the outcome of marketing efforts, and hence negatively with technology-uncertainty. On the other hand, it would also seem significant to our argument that higher levels of resource scarcity are associated with lower levels of CME responsibility.

In terms of the budgeting process, as might be expected CME responsibilities correlate negatively with the influence of other departments over the marketing budget, but positively with marketing department participation in the resource allocation process.

CME Status. As already noted, the status variables correlate positively with CME responsibilities, and with certain aspects of the integration of functions. In Table 12.9 it is seen that positive relationships also exist with departmental rank and the control of sales forecasting. In the political area, CME status correlates positively with sales forecasting influence and correspondingly negatively with the influence in this area of the corporate planning department. In the budgeting process, there is, as might be expected, a negative correlation between CME status and top management intervention in the marketing budgeting process.

Marketing Department Power Rank. As already seen, the indicators of marketing department perceived power rank correlate positively with relative marketing manpower and CME responsibilities and status. There is a similar relationship, shown in Table 12.10, between perceived rank and control of sales forecasting.

Rank also correlates positively with the political variable of of sales forecasting influence, as well as with the strategic contingencies of connectedness (with the finance department), immediacy and influence.

Table 12.8: Simple Correlations with CME Responsibilities

	POW7 – CME marketing mix responsibilities	POW8 – CME strategy responsibilities	POW9 – CME total responsibilities
POWER			
POW7 – CME marketing mix responsibilities	1.00	.61	.99
POW8 – CME strategy responsibilities	.61	1.00	.70
POW9 – CME total responsibilities	.99	.70	1.00
POW10 – CME status vs. production	.30		
POW11 – CME status vs. finance/accounting	.35		.32
POW12 – CME status vs. sales	.34		.31
POW13 – CME status – average	.38		.36
POW14 – Marketing department perceived rank	.38		.37
POW15 – Marketing department perceived rank change	.32		.30
POW16 – Control of sales forecasting	.31	.31	.34
POLITICS			
POL1 – Marketing department information access	.31		.30
POW4 – Sales forecasting influence	.43	.33	.45
STRATEGIC CONTINGENCIES			
STRCON2 – Connectedness (finance)	.37		.37
STRCON3 – Connectedness (production)	.40		.39

	POW7 - CME marketing mix responsibilities	POW8 - CME strategy responsibilities	POW9 - CME total responsibilities
STRCON4 - Connectedness (R&D)	.32	.38	.37
STRCON5 - Connectedness (all departments)	.45	.35	.47
STRCON6 - Immediacy	.41		.41
STRCON7 - Influence	.45		.46
POLITICAL CONTINGENCIES			
POLCON5 - Uncertainty (technology)	-.32		-.35
POLCON7 - Scarcity (this year)		-.37	
POLCON10 - Scarcity (trend)		-.36	
POLITICS OF OTHER DEPARTMENTS			
OTHPOL2 - Others information access	-.31		-.30
OTHPOL3 - Others information control	.34		-.33
OTHPOL4 - Others sales forecasting influence	-.34		-.36
BUDGETING			
BUD4 - Marketing department participation	.32		.33
BUD8 - Corporate planning influence	-.34		-.33
BUD9 - All other departments influence	-.36	-.30	-.37

Table 12.9: Simple Correlations with CME Status

	POW10 – CME status vs. head of production	POW11 – CME status vs. finance/ accounting	POW12 – CME status vs. head of sales	POW13 – CME status – average
POWER				
POW10 – CME status vs. production	1.00	.52	.61	.86
POW11 – CME status vs. finance/accounting	.52	1.00	.50	.80
POW12 – CME status vs. sales	.61	.50	1.00	.85
POW13 – CME status (average)	.86	.80	.85	1.00
POW14 – Marketing department perceived power rank				
POW16 – Control of sales forecasting	.33	.30	.31	.35
POLITICS				
V75A – Sales forecasting influence	.31	.30		.35
V80A – Corporate planning's sales forecasting influence		-.44	-.45	-.43
BUDGETING				
BUD3 – Top management intervention in marketing budgeting				-.30

Table 12.10: Simple Correlations with Marketing Department Rank

	POW14 – Marketing department perceived power rank	POW15 – Marketing department perceived power rank change
POWER		
POW16 – Control of sales forecasting	.44	.39
POLITICS		
POL4 – Sales forecasting influence	.40	.33
STRATEGIC CONTINGENCIES		
STRCON2 – Connectedness (finance)	.33	
STRCON6 – Immediacy	.49	.39
STRCON7 – Influence	.33	
POWER OF OTHER DEPARTMENTS		
OTHPOW2 – Rank of finance department		-.40
OTHPOW3B – Rank of all other departments		-.36
OTHPOW4 – Production department rank change	.49	.30
OTHPOW5 – Finance department rank change	-.40	-.45
BUDGETING		
BUD2 – Marketing department control of process	.30	.31

It follows that we would expect marketing department power indicators to correlate negatively with measurements of the power of other departments, and this is the case for the current ranks of other departments and the rank change of the finance department. However, there is a positive correlation with the present rank and change in rank of the production department – suggesting that marketing and production ranks may change in line, possibly in joint opposition to the rank of the finance department (see pp. 347 – 9 above).

In the budgeting process, as might be expected, perceived rank correlates positively with marketing department control of the budgeting process.

Control of Sales Forecasting. It has already been shown that the control of sales forecasting correlates positively with the other power measurements of integration of functions, relative manpower, representation, responsibilities, status, and perceived rank. As would be expected there is also a positive relationship with the political variable of sales forecasting influence, as shown in Table 12.11. Control of sales forecasting also shows a positive relationship with the strategic contingencies of connectedness (with the finance department), immediacy and influence, and a negative relationship with the rank of other departments.

Marketing Paradigm. The only significant correlation here, shown in Table 12.12, is between marketing orientation and the political variable of information access.

Implications. While it is apparent throughout the preceeding discussion that the correlations are frequently low, it would seem that we may point to a number of consistent and significant relationships: between the positional/ structural, participative and perceptual dimensions of power; between certain of the power measurements and political variables; between certain of the power measurements and the key strategic and political contingencies; and perhaps most importantly between certain aspects of power and budgeting process variables and resource outcomes.

POLITICS AND THE MARKETING DEPARTMENT

Discussion of Intercorrelations

Information Control. Examining the data in Table 12.13, while it would appear quite reasonable that the access of the marketing department to corporate and other information should correlate positively with CME responsibility levels and paradigm strength, what is more surprising is the

Table 12.11: Simple Correlations with Control of Sales Forecasting

	POW16 - Control of Sales Forecasting
POLITICS	
POL4 – Sales forecasting influence	.61
STRATEGIC CONTINGENCIES	
STRCON2 – Connectedness (finance)	.31
STRCON6 – Immediacy	.31
STRCON7 – Influence	.32
POWER OF OTHER DEPARTMENTS	
OTHPOW3A – Rank of other departments	−.52
OTHPOW7 – Other departments rank change	−.38

Table 12.12: Simple Correlations with Marketing Orientation

	POW18 - Marketing paradigm strength
POLITICS	
POL1 – Marketing department information access	.40

Table 12.13: Simple Correlations with Information Control

	POL1 – Marketing department information access	POL2 – Marketing department information restriction	POL3 – Marketing department information control
POWER			
MPTREND – Marketing manpower trend	-.35		
MPST – Relative marketing manpower trend	-.38		
POW7 – CME marketing mix responsbilities	.31		
POW9 – CME total responsibilities	.30		
POW18 – Marketing paradigm strength	.40		
POLITICS			
POL1 – Marketing department information access		-.37	
POL6 – Politicisation of marketing manpower allocations		.31	-.31
POL8 – Politicisation of all marketing resource allocations		.30	
POLITICAL CONTINGENCIES			
POLCON10 – Scarcity (trend)	-.30		
OTHER DEPARTMENT POWER			
OTHPOW3A – Rank of other departments	-.35		
BUDGETING			
BUD2 – Marketing department control of process			.30

Table 12.14: Correlations with Sales Forecasting Influence

POWER	PCL4 – Marketing department relative sales forecasting influence	V75A – Marketing department absolute sales forecasting influence	Z – Other departments sales forecasting influence
POW1 – Integration of marketing functions		.33	
POW2 – Integration of specialist personnel in marketing department	.32	.41	
POW3 – Relative marketing manpower	.47	.49	
POW6 – Marketing's board representation		.36	
POW7 – OME marketing mix responsibilities	.43	.49	
POW8 – OME strategy responsibilities	.33	.41	
POW9 – OME total responsibilities	.45	.51	
POW10 – OME status vs. head of production		.31	
POW11 – OME status vs. head of finance and accounting		.30	
POW13 – OME status – average		.35	
POW14 – Marketing department perceived power rank	.40	.50	
POW15 – Marketing department perceived power rank change	-.33	.38	
POW16 – Control of sales forecasting	.61	.77	

	POL4 – Marketing department relative sales forecasting influence	V75A – Marketing department absolute sales forecasting influence	Z – Other departments sales forecasting influence
STRATEGIC CONTINGENCIES			
STRCON2 – Connectedness (finance)		.35	
STRCON3 – Connectedness (production)		.33	
STRCON5 – Connectedness (all other departments)		.37	
STRCON6 – Immediacy		.44	
STRCON7 – Influence	.33	.38	
OTHER DEPARTMENT POLITICS			
OTHPOL3 – Other department information control	.30	.31	
BUDGETING			
BLD3 – Top Management Intervention			.37
BLD8 – Corporate planning influence	-.30		.32
BLD9 – Other department influence			.35

negative correlation with absolute and relative marketing manpower trends. However, this suggests that when manpower growth is lower (which we know to be associated with larger department size) then information access is higher, while high growth (and smaller size) is associated with lower information access, which does not appear unreasonable in terms of our earlier discussion.

Of some interest is the negative correlation between information access and resource scarcity - suggesting that information access is lowest when resources are most scarce, and vice versa. Similarly, a negative correlation between information access and the rank of other departments is compatible with our political hypothesis, in the sense that access is apparently gained most when other departments' ranks are lowest.

Information restriction by the marketing department is associated positively, as would be expected, with process politicisation, although the negative correlation with information access is again possibly worthy of note. The suggestion is that when access to corporate information is high, information restriction is low and vice versa, so that information sharing is either in both directions or not at all.

The balance between access and restriction - information control - correlates positively with the marketing department control of the budgeting process, which is a significant relationship for our thesis here. Less easily explained is the negative correlation between politicisation (of manpower allocation) and information control. If we argue that information control is highest when politicisation is perceived as lowest, then it might be the case that the marketing department gains control of information only when politicisation (and hence the political value of information) is low, or it may be that those who have gained higher information control, no longer see or admit processes to be political.

Sales Forecasting Influence. The most pervasive of the political measurements are those relating to the relative and absolute influence of the marketing department over the central informational process of sales forecasting, as shown in Table 12.14.

Absolute sales forecasting influence correlates positively with almost all the measures of positional, participative and perceived power, and most highly with CME responsibilities, perceived department rank, and formal control of sales forecasting. Similarly, there are positive correlations with the strategic contingencies of connectedness, immediacy and influence.

Less markedly, but in the same way, the residual of relative sales forecasting influence shows positive correlations with positional, participative and perceived power measures, and with the strategic contingency of influence.

Perhaps more surprising is the positive correlation between both absolute and relative marketing department sales forecasting influence and information control by other departments. However, quite reasonably this suggests that marketing department sales forecasting influence is higher when other departments are least successful in controlling information access, and conversely the marketing department's sales forecasting influence is lowest when other departments are most successful at controlling information.

Relative sales forecasting influence also correlates negatively with the influence of the corporate planning department in the budgeting process, while the residual of other departments' influence in sales forecasting correlates positively with top management intervention, and other department influence in the marketing budgeting process.

Politicisation. By comparison, the politicisation variables showed relatively few significant relationships with the other measures, as shown in Table 12.15. It has been noted already that politicisation correlates positively with marketing department information access and negatively with information control. Table 12.15 shows that the politicisation of marketing processes also correlates highly with corporate politicisation, as would be expected. It was found too that politicisation correlated negatively with information access gained by other departments and with their information control. This suggests that when politicisation was at its highest the success of other departments in gaining access to information and in controlling information was at its lowest, in line with the hypothesis that the more political processes are (or are perceived to be) the greater the competition for information.

Implications. As in the case of the power measures, while the correlations are frequently low, there would seem to be a number of significant relationships highlighted: between the political variables of information control, sales forecasting influence and politicisation, and strategic and political contingencies, power and politics in other departments and the marketing budgeting process.

FACTOR ANALYSIS OF POWER, POLITICS AND CONTINGENCIES

Because of the large number of variables and indices, to reduce the data, prior to attempting to model the relationships with resource allocations processes and outcomes, the variables discussed above were factor analysed, with the

Table 12.15: Simple Correlations with Politicisation

	POL5 – Politic- isation of marketing budgeting	POL6 – Politic- isation of marketing manpower allocations	POL7 – Politic- isation of other marketing resource allocations	POL8 – Politic- isation of marketing resource allocation
POLITICAL CONTINGENCIES				
POLCON6 – Company politicisation	.60	.61	.56	.65
OTHER DEPARTMENTS				
OTHPOL1 – Other department information access		-.31		-.30
OTHPOL3 – Other department information control	-.34	-.31		

results shown in Table 12.16, producing the factors described in Table 12.17, and discussed below.

The Politics of Information Access Factor

This factor was created mainly from the variables measuring the access of the marketing department to information held by other departments. That information included: 'marketing information', such as product and marketing costs; financial data including company-wide budgets and corporate profitability; data relating to other functions, e.g. production schedules; and corporate information, such as company-wide investment and corporate plans. It will be recalled from Chapter 10 (pp. *305–306*) that it was argued that these information items were politically significant in that they were: liable to be defended with barriers of secrecy and confidentiality, important at least symbolically to involvement in strategic decision making, and susceptible to dispute over access.

In addition, this factor included the strength of the marketing paradigm, which was noted earlier to correlate with information access. These factors were negatively related to the relative trend in marketing manpower (where the trend in marketing manpower is related to the trend in sales revenue). This last relationship may be explained in the light of the fact that it was found earlier that manpower growth is lower in established, integrated marketing departments, so that those departments with a low relative growth rate are likely to be the most established with high information access and paradigm acceptance.

Positional/Participative Power Factor

This factor includes the measures of power relating to integration of functions into the marketing department, CME responsibilities, sales forecasting control, and thus reflects both positional and participative aspects of the power of the marketing department. This factor is also loaded with the strategic contingencies of influence over other departments, connectedness and immediacy reflecting the centrality and pervasiveness dimensions of strategic contingencies discussed earlier. Together these variables are taken to describe the positional and participative power of the marketing department.

Process Politicisation Factor

This factor is made up of the perceived politicisation of different marketing resource allocation processes - manpower, other marketing resources and budgets - and corporate politicisation - including the importance to success in the

Table 12.16: Factor Analysis of Power and Politics Variables*

		Factor 1	Factor 2	Factor 3	Factor 4	Factor 5	Factor 6
POL1/V65	– Information access (R&D)	.83					
POL1/V61	– Information access (company profitability)	.82					
POL1/V66	– Information access (corporate plans)	.82					
POL1/V59	– Information access (product costs)	.81					
POL1/V62	– Information access (company budgets)	.78					
POL1/V60	– Information access (marketing costs)	.76					
POL1/V63	– Information access (company investment)	.75					
POL1/V64	– Information access (production schedules)	.72					
POL1/MPST	– Relative marketing manpower trend	-.46					
POW1	– Marketing paradigm	.43					
STRCON7 (V162)	– Influence (over production department)		.72				
STRCON3	– Connectedness (production department)		.65				
STRCON7 (V161)	– Influence (over finance department)		.65				
STRCON6	– Immediacy		.64				
POW7	– OWE marketing mix responsibilities	.35	.62				
STRCON2	– Connectedness (finance department)		.60				
POW1 (V4A)	– Integration (distribution)		.53				
POW1 (V5A)	– Integration (customer service)		.51				
STRCON7 (V163)	– Influence (over R&D department)		.51				
STRCON4	– Connecteaness (R&D department)		.48				
POW1 (V3A)	– Integration (sales)		.48	-.31			.32
POW3 (MP)	– Relative marketing manpower		.44				
POW16	– Sales forecasting control		.44				
POW8	– OWE Strategy responsibilities		.43			.36	
POL4 (SFBAL)	– Sales forecasting influence		.42				
POW1 (V8A)	– Integration (export)		.37				.38
INMTG	– Integration (marketing personnel in marketing department)		.35				
POW1 (V6A)	– Integration (trade marketing)		.31				
POL6	– Politicisation – marketing manpower allocations			.78			
POLCON6 (V129A)	– Company politicisation (cultivation)			.76			
POL7	– Politicisation – other marketing resources			.74			
POLCON6 (V128A)	– Company politicisation (praising)			.73			
POL5	– Politicisation – marketing budgeting			.71			
POLCON6 (V130A)	– Company politicisation (favours)			.66			
POLCON6 (V127A)	– Company politicisation (informal support)			.58			
POLCON6 (V131A)	– Company politicisation (using rules)		.30	.56			

	Factor 1	Factor 2	Factor 3	Factor 4	Factor 5	Factor 6
POLCON6 (V126A) – Company politicisation (attacking)			.55			
POLCON6 (V125A) – Company politicisation (image)			.49			
POLCON13 (YBLD) – Importance (year before)			-.36			
OTHPOW9 (R) – Control of strategic contingencies (R&D department)		.36				
POL2 (V61A) – Information restriction (market studies)			-.35			
POL2 (V73A) – Information restriction (other marketing research)			.76			
POL2 (V70A) – Information restriction (marketing plans)			.73			
POL2 (V69A) – Information restriction (sales plans)			.71			
POL2 (V72A) – Information restriction (new product plans)			.66			
POL2 (V68A) – Information restriction (customer reports)			.62			
POL2 (V71A) – Information restriction (marketing budgets)			.62			
OTHPOW6 – R&D department rank change			.59			
OTHPOW9 (F) – Control of strategic contingencies (finance department)			-.43			
OTHPOW3 – R&D department rank			-.39	-.83		
POLCON7 – Scarcity (this year)			-.38	-.71		
POLCON8 – Scarcity (last year)				-.70		
POLCON9 – Scarcity (year before)				.62		
POLCON3 – Uncertainty (recession)				-.49		
POLCON11 (TYBLD) – Importance (this year)		.31		-.41		
POLCON4 – Uncertainty (market life cycle)				-.40		
POLCON12 (LYBLD) – Importance (last year)				-.40		
POLCON1 – Uncertainty (demand predictability)						
OTHPOW5 – Finance department perceived rank change					-.71	
OTHPOW2 – Finance department rank						-.65
POW11 – CME status vs. finance						.60
POW14 – Marketing department rank		.39				
POW12 – CME status vs. sales						.56
POW15 – Marketing department perceived rank change						.55
POW10 – CME status vs. production						.55
OTHPOW10 (OUTMTG) – Marketing employees outside marketing department						-.45
OTHPOW4 – Production department perceived rank change						.44
OTHPOW1 – Production department rank						.34
OTHPOL4 (SFCON) – Others' influence over sales forecasting						-.33

* Varimax rotation in six iterations.
Coefficients less than .3 are suppressed.
The 6 factor solution produces an eigenvalue of 3.5 and accounts for 42% of variance.

Table 12.17: Power and Politics Factors

FACTOR LABELS	FACTOR CONTENT	% of Variance Explained	Eigen-values
The Politics of Information Access	+POL1 (V65) Information access (R&D); +POL1 (V61) Information access (company profitability); +POL1 (V66) Information access (corporate plans); +POL1 (V59) Information access (product costs) +POL1 (V62) Information access (company budgets) +POL1 (V60) Information access (marketing costs) +POL1 (V63) Information access (company investment); +POL1 (V64) Information access; (production schedules); -POW5 (MPST)Relative marketing manpower trend; +POW18 Marketing paradigm.	11.3	8.6
Positional/ Participative Power	+STRCON7 (V162) Influence (production department); +STRCON3 Connectedness (production); +STRCON7 (V161) Influence (finance department); +STRCON6 Immediacy; +POW7 OVE Marketing mix responsibilities; +STRCON2 Connectedness (finance department); +POW1 (V4A) Integration (distribution); +POW1 (V5A) Integration (customer service); +STRCON7 (V163) Influence (R&D department); +STRCON4 Connectedness (R&D department); +POW1 (V3A) Integration (sales); +POV3 (MP) Relative marketing manpower; +POW16 Sales forecasting control; +POW8 OVE strategy responsibilities; +POW4 (SFBAL)Sales forecasting influence; +POW1 (V8A) Integration (Export); +INMTG Integration (marketing personnel in marketing department); +POW1 (V6A) Integration (trade marketing).	8.6	6.83
Process Politic-isation	+POL6 Politicisation - marketing manpower allocations; +POLCON6 (V129A) Company Politicisation (cultivation); +POL7 Politicisation - other marketing resources +POLCON6 (V128A) Company politicisation (praising); +POL5 Politicisation - marketing budgeting; +POLCON6 (V130A) company politicisation (favours); +POLCON (V127A) Company politicisation (in formal support); +POLCON6 (V131A) Company politicisation (using rules); +POLCON6 (V126A) Company Politicisation (attacking); +POLCON6 (V125A) Company politicisation (image); -POLCON13 (YBBLD) Importance (year before); +OTHPON ((R) control of strategic contingencies	7.2	5.66

FACTOR LABELS	FACTOR CONTENT*	% of Variance	Eigen Values
The Politics of Information Restriction	+POL2 (V67A) Information restriction (market studies); +POL2 (V73A) Information restriction (other marketing research); +POL2 (V70A) Information restriction (marketing plans); +POL2(V69A) Information restriction (sales plans); +POL2 (V72A) Information restriction (new product plans); +POL2 (V68A) Information restriction (customer reports); +POL2 (V71A) Information restriction (marketing budgets); -OTHPOW6 R & D department rank change; -OTHPOW9(F) Control of strategic contingencies (finance department); OTHPOW3 R & D department rank.	5.1	4.05
Political Contingencies	-POLCON7 Scarcity (this year); -POLCON8 Scarcity (last year); -POLCON9 Scarcity (year before); +POLCON3 Uncertainty (recession); -POLCON11 (TUBLD) Importance (this year); -POLCON4 Uncertainty (market life cycle); -POLCON2 (LYBLD) Importance (last year); -POLCON1 Uncertainty (demand predictability).	4.9	3.85
Relative Perceived Power	-OTHPOW5 Finance department perceived rank change; -OTHPOW2 Finance department rank; +POW11 OWE Status vs. Finance; +POW14 Marketing department rank; +POW12 OWE Status vs. Sales; +POW15 Marketing department rank change; +POW10 OWE Status vs. Production; -OTHPOW10 (OUTMTC) Marketing employees outside marketing department; -OTHPOW1 Production department perceived rank; +OTHPOW4 Production department rank change; -OTHPOL4 (SFCON) Others influence over sales forecasting.	4.4	3.49

*Factor scores were calculated by summing the values of loaded variables and substituting mean-scores for missing values.

company of such political influence acts as: cultivating the influential, praising others to gain support, creating obligations and favours, gaining informal support for proposals, knowing the rules and using them, attacking or criticising other departments, and image in the company. These are related to the control of critical success factors, by one of the other departments, and negatively to the scarcity measurement of the year before. This latter factor suggests that earlier scarcity impacts on current perceptions of politicisation in the sense that when earlier resource scarcity was high, politicisation is currently perceived as lower, and vice versa – which may reflect a number of factors, such as increased management control, or the perceptions of politicisation being lower among those who have been successful in gaining resources. Overall, this factor is taken as a measure of the politicisation of marketing resource allocation processes.

The Politics of Information Restriction Factor

This factor is loaded mainly with different aspects of the restriction of the access of other departments to marketing information by the marketing department – including market studies, marketing research, marketing and sales plans, new product plans, customer reports and marketing budgets. In addition, the factor includes negative relationships with the positional power of other departments – the rank and rank change of the R&D department, and control of critical success factors by the finance department. This is compatible with our frame of reference if we argue that information restriction is highest when the power of others is low – i.e. the ability of the marketing department to control information flows is negatively related to the power of others to prevent this. Conversely, information restriction is low when the power of others is relatively high – i.e. in the face of competing departments which are powerful, and which control the critical contingencies facing the firm, the marketing department is not in a position (or has little to gain) in restricting the flow of marketing information to others. (Indeed, it will seen shortly that this factor correlates positively with both the Positional/Participative and Relative Perceived Power factors.)

This group of variables is taken as a measure of the politics of information restriction.

Political Contingencies Factor

This factor links together the contingencies of uncertainty, scarcity and importance and is taken therefore as a measure of political contingencies as they were discussed earlier.

Relative Perceived Power Factor

This factor groups a number of positive indicators of the perceived power of the marketing department - CME status versus the finance department, and versus the heads of production and sales, and marketing department rank and rank change. These are related negatively to the perceived rank of finance and the change in that rank and to the disintegration measures of the number of 'marketing' personnel located outwith the marketing department. The only anomaly would seem to be the positive correlation with production department rank and rank change, although this was discussed earlier (pp. *390-95*).

This factor is taken as a measure of the perceived power of the marketing department relative to other departments.

Power and Politics Factors and Resources

The correlations between the power and politics factors and relative budget size were mostly low, and the only significant correlations greater than R=0.30 were found with Process Politicisation and Relative Perceived Power.

Process Politicisation correlated positively with sales promotion budget size (R=0.36), other marketing expenditure (R=0.33), and total marketing expenditure (R=0.41). The suggestion is that larger budgets in absolute terms are more highly associated with political activities and processes.

Relative Perceived Power was correlated positively with the absolute size of all budget components: with advertising (R=0.35), with sales promotion (R=0.45), with other marketing expenditure (R= 0.37), and with total marketing expenditure (R=0.54). This suggests that perceived power is also significantly associated with budget size.

However, these relationships persisted (or were stronger), in examining relative budget size (see Table 12.22). Process Politicisation was positively correlated with: advertising expenditure ratios (R=0.40); sales promotion expenditure ratios (R= 0.35); and the total marketing expenditure ratio (R=0.43). In fact, in considering non-linear functions the logarithm of Process Politicisation displayed an even closer relationship: with advertising (R=0.45); with sales promotion (R=0.41); with other marketing expenditures (R=0.40); and with total marketing expenditure (R=0.55).

Relative Perceived Power was positively correlated with: advertising ratios (R=0.62); sales promotion ratios (R=0.42); and total marketing expenditure (R=0.52). The suggestion again is that the politicisation of processes and the perceived power of the marketing department are significantly associated with high budget outcomes.

RESOURCE ALLOCATION PROCESS FACTORS

The descriptive results obtained with the resource allocation process variables measured were presented in Chapter 11 (pp. *362-77*), and the variables are listed and described in Appendix C.

These measures describe some eight attributes of marketing resource allocation processes, including the sophistication of budgeting methods, control of the allocation process made by the marketing department, top management intervention, the degree of marketing department participation in budgeting decisions, and the influence of other departments over marketing budgets.

Again to reduce the data, the budgeting variables were factor analysed, with the results shown in Table 20.18, producing the three budgeting process factors described below.

General Management Control of Marketing Budgeting Factor

This factor links top management intervention in marketing budgeting, which was measured as the adjustments made to marketing budget requests, with the perceived influence over marketing budgeting of the finance department and the corporate planning department. These variables are taken together as a measure of general management control over the marketing budgeting process.

Marketing Department Budgeting Control Factor

This factor reflected the measurement of the type of marketing budgeting process - running from 'top-down' with low marketing department control, to 'bottom-up' with high marketing department control - together with the participation or jurisdiction of the marketing department in budget-setting, and the sophistication of the budgeting methods used (suggesting that moving away from simpler '% of sales' and 'affordability' measures is associated with greater marketing department control).

These variables are taken together as a measure of the marketing department's control over the budgeting process.

Production/R&D Marketing Budgeting Influence Factor

The third factor links together the influence of the production and R&D departments over the marketing budgeting process.

Resource Allocation Process Factors and Power and Politics

The only significantly high correlation (R= 0.41) emerged

Table 12.18: Factor Analysis of Budgeting Process Variables*

	Factor Loadings Factor 1	Factor 2	Factor 3
	GENERAL MANAGEMENT CONTROL OF MARKETING BUDGETING	MARKETING DEPARTMENT BUDGETING CONTROL	PRODUCTION/R&D MARKETING BUDGETING INFLUENCE
BUD3 – Top management intervention	.75		
BUD8 – Corporate planning department influence	.70		.38
BUD5 – Finance department influence	.58		
BUD2 – Marketing department control		.73	
BUD4 – Marketing department participation	–.41	.69	
BUD1 – Sophistication of budgeting methods		.69	
BUD6 – Production department influence			.82
BUD7 – R&D department influence			.58
% OF VARIANCE EXPLAINED	25.2	16.9	13.2
EIGENVALUES	2.02	1.35	1.05

* Varimax rotation in 5 iterations. Coefficients less than .5 are suppressed. The 3 factor solution produced an eigenvalue greater than 1 and was accepted according to the Kaiser criterion.

between the Positional/Participative Power of the marketing department, and Marketing Department Budgeting Control. This suggested that such power is reflected in the resource allocation process as in the other areas studied.

Resource Process Variables and Resource Outcomes

Correlations between the resource process variables and resource outcomes were mostly remarkably low, and again yielded few significant correlations. To begin with there was no sign of correlation between the budgeting process variables or factors and absolute budget size.

In relative budget sizes the marketing department control of process variable (BUD2) did correlate with sales promotion budget size ($R=0.38$) and total budget size ($R=0.38$), and marketing department participation (BUD4) correlated positively with the 'other' marketing budget ratio ($R=0.34$). The Marketing Department Budgeting Control factor correlated positively with log transformations of other marketing budget ($R=0.45$) and total budget ($R=0.42$). The Production/R&D Marketing Budgeting Influence factor correlated negatively with the trend in advertising expenditure ($R= -.30$).

There is some suggestion thus that the control and participation achieved by the marketing department in the budgeting process is positively related to budget size, although not always in a linear fashion. Similarly the greater influence of technical departments in the marketing budgeting process is associated with small growth or declines in advertising expenditure.

POWER, POLITICS, RESOURCE ALLOCATION PROCESSES AND MARKETING RESOURCES

Precedent in Budgeting

It should be first noted that clearly the best predictors of all budget sizes and ratios are the other budget ratios, as shown in Table 12.20. This is particularly the case with advertising and sales promotion budgets - e.g. this year's advertising budget has $R=0.95$ with last year's advertising budget and $R=0.74$ with last year's sales promotion budget. It is of some note, however, that the 'other marketing budget' category does not correlate highly with advertising or sales promotion budgets - only with earlier expenditures in the same category, and to some extent with the total marketing budget. In fact though, by far the best predictor of this year's other marketing expenditure is last year's ($R=0.99$) and the same applies to the total marketing budget ($R=0.98$).

Indeed, this effect is even more marked with absolute

Table 12.19: Marketing Budget Intercorrelations

	Advertising budgets (£)			Sales Promotion budget (£)			Other Marketing expenditure (£)			Total Marketing budget (£)		
	This Year	Last Year	Year Before	This Year	Last Year	Year Before	This Year	Last Year	Year Before	This Year	Last Year	Year Before
Advertising budget (£)												
– This Year	1.00	.99	.99	.97	.96	.96	.45	.42	.44	.96	.96	.96
– Last Year		1.00	.99	.96	.96	.95	.46	.43	.45	.96	.96	.95
– Year Before			1.00	.98	.98	.97	.46	.43	.45	.97	.97	.97
Sales promotion budget (£)												
– This Year				1.00	.99	.99	.45	.42	.45	.97	.96	.97
– Last Year					1.00	.99	.45	.43	.45	.96	.96	.97
– Year Before						1.00	.44	.41	.44	.96	.96	.97
Other marketing expenditure (£)												
– This Year							1.00	.99	.99	.65	.66	.64
– Last Year								1.00	.99	.62	.64	.62
– Year Before									1.00	.64	.66	.64
Total marketing budget (£)												
– This Year										1.00	.99	.99
– Last Year											1.00	.99
– Year Before												1.00

Table 12.20: Marketing Budget Ratio Intercorrelations

	Advertising Budget Ratios			Sales Promotion Budget Ratios			Other Marketing Expenditure Ratio			Total Marketing Budget Ratio		
	This Year	Last Year	Year Before	This Year	Last Year	Year Before	This Year	Last Year	Year Before	This Year	Last Year	Year Before
Advertising												
– This Year	1.00	.95	.94	.71	.74	.78	.19	.15	.17	.84	.78	.79
– Last Year		1.00	.98	.73	.72	.73	.17	.16	.18	.81	.80	.79
– Year Before			1.00	.76	.72	.72	.21	.20	.19	.83	.81	.81
Sales promotion												
– This Year				1.00	.98	.98	.23	.19	.15	.84	.80	.79
– Last Year					1.00	.99	.19	.19	.16	.83	.82	.80
– Year Before						1.00	.16	.15	.13	.83	.80	.78
Other marketing expenditure												
– This Year							1.00	.99	.97	.61	.65	.65
– Last Year								1.00	.99	.58	.64	.65
– Year Before									1.00	.56	.63	.65
Total marketing budget												
– This Year										1.00	.98	.98
– Last Year											1.00	.99
– Year Before												1.00

budget sizes, as shown in Table 12.19. Here the money values of budgets correlate extremely highly with previous years – for advertising, sales promotion, other expenditure and the total marketing budget, this year's budget has R=0.99 for both previous years. Again while sales promotion and advertising budgets are highly correlated, this is far less true for other marketing expenditure.

In justice it must be noted from Table 12.21 that the same relationship applies to sales revenue and net profit in – the best predictors are previous years, although this is markedly less true for the profitability ratio and most particularly not the case for the sales revenue to net profit correlations and the net profit (£) to net profitability correlations. It is perhaps of particular note that sales revenue is only weakly correlated to profitability and that for the current year this is a negative correlation, while net profit are also only weakly related to profitability, suggesting that (within the limited size range studied) size is not a strong predictor of profitability.

At one level it seems one may point to evidence of a high degree of precedent and incrementalism in the setting of marketing budget levels – in absolute money terms, but also in terms of budget/sales ratios – confirming the earlier suggestion that marketing budgeting was largely incremental in nature (pp. 63 - 70). In addition, these figures show evidence of stability in budget/sales ratios which also offers some confirmation of the claim that this ratio remains a primary and stable determinant of budget levels (pp. 38 - 39).

However, in terms of our present interest, these figures, by supporting the importance of precedent and incrementalism, suggest that the budgeting decision making process is concerned with changes from a base, although clearly some interest remains in what determines that base in the first place.

In the models below, the direct impact of previous budget size is excluded.

Simple Correlations

Table 12.22 shows the Pearson correlations between the factors extracted and marketing resource outcomes. While the coefficients are generally low, a number of points may be made.

The Politics of Information Access factor shows generally low negative correlations with budget components, suggesting that information access is at its highest when budget ratios are lowest, although as noted earlier this relationship may reflect company size (see pp. 395 - 400). There are positive relationships with manpower and other resource trends.

Table 12.21: Company Performance Indicator Intercorrelations

	Sales Revenue (£)			Net Profit (£)			Profitability		
	This Year	Last Year	Year Before	This Year	Last Year	Year Before	This Year	Last Year	Year Before
Sales Revenue (£)									
– This Year	1.00	.99	.99	.17	.97	.99	-.07	.03	.07
– Last Year		1.00	.99	.22	.95	.99	-.07	.03	.06
– Year Before			1.00	.14	.97	.99	-.07	.04	.06
Net profit (£)									
– This Year				1.00	.99	.99	.20	.13	.14
– Last Year					1.00	.99	.12	.14	.14
– Year Before						1.00	.10	.11	.15
Profitability									
– This Year							1.00	.83	.59
– Last Year								1.00	.69
– Year Before									1.00

The Positional/Participative Power factor is positively correlated with sales promotion, other expenditure and total budget ratios and trends, in the way that has been hypothesised. The exceptions are advertising budgets, manpower and other resources. The latter issues were discussed earlier (pp. *384-86*), and more note is taken of the negative correlation with advertising budget ratios. It may be that advertising should be distinguished for other areas of expenditure, in the ways argued earlier (pp. *23-4*) as more susceptible to management intervention and control.

The Process Politicisation factor correlates significantly and positively with all the financial budget measurements, in line with the case argued here. The only exceptions are low negative relationships with manpower and other resource trends.

The Politics of Information Restriction factor generally relates negatively to budget components and positively to manpower and other resource trends, while the Political Contingencies factor relates positively to budgets and negatively to resource trends - in both cases with low coefficients and levels of significance.

The Relative Perceived Power factor correlates positively and significantly with all financial budget components and trends - particularly in the areas of advertising and sales promotion.

As would be expected the Marketing Department Budgeting Control factor is positively associated with budget sizes and trends - most highly in the other expenditure area - while the General Management Control of Marketing Budgeting and Production/R&D Marketing Budgeting Influence factors generally correlate negatively with budget size.

This far, we have support for our model of the power and politics of marketing resource allocation mainly in associating politicisation and the perceived power of the marketing department with budget size, together with relative control of the marketing budgeting process.

Regression Models

For each of the marketing resource types studied, multiple regression models were built taking the resource as the dependent and the power and politics and resource allocation process variables or factors as independent variables, with the results discussed below.

Advertising Budgets. Tables 12.23 and 12.24 show the relationship between advertising expenditure in the three years studied and the power and politics factors, and resource allocation process variables.

In Table 12.23, in regressing the power and politics factors and resource allocation process variables with

Table 12.22: Simple Correlations of Power and Politics, and Resource Allocation Process Factors with Resources

	Advertising budget ratio			Advertising budget trend	Sales promotion budget ratio			Sales promotion budget trend
	This Year	Last Year	Year Before		This Year	Last Year	Year Before	
Power and Politics Factors								
Politics of Information Access	-.09	-.10	-.11	-.02	-.03	-.02	-.02	.03
Positional/Participative Power	.02	-.04	-.04	.24	.04	.02	.03	0
Process Politicisation	.35	.34	.40	.11	.35	.34	.35	.17
Politics of Information Restriction	-.15	-.08	-.11	-.09	-.12	-.10	-.14	.13
Political Contingencies	.10	0	.01	.13	.01	.02	.17	-.21
Relative Perceived Power	.58	.62	.60	.13	.42	.41	.41	.22
Resource Allocation Process Factors								
General Management Control of Marketing Budgeting	-.09	-.12	-.08	-.14	-.03	-.06	-.08	-.09
Marketing Department Budgeting Control	.05	.04	.05	.06	.22	.16	.12	.26
Production/R&D Marketing Budgeting Influence	-.10	-.12	-.07	-.08	-.13	-.16	-.11	-.13

	Other marketing budget			Other budget trend	Total marketing budget ratio			Total budget trend	Marketing manpower trend	Other marketing resources trend
	This Year	Last Year	Year Before		This Year	Last Year	Year Before			
Power and Politics Factors										
Politics of Information Access	-.11	-.10	-.10	-.13	-.10	-.12	-.10	.05	.25	.05
Positional/Participative Power	.22	.22	.28	.05	.14	.10	.13	.08	-.20	-.01
Process Politicisation	.17	.18	.24	.10	.39	.39	.43	.04	-.08	-.07
Politics of Information Restriction	-.02	.06	.12	-.11	-.10	-.07	-.03	.11	.10	.08
Political Contingencies	.05	.04	.21	-.13	.08	.03	.18	-.20	-.19	0
Relative Perceived Power	.15	.11	.08	.22	.52	.48	.46	.17	.01	-.04
Resource Allocation Process Factors										
General Management Control of Marketing Budgeting	-.04	-.10	-.08	.11	-.05	-.11	-.11	-.22	-.01	01
Marketing Department Budgeting Control	.37	.40	.38	.07	.27	.25	.23	.18	-.01	-.01
Production/R&D Marketing Budgeting Influence	-.08	-.11	-.13	.09	-.11	-.16	-.13	-.30	-.13	.02

Table 12.23: Power and Politics Factors, Resource Allocation Process Variables and Advertising Budgets*

Variables in the Equation**	B	Beta	R	R^2	F	Significance of F
(a) This Year						
Factor 6 – Relative Perceived Power	.000909	.66	.70	.49	28.66	0.0000
Factor 5 – Political contingencies	.00000000369	.28				
(Constant)	.293					
(b) Last Year						
Factor 6 – Relative Perceived Power	.000903	.68	.68	.47	47.09	0.0000
(Constant)	.35					
(c) Year Before						
Factor 6 – Relative Perceived Power	.00769	.57	.73	.53	18.68	0.0000
Factor 3 – Process Politicisation	.00651	.42				
Factor 5 – Political Contingencies	.00000000112	.30				
(Constant)	.000403					
(d) Three Year Trend						
Factor 2 – Positional/Participative Power	.000273	.36	.36	.13	7.85	0.0070
(Constant)	2.16					

* Measured as power and politics factors, resource allocation process variables and advertising expenditure/sales ratios.

** Method of regression was stepwise removal and entry of variables with probability F-to-enter = 0.05 and probability F-to-remove = 0.10.

Table 12.24: Power and Politics Factors, Resource Allocation Process Variables and Advertising Budgets (double log transformation)*

Variables in the Equation**	B	Beta	R	R²	F	Significance of F
(a) This Year						
BUD3 – Top management intervention	-1.62	-.35	.47	.22	7.73	0.0011
Log Factor 3 – Process Politicisation	1.47	.30				
(Constant)	-4.56					
(b) Last Year						
Log Factor 3 – Process Politicisation	2.09	.43	.63	.39	9.57	0.0000
BUD3 – Top management intervention	-1.39	-.30				
BUD6 – Production department influence	-2.34	-.26				
(Constant)	-4.86					
(c) Year Before						
Log Factor 3 – Process Politicisation	1.91	.38	.53	.28	8.59	0.0007
BUD3 – Top Management Intervention	-1.61	-.33				
(Constant)	-6.83					
(d) Three Year Trend						
Log Factor 2 – Positional/Participative Power	0.399	.41	.41	.17	9.67	0.0037
(Constant)	-1.27					

* Measured as logarithms of power and politics factors, resource allocation process variables, and logarithms of the advertising expenditure/sales ratios.

** Method of regression was stepwise removal and entry of variables with probability F-to-enter = 0.05 and probability F-to-remove = 0.10.

advertising ratios, the best model (R=0.73) was for advertising in the year before, taking the form:

$$AD_3 = e + aP_6 + bP_3 + cP_5$$

where: AD_3 = Advertising/Sales ratio in year 3
P_6 = Relative Perceived Power Factor
P_3 = Process Politicisaton Factor
P_5 = Political Contingencies Factor
e = Constant

In Table 12.24, using a double-log transformation, the best model (R=0.63) was for expenditure in the last year, and this took the form:

$$\log AD_2 = - e + a\log P_3 - bB_3 - cB_6$$

where: AD_2 = Advertising/Sales ratio in year 2
P_3 = Process Politicisation Factor
B_3 = Top management intervention
B_6 = Production department budgeting influence
e = Constant

The double-log transformation also produced a better prediction of advertising budget trend based on Positional/Participative Power (R=0.41).

As far as advertising budget ratios are concerned, it would seem that significant positive predictors of budget size are the relative perceived power of the marketing department (with particularly high beta values), the politicisation of process and the occurrence of political contingencies. Similarly budget trend is predicted by the positional and participative power of the marketing department. Negative predictors of budget size are top management intervention and the influence of other departments.

It seems therefore that in the advertising area, our central argument receives support – in this sample of companies it is possible to predict up to 50% of budget variation from the power and politics of the marketing organisation. There are qualifications to this conclusion to which we turn shortly, but at this stage we have support for the logic of our model of the power and politics of marketing budgeting.

Sales Promotion Budgets. Table 12.25 shows the regression models for power and politics factors, resource allocation process variables and sales promotion budgets, where the best model (R=0.57) is that for the year before budget, and takes the form:

Table 12.25: Power and Politics Factors, Resource Allocation Process Variables and Sales Promotion Budgets*

Variables in the Equation**	B	Beta	R	R^2	F	Significance of F
(a) This Year						
Factor 6 – Relative Perceived Power	.000511	.34	.42	.17	6.06	0.0040
BUD4 – Marketing department participation	.291	.24				
(Constant)	-.155					
(b) Last Year						
Factor 6 – Relative Perceived Power	.000477	.33	.33	.11	6.66	0.0126
(Constant)	.611					
(c) Year Before						
Factor 6 – Relative Perceived Power	.000448	.34	.57	.33	7.84	0.000
Factor 5 – Political Contingencies	.0000000187	.50				
Factor 3 – Process Politicisation	.000456	.30				
(Constant)	.108					

* Measured as power and politics factors, resource allocation process variables, and sales promotion expenditure/sales ratios.

** Method of regression was stepwise removal and entry of variables with probability F-to-enter = 0.05 and probability F-to-remove = 0.10.

$$SP_3 = e + aP_6 + bP_5 + cP_6$$

where: SP_3 = Sales Promotion/Sales ratio in year 3
         P_6 = Relative Perceived Power Factor
         P_5 = Political Contingencies Factor
         P_3 = Process Politicisation Factor
         e = Constant

Table 12.26 shows the result of a double-log transformation of the budgets and factors and the best model (R=0.68) is again that for budgets in the year before, but now takes the form:

$$\log SP_3 = - e + aB_2 + b\log P_5 - cB_6$$

where: SP_3 = Sales Promotion/Sales ratio in year 3
         B_2 = Marketing department control of process
         P_5 = Political Contingencies Factor
         B_6 = Production department influence

As shown in Table 12.27, the best model for the sales promotion budget trend was based on the Marketing Department Budgeting Control and Relative Perceived Power Factors, but with a fairly low R value (0.40).

In the sales promotion area positive predictors of budget size are found to be perceived power, the politicisation of process, and the occurrence of political contingencies, but also control of the budgeting process and the degree of marketing department participation in marketing budget decisions. The main negative predictor found was production department influence on marketing budgets. Thus far, the equations fit the model of the power and politics of marketing budgeting - budget size is related positively to marketing department power and politics and negatively to the influence of others - and we have further support for that model. One interesting exception is that in equation (b) in Table 12.26, finance department influence also acts as a positive indicator of budget size. This would follow if we argue that as budget size increases and there is more at stake, it is not unreasonable to expect a finance department to be more involved in budgeting, but what we cannot support is the implication in our conceptual model that such involvement will reduce budget size.

In a similar way, the trend in sales promotion budget is predicted by the relative perceived power of the marketing department and marketing department budgeting control. Again, this is in line with the argument and the conceptual model of the power and politics of budgeting.

It would seem that the sales promotion budget is also predictable through the power and politics model, and that up

Table 12.26: Power and Politics Factors, Resource Allocation Process Variables and Sales Promotion Budgets (double log transformation)*

Variables in the Equation**	B	Beta	R	R²	F	Significance of F
(a) This Year						
Log Factor 3 - Process Politicisation	2.37	.35	.54	.29	7.21	0.0004
BUD6 - Production department influence	-3.72	-.30				
Log Factor 5 - Political Contingencies	.38	.24				
(constant)	-9.45					
(b) Last Year						
Log Factor 3 - Process Politicisation	3.16	.48	.55	.30	10.00	0.0002
Bud 5 - Finance department influence	1.25	.29				
(constant)	-18.6					
(c) Year Before						
BUD2 - Marketing department control of process	2.34	.40	.68	.46	12.11	0.0000
Log Factor 5 - Political Contingencies	2.01	.40				
BUD6 - Production department influence	-3.18	-.25				
(Constant)	-16.84					

* Measured as logarithms of power and politics factors, resource allocation process variables, and logarithms of sales promotion/sales ratios.

** Method of regression was stepwise removal and entry of variables with probability F-to-enter = 0.05 and probability F-to-remove = 0.10.

Table 12.27: Power and Politics Factors, Resource Allocation Process Factors and Sales Promotion Budgets (double log transformation)*

Variables in the Equation**	B	Beta	R	R^2	F	Significance of F
Three Year Trend						
BUDFACTOR 2 – Marketing Department Budgeting Control	0.151	.31	.40	.16	6.69	0.0022
Log Factor 6 – Relative Perceived Power	0.367	.22				
(Constant)	0.418					

* Measured as logarithms of power and politics factors, resource allocation process factors, and logarithms of sales promotion/sales ratios.

** Method of regression was stepwise removal and entry of variables with probability F-to-enter = 0.05 and probability F-to-remove = 0.10.

to 46% of variation in budget size can be predicted in this way.

Other Marketing Expenditure. In regression on the 'other' marketing expenditure budget component, using the power and politics and resource allocation process variables, as shown in Table 12.28, the best model (R=0.40) is for the most recent year's budget, with the form:

$$OB_1 = e - aB_3 + bB_5$$

where: OB_1 = Other Budget in year 1
        B_3 = Top management intervention
        B_5 = Finance department influence
        e = Constant

A better fit (R=0.66) was obtained with a log transformation of the other budget ratio (Table 12.29), giving the equation:

$$logOB_3 = - e - aB_3 + bB_2 - cB_1$$

where: OB_3 = Other Budget in year 3
        B_3 = Top management intervention
        B_2 = Marketing department control of process
        B_1 = Sophistication of budgeting methods

A similar result was obtained with a double-log transformation (Table 12.30), where there were signs of a positive association between the Marketing Department Participation Factor and budget size, but the best model (R=0.64) was:

$$logOB_3 = - e - aB_3 + bB_2 + clog\,P_5$$

where: OB_3 = Other Budget in year 3
        B_3 = Top management intervention
        B_2 = Marketing department control of process
        P_5 = Political Contingencies Factor

In taking the budgeting process factors, instead of the variables, in Table 12.31, the major predictors of budget size were found to be the Marketing Department Budgeting Control and Process Politicisation Factors.

In the area of other marketing expenditure, the regression models suggest that positive predictors of budget size are marketing department participation in budget setting, marketing department control of the budgeting process, political contingencies and the politicisation of process. Negative predictors are top management intervention in budgeting and the sophistication of budgeting

Table 12.28: Power and Politics Factors, Resource Allocation Process Variables and Other Marketing Expenditure*

Variables in the Equation**	B	Beta	R	R^2	F	Significance of F
(a) This Year						
BUD3 - Top management intervention	-0.986	-.35	.40	.16	5.23	0.0075
BUD5 - Finance department influence	0.474	.25				
(Constant)	2.18					
(b) Last Year						
BUD4 - Marketing department participation	0.696	.35	.35	.12	7.07	0.0105
(c) Year Before						
BUD4 - Marketing department participation	0.783	.37	.37	.13	7.56	0.0083

* Measured as power and politics factors, resource allocation process variables and other marketing expenditure/sales ratios.

** Method of regression was stepwise removal and entry of variables with probability F-to-enter = 0.05 and probability F-to-remove = 0.10.

Table 12.29: **Power and Politics Factors, Resource Allocation Process Variables and Other Marketing Expenditure (log transformations)***

Variables in the Equation**	B	Beta	R	R²	F	Significance of F
(a) This Year						
BUD4 – Marketing department participation	1.47	.41	.45	.20	7.10	0.0018
BUD5 – Finance department influence	0.92	.24				
(Constant)	-8.53					
(b) Last Year						
BUD4 – Marketing department participation	1.51	.41	.41	.17	10.04	0.0021
(Constant)	-6.49					
(c) Year Before						
BUD3 – Top Management intervention	-2.76	-.45	.66	.43	11.77	0.0000
BUD2 – Marketing department control of process	2.14	.39				
BUD1 – Sophistication of budgeting methods	-0.000196	-.30				
(Constant)	-5.02					

* Measured as power and politics factors, resource allocation process variables and logarithms of other marketing expenditure/sales ratios.

** Method of regression was stepwise removal and entry of variables with probability F-to-enter = 0.05 and probability F-to-remove = 0.10.

Table 12.30: Power and Politics Factors, Resource Allocation Process Variables and Other Marketing Expenditure (double log transformation)*

Variables in the Equation**	B	Beta	R	R^2	F	Significance of F
(a) This Year						
BUD4 – Marketing department participation	1.36	.37	.37	.14	8.22	0.0060
(Constant)	-6.06					
(b) Last Year						
BUD4 – Marketing department participation	1.52	.41	.41	.17	8.99	0.0044
(Constant)	-6.75					
(c) Year Before						
BUD3 – Top management intervention	-2.87	-.46	.64	.41	9.51	0.0001
BUD2 – Marketing department control of process	1.72	.31				
Log Factor 5 – Political Contingencies	1.29	.26				
(Constant)	-9.16					

*   Measured as logarithms of power and politics factors, resource allocation process variables and logarithms of other marketing expenditure/sales ratios.
** Method of regression was stepwise removal and entry of variables with probability F-to-enter = 0.05 and probability F-to-remove = 0.10.

Table 12.31: Power and Politics Variables, Resource Allocation Process Factors and Other Marketing Expenditure (double log transformation)*

Variables in the Equation**	B	Beta	R	R^2	F	Significance of F
(a) This Year						
BUDFACTOR 2 – Marketing Department Budget Control	0.572	.29	.44	.19	9.37	0.0002
Log Factor 3 – Process Politicisation	1.602	.27				
(Constant)	-14.02					
(b) Last Year						
BUDFACTOR 2 – Marketing Department Budget Control	0.811	.31	.48	.24	10.37	0.0001
Log Factor 3 – Process Politicisation	1.93	.29				
(Constant)	-16.14					
(c) Year Before						
BUDFACTOR 2 – Marketing Department Budget Control	0.811	.33	.52	.27	11.63	0.0000
Log Factor 3 – Process Politicisation	1.93	.31				
(Constant)	-18.67					
(d) Three Year Trend						
Log Factor 6 – Relative Perceived Power	.16	.27	.27	.07	5.24	0.0252

* Measured as logarithms of power and politics factors, resource allocation process factors, and logarithms of other marketing expenditure/sales ratios.
** Method of regression was stepwise removal and entry of variables with probability F-to-enter = 0.05 and probability F-to-remove = 0.10.

methods. Surprisingly, as with sales promotion, finance department influence is a positive predictor.

While the predictive variables are somewhat different - relating primarily to the resource allocation process as such - this area too offers support to the model, in the sense that control of the process by the marketing department together with its politicisation appear to predict budget size, and up to 40% of budget variation.

The trend in other marketing expenditure is predicted by the perceived power of the marketing department (R=0.27) - again offering support to the argument developed.

Total Marketing Budgets. In regressing the power and politics factors and allocation process variables on total marketing budget size, the results are shown in Table 12.32. The best model here (R= 0.70) was for the year before budget, and took the form:

$$MB_3 = -e + aP_6 + bB_4 + cP_5 + dP_3$$

where: MB_3 = Marketing Budget in year 3
P_3 = Process Politicisation Factor
P_5 = Political Contingencies Factor
P_6 = Relative Perceived Power Factor
B_4 = Marketing department participation
e = Constant

Taking a double-log transformation gave the model for the last year's budget (R=0.72) as shown in Table 12.33:

$$\log MB_2 = -e - aB_3 + b\log P_3$$

where: MB_2 = Marketing Budget in year 2
B_3 = Top management intervention
P_3 = Process Politicisation Factor
e = Constant

The best model of the trend in total marketing budget size (R=0.43) is shown in Table 12.33 and took the form:

$$\log MB_T = e - aBF_3 + b\log P_6 - c\log P_5$$

where: MB_T = Marketing Budget Trend
BF_3 = Production/R&D Marketing Budgeting Influence Factor
P_5 = Political Contingencies Factor
P_6 = Relative Perceived Power Factor
e = Constant

In turning to total marketing budget size, the models suggest that positive predictors of the size of the marketing budget and its trend are the relative perceived power of the

Table 12.32: Power and Politics Factors, Resource Allocation Process Variables and Total Marketing Budgets*

Variables in the Equation**	B	Beta	R	R^2	F	Significance of F
(a) This Year						
Factor 6 – Relative Perceived Power	0.0188	.45	.54	.29	11.89	0.0000
BUD4 – Marketing department participation	0.836	.28				
(Constant)	-0.431					
(b) Last Year						
Factor 6 – Relative Perceived Power	0.0175	.42	.54	.29	11.09	0.0001
BUD4 – Marketing department participation	1.098	.32				
(Constant)	-0.916					
(c) Year Before						
Factor 6 – Relative Perceived Power	0.014	.34	.70	.48	11.29	0.000
BUD4 – Marketing department participation	0.646	.18				
Factor 5 – Political Contingencies	0.00000000589	.50				
Factor 3 – Process Politicisation	0.022	.47				
(Constant)	-0.08					

* Measured as power and politics factors, resource allocation process variables and total marketing expenditure/sales ratios.

** Method of regression was stepwise removal and entry of variables with probability F-to-enter = 0.05 and probability F-to-remove = 0.10.

Table 12.33: Power and Politics Factors, Resource Allocation Process Variables and Total Marketing Budgets (double log transformation)*

Variables in the Equation**	B	Beta	R	R^2	F	Significance of F
(a) This Year						
BUD3 – Top management intervention	-1.24	-.48	.68	.46	22.63	0.0000
Log Factor 3 – Process Politicisation	1.19	.45				
(Constant)	-1.87					
(b) Last Year						
BUD3 – Top management intervention	-1.25	-.48	.72	.51	25.82	0.0000
Log Factor 3 – Process Politicisation	1.32	.48				
(Constant)	-2.54					
(c) Year Before						
BUD3 – Top management intervention	-1.68	-.46	.67	.45	17.75	0.000
Log Factor 3 – Process Politicisation	1.63	.43				
(Constant)	-3.41					

* Measured as logarithms of power and politics factors, resource allocation process variables, and logarithms of total marketing budget/sales ratios.

** Method of regression was stepwise removal and entry of variables with probability F-to-enter = 0.05 and probability F-to-remove = 0.10.

Table 12.34: Power and Politics Factors, Resource Allocation Process Factors and Total Marketing Budgets (double log transformation)*

Variables in the Equation**	B	Beta	R	R²	F	Significance of F
(a) This Year						
Log Factor 3 - Process Politicisation	0.712	.23	.60	.36	11.70	0.0000
BUDFACTOR 2 - Marketing Department Budget Control	0.236	.23				
Log Factor 2 - Positional/Participative Power	1.082	.25				
Log Factor 6 - Relative Perceived Power	0.880	.23				
(Constant)	-14.18					
(b) Last Year						
Log Factor 3 - Process Politicisation	1.22	.45	.52	.27	13.47	0.0000
BUDFACTOR 1 - General Management Control of Process	-0.25	-.23				
(Constant)	-2.81					
(c) Year Before						
Log Factor 3 - Process Politicisation	1.54	.42	.42	.17	14.56	0.003
(Constant)	-6.09					
(d) Three Year Trend						
BUDFACTOR 3 - Production/R&D Marketing Budgeting Influence	-0.159	-.27	.43	.19	5.22	0.0026
Log Factor 6 - Relative Perceived Power	0.171	.25				
Log Factor 5 - Political Contingencies	-0.054	-.23				
(Constant)	0.978					

* Measured as logarithms of power and politics factors, resource allocation process factors, and logarithms of total marketing expenditure/sales ratios.
** Method of regression was stepwise removal and entry of variables with probability F-to-enter = 0.05 and probability F-to-remove = 0.10.

Table 12.35: Marketing Manpower Trend*

Variables in the Equation**	B	Beta	R	R²	F	Significance of F
(a) Power and Politics Factors						
(i) Factors to Manpower Trend						
Factor 1 – Politics of Information Access	0.000195	.27	.33	.11	6.97	0.0014
Factor 2 – Positional/Participative Power	-0.00171	-.22				
(Constant)	3.585					
(ii) Factors to Log Manpower Trend						
Factor 5 – Political Contingencies	-0.000000002	-.21	.29	.09	5.25	0.0066
Factor 1 – Politics of Information Access	0.0000057	.20				
(Constant)	0.97					
(iii) Log Factors to Manpower Trend						
Log Factor 1 – Politics of Information Access	0.495	.38	.50	.25	11.40	0.0000
Log Factor 5 – Political Contingencies	-0.116	-.23				
Log Factor 2 – Positional/Participative Power	-0.466	-.21				
(Constant)	3.91					
(iv) Log Factors to Log Manpower Trend						
Log Factor 1 – Politics of Information Access	0.166	.32	.47	.22	9.36	0.0000
Log Factor 5 – Political Contingencies	-0.049	-.24				
Log Factor 2 – Positional/Participative Power	-0.181	-.21				
(Constant)	1.45					

Variables in the Equation**	B	Beta	R	R^2	F	Significance of F
(b) Power and Politics and Budgeting Variables						
(i) Factors to Manpower Trend						
Factor 2 - Positional/Participative Power	-0.000239	-.28	.28	.08	6.24	0.0148
(Constant)	4.07					
(ii) Log Factors and Budgeting Variables to Manpower Trend						
Log Factor 1 - Politics of Information Access	.56	.36				
Log Factor 5 - Political Contingencies	-.155	-.28				
BUD4 - Marketing department participation	.268	.23				
(Constant)	.345					
(iii) Log Factors and Budgeting Variables to Log Manpower Trend						
Log Factor 1 - Politics of Information Access	.22	.35	.46	.22	5.94	0.0012
Log Factor 5 - Political Contingencies	-.06	-.28				
BUD4 - Marketing department participation	.13	.27				
(Constant)	-.14					

* Measured as marketing employees this year/marketing employees the year before.
** Method of regression was stepwise removal and entry of variables with probability F-to-enter = 0.05 and probability F-to-remove = 0.10.

marketing department, the existence of political contingencies (except in the case of budget trend), process politicisation, and the positional/participative power of the marketing department, together with the budgeting process variable of marketing department participation and the marketing department budgeting control factor. On the other hand, negative predictors are top management intervention, and the resource allocation process factors of general management control and production/R&D influence.

In this sense, the model of marketing resource allocation developed here, and its underlying hypothesis receive support - marketing budget size can be predicted on the basis of marketing department power and political strength, and the control by the marketing department or others of the resource allocation process. The models developed explain up to 50% of budget variation in this way.

Marketing Manpower Trend. As shown in Table 12.35, the best model for marketing manpower trend (R=0.50) took the form:

$$MP_T = e + a\log P_1 - b\log P_5 - c\log P_2$$

where: MP_T = Manpower Trend in Marketing
P_1 = Politics of Information Access Factor
P_2 = Positional/Participative Power Factor
P_5 = Political Contingencies Factor

It would seem that the position regarding marketing manpower trends and power and politics is a little different to that found with financial marketing budgets.

Positive predictors of manpower trend were found to be: the politics of information access, and marketing department participation in the budgeting process, while negative predictors were the positional/participative power of the marketing department and the existence of political contingencies. We have already associated information access with manpower growth, so its predictive value comes as no surprise. Similarly, we established earlier that manpower growth was negatively related to size, which would be expected since proportional changes are larger for smaller organisations anyway, but the relationship persists in spite of log transformations because growth rates are apparently lower for established, integrated marketing departments than for those in the process of growth (see pp. *382-88*). The models are therefore consistent with our earlier findings.

In this area we have not been able to establish any clear positive link between power and politics and manpower increments, in the way suggested by our model of the power and politics of marketing. To some extent this may reflect the contamination of our power measures with structural/manpower-related characteristics, but our model is not supported in this resource area.

Other Marketing Resources. The trend in other marketing resources showed little relationship to the other variables and the only results reported are those in Table 12.36, where the Politics of Information Access factor shows a small relationship with other marketing resource trend (R=0.18).

As far as other marketing resources trends are concerned, broadly similar conclusions are drawn as in the case of manpower trends – the predictive value of the model is low, the R^2 is very small, and we believe the politics of information access to be to some degree a size-related variable.

As in the case of manpower trends, our model of power and politics finds no support for this resource type.

Discussion

The regression models described above demonstrate the relationships found between the marketing department power and politics factors, the marketing resource allocation process variables and factors, and resource outcomes in terms of budget to sales ratios, marketing manpower trends, and the trend in other marketing resources. For the most part these relationships were not linear and the variables had to be transformed into linear functions through the use of logarithms, as described in the preceding sections.

In general terms, we demonstrated evidence of what is taken to be the impact of precedent and incrementalism in marketing budget setting, and further we have found it possible to predict resource outcomes using the measurements of marketing department power and politicisation as positive predictors, and the power, influence or intervention of others in resource allocation as negative predictors. In this sense, having pursued the exploratory objectives discussed earlier, we find support for the model of the power and politics of marketing budgeting, although it should be noted that this support is found mainly in relation to financial budgets, rather than in marketing manpower or other resource increments.

However, the comments above are organised around the resource outcomes modelled, and this requires the consideration now of the implications of the models for our hypotheses regarding power, politics and resource allocation processes as general organisational attributes.

Power and Resource Outcomes. The hypothesis that the power of the marketing department – or at least its power relative to others – would relate positively to the size of resource allocations and the trend in those allocations, given the

Table 12.36: Other Marketing Resources

Variables in the Equation**	B	Beta	R	R^2	F	Significance of F
(a) Power and Politics Factors						
(i) Log Factors to other Resources Trend						
Log Factor 1 - Politics of Information Access	.22	.18	.18	.03	4.06	0.0461
(Constant)						
(b) Power and Politics Factors and Resource Allocation Process Variables						
Log Factor 1 - Politics of Information Access	.219	.18	.18	.03	4.06	0.0461
(Constant)	1.62					

** Method of regression was stepwise removal and entry of variables with probability F-to-enter = 0.05 and probability F-to-remove = 0.10.

existence of certain contingencies, is supported in a number of ways.

Positional/Participative Power (which includes the key strategic contingencies measures) related positively to the trend on advertising budgets (Table 12.23 and 12.24) and to total marketing budget size in the way predicted by our theoretical argument. This factor, in fact, also related negatively to marketing manpower trend – for the reasons discussed earlier, i.e. mainly that growth rate correlates negatively with existing size.

A more pervasive relationship was between Relative Perceived Power and resource outcomes. This factor related positively to advertising budget size (Table 12.23) sales promotion budget size and trend (Table 12.25), the trend in other marketing expenditure (Table 12.31), and the total marketing budget size and trend (Table 12.32). Interestingly, this factor did not relate significantly to marketing manpower trends or other marketing resource trends. This association is also supportive to our argument (with the qualification expressed below) – to be perceived as powerful relative to others is apparently significantly associated with large and growing resource allocations.

It follows too from the earlier logic that it would be expected that the measure of Political Contingencies would interact with the power measures in predicting resource outcomes (bearing in mind that the Political Contingencies factor is a positive measure of scarcity, importance and certain elements of uncertainty). This was found to be generally so, although mainly in the case of Relative Perceived Power. (This is partly obscured in certain of the models cited which do not show the beta values of those variables marginally failing the F-to-enter criterion for entry to an equation). This was found with advertising, sales promotion, other expenditure and total marketing budgets. In all these instances the Political Contingencies factor is related positively to budget size – i.e. budget size is related positively to our measure of scarcity, importance and uncertainty when taken in conjunction with a measure of power. Interestingly, the Political Contingencies factor also shows a negative relationship with total budget trend and marketing manpower trend – which is believed to reflect the same reason as above, that resource growth rates generally correlate negatively with size and hence with importance of resource allocations.

On this basis it is suggested that the study supports the proposition that power and resource allocation outcomes are related. In the models built we are taking measures of power as predictors of resource outcomes, and in this way they are supportive of the argument developed and its underlying hypotheses.

None the less, it is important to recognise one major

qualification to this case, to which we have referred above. That qualification relates to the direction of causality, since what we have demonstrated is primarily association not known cause-and-effect. While we have argued that the power of a sub-unit leads to certain resource allocations and increments, it could equally well be argued that those resource allocations create and contribute to the sub-unit's power – particularly in the sense of perceived power. The likelihood is that there is some form of dynamic, two-way relationship, in that power creates the ability to claim resources, while that power is influenced by resources gained in the past and is changed by success or failure in gaining further resources. It is not possible to untangle this interaction with the essentially exploratory data collected here – it is enough for present purposes to have demonstrated the power/resource association, which has so far been lacking in the literature of marketing resource allocation.

Politics and Resources. The relationship between the political behaviour phenomena measured and resource allocations also provides some support for the hypotheses developed, although not with all the measures used.

The Politics of Information Access factor did not enter any of the budget equations, and appeared only in relation to the trend in marketing manpower and the trend in other marketing resources (Tables 12.25 and 12.26), and then only with a relatively weak predictive value. The Politics of Information Restriction factor did not enter any of the equations.

However, what did emerge as a significant predictor was the Process Politicisation factor. In the models developed this factor demonstrated a positive relationship to: advertising budgets (Tables 12.23 and 12.24) sales promotion budgets (Tables 12.25 and 12.26), other marketing expenditure (Table 12.31) and the total marketing budget (Tables 12.32 to 12.34) with particularly high beta-values in the equations for advertising and sales promotion budgets.

This suggests that the evidence is supportive of our hypothesis that marketing budgeting is capable of analysis as a political process, and that political behaviour is significant to gaining resources.

However, given the nature of the data and its analysis there remains the problem of causality. While politicisation would appear to be a good predictor of budget size, it is necessary to accept that the data are equally supportive of the converse – that budget size is a good predictor of the emergence of political behaviour. As in the case of power and resources, it follows from the earlier argument that there is likely to be a complex interaction between the two variables in question, which is not susceptible to analysis with these present data. Again as in the case of power, though, what we have established is an association between political behaviour or politicisation and marketing resource allocation hitherto not evidenced in the literature.

Resource Allocation Processes and Resource Outcomes. It was argued earlier that the marketing resource allocation process was implicitly political, and it was possible to extract factors relating to the control of that process. These factors related to resource outcomes very much in the way suggested by our conceptual model of the power and politics of marketing budgeting: control of the process by the marketing department was positively associated with budget size, control by general management was negatively related to budget size, and generally other department influences were also negative predictors.

More specifically, the marketing department participation variable was positively related to sales promotion budget size (Table 12.25), but more particularly to other expenditure and to total marketing budget size (Tables 12.30 and 12.32). Interestingly this variable was also related in the same way to marketing manpower trend. In a similar way the marketing department control variable predicted sales promotion and total budgets. This was reflected in the Marketing Department Budgeting Control factor which entered the equations for sales promotion, other marketing expenditure and the total budget. This is in line with the hypothesis that control of process by a sub-unit is associated with larger resource outcomes for that controlling sub-unit.

Following the same logic was the finding of a negative relationship between the top management intervention variable and budget size: in other marketing expenditure and for the total marketing budget. In the case of the total marketing budget, this was reflected in the General Management Budgeting Control factor (Table 12.34). Similarly, the influence of production department was a negative predictor of budget sizes and total marketing budget trend. One exception to this was influence of the finance department which was a positive predictor for sales promotion budget size and trend.

As before, certain qualifications are necessary to any conclusions drawn. In the models presented we have evidence that control of the budgeting process by the marketing department is a positive predictor of budget size, while top management control and generally the influence of other departments are negative predictors, which is supportive of the political model of marketing budgeting which was described earlier. However, what should be accepted is that it may be that large budget size is, in fact, the independent rather than the dependent, and it is this large budget size

Table 12.37: Power and Politics, Resource Allocation Processes, Marketing Resources and Profitability*

Variables in the Equation**	B	Beta	R	R²	F	Significance of F
(a) Profitability (This Year)						
Factor 1 – Politics of Information Access	0.0026	.33	.86	.75	11.07	0.0000
Factor 4 – Politics of Information Restriction	0.3071	.27				
ADPERLY – Advertising/budget (This Year)	2.060	.41				
BUD7 – R&D department budgeting influence	-8.40	-.42				
BUD6 – Production department budgeting influence	-5.01	-.35				
Factor 5 – Political Contingencies	-0.000000039	-.24				
BUD1 – Sophistication of budgeting methods	-1.98	-.23				
(Constant)	26.02					
(b) Profitability (This year)*						
Factor 1 – Politics of Information Access	0.00403	.49	.62	.38	8.99	0.0001
Factor 6 – Relative Perceived Power	0.0229	.36				
Factor 2 – Positional/Participative Power	0.0136	.36				
(Constant)	-1.59					
(c) Profitability (Last Year)						
BUD6 – Production department budgeting influence	-5.87	-.40	.40	.16	6.69	0.0139
(Constant)	12.70					

(d) Profitability (Year Before)

(e) Trend in Profitability (This Year/Last Year)

	B	Beta	R	R²	F	p
OBPERYB – Other marketing budget (year before)	29.17	.66	.73	.53	12.87	0.0000
Factor 5 – Political Contingencies	-0.00000009	-.34				
BUD1 – Sophistication of budgeting methods	45.61	.30				
(Constant)	-64.90					

(f) Trend in Profitability (This Year/Last Year)***

	B	Beta	R	R²	F	p
OBPERYB – Other marketing budget (year before)	19.69	.41	.61	.38	13.31	0.0000
Factor 3 – Process Politicisation	0.37	.37				
(Constant)	59.56					

(g) Trend in Profitability (Last Year/Year Before)

	B	Beta	R	R²	F	p
OBPERTY – Other marketing budget (this year)	-31.64	-.52	.56	.31	7.75	0.0017
Factor 2 – Positional/Participative Power	0.35	.46				
(Constant)	47.85					

(h) Trend in Profitability (This Year/Last Year)

	B	Beta	R	R²	F	p
BUD5 – Finance department budgeting influence	-54.49	-.42	.57	.32	8.03	0.0014
RES21 – Other marketing resources trend	43.47	.37				
(Constant)	137.40					

* Measured as power and politics factors, resource allocation process variables, resource outcomes and profit/sales.

** Method of regression was stepwise removal and entry of variables with probability F-to-enter = 0.05 and probability F-to-remove = 0.10.

*** Measured as power and politics factors, resource allocation process factors, resource outcomes and profit/sales.

which creates the process characteristics. Again, it is noted that the complexity of this interaction defies further analysis with the data available, but it must be accepted that we have demonstrated association, and predictive relationships which support the argument that marketing resource allocation may be modelled as a political process.

POWER, POLITICS AND PERFORMANCE

The final issue deserving some attention is the implication of what has gone before - the power and politics of marketing resource allocation - for the 'bottom-line', i.e. corporate performance in terms of profitability and growth.

This issue has been recurrent throughout, since we note both the lack of analysis of the relationship between politicisation and performance (pp. *471-73*) and the problems inherent in validly measuring corporate performance (pp. *472-73*). We are, in fact, constrained here both by the latter problem and also be a shortage of cases with which to investigate the relationship. None the less, we can model the relationship between marketing resource allocation and performance in the following ways. In each case we have regressed power and politics factors, resource allocation process variables and resource outcomes against a measure of corporate performance.

Profitability

Table 12.37 shows the regression equations for profitability in the three years studied. The best models have R=0.86 and R=0.62 and predict current year profitability with the following forms:

$$PROFIT_1 = e + aP_1 + bP_4 + cADPERLY - dB_7 - fB_6 - gP_5 - hB_1$$

where: $PROFIT_1$ = Profitability in year 1
P_1 = Politics of Information Access Factor
P_4 = Politics of Information Restriction Factor
ADPERLY = Advertising/Sales ratio last year
B_7 = R&D department budgeting influence
B_6 = Production department budgeting influence
B_5 = Finance department budgeting influence
P_5 = Political Contingencies Factor
B_1 = Sophistication of budgeting methods
e = Constant

$$\text{PROFIT}_1 = -e + aP_1 + bP_6$$

where: PROFIT_1 = Profitability in year 1
P_1 = Politics of Information Access Factor
P_4 = Politics of Information Restriction Factor
e = Constant

In the first equation, current profitability is related positively to the main politics factors of information access and restriction and to the previous year's advertising expenditure and negatively to the influence of other departments over marketing budgeting, political contingencies (of scarcity, importance and uncertainty) and the sophistication of budgeting methods.

In the second equation we are predicting profitability through the politics of information access, and the positional/participative power and relative perceived power of the marketing department.

In examining the trends in profitability the best models where R=0.73 and 0.61, took the following forms:

$$\text{PTYPLY} = -e + a\text{OBPERYB} - bP_5 + cB_1$$

where: PTYPLY = Profitability (this year)/profitability (last year)
OBPERYB= Other marketing expenditure/sales ratio (year before)
P_5 = Political contingencies Factor
B_1 = Sophistication of budgeting methods
e = Constant

$$\text{PTYPLY} = e + a\text{OBPERYB} + bP_3$$

where: PTYPLY = Profitability (this year)/Profitability (last year)
OBPERYB = Other marketing expenditure/sales ratio (year before)
P_3 = Process Politicisation Factor
e = Constant

If we then categorise the effect of the various predictors according to whether they are positive or negative, the following picture emerges:

Factors acting as positive predictors of profitability level	Factors acting as negative predictors of profitability level
Politics of Information Access Factor	R&D department budgeting influence
Politics of Information Restriction Factor	Production department budgeting influence
Relative Perceived Power Factor	Finance department budgeting influence
Positional/Participative Power Factor	Political Contingencies Factor
	Sophistication of budgeting

Factors acting as positive predictors of profitability trends	Factors acting as negative predictors of profitability trends
Other marketing budget ratio (year before)	Political Contingencies Factor
Sophistication of budgeting methods	Other marketing budget ratio (this year)
Positional/Participative Power Factor	Finance department budgeting influence
Other marketing resource trend	
Process Politicisation Factor	

The tentative conclusion is that the power and politics of the marketing department relate positively to corporate profitability, together with expenditures on advertising and other resources, while the influence of others in marketing budgeting and political contingencies relate negatively to profit performance.

On the face of the evidence, we might claim that the data suggest that a powerful marketing department with political strength and a consequently high advertising spend creates high profits, apparently using unsophisticated budgeting methods, in contrast with the negative effect of intervention and influence of others in marketing budgeting. This may indeed be a fair interpretation, and it is certainly worthy of note since it is central support to our thesis.

However, a note of caution should be taken, in that it might well be argued that it is, in fact, lower profit performance which brings about management intervention in budgeting (and indeed, the use of unsophisticated budgeting 'rules of thumb' as control devices), rather than vice versa and that it is only when profits are high that companies can 'afford' marketing departments. This creates a somewhat less optimistic picture of the relationship between marketing and performance.

The position regarding profitability trends is similar – power and politics and marketing resources are the main positive predictors, while finance department influence is the main negative indicator. Interestingly, however, the current year 'other' budget for marketing is also a negative predictor, suggesting that when profits have grown the 'other' budget is lower this year, and vice versa. It may be that this anomaly represents addition and subtraction from this budget to influence profitability, although clearly other explanations are possible.

Sales Revenue Trend

The best model of sales growth (R=0.78) shown in Table 12.38 takes the form:

$$STYSLY = e + aADPERYB - bADPERTY + cRES20 + dB_4 - fB_5 - gB_6$$

where: STYSLY = Sales (this year)/Sales (last year)
ADPERYB= Advertising budget ratio (year before)
ADPERTY= Advertising budget ratio (this year)
B_4 = Marketing department budgeting participation
B_5 = Finance department budgeting influence
B_6 = Production department budgeting influence
e = constant

Perhaps the most surprising finding is the negative relationship between current year advertising and sales growth in the current year compared to the last.

If the variables from the equations in Table 12.38 are categorised into those acting as positive predictors and those acting as negative predictors the following picture emerges:

Factors acting as positive predictors of sales growth	Factors acting as negative predictors of sales growth
Advertising Budget ratio (year before)	Advertising Budget ratio (this year)
Marketing manpower trend	Finance department budgeting influence
Marketing department budgeting participation	Production department bugeting influence
Process Politicisation Factor	General Management Control of Budgeting Factor

Table 12.38: Power and Politics, Resource Allocation Processes, Marketing Resources and Sales Trends*

Variables in the Equation**	B	Beta	R	R^2	F	Significance of F
(a) Sales Trend (This Year/Last Year)						
ADPERYB – Advertising budget (year before)	11.46	1.15	.78	.61	10.61	0.0000
ADPERTY – Advertising budget (this year)	-9.56	-.92				
RES20 – Marketing manpower trend	3.47	.31				
BUD4 – Marketing department budgeting participation	2.84	.22				
BUD5 – Finance department budgeting influence	-3.46	-.25				
BUD6 – Production department budgeting influence	-8.08	-.25				
(Constant)	106.67					
(b) Sales Trend (Last Year/Year Before)						
RES20 – Marketing manpower trend	6.06	.29	.29	.09	4.33	0.0432
(Constant)	103.11					
(c) Sales Trend (Last Year/Year Before)						
RES20 – Marketing manpower trend	7.47	.33	.41	.17	5.96	0.0044
Factor 3 – Process Politicisation	0.079	.30				
(Constant)	95.20					

(d) Sales Trend (This Year/Year Before)

ADPERYB – Advertising budget (year before)	11.24	1.20	.71	.51	11.25	0.0000
ADPERTY – Advertising budget (this year)	-9.23	-.91			
BUD4 – Marketing department budgeting participation	3.59	.26			
(Constant)	96.33				

(e) Sales Trend (This Year/Year Before)***

ADPERYB – Advertising budget (year before)	10.45	1.21	.62	.39	8.91	0.0001
ADPERTY – Advertising budget (this year)	-8.20	-1.04			
BUDFACTOR1 – General Management Control of Budgeting	-1.70	-.25			
(Constant)	95.45				

* Measured as power and politics factors, resource allocation process variables, resource outcomes and sales revenue trends.

** Method of regression was stepwise removal and entry of variables with probability F-to-enter = 0.05 and probability F-to-remove = 0.10.

*** Measured as power and politics factors, resource allocation process factors, resource outcomes and sales revenue trends.

451

It would seem therefore that high sales growth may be predicted from earlier advertising expenditure, manpower resources gained by the marketing department and the degree of participation in setting marketing budgets, and the degree of politicisation of resource allocation process. Conversely, current advertising expenditure and control of the marketing budgeting process by others act as negative predictors of sales growth.

Again it would appear that the power and politics of marketing resource allocation are associated with high sales performance, and that this association is supportive of the notion that a high level of marketing department power and politicisation may be associated with high performance.

CONCLUSIONS

What has been described here amounts to an exploratory study of marketing resource allocation, which compares structural, participative, and positional variables taken as measures of the power of the marketing sub-unit, and process variables concerned with the politicisation, and control and influence of resource allocation processes, with resource outcomes, in a study of medium-sized UK manufacturing firms. That study was essentially exploratory and the findings presented are indications of support for the argument developed in the earlier part of the book, rather than conclusive in any real sense.

Firstly, the chapter reviewed the structural and process variables which were measured to indicate the power and politics of marketing resource allocations, and the relationships between these variables were explored, suggesting that the positional, participative and perceptual measures of power showed some consistency, and were related to certain of the political and contingency measurements, and that the political measures of information control, sales forecasting influence and politicisation also showed some consistency and were related to various of the measurements of power and contingencies.

With this foundation provided, the large number of measurements of power, politics and political and strategic contingencies were reduced by factor analysis, providing six marketing department power and politics factors. These factors were the 'politics of information access', reflecting the access gained by the marketing department to corporate and financial information; 'positional/participative power', reflecting the department's integration level, CME responsibilities, and the strategic contingencies of influence, connectedness and immediacy, as well as the marketing paradigm; 'process politicisation' summarising the political nature of marketing resource allocation and the importance to success of various political influence acts;

the 'politics of information restriction' describing the
ability of the marketing department, relative to the power of
others, to control access to marketing information;
'political contingencies' summarising uncertainty, scarcity
and importance; and 'relative perceived power', reflecting
status and departmental ranking relative to others.

A number of significant correlations were found between
the power and politics factors and resource allocations.

The variables relating to the marketing resource
allocation process were also factored to produce three
measurements: 'general management control of marketing
budgeting' which reflected the intervention of top management
in marketing budgeting and the influence of the finance and
corporate planning departments over marketing budgets;
'marketing department budgeting control', summarising the
perceived control of the marketing department over the
process, together with the degree of participation of the
marketing department in the budget decision and the
sophistication of budgeting methods; and 'production/R&D
marketing budgeting influence'.

These factors also showed some relationships with
resource outcomes.

Next we turned to the question of the prediction of
marketing resource outcomes with the factors identified.

Evidence was found that invariably the best predictor of
budget sizes (both absolute and relative) were earlier budget
sizes. This was taken as an indication of the incremental
nature of budgeting and the impact of preceedent, as well as
acting as some confirmation of the stability of budget/sales
ratios in marketing.

Then, the power and politics factors and the resource
allocation process measurements were used to build a number
of regression models to demonstrate the relationship between
the power and politics of marketing and resource allocation
processes and resource outcomes.

These models demonstrated variously that marketing
budget allocations - for advertising, sales promotion, other
expenditure, and in total - could be predicted by the
measures of the relative power of the marketing department,
(incorporating measures of the strategic contingencies of
connectedness, influence and immediacy), political
contingencies, process politicisation, and control and
influence characteristics of the marketing resource
allocation process. These models of association support the
thesis advanced here - that marketing resource outcomes can
be modelled as political outcomes, reflecting the power and
political strength of the marketing department compared to
others in the organisation, although there remains some
inevitable qualification to any drawing conclusions due to
the difficulty of determining the direction of causality.

Finally, we examined the relationship between the

political characteristics and marketing resource outcomes in the companies and corporate performance in terms of profitability and sales growth.

In the case of the level of profitability – again the profit ratio was predicted by the relative power and political strength of the marketing department and the resource outcomes associated with that strength.

In studying trends in sales revenue the position was less clear, but generally high marketing department power and politicisation were associated with high performance.

Having demonstrated a certain degree of support for our model of the power and politics of resource allocation in marketing, what remains to be done is to attempt to synthesise the conceptual argument developed and the exploratory empirical evidence to formulate more precisely an organisational and political perspective on marketing budgeting, and to consider the implications for marketing management of what has been achieved. These concluding sections are presented in Part IV of the book.

PART FOUR

Conclusions

13

Synthesis: An Organisational/Political Perspective on Marketing Budgeting

INTRODUCTION

The study which has been presented here (following, its immediate antecedents (Piercy and Evans, 1983; Piercy, 1985)) included three broad components – two conceptual and one empirical. In the first instance, we reviewed marketing budgeting or resource allocation concepts and descriptions as they are presented in the extant theory of marketing. Secondly, we looked to other disciplines for new insights and empirical findings relevant to the analysis of resource allocation issues in marketing. Thirdly, on the basis of that integration, and the reappraisal of marketing structure and process and decision making outcomes which it implies, an attempt was made to evaluate the resulting information-structure-power model of marketing and the power and politics of marketing budgeting, in an empirical study of UK firms.

The need to conclude this discussion with some attempt at synthesis is implied by the disparate nature of the conceptual and empirical sources upon which we have drawn and the need to relate the empirical findings reported here to the conceptual model developed. That synthesis is, however, brief and with the main purpose of indicating the implications of this work for management – and those implications are expanded in the final chapter.

A SUMMARY OF THE THEORY

The conclusion of the conceptual development was the construction of an information-structure-power model of marketing, which had various implications – most notably a model of the power and politics of resource allocation in marketing. At this stage there is some value in retracing the development of those models.

The Information-Power-Structure (ISP) Model of Marketing

Uncertainty and Organisations. The ISP construct or model was put forward in Chapter 8 and summarised in Figure 8.1. The central thesis was that environments create <u>uncertainties</u> for organisations, which may be conceived of, in turn, as producing the critical factors for corporate success and information processing burdens, which reflect the nature of the environment in terms of various concepts of stability, heterogeneity and complexity.

In relation to market-related uncertainty the implications for the marketing organisation are several. The relative importance and nature of market-related uncertainty may or may not create a pressure for the formation of a specialised, formalised marketing sub-unit. If such a sub-unit or department exists, then it is hypothesised that it gains power in its boundary-spanning location from coping with critical uncertainties in the environment, and through coping with information processing burdens to absorb that uncertainty for the core of the organisation.

This leads to a concept of a marketing department with potential sources of organisational power – through the creation of dependencies in relation to other parts of the organisation – and with a potential for political strength in the control and manipulation of information which is important to decision-making processes and upon which others in the organisation rely.

The implication of this concept of the marketing department is the potential for the existence of conflictual, competitive relationships with others in the organisation – such as other functional sub-units and general management – and possibly with others outside the organisation – specialist agencies, key distributors, and so on.

In turn it was then hypothesised that conflict may be resolved through the use of organisational power and in the emergence of political influence acts in the politicisation of decision making processes. Accepting the qualification that the use of power and politics is dependent on the occurrence of a variety of contingencies, then the suggestion is that processual and resource outcomes in marketing may be analysed as political outcomes.

The sources of this theory are various. The information processing concept as an analytical lever may be traced primarily to the work by Crozier (1964), Thompson (1967) and Galbraith (1972; 1973) and to certain more recent attempts to analyse that uncertainty as a determinant of marketing structures (e.g. Nonaka and Nicosia, 1979; Hakansson <u>et al</u>. 1979; Weitz and Anderson, 1981), largely in terms of the significance of its 'boundary-spanning' role (e.g. Pettigrew, 1973; Aldrich and Herker, 1977; Jemison, 1981; 1984).

Support for this perspective was developed by identifying a corporate environment for marketing decision making, with a number of identifiable dimensions such as corporate culture, organisational climate, management style, and so on. The significance of this corporate environment is, in turn, enhanced, by the transiti␣␣ᴉal nature of marketing as an organisational function and the catalytic effect of new information technology.

Indeed, it is possible to identify a lack of analysis of organisational issues in marketing as a noticeable gap in the received literature, which may be partially remedied through adopting a contingency model of marketing organisation. The main purpose of this conceptual development was to hypothesise that structure and information processing are central to controlling decision making processes and thus to influencing the outcomes of those processes. This conceptual development formed the content of Chapter 4.

From Uncertainty to Power and Politics. The reworking of these concepts into a model of the power and politics of the marketing organisation (Piercy, 1985) drew particularly on the strategic contingencies' theorists (Hickson et al, 1971; Hinings et al, 1974; Hickson et al, 1980) and the concept of structure as power (Pfeffer, 1981), and politics as being largely informational in nature (e.g. Pettigrew, 1973; Pfeffer, 1977).

The supporting analysis of power and politics for this purpose was provided in Chapters 5, 6 and 7. Here we first examined the somewhat problematic concept of organisational power, noting the difficulties of definition, but also the central ideas of the determination of behaviour (and thus by implication outcomes), overcoming resistance, and resource dependence, as providing a working understanding of the phenomenon. Secondly, we examined the received understanding of the corollary notion of organisational politics, and the tactics associated with political influence associated with political influence attempts. Thirdly, the concept of contingencies for the use of power and politics was adopted from Pfeffer (1981), which suggested that power and politics would emerge as decisional determinants only under conditions of high interdependence and differentiation, goal and technology dissensus, resource scarcity, the importance of outcomes, the existence of power differences, and conflict.

In fact it was possible to construct a case for the validity of a political analysis of marketing structures and decision-making processes through demonstrating evidence of the existence of those political contingencies in the corporate environment for marketing, either as contingent with certain decisions or more generally. This material was presented in Chapter 7.

From Power and Politics to Resource Allocation and Budgeting. Finally, we reached the major implication for this present work: that resource allocation in marketing – and particularly budgeting for marketing – was capable of useful analysis in terms of power and politics. This was formulated in a model of the power and politics of marketing budgeting (Figure 9.2).

In essence this model suggested that the central dependents should be seen as the type of budgeting or resource allocation process, and the financial, manpower, and other resources devoted to marketing. The determining factors may then be taken to be the organisational power of the marketing department (in structural terms), political behaviour by the marketing department (in informational terms), acting under the specified strategic and political contingencies on resource allocation processes and outcomes, but relative to the organisational power and political behaviour of others.

Our starting point in developing the argument to sustain that model was simply to note in Chapter 1 the importance of the resources devoted to marketing activities – in terms of absolute size and relative size in particular organisations.

We then proceeded to examine the extant literature of marketing budgeting and resource allocation. In Chapter 2 we examined the normative or prescriptive theories of marketing budgeting, which draw their logic from goals of optimisation, 'rationality', bureaucracy, or judgement to propose approaches to resource allocation based on economic analysis, management science, corporate models of programme or task budgeting, and various judgemental models. However, to those models we added a variety of objections – organisational and technical.

Then in Chapter 3, we examined the available descriptive theories of marketing budgeting – ranging from the description of decision rules to the 'pooled experience' concept of the PIMS and ADVISOR projects. We were able to suggest that the available evidence could be reworked in order that the marketing budgeting process could be characterised, in the style of Wildavsky's (1964) model, as based on precedent, incremental, involving tactical methods of calculation, experiential, and involving devices for simplification. We examined the limited evidence describing budgeting processes in marketing, in the light of the emergence of conflict and budgetary strategies. We were led thus to question the concept of 'rationality' in marketing budgeting and to search for alternative explanations of outcomes.

The secondary empirical support for the model of the power and politics of resource allocation in marketing was laid out in Chapter 9. Here we first established the existence of conceptual and empirical corroboration of the hypothesis that resource allocation and budgeting in organisations was susceptible to analysis in political terms. This was done in the areas of: governmental organisations, in a variety of business organisations, and - in a particularly influential set of studies from the point of view of this present work - in a number of public service organisations such as universities, social services and schools.

Secondly, in Chapter 9 we reviewed the available evidence relating to marketing budgeting, which was seen to be capable of interpretation in political terms. These contributions to the marketing literature generally did not make explicit the involvement of power and politics, but we were able to identify such phenomena in marketing as: the use of informational power and information manipulation; the impact of structural forms on resource outcomes; and the creation of organisational slack through the manipulation of marketing budgets - to conclude that there was some basis and unfulfilled potential for pursuing an analysis of the power and politics of marketing resource allocation processes and outcomes.

A SUMMARY OF THE RESEARCH

The Power and Politics of Marketing

The conceptual development outlined above led to the identification of a number of objectives for exploratory research: to examine the organisational arrangements made for marketing in different situations; to evaluate the consequent standing of the marketing department in terms of such criteria as status, control and pervasiveness; to identify the marketing resource allocation processes and outcomes in different situations; to measure the power of the marketing department in relation to the contingencies identified as significant to the use of power; to measure the politicisation of resource allocation in marketing - primarily in informational terms - under various contingent conditions; and to investigate the relationship between power, politics, contingencies and marketing resource allocation processes and outcomes - in terms of both resource allocations and corporate performance.

The writer undertook a small exploratory survey of marketing organisation and resource allocation in a sample of medium-sized manufacturing firms in the UK, with the findings summarised below.

Marketing Organisational Characteristics. In examining the organisational arrangements for marketing in the sample of companies studied, the findings were somewhat mixed but demonstrated clearly the existence of some heterogeneity and diversity in the organisational characteristics of marketing in the sample of firms. The major points emerging were as follows.

(a) The departmentation of marketing itself was found in less than half the original sample of companies (although problems exist regarding the more general interpretation of that proportion).

(b) Where marketing departments did exist, the integration of 'marketing' functions within them was generally low, and highly variable between companies – only one in six manifested the degree of integration that might be expected from the established theory.

(c) The size of marketing sub-units was typically small, but non-sales marketing employment seemed more stable and resilient than was the case for sales employment.

(d) The decision making responsibilities of the chief marketing executive (CME), both for the 'marketing' variables commonly conceived as constituents of the marketing mix or programme and for broader corporate strategic issues, were overwhelmingly participative or shared rather than absolute. In fact, CME responsibilities provided a criterion for clustering firms according to the role of the marketing department into: 'selling', 'strategy/service', 'integrated full-service' or 'limited/staff role' marketing organisations. This demonstrated the variability of the role played by the marketing department and suggested that it was quite reasonable to expect rather different levels and types of influence to be exerted over outcomes.

The Standing of the Marketing Department. In moving past structure and formal responsibility to examine indicators of the standing or status of the marketing department the findings were somewhat more favourable to the marketing paradigm, though again suggesting the variability between companies in which we were interested. The major findings were as follows.

(a) The status of the CME compared to the chief executives in production, finance and accounting and sales, was most commonly that of equality or superiority in favour of the CME.

(b) The majority of the marketing departments had some board-level representation, although the variability in corporate practice is underlined by the fact that one in five had no such representation.

(c) In approximately half the companies the marketing department was perceived as the most powerful, and this proportion had increased over the previous three years, mainly at the expense of the production function, leaving the major corporate rival to marketing as the finance department.

(d) A further approach to evaluating corporate standing was through the identification of 'critical success factors' and the control of those factors by different departments. On this criterion it was again found that there was high variability between companies, but there was also some suggestion that in the most highly rated areas of new product development and pricing (as well as some of the more minor factors) the incidence of control by the marketing department was negatively related to the importance of the factor to the company. In other words - while the marketing department generally controlled a number of strictly 'marketing' factors, the control of the most critical factors when they were most critical tended to be held by others.

(e) The concept of marketing orientation was supported and claimed by the majority of the companies, although it was suggested that this paradigm may in fact exist or act symbolically, independently of the other status factors studied.

(f) In examining the access to corporate information gained by the marketing department and the access to marketing department information gained by others it was found that there was some evidence of the restriction of information flows by marketing departments. In the related area of sales forecasting, most marketing departmens were formally responsible, but there was evidence of other departments exerting influence over this function.

Marketing Resources and Allocation Processes. The final descriptive element related to the resources allocated to marketing and various aspects of the processes surrounding those allocations. Specific findings may be summarised as follows.

(a) Allocations of resources to marketing - both financial and in manpower - were relatively limited and financial budgets showed some signs of reducing over the previous three years.

(b) The budgeting methods used remained dominated by the relatively unsophisticated.

(c) The pattern of budgeting process types was varied, although the majority reported an intermediate bottom-up/top-down mode.

(d) Marketing budgets were frequently adjusted by top management and these adjustments were usually downward.

(e) The degree of management control over the marketing budget decision was highly variable but frequently was considerable.

(f) The influence of other departments over marketing budgets was common, often significant, but highly variable between companies.

(g) There was some support for the hypothesis that marketing budgeting could be analysed as a political process.

In general terms, therefore, our finding was of marketing departments which lacked the standing suggested by the commonly accepted paradigm of the received literature. This relative lack of standing was reflected both in structure, authority and control of critical success factors, as well as in resource allocation process control, although in status terms the position was rather more favourable.

Power of the Marketing Department. Next from the measurements discussed above a variety of indicators of the power of the marketing department were proposed, including integration of functions and roles, relative marketing department size and trend, representation, responsibilities, perceived power rank and change in that rank, the control of strategic contingencies including sales forecasting and marketing paradigm strength. In correlating these power indicators with other variables various points were made as follows.

(a) There was some consistency in positive correlations between the measures of positional power – integration of functions, integration of personnel, relative department size and representation – participative power, in CME responsibilities, and perceived power, in terms of status and rank.

(b) Measures of positional power correlated positively with the strategic contingencies of connectedness, immediacy and influence, and with the control of critical success factors, including sales forecasting influence.

(c) Integration also appeared to be negatively correlated to the politics of information restriction and with advertising budget size. Of some note was the positive correlation between budget sizes and the number of marketing roles which were outside the marketing department – i.e. the disintegration or non-integration of marketing – although this was to some extent related to company size.

(d) Measures of participative and perceived power related positively to the strategic contingencies measured, as well as to the politics of information access and sales forecasting influence.

Politics and the Marketing Department. The study also examined the informational areas of information control, sales forecasting influence and politicisation. Among the main points made were the following.

(a) Information control correlated negatively with marketing manpower trends and resource scarcity, and positively with politicisation and with marketing department control of the budgeting process.

(b) Sales forecasting influence correlated positively with the marketing department power indicators and negatively with the power and influence of other departments.

(c) The politicisation of marketing resource allocation processes correlated positively with corporate politicisation and negatively with the information control gained by other departments.

The conclusion was that we had a reasonably consistent set of measures of the power and the marketing department and the political behaviour surrounding resource allocation.

Power and Politics Factors. Factor analysis of the measurements taken of power, politics and strategic and political contingencies yielded six factors: the Politics of Information Access, Positional/Participative Power, Process Politicisation, the Politics of Information Restriction, Political Contingencies, and Relative Perceived Power.

Correlating these factors with resource outcomes found Process Politicisation and Relative Perceived Power to be correlated positively and significantly with budget sizes.

Resource Allocation Processes. The measurements describing marketing resource allocation processes were also factored, producing three budgeting process factors: General Management Control of Marketing Budgeting, Marketing Department Budgeting Control, and Production/R&D Marketing Budgeting Influence.

It was found that the control and participation in budgeting achieved by the marketing department was positively related to marketing budget size, though not always linearly.

Resource Outcomes. To begin with resource outcomes were modelled as determined by precedent, and by implication as incremental in nature – beyond any doubt the best predictor of this year's budget is last year's budget, both in money and more significantly in ratio terms. As in the reworking of the earlier empirical and conceptual evidence to fit Wildavsky's (1964) model, we consider marketing budgets to be highly influenced by precedent and incrementalism, and found that budget/sales ratios were pervasively stable.

Secondly, a series of regression models related the power and politics factors and the resource allocation process variables and factors to resource outcomes in the following ways.

(a) The best model of relative advertising budget size ($R=0.73$) used Relative Perceived Power, Process Politicisation and Political Contingencies. A double-log transformation modelled the log of advertising budget size as predicted by Process Politicisation, top management intervention in budgeting and production department influence ($R=0.63$).

(b) The best models for sales promotion budget size

related budget size to Relative Perceived Power, Political Contingencies and Process Politicisation (R=0.57). In this case a double-log transformation produced a model predicting the log of sales promotion budget size by marketing department process control, the log of Political Contingencies and production department influence (R=0.68).

(c) In examining other marketing expenditure, the best model (R=0.40) predicted budget size as reduced by top management intervention, and increased by finance department influence. A better fit was obtained with a double-log transformation (R=0.64) which predicted the log of the other marketing expenditure from the log of Political Contingencies and marketing department control of process and reduced by top management intervention.

(d) Turning to the total marketing budget, the best model (R= 0.70) predicted the marketing budget by Process Politicisation, Political Contingencies, Relative Perceived Power, and marketing department participation in budgeting. A slightly better fit was obtained with a double-log transformation.

(e) Marketing manpower trend was best predicted (R=0.50) by the log of Politics of Information Access, reduced by the log of Positional/Participative Power and by the log of Political Contingencies.

Corporate Performance. In general terms it was also found that corporate profitability and sales growth were also positively related to marketing power, politicisation, and marketing resource outcomes. This offered some refutation (though cautious) of the notion that political processes were necessarily sub-optimal in terms of company performance.

The conclusion was that although interpretation has to be cautious because of the residual ambiguity surrounding the direction of causality, we had succeeded in establishing the existence of a variety of relationships between the power and politics of the marketing department and the resource allocation process and its outcomes, which support the direction of the argument advanced and confirm the underlying logic of our model of the power and politics of resource allocation in marketing.

CONCLUSION

This chapter has summarised the development of an analytical framework for the study of marketing decision making which is considered somewhat novel in the marketing literature. By following the procedures of searching for insight into marketing from other disciplines, we have drawn on the field of organisational behaviour to apply certain of the concepts developed in that field to critical issues in marketing.

Our concern has been essentially with the impact of

466

structure (here conceived in the terms developed by students of organisational power) and process (conceptualised here primarily as political in terms mainly of information control and manipulation), on the outcomes of marketing budgets, manpower level, and other resource allocations. With certain exceptions, which have been noted, this approach flies in the face of the accepted marketing theory of budgeting and resource allocation.

The result of this garnering of concepts and empirical tools from other disciplines was a model of the power and politics of marketing resource allocation.

While it would be invalid to claim that the model of the power and politics of marketing resource allocation (Figure 9.2) had been fully tested in a technical sense, in a relatively limited study of the kind undertaken and reported here, certain reasonably convincing support emerged for that model. The relative power of the marketing department and strategic contingencies are variable and are quite good predictors of budget outcomes; the politicisation of processes is also a good predictor; the control by the marketing department of the resource allocation process is positively related to budget sizes while the control of that process by top management or other departments is generally negatively related to marketing budget outcomes.

While these measures do not predict all variance in resources (at best the models show R^2 of only 0.50) it is suggested that these findings one of some significance to the management of companies, and the management of marketing in particular, and hence are of some note for management teachers and researchers. An attempt to highlight these implications is made in the final chapter.

Our conclusion is that a valid attack has been made on a gap in an important area of marketing theory. To suggest that the empirical work here is exhaustive would be quite wrong, but none the less the contribution made to changing the existing paradigm of marketing budgeting and resource allocation is considered to be significant as a basis and justification for further work in this area.

REFERENCES

Aldrich, H. and Herker, D. (1977) 'Boundary Spanning Roles and Organization Structure', Academy of Management Review, 2, 219-230

Crozier, M. (1964) The Bureaucratic Phenomenon, Tavistock, London

Galbraith, J.R. (1972) Organization Design: An Information Processing View, in J.W. Lorsch and P.R. Lawrence (eds.) Organization Planning: Cases and Concepts, Irwin and Dorsey, Homewood, Ill.

Galbraith, J.R. (1973) Designing Complex Organizations, Addison-Wesley, Reading, Mass.

Hakansson, H., Wootz, B., Anderson, O. and Hangard, P. (1979) 'Industrial Marketing as an Organisational Problem: A Case Study', European Journal of Marketing, 13 (3), 81-93

Hickson, D. J., Hinings C.R. , Lee, C.A., Schneck, R.E. and Pennings, J. (1971) 'A Strategic Contingencies Theory of Intraorganizational Power', Administrative Science Quarterly, 16, 216-29

Hinings, C.R., Hickson, D.J., Pennings, J.M. and Scheck, R.E. (1974) 'Structural Conditions of Intraorganizational Power', Administrative Science Quarterly, 19, 22-44

Jemison, D.B. (1981) 'Organizational Versus Environmental Sources of Influence in Strategic Decision Making', Strategic Management Journal, 2, 77-89

Jemison, D.B. (1984) 'The Importance of Boundary Spanning Roles in Strategic Decision Making', Journal of Management Studies, 21 (2), 131-52

Nonaka, I. and Nicosia, F.M. (1979) 'Marketing Management, Its Environment and Information Processing: A Problem of Organization Design', Journal of Business Research, 7 (4), 277-301

Pettigrew, A. (1973) The Politics of Organizational Decision Making, Tavistock, London

Pfeffer, J. (1977) 'Power and Resource Allocation in Organizations', in B.M. Staw and G.R. Salancik (eds.) New Directions in Organizational Behavior, St. Clair Press, Chicago

Pfeffer, J. (1981) Power in Organizations, Pitman, Marshfield, Mass.

Piercy, N. (1985) Marketing Organisation: An Analysis of Information Processing, Power and Politics, Allen and Unwin, London

Piercy, N. and Evans, M. (1983) Managing Marketing Information, Croom Helm, Beckenham

Thompson, J.D. (1967) Organizations in Action, McGraw-Hill, New York

Weitz, B. and Anderson, E. (1981) 'Organizing the Marketing Function', in AMA Review of Marketing 1981, American Marketing Association, Chicago

Wildavsky, A. (1964) The Politics of the Budgetary Process, Little Brown, Boston

14

Implications for Managing Marketing Actions and Resources

INTRODUCTION

Having attempted to establish the concept of a political analysis of the resource allocation process in marketing and to provide some empirical support, this book concludes by indicating the author's view of the significance of this analysis for the manager, teacher and researcher.

IMPLICATIONS FOR MANAGING

The theoretical positioning of this study was discussed in Chapter 1 (pp. *2 - 13*), but in the final analysis we should attempt to identify the implications of this work for the management practitioner.

A Proactive Management Stance

It was stated at the outset that the underlying goal here was not one of criticism but of analysis and our conclusion is clearly not that the use of power and politics in resource allocation is necessarily something to be avoided, but more closely parallels Bower's (1970) statement based on his study of capital budgeting:

> Top management must recognise the multidimensionality of the resource allocation process ... Ignoring the impact on planning and investment of formal organization, systems of management, information, and reward and punishment is a sure way of generating serious problems. 'Politics' is not a pathology, it is a fact of large organization. Top management must manage its influence on 'political' processes and then monitor the results of its performance. (Bower, 1970)

This said, it is undoubtedly true that at best many marketing analysts' response to this thesis will be 'convinced, but uncomfortable' (Pfeffer, 1981), since the concepts of power and politics constitute such an affront to the managerial ideology of rationality in decision making which has been imported into marketing theory (Anderson, 1982). In particular, there is an underlying assumption that decisions based on power and politics will be inferior to those using more 'scientific' or 'rational' criteria.

Political Outcomes and Corporate Performance

In fact, it was argued earlier that there is little evidence to support such an assumption - a point to which we return in a moment. Let us consider first the value-judgement that power and politics in organisation are 'bad' in some way in themselves (e.g. Velasquez et al, 1983), and then consider the specific question of corporate performance.

There is some weakness in the value-laden objection to power use, in the first instance, on the grounds that the powerful are, by definition, those whose interests have been institutionalised in the organisation. The objector is then left to argue that the wrong interests control an organisation, and indeed this would follow from the argument stated earlier that political behaviour has the ultimate goal of obtaining formal power - so power goes to the politically able rather than others with more 'legitimate' claims.

The counter to this is to argue that organisations, in fact, require and reflect different control systems at different times. For example, consider Mintzberg's (1983) analysis of the emergence of political behaviour, which suggested that what he refers to as 'games of politics' can, in fact, coexist with, be antagonistic to, or substitute for legitimate systems of influence (where legitimate systems of influence are close to what has been regarded here as power). His schema identifies a number of systems of influence - authority, ideology, expertise and politics, which may be related in the following ways: (a) internal systems of influence can act together either to concentrate power in the 'internal coalition', or to diffuse power to serve the broad needs of an organisation; (b) personal control by management in the authority system provides needed focused reponsibility, speed, and decisiveness; (c) bureaucratic control in the authority system provides stability and continuity; (d) the system of expertise distributes power to areas of skill and knowledge, rather than by office and rules or to an ideological conformist, or according to political games.

Most apposite here is Mintzberg's defence of the political system of influence, which, he suggests, corrects deficiencies and dysfunctions in the legitimate systems of authority, ideology and expertise, primarily through providing greater flexibility. In particular, Mintzberg argues that politics acts in 'a Darwinian way to ensure that the strongest members of the organisation are brought into positions of leadership', to take a broader view of issues, and to promote needed organisational change, which may be blocked by the pressure for the status quo from the systems of authority, ideology or expertise. It is proposed that influence systems change over time and in reaction to different situations, leading to the identification of personalised, bureaucratic, ideologic, professional and politicised internal coalitions.

In fact, this typology may be compared to Pfeffer's (1981) contrast between alternative models of organisational decision making (pp. *114-119*), but for present purposes provides a useful defence of politics in organisational functioning, on the grounds that it may complement and indeed provide a succession mechanism for legitimate power, or may act as a substitute when legitimate power is inadequate in one respect or another.

It has been suggested, for instance, that power and politics are part of the 'sense-making' apparatus of the organisation to cope with situations of high ambiguity and low structure, as in the case of information gathering in strategic problem formulation (Lyles and Mitroff, 1984), and we will return shortly to the idea of the 'politically competent manager' as the most effective manager (Hayes, 1984).

If we return now to the question of performance - the underlying assumption of those who object to the model of political decision making is that decisional outcomes are likely to be sub-optimal (or perhaps more sub-optimal than would be the case if 'rational' processes and tools were adopted).

It will be recalled that the empirical work reported here was, in fact, suggestive of a positive association between the power of the marketing department and politicisation, and corporate performance - in both profitability and sales growth - though our interpretation of the data remained cautious.

In fact, there is little indication in the general literature of support for the hypothesis that the greater the use of power and politics the lower the level of organisational performance (accepting that there are difficulties in arriving at acceptable definitions of criteria of organisational performance, and of designing adequate control measures to enable such a test).

One analyst is led to conclude that the available literature and evidence does not support the argument that power and politics leads to performance problems and that there is, in fact, some evidence that the reverse may be true (Pfeffer, 1981). Pfeffer continues his case by asserting, on the basis of case evidence, firstly, that political activities may actually be critical to achieving success, in that they allow the able and creative to get their own way, and secondly that it is 'organizational politicking' which facilitates organisational change and adaptation to environmental turbulence. He also rejects the argument that the amount of time spent in political negotiation and bargaining is necessarily any greater than that which would be directed to 'rational' information gathering and evaluation, and does not accept the condemnatory case that power and politics produce outcomes which are sub-optimal from the organisation's view, since 'To argue that power and politics produces decisions which are sub-optimal is to assume that there is knowledge about the organization and its operations which in all likelihood does not exist, for if it did, there would be much less use of power and politics' (Pfeffer, 1981).

In fact, other views are that the creation of organisational slack through political behaviour is in effect a facilitator of strategic behaviour (Bourgeois, 1981) - to allow experimentation with new strategies (Hambrick and Snow, 1977), to provide funds for innovation (Cyert and March, 1963).

Huff (1984) goes further and suggests that organisational politics, in fact, provide an efficient and desirable means of achieving organisational tasks, and specifically that: (a) politics can generate the type of discussion in which policy alternatives are identified, compared and evaluated, allowing new insights and behaviour; (b) politics can be routinised into an efficient form of control which channels potentially disruptive differences of opinion into activity that benefits the organisation; and (c) political systems developed in this way provide leadership succession and promote adaptation in organisational culture.

Certainly, in studying marketing strategy and the deviations between the dictates of prescriptive theories and actual behaviour, one researcher suggests that 'the managers' decision rules may lead to better decision than do prescriptive models. The deviations, then, may be "smart" deviations' (Burke, 1984). In this sense, power and political influence may, in various ways, exert a positive influence on performance.

Indeed, in the specific budgeting context, the Wildavsky work cited earlier came to the conclusion that the political system of budgeting actually worked reasonably well as a mechanism for coping with uncertainty and complexity, and it was noted that 'The overriding concern of the literature on budgeting with normative theory and reform has tended to obscure the fact that we know very little about the budgetary process ... the present budgetary process, though far from perfect, performs much better than has been thought, and is in many ways superior to the proposed alternatives' (Wildavsky, 1964).

If we accept the proposition that resource scarcity in an organisation leads to conflict, then it must be accepted too that conflict may produce both negative and positive effects. Positive effects include building sub-unit cohesiveness and sense of purpose, clarifying objectives, and greater analysis of cause-and-effect (Strauss, 1964; Notz et al, 1983). The implication is that the management problem is to minimise negative effects but to take advantage of the positive effects of conflict in budgeting - i.e. the role of 'manager as arbitrator' (Notz et al, 1983).

The claim, implicit in much of what has gone before, is that the conclusion that power and politics may have positive benefits to organisational performance remains, by and large, as true or truer in budgeting for marketing as is the case elsewhere.

Management Responses

The outcome of such arguments is that some suggest that the managerial response should be to recognise the opportunities to manage political systems as political systems, rather than obsuring issues with ineffective controls that simply drive politics underground.

For example, Pfeffer (1981) draws on George (1972) to argue for a 'multiple advocacy system' to manage conflict, where:

> Instead of utilizing centralized management practices to discourage or neutralize internal disagreements over policy, an executive can use a multiple advocacy model to harness diversity of views and interests in the interest of rational policy making. Diversity is also given scope in 'bureaucratic politics' and 'partisan mutual adjustment' but in contrast to these unregulated pluralistic systems, multiple advocacy requires management to create the basis for structured, balanced debate among policy advocates drawn from different parts of the organization. (George, 1972)

Such a model recognises the creative aspects of conflict and the attraction of 'legal' argument to a 'magistrate figure' leading to decision - or the role of manager as arbitrator discussed earlier (Notz et al, 1983). The parallel is with the situation created by the matrix organisation in marketing (Corey and Star, 1971; Piercy, 1985), with its implicit conflict between managers of resources and managers of programmes. We return shortly to this question.

Indeed, more broadly it has been argued that power and politics may act as just the type of internal capital market that organisational theorists have associated with the multidivisional form as a mechanism to cope with uncertainty and diversity (e.g Chandler, 1962; Williamson, 1975), in the sense that organisations could be viewed as quasi-markets in which power is the medium of exchange (Pfeffer and Salancik, 1977).

Less extreme is the view that at the very least power and politics should be recognised as a normal part of corporate behaviour, to be actively managed as corporate variables for control of outcomes - for instance, Mintzberg (1983) argues that we should conceive of a 'portfolio' of controlling forces, which should be mixed according to different strategies and changing circumstances.

Indeed, it is in the problems of creating and managing change of various types in organisations where these issues typically receive greatest explicit note. For instance, in this area De Luca (1984) has argued that the 'socio-political context' provides the starting point in planning organisational change, in a similar way to Keen's (1979) earlier work on information systems change, while Kakabadse (1984) claims similarly of change in organisations that:

> Change is about renegotiating certain dominant values and attitudes in the organization in order to introduce new systems or sub-systems. (Kakabadse, 1984)

Indeed, it has been argued that this view is of particular relevance in times of cut-back and retrenchment. In a study of public sector budgeting-cutting, one study suggests that 'emergent policy reframing' - in essence a political process of negotiation, delay, bargaining and conflict - accomodates the problems of coping with that period of time when the old and new frames of reference must co-exist, until people adjust to the new situation. It was suggested that:

> relinquishing past ways of doing things in an organization can mirror the stages of coping with death itself. Individuals need a period of time in which to register shock, denial, grief and mourning. The acceptance of new ideas depends upon this process of relinquishing the past. EPR undercovers how organizations can work to encourage the death of no longer appropriate frames of understanding. (Pondy and Huff, 1983)

In this sense also the management of change draws on an understanding of the systems of power and politics and the culture of an organization.

A Continuum of Management Action

Accepting the existence of management choice in such areas, one may draw on the debate above to suggest a number of implications for managing marketing processes to influence outcomes, which may be taken as representing points at various stages on a continuum.

First, if management rejects the notion of politics as a suitable determinant of outcomes, then attempts may be made to centralise power and to reduce the scope for political action, in so far as that is possible (Pfeffer, 1981).

It has been suggested of budgeting systems, for example, that:

> Not only must the system provide procedures for the rational, economic analysis of budget proposals, but it must also provide procedures for the resolution of intergroup conflict over scarce resources that will inevitably arise. (Pondy, 1964)

The dangers in driving political behaviour out of sight have been outlined earlier, but it is certainly true that advances in technique and the availability of new information technology do suggest a potential for more effective centralised control over marketing resources.

Second, there is, none the less, some value in noting and comprehending the political nature of the organisational environment for marketing decision making – whether one's aim is to eradicate the influence of power and politics or to adapt to their influence.

There is much precedent for the view that the management of strategic change is more likely to be effective if its planning incorporates planning to cope with the implied impact on the power structure and the emergence of political behaviour.

Third, it may be that management should recognise the emergence of political decision making as a valid response to surrounding contingencies and to attempt to manage marketing resource allocation as a political process.

For example, Huff (1984) suggests that politics in organisations can be routinised into an efficient form of 'governance or control'. Her proposal is that:

> repeated decisions, especially routinized cycles of planning and budgeting decisions, provide a useful focus for political activity. These decisions simultaneously limit options for dissent and provide well specified possibilities for future dissent. (Huff, 1984)

The argument is that a well established cycle of decision making highlights a limited set of outcomes as recurring benefits, thus reducing the escalation of demands and the growth of animosity between winners and losers. The conclusion is that:

> Conflict is most likely to be positive if those who oppose current activity are able, under controlled circumstances, to develop their complaints into a well articulated program for action which can be compared to

the organization's current strategy ... Conflict is thus most likely to be positive if it takes place in a stabilized political system which discourages "do or die" attempts to change the organization in favour of waiting for well specified opportunities for influence ... In the long run the political system can help adapt to the ambiguity and change which faces all organizations, by keeping a variety of potentially useful perspectives alive. (Huff, 1984)

Managing the power and politics of marketing might involve the application of the matrix concept and making explicit the 'multiple advocacy' paradigm considered earlier. There is some precedent which may be implied for such an approach to marketing management. For instance, Anderson's (1982) contribution to a 'marketing theory' of the firm', which was introduced in Chapter 1 (pp. *11 - 13*) follows the well-known Mason and Mitroff (1981) logic to argue that:

Strategic conflicts will arise as functional areas ... vie for the financial resources necessary to occupy their optimal long-term positions. Corporate management as the final arbitrator may occasionally favor one area over another ... Indeed, it is possible that marketing considerations may not have a significant impact on strategic plans unless marketers adopt a strong advocacy position within the firm. (Anderson, 1982)

Such a view is compatible with Quinn's (1981) model of strategy formulation as a combination of formal/analytical and power/behavioural approaches. In this model, strategies are not created by the formal planning system, which provides merely a framework, but they emerge incrementally over relatively long time periods - time periods during which management negotiates and bargains to obtain the support and commitment of coalitions within the firm (Quinn, 1981). Anderson's derived view of the marketing role in the firm is that:

marketing must negotiate with top management and the other functional areas to implement its strategies. The coalitional perspective suggests that marketing must take an active role in promoting its strategic options by demonstrating the survival value of a consumer orientation to the other internal coalitions. (Anderson, 1982)

This returns us to the last point above - to act effectively as 'a strong advocate for the marketing concept' requires an understanding of the distribution of power and political strength in the organisation. We argued earlier that an implicit understanding of the power structure may be a characteristic of 'good' management, which we have sought to incorporate more explicitly into the marketing paradigm.

In a related way, McCall and Warrington (1984) attempted to describe a non-cultural approach to 'marketing by agreement', which conceptualises marketing plans as negotiated, agreed instruments where the focus is on the analysis of influences and skills in the negotiation interaction. Their study focuses primarily on inter-organisational relationships, but their model is equally applicable to intraorganisational negotiation and the grey area of 'quasi-integrated' organisations (see pp. *105-6*). Again the implication is that effectiveness may rely on advocacy and bargaining skills and a form of situational analysis not generally recognised by marketing.

Indeed, it may be desirable in some situations to go as far as writers like Hayes (1984), who argues that the most effective managers are, in fact, the 'politically competent' who manifest 'a set of skills to do with influencing others and the exercise of power' (Hayes, 1984). The implication drawn by Hayes is that it is possible advantageously to introduce structural and procedural changes which have the effect of making decision making more rather than less susceptible to the use of power and political influence.

More deterministically, to return to our main theme, if the intention is to influence the outcomes of a political process such as marketing budgeting, it may be that the most effective way of doing so is to operate not simply on formal authority systems (except in so far as they influence power and politics) but to reallocate sources of power - in terms, for instance, of reallocating boundary-spanning functions and the strategic influence they bring (Jemison, 1984) - to redesign structures - for example, to modify the institutionalisation of rules and procedures by power holders (Wilson et al, 1983) - to modify information flows - for instance, by the use of new information technology (Piercy, 1984) - and to influence social interaction patterns, to change the power balance, the opportunities for political behaviour, and hence outcomes.

In other words, effective control of the political process of marketing resource allocation may involve acting on structure (power), and information and process (politics) to reshape those factors which determine outcomes (resources).

Indeed, we are not alone in reaching this conclusion, for example it has been noted elsewhere that 'the influence of organizational structure on marketing has seldom been studied systematically ... One set of these relationships deals with managers within an organization. Unless the structure of work relationships in a firm has been designed to optimize managerial effectiveness, the company-customer transactions will suffer and, in turn, negatively impact on the firm's long-term profitability' (Deshpande, 1982). In a broadly similar way, John and Martin (1984), in studying marketing planning, have argued that marketing structure is a crucial determinant of organisational outcomes, though restricting their analysis to formal aspects of structure.

Our present contention is that attention to structure in marketing would be shortsighted in the extreme were it to be reserved to formal, overt characteristics, and that it should focus on the power and politics of marketing structure and process.

IMPLICATIONS FOR MANAGEMENT EDUCATION AND DEVELOPMENT

To the extent that the case made here is accepted, then it has implications not only for management strategies, in both general management control of marketing in the firm and functional management that activity, but for the ways in which managers are educated and developed.

While the debate about the standing of marketing as an art or a source has never been resolved, and probably is unlikely so to be, it would seem true that the ethos of marketing education and development has grown to be one of increasing 'professionalism' and the application of 'scientific methodology'.

This is not the place for a re-evaluation of the marketing curriculum, but it is apt to note a more general conclusion about the business school ethos:

> Business schools impart both the ideology and skills of analysis, especially economic and quantitative analysis. This is a maximizing ideology, which emphasizes the role of numerical procedures and the belief that there are best or optimal answers ... Students emerge from such a program believing that there is an optimum answer or set of answers discoverable through quantitative analysis. It is quite possible that they are thus desensitized both to the issue of multiple goals and to the use of data to construct arguments, explanations and justifications. They are trained in specialized language and techniques which make them excellent allies in political struggles, for they can assist in producing the appearance of non-substitutability and expertise, as well as the numbers and analyses that support one particular position. At the same time it is clear that they may be ineffective themselves in such political contests, in large measure because they are insensitive to the game which is being played or its rules. (Pfeffer, 1981)

At one level, if our concern in marketing education and training is with developing the abilities and skills relevant to the control of the marketing activities of an organisation, then at its simplest there is much to be said for far greater attention to issues of structure and process and the politics of organisational decision making – a gap which certainly exists in both undergraduate and postgraduate marketing programmes in the UK (Evans and Piercy, 1980; Piercy et al, 1982).

At the level of training it may be that politicisation should be recognised more explicitly as the context for marketing operations in which individuals must survive.

Essentially the implication is that the incorporation of management science into marketing theory may be valid in coping with complexity, but it does not provide anything like the panacea which is sometimes claimed. At the very least the implementation of rational decision making models in marketing depends on the nature of the corporate environment, but more fundamentally formal/analytical skills are only part of the total amalgum of managerial characteristics which should be analysed as part of the marketing curriculum. The formal/analytical needs to be balanced with the power and politics of structure and process in marketing decision making, in developing theoretical and practical courses in marketing.

IMPLICATIONS FOR RESEARCH IN MARKETING

It is perhaps inevitable that a work of this nature should raise more issues that it resolves. As a consequence our closing point is with proposals for areas of application of the approach taken here to marketing resource allocation, not in an attempt to explain all outcomes as political, but in identifying more thoroughly those situations and decision areas where power and political inputs may be identifiable as explanatory factors.

Attempts have already been made to introduce concepts of power and politics to the design of marketing information systems (Piercy and Evans, 1983) and to the re-evaluation and design of the marketing organisation (Piercy, 1985), as well as explaining in this present work the implications for resource allocation in marketing.

Additional areas capable of analysis in terms of the information-structure-power model are seen as including the following: (a) the choice of product-market strategy, in such issues as market selection, diversification and risk perception and tolerance; (b) the product policy choices made in terms of such factors as new product selection, product deletion, choice of price level, and so on; (c) the process of internationalisation; (d) choices of communication strategies and media; (e) the management of changing distribution relationships; (f) the implications of new information technology for marketing; and (g) combining existing marketing theories of inter-organisational conflict and power in the channel of distribution with a model of the intra-organisational power of the marketing department, to analyse the emergence of new marketing strategies and channel structures.

In short, this work and its immediate antecedents are presented only as a very limited contribution to marketing theory - but one which is capable of far greater methodological refinement and extension to other decision and context areas.

REFERENCES

Anderson, P.F. (1982) 'Marketing, Strategic Planning, and the Theory of the Firm', Journal of Marketing, Vol. 46, Spring, 15-26

Bourgeois, L.J. (1981) 'On the Measurement of Organizational Slack', Academy of Management Review, 6 (1), 29-39

Bower, J. (1970) Managing the Resource Allocation Process, Harvard University, Boston, Mass.

Burke, M.C. (1984) 'Strategic Choice and Marketing Managers: An Examination of Business-Level Marketing Objectives', Journal of Marketing Research, 21, November, 345-59

Chandler, A.D. (1962) Strategy and Structure, MIT Press, Cambridge, Mass.

Corey, E.R. and Star, S.H. (1971) Organization Strategy: A Marketing Approach, Harvard University Press, Boston, Mass.

Cyert, R.M. and March, J.G. (1963) A Behavioral Theory of the Firm, Prentice-Hall, Englewood Cliffs, N.J.

De Luca, J.R. (1984) 'Managing the Socio-Political Context in Planned Change Efforts', in A. Kakabadse and C. Parker (eds.) Power, Politics and Organizations: A Behavioural Science View, Wiley, Chichester

Deshpande, R. (1982) 'The Organisational Context of Market Research Use', Journal of Marketing, 46, Fall, 91-101

Evans, M. and Piercy, N. (1980) 'Undergraduate Marketing Curricula in the United Kingdom', Business Education, 1 (2), 151-62

George, A.L. (1972) 'The Case for Multiple Advocacy in Making Foreign Policy', American Political Science Review, 66, 751-85

Hambrick, D.C. and Snow, C.C. (1977) 'A Contextual Model of Strategic Decision Making in Organizations', in R.L. Taylor et al (eds.) Academy of Management Proceedings 1977

Hayes, J. (1984) 'The Politically Competent Manager', Journal of General Management, 10 (1), 24-33

Huff, S.F. (1984) Politics and Argument as a Means of Coping with Ambiguity and Change, Working Paper 1056, University of Illinois at Urbana-Champaign

Jemison, D.B. (1984) 'The Implications of Boundary Spanning Roles in Strategic Decision-Making', Journal of Management Studies, 21 (2), 131-52

Kakabadse, A. (1984) 'Politics of a Process Consultant', in A. Kakabadse and C. Parker (eds.) Power, Politics, and Organizations: A Behavioural Science View, Wiley, Chichester

Keen, P.G.W. (1979) Information Systems and Organizational Change, MIT Centre for Information Systems Research, Cambridge, Mass.

Lyles, M.A. and Mitroff, I.I. (1984) The Impact of Socio-Political Influences on Strategic Problem Formulation, Working Paper 1025, University of Illinois at Urbana-Champaign

McCall, J.B. and Warrington, M.B. (1984) Marketing By Agreement: A Cross-Cultural Approach to Business Negotiations, Wiley, Chichester

Mason, R.O. and Mitroff, I.I. (1981) Policy Analysis as Argument, Working Paper, University of Southern California

Mintzberg, H. (1983) Power In and Around Organizations, Prentice-Hall, Englewood Cliffs, N.J.

Notz, W.W., Starke, F.A. and Arwell, J. (1983) 'The Manager as Arbitrator: Conflict over Scarce Resources', in M.H. Braverman and R.J. Lewicki (eds.) Negotiating in Organizations, Sage, Beverley Hills, Calif.

Pfeffer, J. and Salancik, G.R. (1977) 'Organization Design: The Case for a Coalitional Model of Organizations', Organizational Dynamics, 6, 15-29

Piercy, N. (1984) The Management Implications of New Information Technology, Croom Helm, Buckingham

Piercy, N. (1985) Marketing Organisation: An Analysis of Information Processing, Power and Politics, Allen and Unwin, London

Piercy, N. and Evans, M. (1983) Managing Marketing Information, Croom Helm, Beckenham

Piercy, N., Evans, M. and Martin, M. (1982) 'Postgraduate Marketing Curricula in the United Kingdom', European Journal of Marketing, 16 (1), 3-16

Pondy, L.R. (1964) 'Budgeting and Intergroup Conflict in Organizations', Pittsburgh Business Review, 34, 1-3

Pondy, L.R. and Huff, A.S. (1983) Budget Cutting in Riverside: Emergent Policy Reframing as a Process of Analytical Discovery and Conflict Minimization, Working Paper 970, University of Illinois at Urbana-Champaign

Quinn, J.B. (1981) 'Formulating Strategy One Step at a Time', Journal of Business Strategy, 1, Winter, 42-63

Strauss, G. (1964) 'Work-Flow Friction, Interfunctional Rivalry and Professionalism', Human Organization, 23 (2), 137-49

Velasquez, M., Moberg, D.J. and Cavanagh, G.F. (1983) 'Organizational Statesmanship and Dirty Politics: Ethical Guidelines for the Organizational Politician', Organizational Dynamics, 12 (2), 65-80

Wildavsky, A. (1964) The Politics of the Budgetary Process, Little Brown, Boston

Williamson, O.E. (1975) Marketing and Hierarchies: Analysis and Antitrust Implications, Free Press, New York

Wilson, D.C., Butler, R.J., Cray, D., Hickson, D.J. and Mallory, G.M. (1983) Sources of Power in Strategic Decision Making: The Selective Embodiment of Power, Working Paper, University of Bradford

Appendices

APPENDIX A

SURVEY METHODOLOGY

A.1 SAMPLING METHOD

The sampling method for the postal survey was to draw a systematic random sample of 600 manufacturing firms located in the UK using the sampling frame provided by the Key British Enteprises (1984) directory. The selection method was to select every thirty-third firm, adopting this item if it conformed with the sample criteria, or proceeding sequentially from this point until a firm was found which did conform.

The criteria for selection were that the sample items should: (a) be firms with more than 100 employees; (b) not be holding companies; (c) be firms in manufacturing rather than retailing or other service sectors.

The sampling unit was the named chief marketing executive, or the chief marketing executive addressed by the title 'Marketing Director'.

A.2 QUESTIONNAIRE

The postal questionnaire was designed following the formulation of the research objectives described in the text (pp. *297–300*) and amended following a piloting exercise described in A.3 below.

The final questionnaire used in the main study is reproduced in Figure A.1 below, together with the covering letter explaining the survey objectives to respondents and offering the incentive of a copy of the research findings to those participating in the research.

A.3 PILOTING

Following the design of the pilot questionnaire, a sample of 100 firms was drawn from the Key British Enterprise (1983) directory, using the approach described in A.1 above. The pilot questionnaire and covering letter were mailed out on 4th July, 1983 and after a reminder letter, with a further

Figure A.1: Survey Documentation

Director: Professor Roger Mansfield MA PhD

UWIST
Colum Drive
Cardiff
CF1 3EU
☎ 42588 or 371200

NP/SMB

30th April, 1984

A SURVEY OF MARKETING MANAGEMENT

We are carrying out a programme of research into marketing management in UK companies, and would like to request your help through the completion of the enclosed questionnaire, which should take no more than twenty minutes of your time.

Most of the questions require you to do no more than tick a box or circle a number to indicate your answer. The questions are designed to be answered by the executive in charge of Marketing in your business (company or division).

In return for this help, we would like to offer participants in the survey a free copy of the research report, for use in their companies.

The aim of this present research is to provide a realistic, up-to-date picture of the organisational setting for marketing decisions, the information used, and how the marketing view is represented in firms. It is intended that this will provide managers with a bench-mark for studying their own policies and practices. I would emphasise that this work aims to make a practical contribution to 'marketing out of the recession' by British firms in the 1980s, rather than simply being fact-gathering for its own sake.

I should stress that all questionnaire replies will be regarded as completely confidential, and no report will allow the identification of any respondent.

I would urge you to participate in the survey, and to indicate your willingness to receive a copy of the report of the research findings, which I hope will be of practical value to you in auditing and evaluating your marketing.

Yours sincerely,

NIGEL PIERCY
Senior Lecturer

The University of Wales Institute of Science and Technology : Aberconway Building, Colum Drive.

UWIST

Department of Business Administration and Accountancy

I MARKETING ORGANISATION

Question 1

(a) Is there a Marketing Department in your business? Yes _____ ⬚ *V2*
No _____

(b) If possible, could you send a copy of your organisation chart, to supplement your answers, or alternatively draw a sketch of the organisation structure on the back page of the questionnaire.

Question 2
Please indicate if the following activities are part of the Marketing Department, or if they are organised separately in some way.

	(a) Part of the Marketing Department	(b) Organised separately from the Marketing Department (on their own or in another Department)	(c) Not formally organised as separate activities in our business	
Sales	☐	☐	☐	*V3*
Distribution	☐	☐	☐	*V4*
Customer Service	☐	☐	☐	*V5*
Trade Marketing	☐	☐	☐	*V6*
Advertising	☐	☐	☐	*V7*
Exporting	☐	☐	☐	*V8*
Marketing Research	☐	☐	☐	*V9*

Question 3
In relation to the following executives, how would you rate the status in your business of the 'chief marketing executive'?

The chief marketing executive is of:

In comparison with the following:	Lower Status	Equal Status	Higher Status	
The chief production executive.........................	1	2	3	*V10*
The chief finance/accounting executive..............	1	2	3	*V11*
The chief sales executive...............................	1	2	3	*V12*

Question 4

Please indicate the approximate number of full-time employees in the Marketing Department over the last three years.

	Number of employees	
This year....................	_____	*V13*
Last year....................	_____	*V14*
The year before that........	_____	*V15*

Question 5

Please indicate the approximate number of full-time employees carrying out the following functions, within the Marketing Department, and (where appropriate) in other departments in the business.

	(b) Numbers employed within the Marketing Department in different functions:		(c) If separate from the Marketing Department number employed in other departments working in these functions:
Sales......................	*V16*	....	*V26*
Advertising...............	*V17*	....	*V27*
Product Management.........	*V18*	....	*V28*
Customer Service...........	*V19*	....	*V29*
Distribution..............	*V20*	....	*V30*
Marketing Research.........	*V21*	....	*V31*
Marketing Planning.........	*V22*	....	*V32*
Marketing Services/ Administration...........	*V23*	....	*V33*
Exporting.................	*V24*	....	*V34*
Other.....................	*V25*	....	*V35*

Question 6

How many of the directors on the Board of Directors are 'representatives' of the Marketing Department?

Number of Marketing 'representatives' on the Board

☐ *V36*

Total number of directors on the Board

☐ *V37*

Question 7

Please show in the table below the degree of responsibility of the 'chief marketing executive' for decisions in the areas listed.
(Please circle the most appropriate position on the scales.)

	Full and Sole Responsibility	Major Responsibility but shared with others	Equal Responsibility with others	Some Responsibility but less than others	No Responsibility	
Advertising	1	2	3	4	5	V38
Sales promotion	1	2	3	4	5	V39
Price setting	1	2	3	4	5	V40
Discount structures	1	2	3	4	5	V41
Product planning	1	2	3	4	5	V42
Field sales force operations	1	2	3	4	5	V43
Negotiations with distributors/retailers	1	2	3	4	5	V44
Sales forecasting	1	2	3	4	5	V45
Marketing research	1	2	3	4	5	V46
Marketing planning	1	2	3	4	5	V47
Product design	1	2	3	4	5	V48
Packaging design	1	2	3	4	5	V49
Warehousing	1	2	3	4	5	V50
Transport of finished goods	1	2	3	4	5	V51
R & D strategy	1	2	3	4	5	V52
New product launches	1	2	3	4	5	V53
Investment appraisal	1	2	3	4	5	V54
Diversification studies	1	2	3	4	5	V55
Marketing staff selection	1	2	3	4	5	V56
Marketing training	1	2	3	4	5	V57
Corporate planning/ strategic planning	1	2	3	4	5	V58
Other major responsibilities (please specify)	1	2	3	4	5	

_____

_____

II MARKETING INFORMATION

Question 8

To what extent does the Marketing Department have access to the following types of information from other departments (i.e. the Marketing Department <u>can</u> and <u>does</u> request and receive full detailed information from them).

	Marketing has no access to this information	Limited access to partial information	Some access but not as routine	Access to most but not all information	Marketing has complete access to this information	
Product costs	1	2	3	4	5	V59
Marketing costs	1	2	3	4	5	V60
Profitability of company operations	1	2	3	4	5	V61
Company-wide budgets	1	2	3	4	5	V62
Investment plans	1	2	3	4	5	V63
Production schedules	1	2	3	4	5	V64
R & D projects	1	2	3	4	5	V65
Corporate plans	1	2	3	4	5	V66

Question 9

To what extent do non-marketing departments in the business have access to the following types of information (i.e. they <u>can</u> and <u>do</u> request and receive full detailed information from the Marketing Department)?

	Other departments have no access to this information	They have limited access to partial information	Some access but not as routine	Access to most but not all information	They have complete access to this information	
Market studies	1	2	3	4	5	V67
Customer reports	1	2	3	4	5	V68
Sales plans	1	2	3	4	5	V69
Marketing plans	1	2	3	4	5	V70
Marketing budgets	1	2	3	4	5	V71
New product plans	1	2	3	4	5	V72
Other marketing research reports	1	2	3	4	5	V73

Question 10
Please show which part of the business plays the main role in sales forecasting.

(a) Which department is <u>formally responsible</u> for sales forecasting?

Marketing _____	☐
Finance/Accounting _____	☐
Production _____	☐
R & D _____	☐
Corporate Planning _____	☐
Other (please specify) _____	☐

V74

(b) What is the degree of <u>shared responsibility</u> of the various departments in the business, for sales forecasting?

	Full & sole respon- sibility	Major respons- sibility but shared	Equal responsi- bility with others	Some respon- sibility but less than others	No respon- sibility	
Marketing....................................	1	2	3	4	5	V75
Finance/Accounting........................	1	2	3	4	5	V76
Production....................................	1	2	3	4	5	V77
R&D..	1	2	3	4	5	V78
Corporate Planning.........................	1	2	3	4	5	V79
Other (please specify).....................	1	2	3	4	5	V80

III MARKETING BUDGETING

Question 11
Which of the following best describes the usual approach in your business to determining the size of the budget for advertising and sales promotion?

The budget is calculated by:	(a) Advertising		(b) Sales Promotion (below-the-line)	
% of past sales _____	☐	V81	☐	V90
% of current sales _____	☐	V82	☐	V91
% of expected sales _____	☐	V83	☐	V92
what we can afford _____	☐	V84	☐	V93
target share of total industry spend _____	☐	V85	☐	V94
objective and task method _____	☐	V86	☐	V95
accept an agency proposal _____	☐	V87	☐	V96
use a computer model _____	☐	V88	☐	V97
other (please specify) _____	☐	V89	☐	V98

Question 12

(a) Which of the following statements best describes the way in which the marketing budget is determined in your business?

(i) Bottom-up decision process - managers of the subunits in marketing (e.g. product managers, advertising managers etc.) work out how much money they need to achieve their objectives and these amounts are combined to establish the total marketing budget.. ☐

(ii) Top-down/bottom-up decision process - first, the total size of the marketing budget is established by top management, and then the budget is divided up between marketing centres (such as products and markets)...................................... ☐

(iii) Bottom-up/top-down decision process - managers of the subunits in marketing submit budget requests, which are coordinated by the chief marketing executive, and presented to top management, who adjust the total budget size to conform with overall goals and strategies.. ☐

(iv) None of these are even approximately correct. Our budgeting process may best be described as in the space below:.. ☐   *V99*

```
┌─────────────────────────────────────────────────────────────────────────┐
│                                                                           │
│                                                                           │
│                                                                           │
│                                                                           │
│                                                                           │
│                                                                           │
│                                                                           │
│                                                                           │
│                                                                           │
│                                                                           │
│                                                                           │
└─────────────────────────────────────────────────────────────────────────┘
```

(b) If your budgeting process is one where the Marketing Department calculates a budget request, which then goes to higher management for approval, is there usually any difference between that request for budget and what is actually received?

Yes ———————————— ☐   *V100*
No ————————————

If 'yes' please estimate the usual level of adjustment made by higher management in recent years.

The budget request is usually:

Increased by:					Decreased by:			
100% or more	75–100%	50–75%	25–50%	less than 25%	less than 25%	25–50%	50–75%	100%
1........	2	3	4	5	7	8	9	10

V101

493

Question 13

Please indicate the degree to which the Marketing Department determines its own budget size, and the extent of top or general management influence over the size of the budget.

It is a Marketing Department decision	The budget is a Marketing Department responsibility but in consultation with others	There is prior consultation with others	The budget is a joint decision with others	The marketing budget is set by top management

1 .... 2 .... 3 .... 4 5   *V102*

Question 14

Generally, how much influence do other departments have in determining the size of the marketing budget?

	A very great deal	A great deal	Quite a bit	Some	Little or none	
Finance/Accounting.........	1	2	3	4	5	*V103*
Production.................	1	2	3	4	5	*V104*
R & D.....................	1	2	3	4	5	*V105*
Corporate Planning.........	1	2	3	4	5	*V106*
Other departments (please specify)...........	1	2	3	4	5	*V107*

_____

Question 15

Please indicate the size of your marketing budget and its major elements in the last three financial years.

	The most recent financial year 19__/19__	The year before 19__/19__	The year before that 19__/19__
Advertising................	£ *V108*	£ *V109*	£ *V110*
Sales Promotion............	£ *V111*	£ *V112*	£ *V113*
Other Marketing Expenses....	£ *V114*	£ *V115*	£ *V116*
TOTAL MARKETING BUDGET......	£ *V117*	£ *V118*	£ *V119*

Question 16

How much has the work-space (offices, space, buildings, etc) taken up by the Marketing Department increased or decreased in the last three years?

Increased					No change	Decreased			
100% or more	75– 100%	50– 75%	25– 50%	by less than 25%	changed by 0%	by less than 25%	25– 50%	50– 75%	75– 100%

1 ..... 2 ... 3 ... 4 ...... 5 .... 6 .... 7 .... 8 ... 9 ... 10   V120

Question 17

Obtaining a budget and other resources is often regarded as very 'political' in companies. Where would you place your company on the following scale?

	Highly 'political'				Not 'political' at all

Financial budgeting for
  marketing......................... 1 .... 2 .... 3 .... 4 5   V121
Gaining manpower for
  marketing......................... 1 .... 2 .... 3 .... 4 5   V122
Gaining office space, etc.
  for marketing.................... 1 .... 2 .... 3 .... 4 5   V123

Question 18

In negotiation for the marketing budget and other resources, how important in your company are the following factors to success in maintaining and increasing budget size?

	Very important				Not important at all

Using information selectively
  to make a case........................... 1 ...... 2 .... 3 ...... 4 5   V124
Departmental image in the company.......... 1 ...... 2 .... 3 ...... 4 5   V125
Attacking/criticising other departments.... 1 ...... 2 .... 3 ...... 4 5   V126
Gaining informal support for ideas and
  proposals................................ 1 ...... 2 .... 3 ...... 4 5   V127
Praising others to win their support....... 1 ...... 2 .... 3 ...... 4 5   V128
Cultivating influential people in the
  company.................................. 1 ...... 2 .... 3 ...... 4 5   V129
Creating obligations and favours 'owed'.... 1 ...... 2 .... 3 ...... 4 5   V130
Knowing the 'rules' and using them......... 1 ...... 2 .... 3 ...... 4 5   V131

495

IV PRODUCTS AND MARKETS

Question 19
How would you rate the major markets with which you deal.

(a) How well can you
predict the demand for
your products?

	Very well and accurately				Not at all	
(a) predict the demand for your products?	1 .... 2 .... 3 .... 4 5					*V132*

(b) In general, how much
can you influence or
change the market
conditions or environ-
ment you face?

	Not at all				A great deal	
(b) ...ment you face?	1 .... 2 .... 3 .... 4 5					*V133*

(c) How easily can
sales results be traced
to specific marketing
actions like adver-
tising and promotion?

	Very well and accurately				Not at all	
(c) ...tising and promotion?	1 .... 2 .... 3 .... 4 5					*V134*

Question 20
How has your major market been affected by the current economic recession?

No effect at all _____
No major effect _____
Some effects but we have coped _____
A big effect causing major difficulties _____
Disastrous, our very survival is threatened___ *V135*

Question 21
How would you consider the long term nature of your major market?

Generally in decline _____
Mature and fairly stable _____
Growth market _____
Relatively new emerging market _____ *V136*

Question 22
What does your company consider to be the key factors to success in your major market and which
department is mainly responsible for them?

(a) Please rank: 1st,
2nd, 3rd, etc.

(b) The department mainly responsible is:

	(a)	Marketing	Production	R&D	Finance	Other (please specify)	
Legal factors and patents	*V137*	1 .... 2 .... 3 ... 4 5					*V147*
New product development	*V138*	1 .... 2 .... 3 ... 4 5					*V148*
Market standing	*V139*	1 .... 2 .... 3 ... 4 5					*V149*
Aggressive selling and promotion	*V140*	1 .... 2 .... 3 ... 4 5					*V150*
Reliable delivery and stocking of spares, etc.	*V141*	1 .... 2 .... 3 ... 4 5					*V151*
Prices	*V142*	1 .... 2 .... 3 ... 4 5					*V152*
Customer service	*V143*	1 .... 2 ..... 3 ... 4 5					*V153*
Distribution network	*V144*	1 .... 2 ..... 3 ... 4 5					*V154*
Brand image	*V145*	1 .... 2 .... 3 ... 4 5					*V155*
Other (please specify)	*V146*	1 .... 2 ..... 3 ... 4 5					*V156*

_____
_____

V OTHER DEPARTMENTS

Question 23

The following scales are an attempt to assess the role of the Marketing Department in your particular business. Please tick the most appropriate box for each.

(a) How easy would it be to replace the personnel in the Marketing Department, either from other departments or outside recruitment or by using external agencies for activities like advertising and marketing research?............ Easy 1 .... 2 .... 3 .... 4 .... Impossible 5   V157

(b) How much is the work of the Marketing Department connected to the work of the other departments listed below: Very many connections / Very few

Finance...................... 1 .... 2 .... 3 .... 4 5   V158
Production................... 1 .... 2 .... 3 .... 4 5   V159
R & D....................... 1 .... 2 .... 3 .... 4 5   V160

(c) To what extent does the Marketing Department influence the following departments: Not at all / To a very great extent

Finance...................... 1 .... 2 .... 3 .... 4 5   V161
Production................... 1 .... 2 .... 3 .... 4 5   V162
R & D....................... 1 .... 2 .... 3 .... 4 5   V163

(d) To what extent does the Marketing Department directly affect the despatch of goods from the factory:.................... A direct immediate impact 1 .... 2 .... 3 .... 4 .... Little impact 5   V164

Question 24

Departments in firms are likely to have different degrees of power within the firm. How would you rank the power of the following departments in your firm at the moment, and how this has changed in the last three years?

Please rank: 1st, 2nd, 3rd, etc.

	(a) the present rankings of departments in power:	(b) the rankings of departments in power three years ago:
Production..............	V165	V170
Finance/Accounting.....	V166	V171
Marketing..............	V167	V172
R & D..................	V168	V173
Other Departments (please specify).......	V169	V174

Question 25

Which of the following best describes the marketing approach of your company:

Make what we can and sell to whoever will buy it _____ ☐

Place major emphasis on advertising and selling to ensure sales _____ ☐

Place major emphasis on prior analysis of market needs, adapting our products to meet them if necessary _____ ☐ V175

VI CLASSIFICATION DATA

Question 26

Please indicate the total number of employees in the company or division for which you have been answering.

Number of employees

The company/division to which the questionnaire applies................. _____ *V176*

Question 27

Please indicate the sales revenue of your company or division in the three most recent financial years.

The most recent financial year 198_/8_ ....£ _____ *V177*

The year before 19_/19_ ....£ _____ *V178*

The year before that 19_/19_ ....£ _____ *V179*

Question 29

What was the approximate pre-tax profit or loss of your company or division in the most recent financial years?

The most recent financial year 198_/198_ ....£ _____ *V180*

The year before 19_/19_ ....£ _____ *V181*

The year before that 19_/19_ ....£ _____ *V182*

Question 29

Please indicate the principal type of product sold by your business.

Durable consumer goods _____

Repeat-purchase consumer goods _____

Capital industrial equipment _____

Consumable industrial goods _____

Services _____

Other (please specify) _____

_____

_____

V183

THANK YOU FOR YOUR HELP AND COOPERATION
Please return the questionnaire, in the 'freepost' envelope to:
Nigel Piercy, Senior Lecturer,
Department of Business Administration and Accountancy, UWIST,
Colum Drive, FREEPOST, Cardiff CF1 IYU

Please indicate here if you would like to receive a free copy of the
survey results.

Yes _____

No _____ *V184*

Please use the next page for your organisation chart or any
any supplementary comments you would like to make.

copy of the questionnaire, there was a total response rate of 13%.

Because of the low response rate on the pilot, non-respondents were contacted and asked for their reasons for not replying to the questionnaire, which generated a further 19 responses, giving a total response rate of 32%.

These replies suggested: (a) that the sampling was crude and included firms without marketing departments, who were not, for one reason or another, prepared or able to give data on their marketing activities, firms in service areas to which the question wording appeared inappropriate, and which would not therefore be likely to respond, and holding companies/divisional headquarters not involved in operational marketing, which similarly would not respond; (b) that the research instrument itself was problematic - being perceived as too long, unclear, and requiring some data which were too confidential to be revealed.

It was concluded that the nature of the research work was such that a relatively low response rate was to be expected - the target for the main survey being an effective response rate of 25% - and that in the main survey it would be necessary to: (a) investigate the structure of the sample selected to discount the effect of questionnaire non-response due to inappropriateness to the particular sample item; (b) to reduce the overall length of the questionnaire, and to clarify the wording on those questions which had proved problematic to respondents; and (c) to reduce the amount of 'sensitive' data requested to a minumum.

A.4 MAIN SURVEY RESPONSES

The main mail-out to 600 companies was carried out on 30 April 1984, including the research instrument, the covering letter (see Figure A.1) and a reply-paid envelope.

Table A.1 Survey Response Analysis

	No.	%
Sample size	600	100
Total response rate	337	56
Total usable responses (i.e. all respondents revealing data other than only reasons for not participating in the survey	284	47
Total of full participants (i.e. answering more than one-third of the questions)	166	28

A 'reminder' letter and a further copy of the questionnaire were mailed to the non-respondents on 1st June 1984, and a final reminder was sent on 1st July 1984, including a copy of the questionnaire but also asking non-respondents to indicate on a separate proforma their reasons for not participating in the survey. The pattern of responses to that last probe is shown in Table A.2. The response is summarised in Table A.1 and the total response rate was 56% representing 337 responses, of which 166 or 28% gave substantial responses and 284 or 47% gave some data.

However, from the piloting exercise it was clear that some of the non-response was due to the unavoidable crudity of the sample selection method used, and a better view of sample completeness is provided by an analysis of reasons for non-response discussed in A.5 below.

Table A.2: **Survey Non-Response Reasons***

Reasons for Non-Response   %

   (a) <u>Marketing Departmentation</u>

The company has no marketing department	35
The company is a holding company, with no marketing operations	5
The company is a subsidiary/branch with no marketing operations	6
The company's marketing expenditure is too low to allow response	12
The company is too small and has no marketing operations	12

   (b) <u>Research Access</u>

The questions are too confidential and too much data was required	46
The company's policy is not to respond to questionnaires	16

     (c) <u>Other</u>

Other reasons	22
	(N=171)

---

* Includes reasons given for non-response to particular questions as well as to the whole questionnaire.

A.5 SAMPLING FRAME STRUCTURE AND SAMPLE COMPLETENESS

It was noted in the piloting exercise described above that the sampling methodology was crude in terms of its inability to distinguish between those firms with marketing departments and those without. This conclusion is confirmed by the analysis of reasons for non-response shown in Table A.2. Whilst some 60% of these respondents did not wish to participate for the normal refusal reasons - confidentiality, company policy, and so on - 40% could not participate for a variety of reasons associated with the lack or low level of marketing departmentation - no department, no formal marketing, and the like. This suggests that of the original sample of 600, it is possible that only 60% of the sample were qualified to participate in the survey. This question is pursued in the text in evaluating the status and departmentation of marketing (pp. *314-18*), but for present purposes it suggests that the effective sample size was, in fact, only some 360, and that thus the full participation by 166 companies represents a 'real' response rate of 46%. For this reason the response rate is taken as adequate for the purposes of this study, though further qualifications to the representativness of the sample are noted in Appendix B.

APPENDIX B

THE SURVEY COMPANIES

B.1 INTRODUCTION

This appendix describes the main characteristics of the companies participating in the postal questionnaire survey described above in Appendix A.

B.2 SAMPLE COMPANY SIZE

The size of responding companies in terms of the most recent year's sales turnover is shown in Table B.1, and in terms of the most recent year's employee level in Table B.2.

Table B.1:   Sample Company Size - Sales

Sales Revenue in Most Recent Year	%
Less than £5M	17
£5M - £10M	29
£10M - £20M	23
£20M - £30M	17
More than £30M	14
	(N = 132)

Table B.2: Sample Company Size - Employees

Employees in Most Recent Year	%
Less than 250	33
250 - 500	31
500 - 1000	19
1000 - 5000	12
More than 5000	5
	(N = 140)

These data suggest that the sample is biased towards what may be termed medium-sized companies, i.e. those with fewer than 500 employees. However, in this sense the sample is clearly not representative of the small firm, i.e. companies with fewer than 100 employees. This fact is noted since small firms of that type account for some 97% of all UK firms (Business Monitor). The comparisons between this sample and the structure of the size distribution of all UK manufacturing firms in Table B.3 confirms this conclusion: the sample is heavily biased away from representing small firms, in favour of the larger organisation.

Table B.3: UK Company Size*

	All UK Manufacturers*		All UK Manufacturers over 100 Employees*		This sample	
	No.	%	No.	%	No.	%
Number of employees						
Less than 100	106,250	89	-	-	5	7
101-200	5,821	5	5,821	47	17	18
201-500	4,339	4	4,339	35	68	49
501-1000	1,408	1	1,408	11	26	19
1001-5000	(908	1	908	7	17	12)
More than 5000	(				7	)
	(N=118,726)		(N=12,476)		(N=140)	

*Source: Business Statistics Office

Broadly the same comment applies to company size in terms of sales revenue since the sample is dominated by companies with sales of less than £20M in the most recent trading year. Taking the parameters used by Hooley et al (1985), of the small company with sales of less than £2.5M, the medium sized firm in the category £2.5M-£20M, and the large firm with sales in excess of £20M, we may make the comparison shown in Table B.4.

Table B.4:   Sales Turnover in UK Companies

Sales Levels (1984)	Hooley et al (1985) No.	%	This Survey No.	%
Less than £2.5M	(506	32	(3	2
£2.5M – £5.0M	(		(	
£2.5M – £20.0M	(554	35	(88	67
£10.0M – £20.0M	(		(	
More than £20.0M	(522	33	(41	31
	(N=1582)		(N=132)	

The bias away from the very small operation is demonstrated by the fact that while Hooley et al's sample (which was itself biased towards larger firms) contained 32% of items with less than £23M sales, in this present sample only 3 firms or 2% of the sample were in this category.

In terms of the representativeness of the sample, it is thus clearly biased towards the medium-sized company, at the expense of both the small enterprise, and to a lesser, though significant, extent also at the expense of the very large organisation. The sources of this bias are: the sample selection methodology, as described in Appendix A.1, which chose to exclude small firms, on the grounds that their organisation and marketing budgeting systems were likely to be at a low level of development and difficult to evaluate; and the complex systems of very large organisations which were likely to have made the questionnaire wording inappropriate (and although not measured it is likely that the limited response/refusal group is biased towards those larger firms).

B.3   SAMPLE COMPANY PROFITABILITY

The reported profitability levels of the responding companies are shown in Table B.5. This may be compared to the finding in the Hooley et al (1985) work and the overall UK position as in B.6. Certainly, applying a Chi Square test (Chi Square = 2.85 with 3 d.f.) suggests no significance difference between the Hooley et al sample and that studied here, in terms of profitability.

Table B.5:   Sample Company Profitability

	This year %	Last year %	Year Before %
Profit level*			
Loss/Break even	16	20	16
0-5%	31	31	37
5-10%	35	30	30
10-15%	8	9	8
More than 15%	10	10	9
	(N=91)	(N=87)	(N=84)

---

* Profitability is measured as Net Profit Before Tax/Sales

Table B.6:   Profitability Comparisons

	Hooley et al (1985) %	This sample %
Profitability*		
Loss/Break Even	16	16
0-5%	30	31
5-10%	31	35
10-15%)	24	8
More than 15%)		10
	(N=1324)	(N=91)

---

* Profitability is measured as Net Profit Before Tax/Sales

B.4 PRODUCT MARKETS

The major product-markets of the sample companies are compared to the Hooley et al (1985) study is shown in Table B.7.

Table B.7:   Product-Markets Compared

	Hooley et al (1985)* %	This sample %
Product/Market Type		
Repeat-purchase consumer goods	31	31
Durable consumer goods	19	23
Consumable industrial products	31	25
Capital industrial equipment	19	22
	(N=1132)	(N=146)

* Service industries are excluded from this comparison

Applying a Chi Square test (Chi Square = 25.0 with 3 d.f.) suggests that the structure of this sample is significantly different (α = 0.01) from that found by Hooley et al, in that this present sample has a higher representation of consumer goods, particularly consumer durables; and a lower representation of industrial products, particularly industrial consumables. This factor is not taken as a disqualification to the present study, since different sampling frames were used, but it does provide a qualification to comparing the two studies.

In this area it is also possible to compare the respondent's perceptions of market life cyles and recessionary effects, as shown in Tables B.8 and B.9.

In the case of market life cycles, a Chi Square test (Chi Square = 27.4 with 3.d.f) suggests a significant difference (α = 0.01) in that this sample contains a higher proportion of firms in mature/stable markets and rather fewer in growth and new markets in particular.

In the case of the impact of economic recession, a Chi Square test (Chi Square = 24.0 with 3 d.f.) again suggests a significant difference between the two samples (α = 0.01), in that this present sample has a higher proportion of firms reporting little or no impact of economic recession, and a lower proportion experiencing significant effects.

Table B.8:   Market Life Cycles

Long-term Nature of Major Market	Hooley et al (1985) %	This Survey %
Generally in decline	20	23
Mature and fairly stable	46	51
Growth market	29	25
Relatively new, emerging market	5	1
	(N=1653)	(N=130)

Table B.9:   Economic Effects

Effect of Current Economic Recession on Major Market	Hooley et al (1984) %	This Survey %
No major effect	13	27
Some effect, but we have coped	55	45
A big effect causing major difficulties	29	22
Disastrous, our very survival is threatened	4	6
	(N=1660)	(N=132)

APPENDIX C

MEASUREMENT OF POLITICAL VARIABLES

The selection of measurements is discussed in Chapter 10 (pp. 300-8), and the questionnaire showing the coding framework is given in Figure A.1.   Table C.1 below lists the variable codes and the content of the indices and indicators computed.

Table C.1: The Power and Politics Variables Measured

	Codes	Descriptions
POWER OF THE MARKETING DEPARTMENT	POW1	Integration of functions in marketing department (average of V3** to V9**)
	POW2	Integration of specialist personnel in the marketing department (INTEG*)
	INMTG	Number of 'marketing' jobs in the marketing department (total V16 to V25)
	OUTMTG	Number of 'marketing' jobs outside the marketing department (total V26 to V35)
	INTEG	Ratio of 'marketing' jobs inside to 'marketing' jobs outside the marketing department (INMTG/OUTMTG)
	POW3	Relative marketing manpower (MP*)
	MP	Relative marketing manpower (V13/V176)
	POW4	Marketing manpower trend (MPTREND*)
	MPTREND	Marketing manpower trend (V13/V15)
	POW5	Relative marketing manpower trend (MPST*)
	MPST	Relative marketing manpower trend (MPTREND/(V177/V179))
	POW6	Marketing's board representation (BDREP*)
	BDREP	Marketing's board representation (V36/V37)
	POW7	CME marketing mix responsibilities (average V38*** to V51***, V53***, V56*** and V57****)
	POW8	CME strategy responsibilities (average V52***, V54***, V55***, V58***)
	POW9	CME total responsibilities (average V38*** to V58***)
	POW10	CME status versus head of production (V10*)
	POW11	CME status versus head of finance/ accounting (V11*)
	POW12	CME status versus head of sales (V12*)
	POW13	CME status - average (average POW10, POW11, POW12)
	POW14	Marketing department perceived power rank (V167*)
	POW15	Marketing department perceived power rank change (V167 and V172 scored as in footnote ****)
	POW16	Control of sales forecasting (V74)
	POW17	Control of critical success factors (CRITS*)
	CRITS	Control of critical success factors (V137 to V156 scored)
POLITICS OF THE MARKETING DEPARTMENT	POW18	Marketing paradigm strength (V175)
	POL1	Marketing department information access (average of V59 to V66)
	POL2	Marketing department information restriction (average of V67*** to V73***)
	POL3	Marketing department inforamtion control (POL1/POL2)
	POL4	Marketing department sales forecasting influence (V75****)
	Z	Other departments sales forecasting influence (average V76*** to V80****)
	SFBAL	Marketing department sales forecasting influence (V75***/Z)
	POL5	Politicisation of marketing budgeting (V121***)
	POL6	Politicisation of marketing manpower allocations (V122***)
	POL7	Politicisation of other marketing resource allocations (V123***)
	POL8	Politicisation of all marketing resource allocations (average POL5, POL6 and POL7)

Codes — Descriptions

	Codes	Descriptions
STRATEGIC CONTINGENCIES	STRCON1	Substitutability of marketing department (V157***)
	STRCON2	Connectedness (finance department) (V158***)
	STRCON3	Connectedness (production department) (V159***)
	STRCON4	Connectedness (R&D department) (V160***)
	STRCON5	Connectedness (all departments) (average STRCON2, STRCON3 and STRCON4)
	STRCON6	Immediacy (V164***)
	STRCON7	Marketing department influence (average V161, V162, V163)
	V161	Influence (finance department)
	V162	Influence (production department)
	V163	Influence (R&D department)
POLITICAL CONTINGENCIES	POLCON1	Uncertainty - predictability (V132)
	POLCON2	Uncertainty - market control (V133***)
	POLCON3	Uncertainty - recession (V135***)
	POLCON4	Uncertainty - market life cycle (V136***)
	POLCON5	Uncertainty - technology (V134)
	POLCON5A	Uncertainty - all market sources (average POLCON1, POLCON2, POLCON3, POLCON4)
	POLCON5B	Uncertainty - all sources (average POLCON1, POLCON2, POLCON3, POLCON4, POLCON5)
	POLCON6	Company politicisation (average V124*** to V131***)
	V124***	Information selectivity
	V125***	Departmental image
	V126***	Attacking/criticising others
	V127***	Gaining informal support
	V128***	Praising others
	V129***	Cultivating the influential
	V131***	Creating obligations
	V132***	Using the rules
	POLCON7	Scarcity (this year) (TYPRO***)
	TYPRO	Scarcity (this year) (V180/V177)
	POLCON8	Scarcity (last year) (LYPRO***)
	LYPRO	Scarcity (last year) (V181/V178)
	POLCON9	Scarcity (year before) (YBPRO***)
	YBPRO	Scarcity (year before) (V182/V179)
	POLCON10	Scarcity (trend) (TYPRO/YBPRO)***
	POLCON11	Importance (this year) (TYBUD***)
	TYBUD	Importance (this year) (V117/V180)
	POLCON12	Importance (last year) (LYBUD***)
	LYBUD	Importance (last year) (V118/V181)
	POLCON13	Importance (year before) (YBBUD***)
	YBBUD	Importance (year before) (V119/V182)

	Codes	Descriptions
POWER OF OTHER DEPARTMENTS	OTHPOW1	Perceived rank of production department (V165*)
	OTHPOW2	Perceived rank of finance department (V166*)
	OTHPOW3	Perceived rank of R&D department (V168*)
	OTHPOW3A	Perceived rank of other departments (V169*)
	OTHPOW3B	Perceived rank of all other departments (average OTHPOW1, OTHPOW2, OTHPOW3, OTHPOW4)
	OTHPOW4	Production department rank change (V165 and V170 scored as in footnote ****)
	OTHPOW5	Finance department rank change (V166 and V171 scored as in footnote ****)
	OTHPOW6	R&D department rank change (V168 and V173 scored as in footnote ****)
	OTHPOW7	Other department rank change (V169 and V174 scored as in footnote ****)
	OTHPOW8	All other departments rank change (average OTHPOW4, OTHPOW5, OTHPOW6, OTHPOW7)
	OTHPOW9	Others control of critical success factors (total for others scored as in POW17 and totalled)
POLITICS OF OTHER DEPARTMENTS	OTHPOL1	Other department information access (average V67 to V73)
	OTHPOL2	Other department information restriction (average V59*** to V66***)
	OTHPOL3	Other department information control (OTHPOL1/OTHPOL2)
	OTHPOL4	Other department control of sales forecasting (average V76*** to V80***)
BUDGETING	BUD1	Sophistication of budgeting methods (V81 to V88 scored)
	BUD2	Marketing department control of budgeting process (V99)
	BUD3	Top management intervention (V101*)
	BUD4	Marketing department participation (V102***)
	BUD5	Finance department influence (V103***)
	BUD6	Production department influence (V104***)
	BUD7	R&D department influence (V105***)
	BUD8	Corporate planning department influence (V106***)
RESOURCES	RES1	Advertising budget (this year) (V108)
	ADPERTY	Advertising budget/sales (this year) (V108/177)
	RES2	Advertising budget (last year) (V109)
	ADPERLY	Advertising budget/sales (last year) (V109/178)
	RES3	Advertising budget (year before) (V110)
	ADPERYB	Advertising budget/sales (year before) (V110/V179)
	RES4	Advertising budget trend (V108/V110)
	RES5	Sales promotion budget (this year) (V111)
	SPPERTY	Sales promotion budget/sales (this year) (V11/V177)
	RES6	Sales promotion budget (last year) (V112)
	SPPERLY	Sales promotion budget/sales (last year) (V112/V178)
	RES7	Sales promotion budget (year before) (V113)
	SPPERYB	Sales promotion budget/sales (year before) (V113/V179)
	RES8	Sales promotion budget trend (V111/V113)
	RES9	Other marketing budget (this year) (V114)
	OBPERTY	Other marketing budget/sales (this year) (V114/V177)
	RES10	Other marketing budget (last year) (V115)
	OBPERLY	Other marketing budget/sales (last year) (V115/V178)

Codes		Descriptions
RES11		Other marketing budget (year before) (V116)
RES12	OBPERYB	Other marketing budget/sales (year before) (V116/V179)
RES13		Other marketing budget trend (V114/V116)
RES14	BUDPERTY	Marketing budget (this year) (V117)
RES15	BUDPERLY	Marketing budget/sales (this year) (V117/V177)
RES16	BUDPERYB	Marketing budget (last year) (V118)
RES20		Marketing budget/sales (last year) (V118/V178)
RES21		Marketing budget (year before) (V119)
		Marketing budget/sales (year before) (V118/V179)
		Marketing budget trend (V117/V119)
		Marketing manpower trend (V13/V15)
		Other resources trend (V120*)

* Standardised to a 5 point scale.

** Reversed variable scale direction and converted to a 5 point scale.

*** Reversed variable scale direction.

**** Power rank change scored as follows:

Rank 3 Years Ago	Rank Now	Score
1	1	4
1	2	3
1	3	1
1	Below 3	5
2	1	3
2	2	2
2	3	1
2	Below 3	5
3	1	4
3	2	2
3	3	1
3	Below 3	5
Below 3	1	4
Below 3	2	3
Below 3	3	1

Author Index

Dahl 142, 148, 149, 293
Deshpande 102, 113, 198, 213, 222, 227, 228
Dollinger 120
Douglas 113
Downey 296, 306
Doyle 39, 103, 104, 107, 108, 109, 110
Duncan 119, 121, 202
Dunn 9, 102

Earl 223, 224, 225, 226
Evans 1, 5, 14, 18, 40, 77, 105, 191, 222, 223, 227, 235, 457

Farris 39, 81, 85
Freeman 210, 253-4, 272
French 150, 153, 194
Foxall 3

Galbraith 119, 123, 149, 155, 163, 179, 225, 230, 306, 458
Gandz 178, 249
Gemmill 194
Gilligan 41, 46, 67, 79, 80, 88, 270
Gilligham 22, 34
Goldhaber 146, 163
Guiltinan 70, 71
Guirdham 48, 119, 120

Hakansson 18, 112, 113, 120, 122, 123, 124, 126, 232, 458
Halbert 8, 10, 11
Haller 103, 107, 109, 211, 265
Hanmer-Lloyd 44, 70, 72, 73, 74, 75, 77, 108, 213, 262-64, 266, 267, 270, 307
Hannan 210, 253-4, 272
Hayes 103
Hayhurst 3, 4, 22, 104, 107, 108, 110, 111, 297, 304, 305, 316, 318, 320, 327
Hedberg 87, 147, 163, 202, 225, 290, 294, 307
Heidrick and Struggles 316, 320

Hickson 49, 146, 150, 152, 154, 156, 157, 160, 166, 194, 195, 196, 229, 232, 286, 297, 291, 296, 459
Hills 252
Hinings 156, 159, 60, 196, 213, 229, 287, 306, 459
Hise 7
Hooley 6, 7, 104, 112, 207, 211, 305, 307, 316, 318, 356
Hopwood 89, 223, 226
Howard 13, 110, 111, 197, 227, 265
Huff 166, 473, 475, 476, 477
Hulbert 214
Hunt 8, 9, 10, 11, 12, 13, 188
Hurwood 37, 39, 91

Institute of Marketing 3
Izraeli 183

Jemison 119, 120, 206, 458
Jobber 67, 79, 80, 224
John 113, 227

Kaplan 157, 195
Keen 48, 189, 288, 475
Kennedy 24, 37, 38, 39, 40, 43, 44, 65, 69, 70, 72, 73, 74, 75, 77, 79, 108, 208, 213, 262-64, 266, 267, 270, 271, 307
Kipnis 183
Korda 141, 166, 167, 183, 188, 189
Kotler 3, 6, 37, 38, 40, 43, 63, 64, 122, 207, 210
Kotter 141, 142

Lancaster 79
Lasswell 179
Lawrence 119, 121, 195, 200, 201, 207

Levitt 6
Lewicki 183
Likert 113
Lilien 40, 44, 66, 67, 68, 69, 72, 79, 81, 85, 88, 270, 271
Lorsch 119, 121, 195, 200, 201, 207
Lowe 77, 164, 19, 255-7
Lutz 10-11
Lysonski 120

McNamara 9, 104
Madison 197, 206, 207, 289, 306
March 11, 62, 69, 77, 87, 107, 116, 118, 156, 162, 164, 175, 202, 204, 207, 242, 244-45, 247, 293, 473
Markus 48, 164, 225, 229, 288
Mayes 176, 177
Mechanic 1149, 151, 154, 163, 180
Meyer 145, 154, 155
Migliore 113
Mintzberg 16, 48, 143, 146, 147, 149, 164, 165, 176, 194, 199, 202, 226, 242, 243, 471
Morein 110

Nicosia 18, 111, 112, 113, 121, 122, 123, 126, 127, 228, 229, 230, 265, 306, 458
Nonaka 18, 111, 112, 113, 121, 122, 123, 126, 127, 228, 229, 230, 265, 306, 458

Palda 37
Parasuraman 7, 102, 104
Parsons 146
Patchen 293
Patti 23, 79
Permut 79
Perrow 92, 142, 196, 207, 291, 305
Peters 102
Pettigrew 119, 148, 149, 151, 155, 156, 160, 163, 164, 166, 175, 176, 179, 180, 191, 193, 195, 213, 286,

287, 289, 291, 304, 458, 459
Pfeffer 11, 16, 17, 36, 41, 48, 49, 87, 91, 92, 114, 116, 117, 126, 142, 143, 144, 145, 147, 151, 152, 154, 155, 157, 158, 159, 160, 161, 162, 163, 165, 166, 176, 177, 179, 180, 190, 191, 192, 193, 194, 196, 200, 202, 204, 205, 225, 226, 227, 229, 232, 235, 243, 250, 252, 253, 274, 286, 288, 289, 292, 293, 294, 304, 306, 459, 470, 472, 473, 474, 476
Phillips 297
Piercy 1, 4, 5, 6, 124, 18, 22, 33, 35, 36, 40, 47, 67, 77, 101, 102, 104, 105, 107, 108, 109, 110, 111, 112, 114, 118, 119, 122, 123, 126, 129, 131, 132, 140, 141, 164, 191, 195, 206, 214, 222, 223, 227, 228, 230, 235, 297-8, 325. 457, 459
Pondy 16, 36, 89, 92, 161, 207, 213, 245-47, 476
Porter 179, 185, 189, 204, 205, 286, 287, 289, 292
Provan 253
Pugh 124, 318

Rabino 79
Rayburn 22, 23-4, 37
Raven 150, 153, 194
Rodger 2
Ruekhart 113, 122, 126

Sachs 103
Salancik 11, 36, 126, 143, 144, 159, 161, 163, 165, 176, 180, 194, 196,

Subject Index

advertising budgeting
see marketing budgeting
advertising effectiveness 43-44
advertising models 43
advertising/sales ratios 21, 38, 39, 64, 79, 80-5, 271
ADVISOR 46, 67, 71-2, 79, 81, 84-5, 460
Aston organisation research 124-6

Beechams 21
behavioural theory of the firm
see theory of the firm
boundary spanning
see marketing, and boundary spanning
brand management
see product management
British Leyland (BL) 21
British Steel Corporation 63, 64, 69, 257-8, 271
budgetary calculations 61-2;
see also marketing budgeting, methods of calculation
budgetary strategies 62-3, 77;
see also marketing budgeting, strategies in
budgeting, bargaining in 65;
see also marketing budgeting, bargaining in
budgeting, and politics 63, 77, 86-90;
see also marketing budget-

ing, and organisational politics
budgeting, and 'rationality' 86-90;
see also marketing budgeting, and 'rationality'
budgeting games 41-2, 59, 63, 242;
see also budgeting, and politics
budgeting, in business organisations 244-50
budgeting, in the public sector 16, 60, 61, 242-3, 250-5
budgeting, and rationality 47-50, 62;
see also marketing budgeting methods
budgeting norms 64, 65, 68;
see also marketing budgeting methods, heuristics
budgeting norms, institutionalisation of 64, 65
budgeting norms, and politics 65
budgeting rules 62;
see also marketing budgeting methods, heuristics

Cadbury Schweppes 20, 21
capital budgeting 245-8

515

channels of distribution 48, 108;
see also marketing, and organisational power
channels of distribution, and new information technology 105, 109, 233
chief marketing executive 4-5, 102, 113, 298, 327-41, 343-5, 390
coalitions of interest 13, 62, 102, 165, 193
communications models
see advertising models
community power 143, 144-5, 290
computerisation
see marketing, and new information technology
conflict 62, 76, 117, 155, 204, 205-8, 245-48;
see also marketing, and interdepartmental conflict;
see also political contingencies
corporate environment
see marketing, corporate environment for
corporate strategy 48-9;
see also marketing, and corporate/strategic planning
cost-cutting in marketing 68, 69
critical contingencies
see critical success factors
critical success factors 106, 206, 213, 230, 232, 233
critical success factors, and marketing 236, 298, 300, 347-53

DAGMAR (Defining Advertising Goals for Measured Advertising Results) 43
decision making, and rationality 13, 17;
see also organisational decision making models;
see also theory of the firm

'disjointed incrementalism' 49;
see also incrementalism in budgeting
Dorfman-Steiner theorem 38, 39

environmental dependency 105
environmental enactment 127, 226, 227, 228, 232
environmental perception 127, 232, 306
environmental resource-dependence 11, 36, 126, 226
experiential budgeting 62

General Electric 80
goal dissensus 201-4, 134, 243;
see also organisational objectives;
see also political contingencies
goal dissensus, in marketing 206-9, 234, 269-70

incrementalism in budgeting 42, 49, 61, 63;
see also marketing budgeting, and incrementalism
information distortion 63, 198, 228;
see also organisational politics, and information
information distortion, and budgeting, 72, 77, 246-7, 258-62, 263
information processing 1, 18, 24, 59, 104-10, 119, 129-30, 223, 228, 230;